A LIFETIME IN THE BUILDING

'Write funny story of furniture in attic (a life)'

Note written to herself by May Savidge, on a scrap of paper
found in a box in the attic of Ware Hall-House

A LIFETIME IN THE BUILDING

The Extraordinary Story of May Savidge
and the House She Moved

Christine Adams

with Michael McMahon

A note from the authors

All quotations in this book are given with their original punctuation. Miss Savidge wrote letters in carefully constructed prose, but her diaries were written as notes.

The names of two or three people have been changed in order to avoid causing embarrassment or offence. Miss Savidge would not have wanted a book written in her honour to hurt anyone.

First published in Great Britain
2009 by Aurum Press Ltd
7 Greenland Street
London NW1 0ND
www.aurumpress.co.uk

A catalogue record for this book is available from the British Library.

ISBN 978 1 84513 396 2

3 5 7 9 10 8 6 4 2
2009 2011 2013 2012 2010

Designed and typeset by SX Composing DTP, Rayleigh, Essex
Printed by MPG Books, Bodmin, Cornwall

I dedicate this book to my amazing children, Daniel and Polly, who have helped me through eight tough years. With their help, and the support of my wonderful friends, I have fulfilled my promise.

Christine Adams

BULAWAYO, RHODESIA.

THE SUNDAY NEWS, DECEMBER 3, 1978

n joggers
being

RHODESIAN joggers seems to
craze sweeping America an
is too scarce to import su

THE HOUSE THAT MISS MAY REBUILT

MISS May Savidge (67),
has almost single-handedly
moved her two-storey cot-
tage brick by brick from its
location 160 km away and
rebuilt it at Wells-next-the-
Sea, Norfolk.

She learnt 11 years ago
that local officials planned
to pull down her 500-year-
old cottage, which then
stood near the village of
Monkey Row, to make way
for a roundabout.

"The house was too
valuable to destroy," said
Miss Savidge, a retired
book illustrator. "I simply
decided to take it with me
and rebuild it."

She has spent every day
from dawn to dusk for the
past 11 years moving the
house. She numbered and
relaid all 10 000 bricks and
8 000 roof tiles herself.
She paid to have the materials moved by lorry.

The house is now almost
finished and Miss Savidge,
who is living in a caravan
on the site, expects to move
in by Christmas with her
cat Pansey and dog Sasha.
Iana-Reuter.

"BRICK BY BRICK" again (B + T. Times, Fri.

Originally thatch storey tiles of brick element some bricks
only frame of lath & plaster (No BRICKS)

III likes as to retire early
Fried of helicopter of frame only - ong.
Pickford - frame complete - reads to normal.

Make sure folks know I haven't been paid by
radio or TV - haven't made anything out of whole
even though BBC. TV. & others(?) used my photos of
before it was dismantled - (I saw it).

Dear Miss Savage Savidges
Please find enclosed one
antique nail. My husband got it
when he was in the building
trade, now retired in ill health
I admire your guts immensley,
it spurs me on to get jobs done
myself around my modern bungalow
I hope I shall be able to view
your house from the outside when
I can get to Norfolk. I hope to
go to Walsingham, Rougham Manor
Norwich & Naunton Hall.
Yours Faithfully
(MKS ap. 57.5)

Miss May Savidge.
(Who re-moved and re-built her house)
__WELLS-NEXT-THE-SEA.__

Norfolk.

Contents

It has been impossible to mention all the people who helped May in her daunting task. A few have been named, but if you read this book and know that you were there, in her many hours of need, I sincerely thank you and hope you enjoy reminiscing about your part in the life of an extraordinary woman.

INTRODUCTION

by Paul Atterbury,
BBC Antiques Roadshow

The Antiques Roadshow is one of Britain's best-loved and most familiar television programmes, yet this perennially popular series still has a few secrets. One of these is something called the Furniture Round, when one of the experts visits the homes of members of the public who have contacted the BBC about large things they are unable to bring to the show. Every Roadshow has a Furniture Round, which is usually spread over a radius of fifty miles around the location and takes place in the days that immediately precede the recording day. A few of the Roadshow team of experts do these Rounds, and they are well versed in the techniques of talking to the owners of the objects under review without giving anything away.

A few years ago I was given the task of carrying out the Furniture Round for the show that was to be filmed at Holkham Hall, in Norfolk. Over the allocated three days a colleague and I visited everyone who had written in for that particular Round, and we were well on the way to completing the final selection of the few things that we would be able to bring in to help the owners. As ever, there were a couple of unresolved issues, usually visits that could not be made because the owners had gone away. One of these was in Wells-next-the-Sea, to a lady who had written in about a desk with some association with Mark Twain. From the photograph it did not look very exciting, but we had persevered, telephoning regularly throughout the three days, partly because the address, Ware Hall-House, sounded promising. There was never an answer and no means of leaving a message.

On the evening of the final day, as we were tying up the loose ends, we decided to give it a final go, and called the number again. Rather to our surprise, there was an answer, and we arranged to visit the lady, who had been away for a few days and had forgotten about her letter to the BBC, immediately. We parked on the green at the heart of Wells and walked up the narrow path that we had been told to follow. There was no sign of any house, just an old door in a high wall. We entered, and were faced at once by what was obviously a major timber-framed building of the medieval era. Yet, somehow it did not look quite right and I was intrigued.

The lady who opened the door introduced herself as Christine Adams and led us in, to show us the desk that was the reason for the visit. As I had guessed, it was relatively unexciting. At that point, I decided I had to put my BBC duties aside, and told Christine I had to know about the house. She asked us if we had plenty of time, which we had, offered us some tea and took us into the wooden conservatory that projected from one side. As soon as we were seated, she launched into the long and complicated story of May Savidge.

She told us about May and her extraordinary life, about the house which she had demolished and rebuilt, and about her compulsive collecting and hoarding. Christine also explained where she fitted in, and how she had devoted much of her life to fulfilling the wishes of an eccentric and demanding woman who was her former husband's aunt. I was completely gripped, not least by Christine's lengthy entanglement in a project that was actually nothing to do with her.

When we left, some hours later, having toured the house and looked at what remained of Auntie May's collections, I knew that we had a story that had to be included in the Roadshow. The challenge was how to do it. It broke all the rules. There was no object to talk about, other than the house and that could not be taken to the show. It was a multi-layered story of great complexity that seemed to demand much more time than the normal few minutes taken up by a typical Roadshow item. And at the heart of it was Christine who was understandably reluctant to expose the extraordinary story of her life to the Roadshow's cameras. She was happy to talk about Auntie May and the house, but it took me a while to persuade her that her story was just as exciting. In the event, we made it work somehow, without breaking the Roadshow's rules about items having to be unprepared and unrehearsed, and when it was transmitted some months later, it provoked a great response, with many people wanting to know more about May Savidge, her house and the story.

Through this process, I came to know Christine quite well, helped by the filming of a follow-up item for the end-of-series Roadshow retrospective programme, which involved more visits to the house and gave me the opportunity to stay there and experience Auntie May's handiwork in a more direct way.

From the very start of this adventure, I knew that what the story really demanded was a book. Television, as ever, could only scratch the surface. I did my best to encourage Christine to write it all down, and to collect together photographs and other material that could bring it all to life. Above all else, I encouraged her to tell her story, which seemed to me in so many ways the most interesting part of the whole saga. During our conversations, I had become aware that Christine was in some ways a prisoner, trapped both by the story and the house. There were many ghosts to be laid, and I was sure that the process of writing it all down would in some ways release her.

This book, which I read in one sitting, seems to me to have done just that. It is exciting, enthralling and occasionally shocking. And through it Christine Adams seems to have gained her freedom. She is the real heroine of the story and a remarkable woman who can now see beyond the limits on her life imposed by Ware Hall-House, which, in the final analysis, is nothing to do with her.

It has often been said that *The Antiques Roadshow* is not just a popular television programme, but something with the power to affect people and the way they live. Christine Adams, and the story of Auntie May, has changed my life, and I like to think that we have changed hers. I am so glad we persevered and kept trying that telephone number.

Paul Atterbury, April 2009

CHAPTER ONE

An End and a Beginning

April 1993

She looked so frail and broken in her tidily arranged bed. I picked up her hand and held it. It was blue. There was no weight in it. The nurse said: 'I don't think she can feel her hands any more. Why don't you stroke her neck? And do talk to her: she's slipping away fast now, but hearing is the last sense to go . . .'

It seemed cruel that someone so fiercely independent should have to die like this. Auntie May should have been the one doing the nursing, not the one being nursed. She was a giver, not a taker. When she had joined the St John Ambulance Brigade in 1938, she had taken both its mottoes – 'For the Faith', and 'For The Service of Mankind' – as her own. She had tended the sick and the wounded, visited the handicapped and housebound, given and organised first aid courses, and run fundraising and recruiting events. Years later, when the Wells Cottage Hospital had been listed for closure, she joined in the battle to keep it open for the benefit of the community; now, aged not quite eighty-two, she was dying in the very Norfolk hospital she had fought to save for others. It just didn't seem right.

•

I first met Auntie May in 1966, when she was fifty-four.* Strictly speaking, she wasn't my aunt, she was my husband's, but he introduced me to her as Auntie May, and I've thought of her as my own auntie ever since. Tony clearly regarded her with affection, but he did warn me that the family thought her eccentric. His mother, Nellie, May's sister, was very fond of her, too, but whenever May's name was mentioned, her eyes would widen – though she wouldn't quite raise them to heaven – and she would say: 'May! Whatever will she get up to next?' She wasn't a typical maiden aunt.

Nellie told me that when she was still in her mid-teens, May met an older man, a Shakespearean actor; later, they planned to marry, but he died in 1938. Nellie said she never recovered from the loss, and that the signet ring she wore on her wedding finger had been his. Shortly after his death, she had joined the St John Ambulance Brigade and thrown all her energy into it. During the war, she had retrained as a technical draughtswoman and had helped to design the Mosquito. She had been the only female in the team.

Then, when the war was over and the nation faced a housing shortage, May thought it wouldn't be fair for a single woman to occupy a house all to herself, so she bought an old Thames river bus, the *Formosa*, and converted it into a floating home. She did some of the conversion work herself, but she never managed to make the boat's hull totally watertight, and in 1947 she abandoned it for another restoration project, a house that would otherwise have fallen down. It was a semi-derelict, semi-detached cottage – 1 Monkey Row, Ware, Hertfordshire, that had originally been built as a 'hall house': a medieval arrangement in which private living

---

* May Alice Savidge was born in Streatham on 25 May 1911.

space is attached to an open hall.* The council had told her that her house was to be demolished to make way for a relief road and May had dug her heels in and resolved to save the building at all costs. It would be a fight that would occupy the rest of her life.

But when I met Auntie May for that first time, I was surprised: she looked nothing like the person that Tony and his mother had led me to expect. In my mind's eye, I had imagined a bag lady in wellington boots, but Auntie May came to our wedding in a neat tapestry suit with a matching pillbox hat. In our wedding photographs, she looks elegant, happy and relaxed.

This very positive first impression was confirmed by her choice of wedding present – though it was the first of many signs that showed she had an unconventional approach to life. She gave us a home-made first aid kit, containing items that she had chosen herself. It was a particularly appropriate gift, for Tony and I had planned to drive to the Sahara and back for our honeymoon. Tony – who has more than a small share of the Savidge family's independence of spirit – had bought a long-wheel-base truck and converted it into a motorhome, and we took it across Europe to the Middle East, returning via north Africa. Auntie May's first aid kit contained something for every imaginable emergency. There were splints, slings and bandages for injuries, medicines for food poisoning – and there was even a tourniquet for snakebites.

I took to Auntie May immediately. She was certainly a character. There was something strong, and centred and certain about her – but something kind and gentle, too. I remember being surprised to find her shy. It seemed strange that someone who had ploughed such an independent furrow should be so undemon-

---

* When she re-erected the building, she named it Ware Hall-House, not Ware Hall House; the hyphen emphasises that it is an example of this particular architectural style.

strative and softly spoken. I was happy to have her as an auntie. I felt proud of her and yet, at the same time, there was something about her that made me feel protective – though I could see that it wouldn't be a good idea to show it.

Our honeymoon was a great adventure – though that's another story – and the next time I met Auntie May was the following spring, when Tony took me down to see her in the cottage she was fighting to save from demolition. It was obvious that her time in Ware was running out. The building that was 1 Monkey Row and 36 Baldock Street now stood in a rubble-strewn car park. Auntie May's half looked presentable enough, but the other side, which had been a bakery, looked long abandoned.* I remember peering through its grubby shop-front window. The place was empty, apart from a dusty glass cabinet containing a couple of brown and white bowls and jugs.

But when we stepped inside Auntie May's half, we found a very different ambience. It was warm and cosy, and full of an incredible quantity of clutter. Every surface was piled high with so many bits and pieces that it looked like an overstocked curiosity shop. There were books, ornaments and mementos everywhere. Tony told me that there was much, much more stuff like it – everything from a stripped-down motorbike to a vast collection of matchboxes – in the two-storey workshop at the bottom of the garden. Tony and I had brought our honeymoon slides to show her and when we asked where we could plug in our projector, she pointed to the light socket hanging from the centre of the room. It was a monkey-puzzle of interconnected two-way adapters, from which wires ran in every direction. Tony said that if we plugged anything else into it, the circuit would blow. But Auntie May insisted – and there was

---

* I later learned that it had been empty since the local council purchased it in 1959.

indeed a bang, a flash and a puff of smoke. She seemed to have a blind spot when it came to electricity.

Auntie May didn't show us the workshop, but she did show us around the house. She was proud of it. She had stripped out the 'improvements' of several centuries to expose features that showed the building to be ancient. She had uncovered a window that had been identified as fifteenth century. She had exposed heavy oak beams that bore the marks of medieval carpenters. She had lifted crumbling lino to reveal the wide, oak floorboards that those carpenters had cut by hand. She had uncovered fireplaces that were unmistakably Tudor. And when she had shown what she had found to architectural historians, they had told her she was living in a building that was a fine example of a medieval hall house. It was a rare example, too, for most hall-houses are considerably larger.

Auntie May told us she was determined to save such an important part of national heritage even if she had to take it apart beam by beam and board by board, and rebuild it in another part of the country. She had been looking at possible sites in Devon or Cornwall, but was now thinking of moving to Norfolk. She had spent several happy holidays there in the past, and she had found a plot of land, an old rope-walk garden in Wells-next-the-Sea, on the North Norfolk coast, where ships' rigging had been made for generations. The idea seemed half-crazy, but I did think that if anyone could do it, Auntie May could. After all, she had done a pretty good job renovating the house where it stood.

And so, in 1969, when the bulldozers finally reached her front gate, Auntie May had taken the building to pieces and moved it a hundred miles to Norfolk – and set about rebuilding it with her own hands. 'That house!' Nellie would exclaim; it was a project she dismissed as bordering on madness.

Now, twenty-three years later, Auntie May was dying, and 'that house' was still far from finished. The walls were up and the roof was on, but the place was little more than a shaky shell. There were no internal partitions upstairs, and many of the windows were just timber frames covered in plastic sheets. And the building was filled from top to bottom with boxes containing a lifetime's accumulated junk. So was the outhouse and the caravan in which May had lived for years, and the garden contained almost as much again, piled up under makeshift polythene shelters that were half-buried in nettles and brambles. God only knew what all those boxes might contain. Sorting them all out would be somebody's nightmare, to say nothing of the work still to be done to the building itself. Tony and I had only just finished rebuilding our own home, a cottage in Cambridgeshire that we had worked hard on for years, and in recent years, as we had watched May's project slow down and seem more and more hopeless, he had said to me many times: 'Don't ever let me take on that house!'

•

I leaned over her, stroking her neck. Then Auntie May opened her eyes and struggled to speak. She had just enough strength left for her face to show anxiety. 'Sorry,' she said.

I didn't know what she meant. What had she got to apologise for? She had done nothing in her lifetime that had caused me pain or hurt. I opened my mouth to say something comforting and non-committal, but the words that came were not the words I planned to speak. It was one of those moments when you seem to have stepped outside yourself, and have no control over what you hear yourself saying.

'Don't worry, Auntie May, whatever you want us to do, we'll do; whatever your final wishes are, we'll carry them out. I promise.' She sighed and closed her eyes. She seemed at peace.

Then it struck me why May might have felt the need to say sorry. Surely she hadn't left us the house?

CHAPTER TWO

An Extraordinary Inheritance

In which I describe what we found in Ware Hall-House after Auntie May's death

I bought lilies for the funeral. We stopped off at Ware Hall-House before the service. The place was damp, and dark, and lifeless. Wind had torn away the plastic that May had used to cover the window frames that hadn't yet been glazed, and when we pushed open the front door, we could tell the weather had started to get in, for there was a musty, earthy smell – like mushrooms in a damp paper bag. There was something else in the atmosphere, too: a feeling of absence. The place felt abandoned. It didn't seem right to leave it unattended. I went back to the car, got the flowers, found a vase and put them on Auntie May's table, beside her clock. Their strong, sweet scent lingered for weeks.

The will was read to Tony and me, and to Auntie May's executors, Betty Leftley and Pat Terrington, in the Wells office of the solicitors Hayes & Storr. The firm occupies a Georgian-fronted building just across the village green, known as 'the Buttlands', and is very near Ware Hall-House. The street it stands on is called Chancery Lane. I hadn't noticed the name before: it made me smile. The contrast between the great thoroughfare at the heart of London's legal district and a narrow alleyway in a north Norfolk seaside town couldn't be greater. For some reason, the name made me think of Charles Dickens, and shortly after we climbed the dark, narrow stairs to the first-floor office, and the solicitor had placed two large, decrepit and very dusty leather handbags on to the table, I found myself wondering whether I hadn't walked into a scene from one of his novels.

The will wasn't quite as complicated as the one in *Bleak House*, but there was definitely something Dickensian about it. It ran to eight pages and listed scores of family heirlooms, each with a carefully recorded provenance. I still have a copy of it:

4. I GIVE the following items free of inheritance tax:
(1) To my sister Nellie Henrietta Adams . . . (knowing that she would not want my house*) or if she shall predecease me then to the said Anthony Brian Adams, the following jewellery which came to me from our mother Henrietta Geertruida Carolina Augusta Savidge (born Hovelson) or from our grandmother Cornelia Johanna Hovelson (born Kikkert) or from our great-grandmother Maria Adriana Judith Kikkert (born Coninck Westenberg) namely:
(a) My gold chain – approximately fifty-five inches long with watch clip . . .
(n) My striking clock black enamel on iron with a lion's head at each end and a gilt cream face, made in USA – approximately fifteen inches times ten inches high which was a wedding present to our father and mother (twenty-eighth July one thousand nine hundred and six) from his father and mother (Joseph Traylor Savidge and Sarah Savidge, born Hampson) together with winding key which is in my large brown purse . . .

* This is something of an understatement!

9

5. I GIVE to the said Anthony Brian Adams free of inheritance
tax:

(2) The following items all of which are from my mother's family:

(a) The christening shawl used in the Kikkert family [her Dutch
ancestors on her mother's side] since one thousand eight hundred
and fifteen or thereabouts . . .

(k) My old wooden black box – sixteen and a half inches times
ten inches times eleven inches high, with handle on top, which
probably belonged to my grandmother Cornelia Johanna
Hovelsen (born Kikkert), which has a left-hand lock and a key
which is in my large brown purse and contains the following
paintings by my grandfather Joseph Traylor Savidge:

(i) Full-length portrait of King Edward VIII – five and three-
quarter inches times three and a half inches . . .

The will goes on for page after page like this, but at the time, it all
went by in a blur, because Tony and I were sitting there pole-axed
by section 3 (1), which confirmed my guess and his worst fear:

I GIVE free of inheritance tax my freehold house situated and
known as Ware Hall-House, Water Pit Lane, Wells-next-the-
Sea, aforesaid . . . to my trustees upon trust for my nephew
Anthony Brian Adams of The Nook, South Street, Litlington,
near Royston, in the county of Hertford, during his life and after
his death upon trust for such of his children living at the death of
my said nephew . . .

(2) I DIRECT that my nephew shall during his lifetime at his own
expense keep the house . . . in good repair and condition . . .

Even though it wasn't a complete surprise, it was still a shock.
Auntie May had not only left us the house, she had left us the task

of finishing it off. We couldn't sell it; we were stuck with it. And we couldn't leave it as it was – it wasn't even watertight. As the list of other bequests rolled on, Betty and Pat must have picked up the uncomfortable atmosphere. One of them – I can't now remember which – said: 'This is family business – we shouldn't really be here.'

The atmosphere continued during the car journey back to Litlington and we spent the next couple of days in a worried trance. Then, one day, we decided we had to bite the bullet. We packed the car with sleeping bags, hot-water bottles, extra jumpers and a primus stove, and set off for Wells.

We had a pretty good idea of what lay ahead of us: we had been to Ware Hall-House only a fortnight ago. Even so, when we opened the gate in the garden wall, we were shocked. Briars now reached beyond the first-floor windows. The house seemed somehow tattier. The garden seemed far more densely packed with clutter. I don't suppose that the amount had actually increased since we had last seen it. When we had been there before, we had given our attention to the person living in the middle of it all; now, there was nothing to look at but her junk.

There was so much of it in the house that we could hardly get in. The front door wouldn't open fully, because right behind it was a pale green 1930s kitchen unit. Tony opened its doors, to find that it contained hundreds of neatly stacked empty jam jars, large and small, ancient and modern, glass and pottery. Behind it, the passage was blocked by a great heap of chairs – a tangle of rusty springs, fraying upholstery and broken arms and legs. We squeezed past them into the great hall, which was filled with boxes and trunks stacked up to the ceiling, with narrow alleys left between them. Tony followed one that led to a window and pulled off the battens that held up the sheet of stained polythene covering its unglazed frame. Spring sunshine tumbled in – just as it does when Pip tears down Miss Havisham's curtains in the 1940s film of *Great Expectations*. It fell like a floodlight on the far corner of the room, in which half a dozen or so headless figures were suspended – coats hanging on hooks fixed in the ceiling. I fiddled my way through the cartons and rusty tin trunks to get a closer look, and saw that one of the hangers carried a St John Ambulance uniform jacket. When I took its cuff in my hand, the sleeve fell in pieces to the floor.

I don't know how long we were transfixed by the atmosphere of the place, but at some point, Tony reminded me that we had come to sort things out, not to gawp – and so we set to work. We started on the chairs. As we disentangled them, we found that nearly all of them were broken. They were all, however, interesting pieces of furniture – at least, they once had been. We struggled with them for the whole morning, shifting them into heaps of matching or near-matching sets, and stacks of chairs worth repairing and beyond repair. When, after a couple of hours, we stood back and looked at what we had achieved, we laughed as it dawned on us that we had achieved precisely nothing. We had just replaced one pile of junk with another. Tony said that he wondered whether sorting through all this rubbish was a waste of time, and we might do better to set light to it all where it was. I am not now entirely sure he was joking. But the only thing we did set light to that evening was the Rayburn, and that took a lot of effort to get going. Once Tony had coaxed it into life, we walked around the corner to the Crown, where we washed in hot water and enjoyed a hearty meal. It was a routine that we were to follow for some years to come – though we didn't realise then quite how many of those years there would be.

A hard day's work, a good supper and a few drinks should have set us up for a well-earned sleep, but our first night in Ware

Hall-House didn't go quite as comfortably as we had planned. We set out our sleeping bags in the space that would eventually be the main bedroom, but one of the walls was still open studwork and the door hadn't yet been hung. This wouldn't have mattered if it hadn't been for the rats. We knew they were about, because we had the rat man come before our arrival and he had found evidence of them everywhere. We didn't fancy being visited by rats as we slept, so Tony built us in and them out by nailing sheets of perspex to the inside of the studwork. When he had fixed the last piece over the doorway, we felt safe. But not for long.

We had only just climbed into our sleeping bags when we heard scuffling and scratching noises from the ground floor. 'Rats!' said Tony, cheerfully, but then the scuffling and scratching got louder. There must have been scores of them. We could hear them fighting over the little plastic trays in which the rat man had put out his poisoned bait. The sound of plastic scraping on concrete echoed around the house. I looked at Tony and his face wasn't quite so cheerful. I expect mine was showing terror. I certainly felt it. Without speaking, Tony reached across to the pile of tools we had been using, picked up a claw hammer and passed me a hand axe. We sat up for what seemed like ages, until the scrabbling noises faded away and we could no longer fight off sleep.

When I woke up the next morning, my first thought was that I had been having a nightmare, until I turned over and found myself lying on an axe. I sat up and looked around me. What on earth were we doing here, sleeping in a building site? We had endured only one night of it, but Auntie May had been roughing it like this – and much worse – for twenty-three years. I got up, stretched and pulled away the sheet of perspex that had served as a door. The rest of the first floor had no boards down and I could see all Auntie

May's junk heaped up as high as the joists. How could she – how could anyone – live like this?

Then the birds began to sing in the overgrown garden, and I heard sparrows hopping and skipping on the tiles above my head. As I stood there, watching the morning sun spilling in to fill the gaps between the boxes that May had crammed with all the things she had been sure she would one day find a use for, the answer came to me. May had had hope. I felt her hope rise within me. We would complete her task. I was sure of it.

CHAPTER THREE

A Matter of Record

In which I discover Auntie May's diaries and
realise their significance

In the spring and summer of 1994, we came back to Ware Hall-House every weekend. Mind, we never again heard any rats – the poison must have worked. They had certainly tucked into it keenly enough! We did, however, hear other creatures in the house – creatures that Auntie May had unknowingly brought with her from Ware. One night at the end of April, we found ourselves lying awake listening to a noise that sounded like distant pneumatic drills, but which seemed to be coming from somewhere indoors. When we got up the next morning to investigate, we spotted a couple of brown insects walking along a dusty oak beam. We had death watch beetles. When we found out how much it would cost to eradicate them, we decided we could live with them.*

By then, the project had taken hold of us and as the months went by, it tightened its grip. On Friday nights, as soon as Tony came home from work, we would pack up and head off in our Land Rover to Wells, let some air into the house, light the Rayburn and pop around the corner to have supper in the Crown. On Saturday

---

* I still do!

mornings, we would drive to Jewson's to pick up whatever building materials we needed for that weekend's tasks. The first was to sort out the plumbing. The downstairs loo worked well enough and there was a cold-water tap over the sink in the scullery – though we had to empty the room of boxes and boxes of junk to get comfortable access to it. It was the upstairs bathroom that was the problem – not that there was actually a room around the loo and the old, cast-iron bath above which a huge, ancient electric water heater was tied with binder twine to a beam. We ripped the whole lot out and threw it in a skip.

It was on one of those early visits that I heard my first nightingale. It was a still, late spring night and I was lying in May's bed with the windows open when I heard the most wonderful sounds coming from the little clearing we had made in the front garden. The song was sweet and pure and various: trilling, chirping, chattering and whistling. The gaps between the phrases were filled with a kind of awestruck silence, as if the rest of nature was holding its breath until the performance finished. On another occasion, I was cutting my way past the old apple tree that stood – that still stands – near the western corner of the house, when a blackbird flew up and settled on a branch a couple of feet from my face. It stood there, looking at me, and I stood there, looking back. We can only have been staring at each other for a second or two, but it was one of those moments when time seems to stop. A strange thought alighted and lingered. Was this May, making a fleeting, reassuring visit, telling me that she was at last at peace?

A couple of wing beats and it was gone – and a second, less fanciful thought occurred to me. So that was why May had always refused to let us cut down the weeds for her. She had wanted them left for the birds. She hadn't kept a garden; she had kept a wildlife sanctuary. In the summer, it was full of birdsong, butterflies and bees . The atmosphere was magical.

But we had to break the spell in order to work on the house. The nettles on either side of the path now touched each other, and the shed and Auntie May's old caravan were invisible through the tall, tumbling tangle of undergrowth that filled the site from wall to wall and fence to fence. We knew that somewhere under it all there were piles of building materials that we would want to use, including all the panes of glass Auntie May had carefully removed and labelled in 1969. We would need them to make the house properly weathertight before the next winter.

So, we set to, hacking and slashing towards where we knew the caravan to be. But the task was even harder than it looked. On only my second or third swipe, my hook struck something heavy and metallic – a stack of scaffolding poles, as it turned out – and once I had worked my way round those, I hit something solid again: an ancient mangle. The ground was almost entirely covered in junk. The brambles, briars and nettles had grown through it all, knitting it to the soil. The only way to get through was by cutting down what I could with the hook, then using a hand fork and a trowel to scrape away at the ground like an archaeologist. Working like this, I unearthed four fireplaces and grates, and two huge bread-oven doors, all of them beautifully made and finely decorated – but useless. Auntie May had rebuilt her house without a chimney. There was no need for fireplaces. They were just things that had come into her possession and were thus destined to be kept.

The caravan was only twenty yards from the house, but it took us all morning to reach it. Apart from the scaffold poles, none of the stuff that we uncovered could be of any use. We did find a neat stack of ancient floorboards, but when we tried to pick them up they turned to dust. When we finally reached the caravan, her name was still visible in the paintwork that was peeling off in patches: Blue Lady. We cut our way carefully to the door, turned the handle and pulled. It was unlocked.

The last time we had peeped inside – some twenty years earlier – the stove had been lit, the kettle was boiling on top of it and one of May's cats had been curled up sunning itself in the window. Today, the place stank of damp. The fibreboard walls and ceilings were soft and sagging. We couldn't get in for all the stuff that May had stored there. It was stacked front to back and side to side with boxes, chests and cupboards. Under the table were several piles of old 78-rpm gramophone records. When Tony reached in to pull a couple out, the paper covers came to pieces in his hands. The edges of the discs were covered in tiny silver snail trails, but the snails themselves were nowhere to be seen. We soon worked out why. As we pulled out all the clutter, we found rat-holes in the floorboards. And when we looked under the caravan, we saw several neat wheels of carefully woven grass – rats' nests. Each was filled to the brim with the unbroken, empty shells of snails.

We pulled out all the caravan's contents, and stood there looking at it, set out on the stumps and stubble of the clearing that we had made. None of the furniture was worth keeping, but we thought we ought to go through cupboards before we burned them. I am very glad we did. One old wooden cabinet contained several cardboard boxes labelled 'SJAB'. In them, we found all of Auntie May's St John Ambulance papers, dating back to the certificate qualifying her to render 'first aid to the injured' in September 1938. There was a pile of cashbooks recording every financial transaction of the Ware branch of the SJAB. There were rolled up wartime recruiting posters depicting angelically beautiful SJAB nurses, at work against the background of the London Blitz. There were all of May's personal record cards, noting her annual refresher courses in first aid, the number of divisional instruction meetings attended (forty-four of them in 1941; fifty-one in 1965), the number of hours she contributed to public and other duties, and the dates on which she was awarded her service chevrons (1942, 1945, 1948 and 1951). There were her medals and her belt buckles wrapped in tissue paper. There was the certificate recording her appointment as a divisional superintendent in Ware, dated 9 June 1958. There were photos of first aid demonstrations, newspaper cuttings and minute books. There were folders of correspondence relating to Auntie May's wartime service medal and bars. One box contained a dozen or so unworn nurses' bonnets, a pile of unissued black uniform stockings and several starched, white detachable cuffs. Another contained three blue uniform dresses and her uniform hat with cockade.

Everywhere we looked, we found hoards of things stored according to various themes. In the crumbling brick and tile shed at the northern end of the garden, we found ancient boat lights, railway lamps, Tilley lamps and hurricane lanterns, ornate Victorian paraffin lamps – one with a beautifully engraved bat etched on the chimney. Beside them were all kinds of tools, ancient and not-quite modern: hammers, axes, saws, chisels, files, clamps, cramps, spokeshaves and any number of implements that we couldn't identify. There were lengths of chain, coils of rope and all sorts of bits and pieces of brass that looked as if they had once been attached to a boat. And behind them all we found the rusty frame of the old Velocette motorcycle that Auntie May had bought during the war.

In a corner of the garden, under a cover of old gabardine mackintoshes and yellowing polythene, we found a stack of side-saddles. I pulled out one, then another, then another, then another . . . there were nine of them in varying stages of decay. How on earth would Auntie May have come by nine side-saddles? She had, as far as I knew, never ridden a horse – though I had seen the back end of what looked like a stuffed one among the heap of furniture in the front passage of the house. I wondered if there might be any connection, so I spent some time shifting chairs and wardrobes so I could get a better look. When I got to it, though, it turned out to be some kind of vaulting horse – at least, that's what I thought at first. When I looked more closely, I realised it couldn't be. There was a carpeted step on one side to allow someone to mount it, and the top wasn't straight, like a piece of gym equipment, but indented, like the back of a real horse. I dragged in one of the saddles. It fitted perfectly. But what was it for? And why were there eight more? I couldn't work it out.

Some long time later, we had a visitor who knew a bit about horses and so we asked her what all that horsey stuff meant. 'Do you have any painters in the family?' she asked. Tony said yes: his great-grandfather had been a portrait painter, but that we didn't have any of his pictures, because all his work was commissioned and therefore sold. 'Well, that's it, then,' said our friend. 'He must have painted ladies on horseback. A real horse wouldn't have stayed still enough during the sittings, so the subject would have sat on the dummy. The rest of the horse would have been painted in later.'*

We had always known Auntie May had been a hoarder, but as we opened box after box of her possessions, it became obvious that the reason there were so many of them was that she had, quite literally, never thrown anything away, ever.

---

* Years later, I found a copy of a letter Auntie May had written (just before she moved) to the BBC's scenery and properties department, offering them the side-saddles in return for a donation to the SJAB: 'If the saddles are of no use, I will take them with me, as part of a display of bygone relics that I hope to have in the attics.'

One box was so light that at first we thought it must be empty, but we found that it contained several hundred paracetamol packets. In each of them, Auntie May had replaced the blister-sheets that had originally held the tablets. On the top of each packet, she had written the date, time and quantity of each dose she had taken. I was about to throw the lot away when it occurred to me to look at those dates and dosages more carefully. She had got through the lot in the last three years. She had taken the maximum dose every day. There were three years of suffering in that box.

Another strange find was a brown paper bag like a little stuffed cushion. When I opened it, I dropped it in horror. It was stuffed with human hair. Later, we found dozens more wedged in between many of the tea chests, packing cases and furniture. My first thought was that this was more than eccentricity, this was madness, but Tony said he wondered whether she had kept it to mix with the wall plaster. We knew that she was a stickler for architectural accuracy, after all, and medieval plasterers did add hair to their mix – but that was horsehair, not human hair. And not dog hair either – we found loads of paper bags filled with that, too. We hated finding them; we found the very feel of them revolting. One day, Tony threw one to me with a grin. I caught it and realised that although it was unusually heavy, it clearly contained hair. I opened it hesitantly to find a long, black, wiry hank with two white streaks in it. I was holding a sporran. Months later I found a sepia photo of a man wearing it.

Another frequent find was an old-fashioned soap-powder packet – Omo, Oxydol, and the like. These, it turned out, were just the right size to contain the scores of matchboxes that Auntie May had filled them with. We came across hundreds of them. Each contained fifty or sixty matchboxes. Many held the original matches, now spent; others held small items ranging from bits of broken pottery to coins, beads and buttons.

There was a sack of paper bags full of milk-bottle tops – thousands of them, all carefully washed and pressed flat. Later, we found a pile of pans and aluminium kettles in the garden, obviously saved for recycling. Each had been used until the bottom had burned through.*

One discovery that held me captivated for hours, and which I returned to frequently, was the stack of old scrapbooks I found in one of the bedrooms. There were dozens of them, all filled with neatly arranged items that seemed to have been chosen just for their prettiness: seed packets, photos of sailing ships, Rupert Bear comic strips cut from newspapers, fruit tin labels, postcards, pieces of coloured wrapping paper . . . They were magpie collections made by someone with a keen eye for design. The earliest of the books dated from Auntie May's teenage years – I wondered if she had kept them as ideas for the wallpaper patterns she was then creating.†

There were hundreds of odd editions of the *Times*, the *Telegraph*, the *Daily Express*, the *Daily Mirror*, the *Evening News*, the *New Statesman*, *Tribune*, *Daltons Weekly*, the *Daily Herald*, the *Daily Mail*, the *Hertfordshire Mercury*, the *Eastern Daily Press*, the *Dereham and Fakenham Times* and the *Lynn News and Advertiser*. Most of them appeared to have no particular significance: they are clearly just papers she happened to buy on a particular day. But she bought some on special occasions, too. Browsing through one box, I found the 4am edition of the *Daily Mail* of Thursday, 7 February 1952:

---

* Later still, we gathered all this scrap metal together, along with the aluminium panels of the caravan, and donated it to Guide Dogs for the Blind, a charity Auntie May supported throughout her life. It raised enough to buy and train a dog.

† Alas, the collection of scrapbooks was stolen in a break-in a couple of years after I found them.

THE QUEEN FLYING HOME

The King to Lie in State for Seven Days in Westminster Hall

VALET FOUND HIM DEAD IN BED AT 7.15 A.M.

Premier Broadcasts Tonight After Meeting
Royal Party at Airport

Turning the pages was like going back in time. The story was full of touching details that reflected the shock felt by the nation, by the Commonwealth and by the young princess who was to become Queen.

> The princess had spent some of the happiest hours of her visit at Treetops during the night, watching the wild game by the light of the moon.
>
> Before breakfast this morning she sat writing letters and when she had finished she joined the rest of the party. She talked about her father a great deal during breakfast and seemed particularly happy.
>
> She told Colonel Sherbroke Walker how well her father had looked lately and how much stronger he was getting, and said he had been shooting and enjoying himself.
>
> When she got back to the lodge one of the household said to her: "You look tired, but you look much better for your rest."
>
> It was about an hour after this that the news was heard.

Further down the same box, another paper from that year caught my eye. It was a copy of the *Daily Express*, dated Thursday, 25

September. In the middle of the top half of the front page is a picture of a woman in a beret being rescued in a boat. The headline reads, 'Miss May, on holiday, drifts in a gale' – it's Auntie May!

RESCUED – WITH HER
DOG AND CAT

HOLIDAYMAKERS in macintoshes, dodging the spray on Westcliff, Essex, esplanade yesterday, saw a 35ft. cabin cruiser bobbing in gale-swept seas.

The anchor had broken. The boat drifted towards a sea wall and threatening breakwater. On deck, Miss May Savidge, of Ware, Herts., having a holiday afloat, shouted and waved. Police were called.

Two men – Mr. Gill Pyke and his son Arthur – launched a small boat, took out a spare anchor and managed to tow the boat to new moorings.

In the picture they are bringing Miss Savidge ashore. Her pet dog and cat were with her.

AND here an officer takes a few notes . . . Miss Savidge, her dog Julie beside her, takes tea . . . and Twinkle the cat? She is in the larger bag.

We found huge bundles of journals that reflected Auntie May's curiously wide range of interests: *Flight*, the *Draughtsman*, the *Schoolmaster*, *Radio Constructor*, *Apollo*, Woolworths and ICI house magazines, the weekly newsletter of the Cancer & Polio Research Fund, and the *Journal of the East Hertfordshire Archaeological Society*. There was a foot-high pile of *Rupert the Bear* comic strips cut from the *Daily Express*. There were stacks of special editions, supplements and souvenirs commemorating the great national events that had occurred during Auntie May's lifetime – including all the royal marriages and deaths, the coronation of Queen Elizabeth II, the death of Winston Churchill and the investiture of the Prince of Wales. There was a calendar for every year of her adult life – she had written nothing on any of them, and had not torn off any of the days or months as they had passed.

Squatting in the gloom of that dusty house, I sorted through those piles and found the day of my birth on a 1944 calendar. I felt rather strange, as if I had actually returned somehow to that very year, just for a moment. I suddenly wanted to know what day of the week my sister was born on, eleven years before me. In that dingy corner, peering through May's paraphernalia, I happily lost sight of the enormous task that faced me.

There were hundreds of programmes of plays and films she had seen, and public events she attended, including the British Empire Exhibition of 1924, when she was thirteen, and the Empire Day Festival in Hyde Park in 1929.*

There were folders containing every single letter, flyer and pamphlet put through her letterbox during every national and local election campaign conducted during her adult lifetime. There were hymn sheets and orders of service for religious occasions great and small, including the Thanksgiving for Victory service that marked the end of the Second World War.

And then there was a collection within a collection. Behind a broken-down chaise longue in the kitchen, we found pile after pile of copies of the *Radio Times*, stacked in date order. Auntie May had used them as a filing system: tucked into each issue were the receipts and bills relating to all the purchases she had made during

---

* I later sold most of these to help pay for further renovations of the house.

that week. Among them were thousands of train, bus and trolley bus tickets – some printed on card of gentle shades of pink, green, yellow or blue, and others on flimsy white paper. She even kept notes left for and by the milkman. One scrap of paper carried the message, 'Mrs Savage [*sic*]. Sorry only one blue top. I broke the bottle on the way round and I don't carry any extra. Sorry for any inconvenience.'

There were trunks containing neatly stacked chocolate boxes, their contents consumed but each individual frilled paper case and smoothed-out silver paper put back in its place. There were hundreds of carefully flattened and folded paper bags, plain and fancy. Many of them were printed with advertisements for Fyffes or Geest bananas; some had historic interest (though I don't think this is why Auntie May kept them). Several carried pictures of the Queen or her coat of arms, marking her coronation. Some carried the names of department stores that have long ceased to exist – Bourne & Hollingsworth, Swan & Edgar, Derry & Toms; some were plain; and some carried a carefully pencilled note describing what they once contained: '<u>LOAF. 9.11.90</u>'.

May seemed to have kept all the packaging that anything she ever bought came in. We found flattened PG Tips tea boxes on which she had written notes and shopping lists; we found packets that had contained Austin's Cloudy Ammonia ('For the bath, the addition of three tablespoonfuls acts as an invigorating and refreshing tonic') on the back of which she had written drafts of her domestic accounts. We found the packets of all the medicines she had ever taken, filed after she had finished them between the appropriate pages of the *Radio Times*.

There were neatly slit breakfast cereal and 'mansize' tissue boxes flattened and used as filing folders; there were hundreds of Kit Kat wrappers and hundreds more dog-food can labels, all

ironed flat for use as note paper, clipped together with clothes pegs
to form little booklets. Many of the labels had carefully written
memos or shopping lists on the back. From the dates on the notes
and the old-fashioned design of the labels and packaging, it was
clear to us that Auntie May had been reusing things for decades
before recycling became fashionable. But we also found stuff that
had no imaginable further use, including scores of cellophane
Cambridge Stocking packets, and various instruction leaflets
printed on both sides. One box that Tony picked up jingled as he
moved it. When he opened the lid, he found it contained scores of
empty medicine bottles. Most of them had contained J Collis
Browne's Mixture, the Victorian cure-all for tickly coughs and
upset stomachs.

We found all this stuff and more on our first couple of visits.

Then, one day, I opened a box to find that it contained copies
of all the letters Auntie May had ever received. She had filed them
carefully according to the name of the correspondent, and stored
them in yellow folders, arranged alphabetically. There were about
fifty of them, and most of them contained scores of letters in date
order, each in its original envelope.* There were postcards, too.
The earliest of them dated back to the 1920s, when Auntie May
was a teenager. I had always thought of Auntie May as a lonely,
private person, but all these letters showed that she had made – and
kept – lots of friends. In the same box were dozens of similar files
– labelled 'Christmas' or 'Birthday' followed by the year. They
contained all the greetings cards she had received. I picked out one
of the letter folders at random. It was labelled 'NELLIE ADAMS
(MRS)'. It contained several hundred letters and postcards from
Auntie May's older sister. It fell open at a letter written with a

---

* Many of the stamps on them turned out to be valuable. We sold these to help fund the
building project.

fountain pen in careful, old-fashioned longhand. It was dated 19 September 1945.

> *Dear May,*
>
> *Thanks for your letter telling me about your "Formosa". It really sounds a very nice boat and I do feel most interested in it and shall be very pleased to hear some more particulars when you have time to write again, such as sanitation, heating and cooking etc . . . I do hope you will be moored near some other people as I don't like to think of you all alone on it, specially wintertime . . . if you found it was too damp and dreary to spend every winter on it you could perhaps go into digs of some sort for the worst months . . .*
>
> *Love from Nellie*
>
> *P.S. Has it got a lav? Or what do you do about it?*

I could hear Nellie's voice as I read it. There was a particular tone she adopted when speaking to her younger sister: it was kindly, concerned, and just a little disapproving.

I wondered where Auntie May had kept copies of her half of these exchanges: if she had kept useless ephemera such as bus tickets and shopping lists, she must have kept copies of the letters she had written. I found them almost immediately, because they, too, were in boxes near her desk. There were thousands of them, all filed under date. I pulled several out and read them. Pulling out one at random now, I find a typed carbon copy dated 3 February 1964 and sent from 1 Monkey Row.

> *Dear Marion,*
>
> *Sorry to hear you had been ill again . . . sorry not to have written sooner . . . thank you for all your presents . . . Poor old Moxy, my stray puss, has had to be put to sleep . . . how are your pets?*

And then a charming little reference to Auntie May's charitable work with the elderly and sick:

> *One old soul, who I visit for St. John and the Old People's Welfare Assn. got it into her head, just after Christmas, that she still had to do 'black out', and in climbing up to fix a thick curtain, fell, and is still in bed, so I have had to spend a good deal more time there than I usually do. It is pathetic the way some of these old people battle along on their own.*

•

Going through Auntie May's things was fascinating, but it was taking up a lot of time. Summer was dribbling away and the days were getting shorter, and all we seemed to have achieved was to move Auntie May's junk around from one place to another, creating temporary little spaces in which to work. Tony was scornful of her hoardings – he wanted them out of the way so that we could get the building and decorating finished as quickly as possible. We weren't making anything like enough progress and we weren't going to, until all those boxes were out of the way. But we couldn't just dump them.

We wondered what on earth we could do to speed things up. In desperation, I thought about writing to the BBC to offer the job to the *Challenge Anneka* programme, in which the presenter, Anneka Rice, took on all sorts of seemingly impossible tasks. But before I could do so, Tony had a better idea. If I gave up my teaching job, I could move up to Wells permanently, sort through May's boxes, throw out any junk, identify anything that had any value, and sell it. He reckoned doing this might raise as much money as I had been earning – maybe more – and it would get

May's stuff out of the way so that we could finish work on the building. It seemed the perfect solution. I handed in my notice at the school. My colleagues gave me a cordless electric screwdriver as a leaving present.

I moved to Wells in the summer holiday and began in earnest. The plan was to spend half the time sorting through boxes, and half the time getting on with light building work. Tony would do the heavier stuff at the weekends.

It was a good plan, but I just couldn't stick to it. I found the boxes too tempting and spent far more time rummaging than painting or plastering. My good intentions were derailed almost immediately, when I opened a box that was under the table at which she ate her meals, near the chair in which she sat and slept. (We had worked out some time ago that she couldn't ever have slept in her bed. The space upstairs that she had never got round to building walls for did have a bed in it, but it was covered with boxes that were piled up as high as the ceiling.) The box contained more boxes – twenty-six of them. Most had originally contained Cadbury's Marvel milk powder; a couple of them had once held Norfolk House Brazilian blend instant coffee; one was an old 2lb ICI washing soda crystals box. They were all roughly the same size. Their top flaps had been neatly cut off – later, I was to find them with notes or shopping lists written on them – and each box was filled with twenty or so little notebooks from which the outside covers had been removed.

I pulled out one of the Marvel boxes at random and fished out one of the books. It was ruled for cash accounting but had been used as a diary. At the top of the first page was the number '393'. The first entry read 'TU: 23.6.87 Cont^d.' Under it, in Auntie May's neat, tiny handwriting, was a list of all her actions that day. She had gone to the post office to post a printed card to Mr Beales (of

Hertford Planning) and another to Councillor P Bellam. Both had been 'filled in on typewriter'. Both cards had been pre-printed (with, I guessed, a message expressing an opinion on some planning matter) by the 'Hertfordshire Restoration Society (61b Ware High Street)'. Each had been sent by first-class mail, at a cost of 18p, which was noted in a cash column on the right of the page under a running balance of £87.45. She had returned via the east side of the Buttlands and arrived home by 4pm. The last entry for the day read 'L.C.', followed by a tick. I didn't know what that meant.

Below this was the entry for 'WED: 24.6.87. MIDSUMMER DAY!!!', under which Auntie May had recorded that she got up at 6.45am, listened to the radio, dozed off again in her chair, 'slept a bit', unlocked the gate at 8am, taken a telephone call at 8.20am, which was a 'wrong number (young woman)'. The milk had arrived at 9.10am. At 3.10pm she had left for an 'optical test' at 3.40pm with Mr Keith Waring, '(partly bald – full beard)', taking with her (as the appointment card required) her 'old specs – 5 pairs', including her 'broken bifocals – 20 yrs old, pair for close work – about 23 yrs old, pair for distances – about 30 yrs old . . . He said my eyes had not altered much.' Having her bifocals made 'will take about two months'. She returned 'across Buttlands' and was 'home by 4.10pm' when she had 'tea'. That day's weather was 'some sun and clouds'. 'L.C.' and the tick are written twice. (I wondered whether it might mean 'exercised Lorraine and the Cats'.)

I could hardly believe it. There were 440 books filled with meticulous records like these. I flicked through the rest of volume 393, and all sorts of details caught my eye. Many were records of medical problems. 'Cut piece of lint – 15″ long – to cover all ulcers'; 'Savlon on inner side of leg, more painful than heel'; 'hot and humid – so sudden – no energy'; 'had to rest R. leg, so could not finish jobs'; 'ankles very tired – too weary'; 'dozed off again in brown chair'; 'left leg again discharging – left knee inclined to bend more than necessary'; 'extraction of L. upper broken tooth'; 'dentist removed 2 more . . . I still have 3 upper teeth.' Poor Auntie May. In all the years I had known her, I had never once heard her complain of ill health; only now could I see how much she had suffered.

But there were all sorts of other things noted, too. She listed everything she ever bought, where she bought it and how much she paid. In volume 393, at least, every list of shopping bought each Friday is almost exactly the same, except in fractions of weight or price. On Friday, 10 July 1987, she got up at 4.40am to find that it had rained a little in the night, though it was sunny and breezy by 9.30am, and warmer and humid by 11am, when she went out. She bought five wholemeal loaves at 54p each from the baker's. She ordered two gallons of paraffin (for £3.20) from Walsinghams. She bought six bananas at 48p per lb at the Yellow Fruit Shop. They weighed 2lb 11½oz. and cost £1.31. She collected the *Fakenham & Wells Times* (18p) and the *Radio Times* (35p) from Martin's, the newsagents. At Howells, the butcher's, she bought a pound of ox liver (46p) and 2lb of pet mince (40p) for the 'pets'. She didn't buy ox heart, which she notes was 68p per lb. (She records a conversation between Mr Howell and two lady customers who are visiting on holiday. The older one said that her daughter in Kent would like to move to Wells.) She bought two 40-watt light bulbs (90p) from Montforts, and a large tube of Savlon from Kinghams (£1.19). In the Station Road post office, she collects two weeks' worth of pension @ £39.91, totalling £79.82) and meets someone called 'ROS' who has just spent a week's holiday in northern Scotland, touring around and staying in a hotel, which was 'lovely'. Auntie May then went to the high street, and Leftley's, where she bought:

Bananas (ripe) – 42p per lb.	.80
Cup-a-Soup – pkt of 4	.51
Orange cream biscuits (NISA) 300g	.36
Marg – (LOW salt) sunflower – NISA 250g	.24
Peach jam 1lb green	.35
Strawberry jam 1lb green	.35
Tea – NISA 125g	.39
Cheese – 9⅝ oz. Mild Cheddar NISA – 1.29 lb.	.77
Kitekat tins – 400g – 2	.62
Pkt CHUM MIXER (no bags) 700g	.61
Strawberries – LOCAL – punnet – 1lb 2oz	.55

When she got home (at about 1pm, via Green Dragon Lane) she checked her totals and noted that Leftley's had undercharged her by 5p.

Of the 440 numbered volumes in those boxes, the earliest entry is dated 8 November 1946. The last one is Friday, 4 December 1992. How on earth did Auntie May find the time to write them all, and why on earth would she want to in the first place? Why such detail? How could it possibly be of interest that she returned via Green Dragon Lane, or across the Buttlands, or via the east side of it? How can the very order in which she visited the shops be so important that she corrected it with arrows at various points? How could anyone survive on a diet of bread, jam, cheese, biscuits, Cup-a-Soups and bananas? All the shopping lists in later years contain these items and little else.

Standing in the narrow passageway between the piles of boxes, stacks of furniture and heaps of clutter that filled almost every cubic foot in the house, I realised that the answers to these questions were all around me. If I chose to, I could reassemble Auntie May's whole life in the same way that she had reassembled her whole house. I could fit together a detailed picture of everything she had ever done, matching diary entries of bus journeys with the very ticket she had used, finding the packet that had contained the Cup-a-Soup for which she had paid 51p at Leftley's on the morning of Friday, 10 July 1987, and the label from the tin of Lassie dog food for which she had paid 13½p on 22 April 1975.

And then I had a strangely unsettling thought. There was a sense in which Auntie May was still present. The life-force that had once held all those things together, giving them meaning, had not disappeared, but had taken up a fragmented existence in all those boxes, papers, letters, diaries, photographs, newspapers, magazines, shopping lists, jam jars, medicine bottles, clothes, notebooks, bus tickets, invoices, Christmas cards and pieces of whole or broken furniture. A little of the personality of Auntie May, a tiny part of her being, was still in everything she had ever touched and kept. There was something of her in every till receipt and cinema ticket, every Kit Kat label and cornflake packet, every bill left by and note left for the milkman.

It was like a huge jigsaw puzzle, but without the picture on the lid of the box. The picture of Auntie May in my mind turned out to be far simpler than the one that began to emerge as I started sorting through and making sense of all she had kept. I didn't decide to start putting those pieces back together again, I just found myself doing it. And once I had started, I couldn't stop. It was a challenge that I didn't even think about refusing. It was a responsibility that had fallen to me.

CHAPTER FOUR

Distractions and Detective Work

In which I am side-tracked by some puzzling and
unexpected finds

So, during that first week alone in the house, when I was supposed
to be getting on with the plastering, I found myself compulsively
rifling and rummaging. One early find was a folder made from a
flattened cornflake packet, labelled 'Stories to write'. Tucked inside
were about forty scraps of paper and old envelopes on which she
had written the outlines of short stories. She doesn't seem to have
got round to writing the stories themselves – I certainly haven't
found any. The earliest was dated 1962 and the latest, 1983, but
most were written a little before or a little after Auntie May's move
from Hertfordshire to Norfolk. Her imagination seems to have
been operating in overdrive at the time. As I sat at her desk reading
her notes, I found several interesting clues as to how her highly
original mind must have worked.

1.6.1969

The Fantasy of the Phantoms, OR, The Re-erection of the Wraiths
How about a story about moving an old house and the associations

35

*that go with it? Perhaps some [ghosts] would go with the house &
others stay in the place where it was . . .*

30.9.71

*There may be a note of this on some other scrap of paper – I've thought
about it before, anyway. After decimalisation of currency – what about
decimalising the clocks – 100 hour day(?) – 100 minutes to the hour,
anyway – just now, seeing . . . 2 minutes 50 seconds, I automatically
thought of 2½ minutes – due to decimal currency!*

2.10.71

*This one should point out that some of the lonely folks (old or
otherwise) wait for someone to call on them (or do things for them)
instead of making an effort themselves . . .*

4.10.71

*An interesting story could be worked out from the flashes when one
feels one has "been there before" – I think there is a word* [for this] –
I think some people put it down to reincarnation – but suppose it was
passed on by one's parents – an <u>inherited memory</u> which only discloses
bits of itself when something stimulates it to do so – or perhaps only
some persons have it (or have little "flashes") – it might be in all of
us, like all the other things we inherit (looks, ability, etc.) – if only
we could get at it. A character in the story could have a much greater
than usual number of "flashes" – something triggers them off (could
also occur in dreams) – but always they are "memories" passed down
from parents – things that they actually knew about & perhaps their
desires to know what was kept secret from them – this could stir a
character to know what was hidden from some ancestor – not*

* *Déjà vu.*

36

necessarily very far back. The way family likenesses are passed on makes one feel that the memories could be there, to be tapped, if one knew how — take the likeness of Mark's eldest daughter to Alan and Uncle Will & the two cousins born in Australia (Uncle Ben's) — the little girl reminded me of Grandma as soon as I saw the photo, years ago — she might have hidden, untapped memories of England — that could lead to another interesting part — when one goes to a strange town & one feels one has been there before, is it possible that one of one's ancestors had been there? — not too long ago, as towns often change.

This theme has possibilities — someone who feels she has "been to some place before", but that it was a bit different — thinks she may have been there as a small child, but finds that the "difference" occurred before that and that her Mother or Grandmother had been there before it happened — not an item that one might see on a local view card — or if it is, she finds that she automatically knows something about it that is not in any picture.

4.3.72

Write a funny (or light-hearted) story in opposition to the outlook on spinsters — that they are objects to be pitied — no-one wanted to marry them — they have "missed out" on life — they are lesser mortals than the girls & women who did get married . . . Spinsters need some sort of status, not just as "maiden aunts".

Many other things I found were quite puzzling. Browsing through Auntie May's piles of the *Radio Times*, I found dozens of scraps of paper on which she had written odd little notes. They didn't seem to make much sense at first:

'Could you hear the singing yesterday?'; 'The dresses were pretty,

weren't they?'; 'WE USED TO MAKE PAPER FLOWERS FOR THE CHILDREN, FOR THE SCHOOL PLAY'; 'WE TIED THEM ON TO TWIGS'; 'Mrs NEWBOULD, who looked after the HANDICRAFTS EXHIBITION'.

At first, I wondered whether Auntie May's obsessive orderliness had extended to planning what she was going to say in advance – she surely can't have written notes to prompt herself?

Then it dawned on me. Many of the notes were in unjoined-up writing, or in block capitals. They had been written clearly so that they could be read by someone with poor eyesight:

'I CAN HEAR THE BATTERY NOISE'; 'IF YOU PRETEND YOU CAN HEAR, YOU MAY SAY YES WHEN YOU MEAN <u>NO</u>.'; 'You are better off, because a deaf-aid does help you.'

They were her half of conversations she had had with the old people she had visited who were deaf. She had written them so that they could read what they couldn't hear. And I could hear them now: chatty, kindly, encouraging, reassuring. It didn't take much imagination to guess the unrecorded sides of the conversations, too:

'Another young man I know is now so deaf that a deaf-aid cannot help him.'

'Oh, really? How does he manage?'

'He has to lip-read.'

'What do you mean, "lip-read"?'

'He has to look at people's lips.'

'I feel very cold today.'

'Put your wool scarf on.'

Later, I was to find other pieces of that corner of the jigsaw.

One was a little coloured engraving in a Hogarth frame with the title: 'The Priory, Ware, Hertfordshire'. With all the moving of boxes and furniture going on, I thought I had better take it down in case it got knocked off its nail. On the back was written 'Presented to Miss May Savidge by Ware Old People's Welfare Association in recognition of services to the elderly, May 1970.' Later still, when I had time to go through all those diaries, I could see that it was a gift that Auntie May had thoroughly deserved.

When Tony came up to join me at the end of the first week, he looked around, saw how little work I had done and sighed deeply. I can't say I blame him. He had telephoned to ask how I had been getting on and I had lied about how much plastering I had done. I hadn't dared admit that I had spent most of the time losing myself among Auntie May's memories. On the Friday, I rushed to do as much as I could before he arrived, but it must have been obvious that I hadn't done a week's work.

He wasn't best pleased. He said that I seemed more interested in what he called 'her junk' than in honouring my promise of finishing the building. Even as I was denying it, I knew that he was right. He reminded me that until we dealt with the contents we couldn't possibly deal with the house. Even if some of her things were valuable, there was more value in having them out of the way. The best thing we could do would be to drag them all out into the garden and set fire to them – no, he had a better idea: we should set fire to them where they were, and get rid of the whole house, too. He had never wanted it in the first place.

I knew why he was upset. Auntie May's house and property had taken over his life, my life and our joint lives, totally. He had already told me several times that I was turning into her and that it wasn't healthy. I had taken early retirement to devote myself to the project Auntie May had bequeathed to us, but I had been side-tracked. I wasn't pulling my weight with the building work and I wasn't turning up things that could be sold.

To demonstrate his point, Tony picked up one of the boxes I had been going through, carried it out into the garden, and tipped its contents onto the heap of rubbish that was destined for the bonfire. 'No, not that one!' I cried – though I am sure I would have said the same of whichever box he had taken. This, though, did indeed contain something remarkable: one of the items that Auntie May had listed as left to Tony in her will. It was the prototype of a musical instrument that Auntie May had invented. She had called it the 'Selectatune'. It was a cross between a music box and a zither. Its purpose was 'to provide amusement combined with occupational therapy' and 'a means of training the ear in cases of tone deafness and speech therapy'. It was a flat plywood sounding board with strings that had sliding bridges that could be set out to play a predetermined tune, using a plectrum. The original drawings and design notes were also in the box.

The Selectatune and its documents lay on the rubbish heap for weeks, daring me to rescue them. Then one day, I came home to find that Tony had lit a bonfire. The Selectatune was gone, but the wind had blown the scorched papers into the hedge. I took them into the house and hid them under the cupboard in the kitchen, where Tony wouldn't find them.

CHAPTER FIVE

Discoveries of Value

In which I sell some very ordinary things for a lot of
money and part with something very special for
much less than it is worth

Tony was right. We needed to sort out what could be sold to pay
for building materials. If we didn't, the project would grind to a
halt. I got a man from Sotheby's to come in and look at the
furniture, but he said there wasn't much of any value apart from the
upturned chaise longue in the old parlour and a couple of ancient
cupboards. But he did point out something that hadn't occurred to
me: that though all those ancient bus tickets, chocolate boxes and
magazines might look like junk, there were collectors willing to
pay very good money for them. He said the best way to meet them
was to join the Ephemera Society, so he gave me the address.

Just before the Sotheby's man's visit, I had found Auntie May's
Marks & Spencer boxes and decided to find out what they might be
worth. She had worked for the company in the late 1920s and –
needless to say – she had kept every piece of paper that had come
her way.

I telephoned Marks & Spencer's head office and asked if they
had an archivist: they did, and she was called Angela Burns. When
I told her that Auntie May had worked for M&S in the 1930s, she

didn't seem particularly interested – until I mentioned that I had some early numbers of the company's magazine. 'Oh yes,' she said, 'they go back to 1937.' 'But I have got volume one, number one,' I replied, 'and it's dated 1934.' There was a silence and then she asked whether I'd care to come up to London and join her for dinner. I did, and we became friends. It turned out that the magazines Auntie May had left were issues that had been produced unofficially, before the project had been adopted by the management. They were very rare – in fact, no one in the M&S archives department had known of their existence – and they were potentially very valuable.

Angela came to Wells to look through Auntie May's M&S memorabilia – and I sold a box full of company pattern books, price lists and product catalogues directly to the Marks & Spencer museum. I asked her what I should do about valuing Auntie May's other bits and pieces and she, too, suggested I join the Ephemera Society, of which she was a member. So I did. At one of its meetings, I met the collector Robert Opie, who had founded the Museum of Brands, Advertising and Packaging, which is now housed in Notting Hill. He bought a number of old toothpaste tins, Kit Kat wrappers and other bits and pieces of old packaging that I had very nearly thrown away. He was a good man and paid me well for them – he was intrigued by the myriad saved chocolate wrappers, for they had the date she had bought them written on the back. I also got an excellent price for Auntie May's bus tickets. She had kept every one she'd ever bought and filed them between the pages of the *Radio Times* that carried the date on which she used them.

Not everyone I met was quite so generous. When I told one collector about my struggle to sort out Auntie May's stuff, she insisted on coming back to help me value it. She spent a whole day with me, estimating values and putting aside things that might get a good price. By tea time, we were both exhausted, and I offered to pay her for her efforts. At first, she refused to accept anything but, when I insisted, she said something she had seen caught her fancy – and it would be reward enough to be allowed to buy it from me. It was the little photograph of Queen Victoria that had been left to Auntie May by her own maiden aunt, Alice May Savidge, after whom she had been named. It was a pretty little picture, in which the Queen is holding a fan – and was taken by William Downey, who was, I later discovered, a much sought-after nineteenth-century photographer. Alice May Savidge had been employed by him to paint colour on his black and white prints. On the back of it, the Queen's equerry had written a note to Downey himself, instructing him to make a coloured copy and to be particularly careful of the colouring of the chin.

'It's not so much the picture that I like, as the mounting,' said my new friend. 'I know it's a bit quaint, but I think it's rather pretty.' I felt torn: I was truly grateful for all the help I'd had, but I didn't really want to part with something that Auntie May had kept as a family treasure. She told me it was worth about £30, and she'd be happy to buy it for that. I gave in and sold it to her. A few months later, I heard on the radio that it had been auctioned for a sum that would have paid for a builder to finish the work on the house twice over. I felt physically sick.

•

But – as far as I know any way – that photo was the only thing of Auntie May's that I sold badly. I started to develop an eye for things that had no sentimental value and that collectors might want.

A steady trickle of money was coming in and we spent it all on the house. Soon, we had finished the main bedroom, the scullery, the loos and the bathroom, though the rest of the place was still a cross between a junkyard and a building site. The house was still raked by draughts. Most of the windows were still unglazed, their frames covered with plastic sheeting. The house was cold. I had managed to get Auntie May's Rayburn to work, but the only way to get any real heat out of it was to build the fire up so far that the water boiled in the tank, so I had to leave the taps running while I cooked. The house was impossible to clean. Where there wasn't dust, there was mould. When it rained, water ran down the inside of the windows and, at times, it would drive straight through the walls.

Worse still, when the wind was in the north, the whole building swayed like a ship in a storm. The plastic that covered the windows flapped and snapped like sails. The house timbers – which were only held together with oak pegs – shrieked and graunched as they rubbed against each other. The movement would start erratically, gather momentum and then reach a resonant frequency that you could feel in your bones. Then the wind would ease, the vibration would stop and the whole house would shudder to a halt.

The first time this happened I was terrified. It was during the week, so I was alone in the house. I was so frightened the place would collapse that I hid under the bed. It happened again one weekend while Tony was there. We were woken in the middle of the night. He couldn't stop the swaying, but he did manage to lessen the noise. He went round the house with a lighted candle, pouring wax into the gaps around the pegs and joints in all the beams.

It couldn't have swayed and rocked like that originally, surely? What was wrong? Then we realised. Auntie May had taken great pains to restore the house authentically, but the one detail she had overlooked was the relationship between its design and its site. She had carefully orientated it in the medieval manner, with the solar facing south to catch the sun and the dairy facing north to keep cool. But in Ware, it had stood in a sheltered valley; now, it was on top of a hill and sideways-on to the prevailing wind. The frame would need strengthening. More expense!

CHAPTER SIX

A Surprising Correspondence

In which I find a broken heart wrapped up in a
brown paper parcel

I don't think Tony was right when he said I was turning into
Auntie May, but I can see that there were certainly some
similarities. She had started the rebuild immediately on her
retirement and I had retired in order to help finish her task. She
had been happy to live surrounded by the clutter she accumulated
throughout her lifetime, and I was delighting in that clutter, like a
child given free run of a toy shop. She had lived there alone and,
for five days of the week, I was living alone there, too. She had
captured and stored a lifetime's worth of emotions and, as I
unpacked them, her emotions came alive in me.

One afternoon, I found a brown paper parcel buried under some
bags and boxes at the very back of the attic. It contained a mounted
and framed black and white photograph of a man wearing
Elizabethan dress. I could see straight away that it was an actor
playing the part of Hamlet. He sits in sombre reflection, looking
deep into the dark middle distance. Tucked into the frame were
scores of letters in their original envelopes, along with numerous
pieces of paper covered in Pittman's shorthand. Sitting on the glass
were bundles of documents that included old theatre programmes,

newspaper cuttings and a passport issued in 1926 and bearing the name of Mr Denis Elliot Watson, a designer, born Newcastle upon Tyne on 9 September 1881. The passport photo and the Hamlet picture are of the same man.

When I pulled out the letters and began to read them, I was taken aback. They were love letters. Nellie had told me her sister had had a fiancé who had died before the war, but the reality of that relationship had never sunk in. In all the time I had known her, Auntie May had seemed a very solitary, self-sufficient person. I knew that she had had lots of friends and acquaintances, but I had never imagined her capable of anything like intimacy. All the evidence around me pointed to a life filled to overflowing with single-minded busy-ness. The idea that she might have found time even to think of romantic companionship just hadn't occurred to me. But looking through those letters, I could see that she had not become a loner through choice.

I skim-read them with guilty excitement. I had been immersed in Auntie May's life for months and thought I understood her: now I had found a side of her that I would never have imagined. There, spread out before me upon a great sheet of brown paper, were all the mementos of a relationship that had started as a tentative friendship, grown into love and been ended by death. Auntie May had wrapped her broken heart in a parcel, tied it with string and hidden it at the back of the attic.

Who was this designer and Shakespearean actor, and how had Auntie May met him? The expression in the photograph in his passport was as Hamletic as the younger face in the picture in the frame. In each, the eyes seem focused not on things, but on thought. In the passport, a middle-aged man wears a stiff collar and tie, and large, round, wire-rimmed pince-nez spectacles. His backcombed hair is receding. He is not young.

I did a little sum in my head. Auntie May was born in 1911; Denis was born in 1881. He was thirty years her senior. I did another little sum, too. Her copy of the first letter she wrote to him is dated 2 January 1928. She was only sixteen. I found myself wondering whether I ought to be shocked.

I didn't wonder for long. The correspondence begins innocently – and it is Auntie May who initiates it. She writes to thank Mr Watson for passing on her address to a potential new employer. They must have met at Heffer Scott's, the wallpaper design studio at which Auntie May had worked, and for which, I guess, Mr Watson had done work, too. Heffer Scott's was laying off staff – and Auntie May needed a job.

Dear Mr Watson,

Thank you very much for letting Mr P. have my address, so quickly; I am sure it is very kind of you to bother about me, and I thought you might be interested to know what has happened.

The letter is polite, friendly and chatty – but puzzlingly signed, 'I am, yours sincerely, Wendy.' Mr Watson's early letters address her as Wendy, too. He must have given her the nickname before they started writing to each other.

As I sat on the attic floor with all those letters round me, I wondered if the name 'Wendy' had any significance. And then it struck me. He called her Wendy because he saw himself as Peter Pan – the boy who wouldn't grow up. It seemed a rather telling choice of nickname. I guessed he was justifying their friendship by defining it as innocent. But just as there are hints of flirtation between Peter Pan and Wendy in JM Barrie's play and stories, there are flickers of more than friendship in even the early letters between Mr Watson and Auntie May.

For years, they seem to write more often than they meet. Early in the correspondence, Mr Watson gives up his job in the design business and tries to make a living as an actor. I could see from the theatre programmes in the bundle with the love letters that he had already had a lot of amateur experience. His name, often in the form Elliot Watson, is nearly always top of the bill. The earliest programme dates from 1916. In 1924, he played Leontes in the Kemble Society's *A Winter's Tale*, which he also produced, and in 1926 he produced and played the title role in the same company's *Henry V* – and produced its *Julius Caesar*, in which he played Marc Antony. By 1928 he has joined the Bensonians, taking the parts of Marcellus and the Player King in *Hamlet* and Gratiano in *The Merchant of Venice*. Each cast includes Sir Frank Benson himself and also Robert Donat, who went on to be a film star and Academy Award-winner. Donat got his film break in 1932 and went on to become a Hollywood star. Denis Elliot Watson was not to be so lucky.

Several cuttings of newspaper reviews were tucked into those old programmes, and criticism of Denis Elliot Watson's performances was mixed. The *Shakespeare Journal*'s review of the Streatham Shakespeare Players' 1926 *Much Ado About Nothing* asserts that D Elliot Watson 'is clearly an actor of great ability . . . But in his boisterous vitality, he overstepped the bounds proper to Benedick.'

Another of the cuttings was from the *Bromley and Kentish Times* of Friday 13 January 1933. Under the headline 'HAMLET – FINE ACTING IN BROMLEY' is a wordy and self-important review full of praise for Watson in the title role. The reviewer found something wonderful, but something imperfect in his performance:

If the history of play-acting in Bromley should ever come to be written, last Saturday will have a prominent place in the list of memorable occasions.

49

For on that day one of the finest performances the town has seen was given at St Mark's Church Hall in the Kemble Society's production of "Hamlet".

Mr Watson . . . laid on the sombre hues with a sure touch, until eventually he had composed a picture only too expressive of all the gloom, the death and the madness which stalk through the piece with ominous tread. If occasionally he was carried away by the feelings of the being he was personating, he never tore passion to tatters . . .

The following year, Mr Watson is doing his best to get into films, but he is finding it a struggle.

> *154 Sinclair Road,*
> *West Kensington, W14*
> *5.10.34*
>
> *My dear "Wendy" – You are a most faithful pal – I was most happy to have your letter and glad to hear your mother is so much better, maybe the new home will be an extra cheer for her – Bless my soul – but time does fly and nearly all people driven potty with anxieties or something – one d–! thing after another – I have had a hell of a time – no work since Jan. but that little bit in "Little Friend". But begin next week – nothing to say, just walking on – in "The Dictator" – and in about three weeks time have a part with lines in a new film – "Abdul The Damned" at Elstree. – I see little of anybody these days – and would like to see Griffiths again – as well as yourself – my fault, I know, for you have had the patience of Job.*
>
> *. . . Is your hair as beautiful as ever? And do you paint your nails – horrible habit – like raw meat! I fear this is a poor letter*

after yours which is so full of interest . . .

My hand is mending – the greatest specialists say it is "mental",
caused through worry – well, I have 1/- left – but am trying not to
worry – Please Wendy keep this to yourself –
As I am very old – I think I may send my love to you –
Yours ever
Denis Elliot Watson

I couldn't read Auntie May's copy of her reply as it and most
subsequent copies were written in shorthand. (I had already found
among her other possessions the fifty-words-per-minute certificate
she was awarded by the RSA in 1932.) I phoned up a good friend,
Jan Paler, who knows Pittman's, and some time later we both sat
at the table in the great hall with Auntie May's reply to Mr
Watson's letter in front of us. Jan said that the shorthand was
'perfect Pittman's that was easy to decipher' – but as she did so,
she wondered whether we really ought to be reading it. We were
peeping into other people's private past.

29th Oct 1934

Dear Mr Watson
    Thank you very much for your letter which I was very pleased to
receive. I am awfully sorry to hear how unlucky you have been and do
hope things will brighten up soon. Perhaps these two new parts you
mention will lead to something . . .
    My mother is keeping fairly well, I'm glad to say. She still has to
go to hospital every two months for examination . . .
    Wishing you the best of luck and hoping you are both quite well
I am yours
For ever
Wendy

But those two new parts Mr Watson mentioned did not lead to anything and, in the following year, the health of Auntie May's mother deteriorated steadily.

154 Sinclair Road, W14
Oct-23-35

Dear Wendy

I was most pleased to have your letter but most sorry to hear your sad news — I know how devoted you were to your mother and the shock of her passing on must have been hard for you, and being alone, harder still — still, time softens all things, and no doubt you will find new interests in life —

You may be surprised to hear that I have returned to designing — my health would not stand the anxiety of stage work — and I am most certainly much happier and getting my health back — also mother is getting on in years and impossible and not right for her to be left alone so I could not go on tour — I have no regrets about leaving acting for the present anyway — could you come over to tea one Sunday or Saturday — or are you always engaged?* I hope you may be able to meet Mother — just let me know by phone.

With all good wishes, and be of good cheer, Wendy,

Yours ever

Denis Elliot Watson

What a strange man Denis must have been! He seems to have had a kind of emotional blind spot. I wondered whether Auntie May had felt, as I did, that his words of condolence, though sincere, are just a little too brief, and that the sudden change of subject — to himself — is insensitively abrupt.

Either way, the relationship seems to have reached a turning

---

* This seems to suggest that he had asked her several times before and she had said no.

point. Auntie May no longer has her sick, widowed mother to look after – though Mr Watson still has his. He has time to spare, now that he has given up acting. It was nearly eight years since the couple started exchanging letters, and he is actually suggesting they might have some kind of date!

Auntie May clearly hit it off with Mr Watson's mother. Several of the letters to Wendy are from her. They make rather sad reading, though, because they are mostly about how unwell she and her son are.

54 Sinclair Road
W.14
Feb. 19th 1936

My Dear Wendy,

I have been going to write for many days, but I am still ill and unable to go about. Denis is much better although not right yet. He does not forget you, dear, and as soon as I am able, you must come and see me. I feel very weary and tired not being able to walk about. The doctor said I had to be careful and not fall. My heart is the great trouble – and my legs. I will not forget your love and kindness and as soon as I can Denis will fix a day for you to come and see us.

With dear love
Your loving friend
Charlotte Watson

Denis's illness is never given a name, but whatever it is, he seems to suffer from depression, as well. Auntie May writes of her own recurrent medical problem, too – the indigestion that dogged her throughout her life. But the tone of her letters is jolly, uncomplaining and generous.

94, *Broadhurst Gardens*
Hampstead
NW6
1.3.36

Dear Mrs Watson

Thank you so much for your letter, which I was very pleased to receive. I was sorry to hear that you are still so weak, though I do hope you are progressing more favourably now. The weather is certainly very trying, and doesn't help anyone to feel any better.

Has Mr Watson found time for any designing yet, I wonder?

I am still sticking to my diet, more or less, and am a lot better. The canteen staff at the office look after me fairly well, but sometimes they forget, and on Shrove Tuesday, what <u>do</u> you think they said? They had forgotten the milk pudding, so would I have pancakes? – About the most indigestible thing on earth, I should imagine!

Hoping you will soon be quite well again, and with love,
Yours affectionately
Wendy

The relationship is picking up speed, but there are three people in it, and the pace seems to be being pushed by Mr Watson's mother. The words 'love' and 'affection' are first exchanged between the two ladies. At this point, Denis is writing not as an individual, but on behalf of his mother and himself. He dismisses himself as too old for a romantic relationship with his Wendy, but he – or his mother – has an idea . . .

154 Sinclair Road

W14

April 27-36

My dear Wendy,

You have been very much in <u>our</u> thoughts of late – and I fear you must think us most negligent – Mother is still far from well and so tired out – in fact I do not know what to do. I may say there is little cooking done, but, that little is more than enough for this ageing man – umph! I am getting greyer and greyer every day – and not gayer. Life seems an awful muddle – and though I am ever so much stronger, am not up to the mark yet. Still drawing and living in hope of something to turn up. Of course, I know there is no help of selling till autumn at the earliest – but I go on – though we have a good woman there always seems to be something for me to do with the house. – – which is a d— bothersome thing.

Now – Wendy, how are <u>you</u> going on – I hope your trouble has passed away, and that taking all things, you have some joy in life – we wish you were nearer to us – do you know anyone who wants a bedroom, etc. – and not much looking after – Mother often says she wishes you were free to come to us – this house is too big . . .

Do write when you can – Mother is in bed – but knows I am writing to you and sends her deep affection to you – and – if I may – being an old crock – do the same –

> *Cheer O*

> *Yours ever*

> *Denis Watson*

I couldn't help wondering whether old Mrs Watson put him up to writing that letter. I could imagine her saying to him, 'Go on, don't be shy – she's devoted to you!' and his reply: 'Don't be ridiculous, I am 55 years old, for Heaven's sake!'

In any case, it seems to have done the trick. Denis's subsequent letters begin with 'My dearest' or 'My beloved dear' and end with 'love', 'devotion' and 'with a big hug and kiss'. By the summer of 1937, they are clearly much more than 'faithful pals'. It is clear that she doesn't move in with Denis and his mother, as the postal correspondence continues. But the exchanges become more intense and more frequent. And they are overshadowed by Denis's rapidly declining health.

154 Sinclair Road
W14
22.7.37

My Beloved Dear — Your two letters were a very great joy to me — indeed they kept me going — yes — it is well to write to the office. Ye Gods! How the days fly — you do write mostly excellent and interesting letters — both of which I shall answer more fully on Sunday. — I have had a very hard and difficult week so far and am dead tired out — Mother is very unwell and most difficult — so am I — I fear. Today I was quite done up after a very restless and non-sleeping night . . . I came home with a crawling walk at 5 p.m. Tomorrow though I have a very full programme. Being weary and hot and rather grubby am off to my bath — this will be posted in the morning — though written at 9.45 p.m. 21.7.37 — Eat, eat, eat and be well, my bonny dear — not boney — Bless you, sweetheart

With devotion and love
Denis
Do excuse scribble.

Four days later, Denis writes: 'Life seems a terrible muddle and I feel the lack of body strength. This weakness is most bothersome.' I can't quote May's replies to these and Denis's later letters, because I can't now find them. Somehow, in all the sorting and sifting of all the hundreds of thousands of pieces of paper that May left behind her, those originals and their longhand transcriptions have come adrift. The irony is as painful as it is obvious: I can reconstruct Auntie May's life in even the most trivial detail, but when it comes to the most intimate and revealing things she ever wrote, the record is now blank. Perhaps it is meant to be.

At some point after October 1937, the letters stop, but then there are lots of short, undated notes written by Denis:

Dearest – It has not been my lot to have my supper put out for me for ever so long. Bless your dear heart and thought – sleep, my beloved, sleep.

Denis.

I sat there wondering why letters sent through the post had been replaced by notes without a date or a sender's address. Perhaps Auntie May moved into 154 Sinclair Road. If she did, she had a room to herself. One little note says: 'Sleep well, my dearest. Denis XXXX'. You don't leave notes like that to anyone sharing your bed.

Another note shows that Denis is doing freelance design work at home again – and that he isn't always finding it easy:

My Dearest –
  Have gone out for a look about – Drawing very slow this day –
Your devoted
  Denis

Then there is a note that says he has gone out for a walk to clear a 'd— awful headache', and one that is evidence of a row:

Dearest —

There will be <u>NO</u> more bursts of temper — I am thoroughly ashamed of myself — I have to begin all over again.

Denis

I had no way of working out what caused that particular outburst, but I found another note that seems to be an explanation following another argument. Denis had made another attempt to get back into professional acting and had failed:

Beloved — I may be very badly bent — very badly — but not yet smashed — the fault is mine — there is little use in going back over the past.

That I am disappointed about Victoria Regina*is most true — but — I am still with a somewhat curious faith in myself — I will win through —

You are all to me — even if I am no longer a youth — but some wake up late in life — I am one.

Sleep — dear — do sleep

Denis.

Then there is one last letter.

Ward B4 — Bed 17
Hammersmith Hospital
Du Cane Road
26.4.38

My dearest Wendy — Most hearty thanks for your good letter — Dr Davies is a wise man and it is fortunate we have taken his advice which is thoroughly sound. — So far I have had 4 medical exams and two

---

* Denis must have auditioned for the Laurence Housman play first produced in 1937.

blood tests (Do not tell Mother about the blood tests) – and more
exams to come, all by different men – when the X Ray will be I do not
know – and do not be surprised if the knife has to be used. I have no
fear – But to tell Mother would be far from wise.

By the way, send or bring on Sunday my volume of Keats' poems
– in Mother's room I think – if you can find same –
I am very weary today.
Cheer up
All devotion
Denis

Underneath this letter was a plain, unsealed envelope. I opened it.
It contained a folded card printed in Palace Script:

Mrs Charlotte Watson wishes to express her very grateful thanks and
appreciation for your kind thoughts and sympathy, in the passing of
her son, Denis, on 9 June 1938.

154 Sinclair Road,
London W14

•

Auntie May must have inherited the theatre programmes wrapped
up with those letters from Denis – some bore dates before she was
born. Later, I found a box downstairs that contained the
programmes of scores of plays that Denis must have watched rather
than acted in, for his name does not appear in any of the cast lists.
One of them was something that he surely must have treasured –
a souvenir programme of the Jubilee tribute given by the theatrical
and musical professions to Miss Ellen Terry on 12 June 1906. He
would have been 25 when he attended it.

I found lots of other things that must have belonged to Denis, too: photographs, papers, notebooks and working scripts of plays he acted in and directed. I knew that Auntie May had inherited Denis's cigarette box and signet ring, along with his mother's necklace – they are mentioned in Auntie May's will. She left them to her friend Winifred Rozee, 'who knew him almost as long as I did'. But as I carried on opening the boxes that filled Ware Hall-House, I kept coming across other Elliot Watson memorabilia, too. There were trunks filled with Denis's mother's carefully folded and mothballed dresses. There was a signed photograph of a Sir Renny Watson, who must have been a Victorian ancestor. There was a photograph of the grave of 'Ernest Watson, native of Newcastle upon Tyne, Eng., born 11 August 1852, died 8 April 1894: at rest'. The photographic company named on the mounting is Payne, of Monrovia, California. Denis's family must have lived there at some point. I found the plan of the ship on which I guess they returned to England – the SS *Berengaria*. The plan was for the use of second-class passengers – on the way back, at least, the family cannot have been rich.

I realised that with time and detective work, I could find out a lot more about the enigmatic Denis Elliot Watson from the things of his that had fallen into Auntie May's careful possession. What I had found already showed that although they had never been fully united in life, their possessions had been intermingled after his death.

CHAPTER SEVEN

Rebuilding a Biography

In which I start to reconstruct Auntie May's life
using the documents she hoarded and the
diaries that she kept

By the end of 1995, I had opened all the boxes and I knew how
Auntie May had organised her diaries, her papers and her
correspondence. Since then, I have read almost all of them and I am
now able to describe her life in some detail – and show how she
came to be the remarkable woman that she was. The earliest
original documents I found in the archive were some letters written
in the 1870s between Savidges then living in New York. I knew of
these people, for Nellie had told me how the lovely black clock
with the golden lions had come from America as a wedding present
to her mother and father. I also knew that one of her interests had
been family history; in her letters to Tony and me, she had often
mentioned new ancestors she had discovered in various parts of
the world. Looking through her letters to other family members, I
saw that she had exchanged information about family history with
them, too, and I found a folder made from a cut and flattened
mansize tissue box in which she had kept extra copies of these
letters and associated notes. With them was a photocopy of letters
patent dated 13 July 1862 signed by Leopold, King of the Belgians,

appointing Johannes Kikkert an honorary vice-consul in Texel, Vlieland and Terschelling.

Nellie had told me that their great grandfather, Johannes Ludovicus Kikkert, had been mayor of the Frisian island of Texel in the 1850s. At that time, the coastline was plagued by wreckers. Johannes knew that if Texel had a lighthouse, ships couldn't be lured onto its rocks. But building lighthouses costs money, and Texel didn't have any. So he wrote to all the kings and queens of the countries whose ships were being plundered, pointing out that it would be in their interest to pay something towards building one. They agreed and the Texel lighthouse was built. That, at least, was how the family version of the story went. I had taken it with a pinch of salt, but I could now see that it was true – and that May hadn't been the first independent-minded person in the family.

Other papers bore out the stories Nellie had told me about their father, another strong character. Frederick Savidge had been a foreman in a metalwork factory in Peckham Rye. During the First World War it had been turned over to munitions production and his job was to supervise the women that worked on the shop floor. The girls must have been fond of him, for they gave him an affectionate nickname – 'Uncle Vidge'. He was the war hero of the family, though he never saw active service. His heroism was shown when the factory ceiling began to collapse under the weight of the machinery set up on the floor above. Nellie told me that her father had rushed into the middle of the room and taken the whole weight of the ceiling on his shoulders until all the girls had scrambled to safety. The strain of it had damaged his heart and led to his early death shortly after the war. Without a husband to provide for her or her daughters, his widow had to give up the family home in Southwark and find cheap lodgings while she looked for work.

I found a folder containing his National Service Volunteer card and the 'scheduled occupation certificate' that was subsequently issued to him, exempting him from military service. With them was a beautiful little handmade card of thanks bearing twenty-three signatures, addressed: 'To Uncle Vidge – a little recompense for your grey hairs.' It is decorated with hand-drawn pictures of artillery shells and the flags of the victorious allies. It must have accompanied the gift they gave to him at the end of the war – the handsome gold pencil holder, which Auntie May inherited and left to Tony in her will. There was also his death certificate, dated 13 May 1921.

The last piece of paper in the folder was a letter from the surgeon that treated him:

KING'S COLLEGE HOSPITAL
DENMARK HILL
LONDON S.E.5
12.vi.21

Dear Mrs Savidge,

In answer to your letter of the 8th, at the post mortem examination it was found that the heart shewed signs of disease of the muscle and one of the valves was not functioning. The whole organ was much dilated, thus causing the final failure. The other organs shewed the changes such as one would expect after a long illness due to heart disease. I am sorry we were not able to do any more for him than we did – but he did not answer to treatment at all.

With much sympathy to you in your loss
Yours very truly,
C.F.J. Earl
House Physician

Reading that little letter brought the physical reality of Uncle

Vidge's death horribly to mind. The death certificate records Mrs H Savidge as 'present at the death'. It must have been a terrible time for May, Nellie and their mother. As I sat there, holding those old papers in my hands, I found myself wondering whether this might have been the defining moment of Auntie May's life. For a ten-year-old girl to lose her father must be quite specially distressing – it's a time when many girls and fathers are at their closest. Was it this that led her later to latch on to Mr Watson, a man more than old enough to be her father? Was this first bereavement so traumatic that it set the pattern for the rest of her life? Perhaps. Perhaps it was also the origin of her refusal to give up her home when the council wanted to take it from her, for after the death of her father, the family never again had a permanent home together. It might even explain Auntie May's hoarding. Her home and the most important person in her life were taken from her when she was young and impressionable. Maybe she hung on to everything because she couldn't cope with any more loss. I don't know – but I did find myself wondering. My thoughts turned to her long, doomed love affair with Denis Elliot Watson. I couldn't bear to imagine how much grief she must have suffered when he died, too.

•

I knew that Auntie May's school days had been cut short by poverty,* but only when I found her school books and papers did I realise what a tragedy that had been. She was scholarly by nature.

---

* Both Auntie May and her sister left school at the age of 14. A cousin, a Mr Hampson, helped Nellie find a job with Marks & Spencer. May got herself a job as an assistant in a design studio, working on patterns for wallpapers and silk scarves. During the Depression, when the design business dwindled, Mr Hampson helped May get a job in Marks & Spencer, too.

Her written work is almost perfect in its presentation and most of it achieves top marks. Her domestic science exercise book begins on 23 April 1925 with 'Demonstration 1: Characteristics of a Good Larder and Care of the Meat Safe'. The lesson is recorded in a flawless, childish hand. Subsequent demonstrations are mostly recipes for meals with precise quantities and costings – a pattern that Auntie May followed in the diaries she kept until the end of her life.

On 7 May 1925, she learnt how to prepare a 'dinner for six' consisting of grilled chops and mashed potatoes followed by ginger pudding. The cost was precisely 3s 6d, including '1 gill of treacle' for 3d. The last lesson is 'Demonstration 13', which took place on 16 July 1925, in which she was taught how to make raspberry buns. But that is not the last entry in the book. The rest of it is filled with recipes that Auntie May found in later life, either cut or transcribed from newspapers and magazines. Then, when she ran out of space, Auntie May tucked in other recipes on pieces of scrap paper. Every entry is dated; the latest is 'Christmas 1983' – 58 years after the exercise book was issued. At the back is a section that lists and dates her experimental recipes for 'Wartime Marmalade' between 10 March 1944 and 12 January 1952. She tried it again on 12 January 1972, exactly twenty years later. The yield of each batch is recorded after the ingredients. When I checked the dates, I was amazed to find that she had been making marmalade, biscuits and fudge during the years that she was living in the Blue Lady caravan.

The artwork I found among Auntie May's school books is skilful rather than imaginative. One of her exercises was to trace a picture and then draw a freehand copy beside it. The two girls in flapper dresses are almost indistinguishable. The patterns that she drew in her first job, in Heffer Scott's design studio, are equally precise. She was clearly someone who strove to get things exactly right. I still have many of the watercolours that she drew in her early years and several pretty drawings of birds. Every now and then, during my rummaging, I would have one of those *déjà vu* feelings – none more so than when I unwrapped a newspaper bundle to find a Chinese vase beautifully decorated with a flowery bamboo pattern. I took it out of its box and placed it on the dusty concrete floor of the great hall. Surely, I had seen this vase somewhere before? But I couldn't have – I had just unwrapped it. Later, of course, I realised that it was in one of her pictures, copied to perfection, and filled with lovely pink tulips.

By then, I had come across a second set of Auntie May's diaries. Unlike the 440 cashbooks I had found earlier, these were printed and bound pocket diaries for individual calendar years – thirty-one of them. The earliest of them was dated 1924, when Auntie May was thirteen, but she hadn't yet started her daily diary habit. The only original entries note a handful of birthdays, including her own, although one made in November 1925 was an uncharacteristically grumpy sentence: 'I seem to spend all my evenings darning and mending clothes.' In 1929, she reused the diary as a cashbook. It doesn't make fascinating reading, but it does give some insights into her life at the time. She buys quite a lot of chocolate, cream buns and peppermints, and she makes several visits to the theatre. She also buys 'films' (at 1s each), 'hypo', 'developer' and 'printing paper'. She has started taking, developing and printing her own photographs – and, of course, she kept them all. One of the albums in which she stuck them is on the table in front of me. There are portraits of family, friends and pets – all the people are smiling and the animals seem to be having fun, too. There are pictures of Auntie May's colleagues at work in the design studio in Berners Street – though there are none of Denis Elliot Watson, with whom she was corresponding tentatively at the time. There are snaps of days out at Hampton Court, Wimbledon Common and St James's Park. All the photos are bright and cheerful and a fair few are significantly overexposed. They all bear dates in 1928 and 1929. They were clearly happy years for Auntie May.

The first year Auntie May used one of these diaries for its original purpose was 1934. Most of the days are blank. All the entries she makes seem to be reminders to meet people at certain times and places. She 'rang up Mr Watson' on Monday, 22 January, when she 'spoke to his mother as he was in Edinburgh', and telephoned again on Saturday, 17 February; the entry for the following Wednesday reads: 'Meet Mr Watson outside Bakerloo Line Station, 5.45', but it has been crossed out and beside it she has written 'Could not come'. She rang him again on Monday, 26 February and on Tuesday, 16 March, but there are no more calls recorded that year – and she has not recorded any calls coming from him. It seems that she was doing the running at this point in the relationship – though he did write to her affectionately in October of that year.

I couldn't find any diaries of any sort for the years 1935, 1936 and 1938. Perhaps there never were any. Perhaps one day they'll turn up. Even after all these years, I am still coming across stuff that I missed the first time round. The 1937 diary is a bit thin, but it does contain details of a holiday Auntie May took in Cromer, on the North Norfolk coast. She writes that it was 'reminiscent of an old Dutch town', and notes the 'sliced stones' used as local building materials. She admired the wild fuchsia and poppies, visited the Cromer lifeboat and saw a wrecked ship at the foot of the cliffs.

I was disappointed not to find Auntie May's 1935 diary, for it was the year of her mother's death. I never did find the copy of the letter she wrote to Mr Watson to tell him of it, the reply to which I had found in the brown paper parcel in the attic. I have not found anything that she ever wrote about it, but I did find something that shows the death affected her deeply. When I was going through the 440 diaries, I came across an entry that at first, I found puzzling. In diary number 164, under 18 September 1968, she writes '33 years'. Under the same date in 1969, she writes '34 years', and so it goes on until the last diary in 1992. I puzzled over these entries for a while before realising their significance. Auntie May was noting the time that had passed since her mother's death. Why she started doing this in 1968, I could only guess – 9 June 1968 had been the thirtieth anniversary of Denis Elliot Watson's death, which she had been recording in the same way since 1966. Perhaps the passing of three decades since then got her thinking about the other losses in her life. I can only guess.

I found a big chocolate box with a ribbon around it that contained dozens of travel brochures dating from 1929 to 1936. Most of them relate to Holland, but there are more adventurous pamphlets, too, including *P&O Cruises in Southern Sunshine* and *Holidays at Sea* arranged by the Free Church Touring Guild. The ones describing early aeroplane holidays have all been sold now, but they were fascinating to read and the pictures of ancient airliner interiors with easy chairs to sit in were totally unlike anything found in aeroplanes today. All these brochures were fascinating, for they offered charming little insights into middle and upper-class holidaymaking at the time. I am sure that Auntie May would have loved to travel on those elegant ocean liners and flown in those early planes – but it was not to be. However, I do know that she travelled to Texel in 1932 with her mother and alone in 1939, because the box contains sets of postcards of places with the dates that she visited them written on the back. The souvenirs that she kept of that second holiday are rather telling. She went alone. She took her bicycle and her camera, and took scores of snaps. The few photographs that include her must have been taken by strangers, as they show her standing with her only travelling companion – her bike. The rest are of churches, dykes, landscapes and ancient buildings, and most have her bicycle in the foreground. But the memento that brought me up short wasn't a souvenir, it was a letter from the Ministry of War, thanking her for the maps, photographs and sketches of the Dutch coastline. On her own, unprompted initiative, Auntie May had spent the holiday she had so long looked forward to contributing to what was soon to be known as the war effort. Auntie May was a patriot.

When war broke out, Auntie May moved with Marks & Spencer to Blackpool, where she carried on with her St John Ambulance work. Two years later, she decided that she wanted to do more for her country.

> *C/o 38, Finsbury Avenue,*
> *Blackpool, S.S.*
> *18.10.41*

The Secretary,
Ministry of Aircraft Production, Recruitment,
Romney House, Westminster, S.W.1.

Dear Sir,

On making enquiries at St. James' Square, for war work, in which drawing would be useful, I was advised to write to you, regarding some secret work. Before taking up my present work (book-keeping) I had five years experience in drawing, painting, tracing, measuring, etc., in a commercial studio, and also attended the Central School of Arts & Crafts, in Southampton Row, for evening instruction.

At present I am in Blackpool in business, my home being in London, but I do not mind where I go, as I am very keen on this kind

of work. I shall be in London in about three weeks' time, for a long
week-end.

Hoping to hear favourably from you,
Yours faithfully,
May Savidge

She sent the same letter to the Admiralty, adding that she was especially interested in anything to do with maps.

The Admiralty replied that there were no vacancies at present, but that if she wished to be considered for future employment, she should complete and return a drawing test, which she did. But the Ministry of Aircraft Production called her in for interview and offered her a job in the jig-and-tool drawing office of De Havilland's. She accepted it. She didn't know it then, but she was to become part of the team that created the Mosquito, a plane of revolutionary design that would play a significant role in the war in the air.* Auntie May's contribution was also revolutionary. Technical drawing was then seen as man's work – she was the only female 'draughtsman' in the team.

She stayed with De Havilland's for three years after the war. When she left, her colleagues collected £3.10 as a leaving present – a significant sum at that time.† They presented it with a charming letter of farewell, signed by all twenty-eight members of the tool drawing office. I found it tucked into a February 1948 *Radio Times*.

MISS SAVIDGE,

WE, THE MEMBERS OF THE TOOL DRAWING

---

* * The Mosquito was extremely light – its fuselage was made of wood – and fast. It had two Rolls-Royce Merlin engines. It was also very versatile – fighter, fighter-bomber, ground attack and photo-reconnaissance models were produced.

† Relative to average earnings, this is the equivalent of about £280 today.

OFFICE, ON THIS DAY OF FRIDAY, 20TH FEB. 1948,
HERE CONVEY OUR HEARTY BEST WISHES FOR YOUR
FUTURE . . . LOOKING BACK OVER THE PAST FIVE OR
SO YEARS, WE HAVE ADMIRED YOUR COURAGE, NOT
ONLY IN THE WAY IN WHICH YOU HAVE HELD YOUR
OWN AGAINST OVERWHELMING NUMBERS OF
DRAUGHTSMEN, BUT ALSO IN THE MARITIME
MANNER IN WHICH YOU HAVE LED THE WAY IN THE
DESPERATE HOUSING PROBLEM.

WE HERE TAKE THE OPPORTUNITY IN SAYING
"BON VOYAGE" AND TRUST YOU WILL ACCEPT A
LITTLE TOKEN BY WHICH YOU WILL REMEMBER US
AND WHICH WILL HELP YOU FACE CHEERFULLY
YOUR NEW DUTIES.

The following Monday, Auntie May took up her new post with 'DOTS', the Drawing Office Technical Service in Hertford. One of her first tasks was to design a new logo for the firm.*

The 'maritime manner' in which Auntie May addressed the post-war housing shortage had been her purchase of an old Thames water bus, the *Formosa*. She paid £150 for it in August 1945, and £5 to have it towed from Bromley Lock to the River Lee at Ware, where she had found a mooring by the Saracen's Head pub,† and rented a workshop in which to store the possessions she couldn't fit in the boat. (The pub had a garden which she treated as her own. She sowed it with wild flower seeds, bought by post from seed merchants. She kept the packets, and stuck them in her scrap books.) She paid £85 to Mr WG Hill of the Rye House Boat Service, Hertford, to help convert the *Formosa* into a floating home

---

* I found this and dozens of her other drawings for DOTS rolled up in a chest in the attic.

† This is the pub in which the famous Great Bed of Ware used to be.

– and she lived on it for over four years. They were not easy or comfortable years and I don't imagine many people – especially women – would have put up with all the difficulties that come with living on a boat. Her diaries and accounts record all the practical problems that arose, and the cost of putting them right. She had a particularly bad year in 1948, when she took the *Formosa* up the Thames for a major overhaul:

> *11.10.48: Formosa left Ware 12 noon*
> *Thurs 14: Formosa keeled over – smashed crockery – up all night clearing up.*
> *Sun 17: Creekside Lock at last (For repairs)*

The *Formosa* file contains a list of all the crockery that was broken. There are thirty-two items on it, including plates, cups, saucers, jugs, a bottle of milk of magnesia and a 2lb jar of marmalade.

In 1949, the workshop that housed her possessions was put up for sale, along with its neighbouring cottage, 1 Monkey Row. The building was semi-derelict, but Auntie May reckoned it was worth buying and doing up. After completing the purchase on 20 September 1947, with a payment of £270, Auntie May immediately arranged for builders to relay the drains and to strip, repair, rebatten and retile the roof. Her first plan was to let the cottage and continue to live on the boat, but she soon realised she had made a terrible mistake.

Her tenants were a Mr and Mrs Miller. They had been introduced by the Hertfordshire Assistance Committee, which I guess must have been a local charity devoted to helping the poor. The Millers moved in on 28 July 1948, and on Saturday, 17 August, Mr Miller came to the *Formosa* with his first week's rent of 15s. It had been due on 4 August. It was a poor start and things rapidly got worse. His early payments were late and erratic, and then they stopped altogether. On Sunday, 26 September, someone broke into the *Formosa* and stole Auntie May's deed box. She suspected the culprit might have been her tenant. By the following May, Mr Miller was twenty weeks behind with his rent. On Saturday, 14 October, Auntie May found that someone had broken into her shed and stolen a pair of riding boots, a standard lamp and an iron. The following Thursday she 'told Mr Miller to go' and telephoned her solicitor to instruct him to give a week's notice to her tenant. On Saturday, 28 May 1949 she wrote: 'Mr M. said he had received the NOTICE.' But getting him to act on it was another matter.

Auntie May's need to get the Millers out was becoming increasingly urgent. It wasn't just that they were dreadful tenants; she needed possession of the cottage so that she could live in it herself. For some time, the *Formosa* had been taking in water and it was now flooding so frequently that it was getting uninhabitable. To begin with, she used first one pump, then two, to get rid of the water; but it got so bad in April 1949 that she had to call the fire brigade. They charged her £6 3s 4½d for the service. She spent most of the Whitsun bank holiday weekend 'looking for the leak', but couldn't find it, and she kept on pumping throughout the summer. Her diary entry for Friday, 9 September reads: 'Home about 9.30. Water partly over floorboards. Pumped for ½ hour then put seats away – got milk etc. Went on pumping – very tired – kept on falling asleep. Finished just after 12 – no tea.' There are many similar entries. On 24 September, it took her an hour and ten minutes to get the water below floorboard level, using both pumps operating at 300 gallons per hour each.

Meanwhile the Millers had simply disappeared, which was bad news, because they hadn't legally vacated the cottage – they had left all their furniture behind.

17.8.1949: Called at Monkey Row – Mr. M still missing. Heard about Mrs Hughes taking out summons against him, for money borrowed . . .

The following day, Auntie May went to the police station to find out if they knew anything of the Millers' whereabouts, and 'heard about them going out playing cards nearly every night – leaving the children, or staying out, or sometimes coming home in a taxi'.

SAT 10.9.49: Called at Monkey Row. Mr M. still away – neighbours said police had been, so I went to Police Stn. They wanted Mrs. M's address, which I gave them. They said that Mrs. M was miles away – not in this county.

SUN 11.9.49: Went to Police Stn. again (twice) as I had heard that Mr. M. had worked his passage to Canada: Police said he had applied for a ration book in NELSON, Lancashire. He had a young woman with him. The Inspector said he would find out if it was an ordinary ration book or just an Emergency Card – and let me know.

SAT 17.9.49: 'Phoned Solicitor told him about Ration Book (in Lancs.) also asked about moving in and letting Mr. M. sue for repossession – but he said it was dangerous – there are all sorts of things he could sue me for.

SAT 1.10.49: Called at Monkey Row – Mrs Gay said Mrs M. had been seen in Ware??? Also that Police had enquired at MOSS'S about bicycle – stolen? – Called at Police Station – no news. 'Phoned Solicitor – he says case can't proceed until summons served on Mr. M.!!! Why didn't he say this before? – or do something about it – Am to phone again in a few days if I can find out where he is.

I could imagine how Auntie May must have felt at the time – but I didn't have to, because I found her feelings expressed in a note she had filed in one of that summer's *Radio Times*. I am not sure whether she wrote it to clarify her thoughts, or as a reminder of questions to ask her solicitor – either way, she is clearly anxious:

Can I get them out – preferably without making an enemy of him – I think he is dangerous – How can I safeguard my furniture in cottage and shed etc.?
Cottage let part furnished.
11 weeks rent owing 1948 plus 1 week.
Tried to sell my wireless set.
? boat burglary.
Can they get a council house if I want the cottage? – are they on the list?
Is the property to come down?
How do I stand as regards to compensation?
Should I do any more repairs? Wall bulging, etc.
Don't want to lose mooring if cottage is coming down.
Do I have to refuse rent?

As if this wasn't enough to worry about, Auntie May was having a terrible time with her motorbike – her old Velocette (the one we had found in pieces at the back of the outbuilding). There are countless references in her diaries to problems with and repairs to the carburettor, the tyres, the spokes, the drive chain, the speedometer drive cable, the compression release and the plugs. She also records ongoing problems with 'Tiny Tim' – a reference I couldn't understand at first, until I later found the Tiny Tim file, in which I discovered that Tiny Tim wasn't a person – it was the brand name of a petrol-powered lighting and power generator. Auntie May was suffering other mechanical problems, too. During the same period, her water pumps kept breaking down and there are many references to promises by electricians to come and repair them. Most of them were not kept.

Another of Auntie May's worries was the fear that her cottage might be scheduled for demolition. The idea seems to have sprung from general rather than particular anxiety, for in those post-war years, quite a lot of old buildings were condemned and pulled down rather than repaired. But Auntie May put such worries behind her when some good news appeared out of the blue:

> *27.10.1949: <u>Mr Miller came back</u> – to see me at boat . . . Mr. M. took what he wanted and made written statement that he was vacating the cottage & stuff left behind was for me in lieu of part of rent.*

She was rid of her dreadful tenants at last. She spent some days clearing up the mess they had left, and made a triumphal entry in capital letters in diary number eighteen on Friday, 11 November 1949:

> *MOVED INTO No. 1, MONKEY ROW.*

The following day, she went to collect her Lotus wireless set, which Mr Miller had taken to be repaired over a year earlier. When the repair man returned it to her, he told her that Mr Miller had offered to sell it to him. It is the last reference to the Millers in Auntie May's diaries.

Auntie May was in her own home on dry land at last and she was determined to make the most of it. She bought herself a Christmas present – a piano, for which she paid £6, plus 10s for delivery. She stayed up until half-past midnight on Christmas Day playing it.

•

Auntie May had no more need for the *Formosa*, and in August 1950 she advertised it for sale in the *Exchange and Mart*:

> **Houseboat** for sale, 60ft. x 10ft. 3in., ex passenger boat, fitted shaft, propeller, rudder, sufficient accommodation for family, partly furnished, lighting plant, full head room, needs slight repairs and painting, lying Ware, Herts. Write for appointment to view, preferably week-ends. Savidge, 1, Monkey Row, Ware, Herts.

She sold it to a Mr Stoddard for £120 the following October, and threw herself wholeheartedly into renovating and decorating the first real home she had lived in since her father had died in 1921.

CHAPTER EIGHT

A Bolt from the Blue

In which Auntie May's peaceful enjoyment of her
home is suddenly threatened

For the next three years, Auntie May lived a life of happy
normality. She got a job at ICI and she was good at it. She
made technical drawings of exploded views of plastic manu-
facturing machinery and, in 1952, she won a Certificate of Merit
from the British Plastics Federation for designs she submitted for
the Worshipful Company of Horners Award. She made new
friends at ICI and kept in touch with those she had made earlier
in life.

One name that appears pretty frequently in her diaries is an old
colleague, Edward Collins. They exchanged telephone calls and
visits and on many he was accompanied by his aged and infirm
mother, though the even more infirm father stayed at home. They
also exchanged letters, postcards and small birthday and Christmas
gifts. The earliest letter in the 'Mr EC Collins' file is dated 29
October 1945. There is a separate file for Mrs Collins, who in the
first letter, dated 11 January 1944, thanked Auntie May for her
Christmas and birthday presents. When I discovered this three-
way correspondence, I couldn't help thinking of Auntie May's

relationship with Denis Elliot Watson, which was also one in which 'mother came, too'. But the letters between Auntie May and the Collinses are friendly rather than affectionate. In all of them he addressed her as 'Miss Savidge' and signed himself 'Edward C Collins'. They contain little more than small talk – mostly about illnesses, work colleagues and the weather.

Nineteen fifty-one was Festival of Britain year and, in June, Auntie May visited the Festival Gardens in Battersea Park. The following August, she bought a copy of the official book of the festival for two shillings and sixpence. She kept it, of course. At the front of it there is a double-page spread with a picture of the Dome of Discovery, that seems uncannily similar to the Millennium Dome erected half a century later. The 1951 version contained stands devoted to up-to-date scientific discoveries, but there were also displays about discoveries made by Britons in the past, including Sir Francis Drake, Captain Cook and Captain Scott; and most of the other pictures in the book show the nation's historic architecture, including Georgian Bath, medieval Canterbury and Regency Brighton. The section called *The Land and the People* is illustrated with photographs of a modern coal-fired power station, a shipyard and a newly built school – but there are pictures of a village cricket match and a horse-drawn plough at work, too. The chapter on the festival church of St John in Waterloo Road begins in capital letters: 'BRITAIN IS A CHRISTIAN COMMUNITY. The Christian faith is inseparably a part of our history.' The festival celebrated a Britain that was moving confidently forward, while taking the whole of its proud heritage with it. It was a spirit that Auntie May embraced. It was a Britain that Auntie May loved.

The diaries from this time record a lot of hard work repairing and redecorating the cottage. Auntie May spent many days removing old plaster, stripping timber, filling holes with putty and applying several coats of new paint to woodwork. She got a man in to replace the old sink and associated drains, and had a new concrete floor laid in the kitchen. On the Saturday of the Whitsun bank holiday weekend, she bought a ladder, nails for the stair carpet, a putty knife, a long-handled tar brush, some window furniture, four panes of glass (5⅛ft × 7¼in) and '1 pr 3-in. hinges (½ price – rusty)'. It was a working holiday, but I suspect she enjoyed it. She wasn't just repairing a house – she was building a home.

Having a full-time job and a run-down house to repair would be enough to use up any ordinary person's energy, but Auntie May wasn't any ordinary person. She always found time to do a lot of voluntary work for others. Most of this was through the St John Ambulance Brigade. One of many stints of SJAB duty she records about this time is Coronation Day, 2 June 1953, when she got up at 3.30am to catch the 5.06 train to Liverpool Street, spent the day attending the crowds in London, and got back at 7pm.

Nineteen fifty-three was also the year she started working on her music therapy Selectatune invention that I was to find more than forty years later:

Sun 31.5.53: am going to look up old musical instruments in Hertford Library and perhaps British Museum, while on 2½ weeks' holiday, for any with strings of same length and diameter as "Selectatune".

SAT. 13.6.53. Caught 6.43 from Ware to Liv. St. 2.11d walked . . . to Embankment, then to Brit. Museum Music Dept. They showed me some books, and recommended V & A Museum. Went there and spent most of day in V & A Library till about 5 p.m. Also saw flowers from Holland in entrance hall – sent to the Queen.

Auntie May's public spirit showed itself in her frequent donations to charity, which – like everything else she spent or received – are recorded in her diaries. She gave 2s a month to the boy that called to collect donations for cancer research. She sent a £1 postal order (which cost her £1 3d) to the Greek Earthquake Appeal on Saturday, 29 August 1953; on the same date, she sent the same amount to the Westminster Abbey Appeal. There are frequent entries throughout all the diaries noting gifts to medical and human and animal welfare charities – and there are signs that Auntie May was kind to needy individuals she came across, too:

FRI 24.4.53: Old man at door again: 6d and box matches.

SAT 25.4.53: Old man came again wanting to do gardening etc. – gave him 1.6d to get to Royston.

Auntie May also performed her duties to the dead.

TUES 8.9.53: Cleared up Denis' grave – weeds – took heavy vase – cast iron – black enamel with white fleck – also some stattii – enquired about having space filled with green chips (semi-transparent).

Auntie May's generosity also expressed itself in the presents she gave to her friends. Her diary entries for December 1953 are dominated, as usual, by Christmas shopping. On Saturday, 12 December she bought twenty presents, including some '4711' toilet cologne for her sister Nellie, a book (*Elizabeth Our Queen*) for Winnie, *The Observer's Book of Music* for Winnie's daughter Ruby and some Yardley talc for Mrs Collins. A couple of days earlier, she bought forty-two Christmas cards at 2d, and eighteen more at 1½d. The spirit of Christmas was in the air.

Then, on Monday, 14 December comes the bombshell. Auntie May has underlined every word of the entry:

Evening – message from Mr. Lucas – San[itation] Ins[pector] (through Mrs. Bell) that he wants to inspect cottages on Sat. morning with view to pulling them all down!

The post-war rush to eradicate the nation's crumbling housing stock has reached Auntie May's ancient corner of Hertfordshire. A shadow has fallen over her cottage. She will never be at ease in it again.

FRI. 1.1.54: Stayed up all night doing jobs in cottage in Case Mr. Lucas comes on Sat morning. (He didn't.)
SAT. 16.1.54: Still expecting Mr. Lucas (San. Insp.) to come.
SAT. 23.1.54: Mr. Lucas did not come.
SAT. 30.1.54: Mr. Lucas did not come.
SAT. 6.3.54: Mr. Lucas did not come. Mrs. Hunt & Mr. John Whitefield came about 3.15 and looked all over cottage. – he says it is Tudor.
FRI. 19.3.54: Up all night – 4th time.
SAT. 20.3.54: Mr. Lucas came at last with Dr. Wildman – Medical Officer of Health. They said Monkey Row was first on the list of property to be demolished.
Afternoon – Mr. John Whitfield called & said that this and No. 36 are scheduled as ancient monuments – section C.

Her first efforts were directed to making the place as spick and span as possible, giving the lie to the local authority's claim that the place was unfit for habitation. Her diaries are full of references to painting and decorating. On Easter Sunday 1954, she painted the whole of the front of the cottage with Snowcem. On Saturday, 1 May, she went to a meeting of the East Herts Archaeological Society at the Shire Hall, and heard a Mr Farthing give a talk on 'old property'. There, she met Mr Gordon Moodey, who was to become a champion of her cause, a frequent correspondent and a good friend.

SAT 8.5.54: 3.15 pm – Mr G. Moodey and Mrs. Hunt came to inspect cottage . . . Mr. Moodey sketched my window.

SAT 15.5.54: About 12.20 Saturday 15th May, 1954: Mr Peter Locke arrived about 2.50 p.m. and inspected all cottages – said he did not think there was any doubt about its being a Hall-House. About 4.40 a reporter and photographer arrived from Evening News – they stayed another 2 hours! – notified by E. Herts Arch. Soc.

The work of the reporter and the photographer was published in the *Evening News* on Wednesday, 19 May. Auntie May cut it out and filed it. The picture shows her looking businesslike, groomed and surprisingly glamorous. She had not yet become the little old lady that I was to meet in 1966. The caption reads: 'Miss Savidge repairing one of the leaded lights of her cottage. Experts say they were installed in Elizabethan times.'

NOW DREAM
COTTAGE MAY
HAVE TO GO
"Evening News" Reporter

MISS MAY SAVIDGE, a technical illustrator, has for four years spent most of her spare time restoring her picturesque centuries-old cottage in Monkey-row, Ware, Herts.

She obtained a license for a builder to repair the roof, but all the rest of the work, including brick-laying, carpentry, re-glazing and stripping plaster from the ceilings and 20 layers of paper from the walls, she has done with her own hands.

Now she has been told that the building may be condemned.

Miss Savidge is not alone, however, in wanting to save the cottage, for the Society for the Protection of Ancient Buildings and East Hertfordshire Archaeological Society are also keenly interested.

While stripping one of the upstairs walls Miss Savidge discovered a six-light medieval window. The huge chimney breast is thought to have been inserted in early Elizabethan times.

Of Great Interest

Mr Peter Locke, who examined the cottage on behalf of the S.P.A.B. said it formed part of a small hall-house of the late 14th or early 15th century.

"Houses of that period had a central hall over which there were no upper floors, and that this was one can be clearly seen by examining the roof timbers," he said. "It is of great interest, because it is one of the smallest houses of this kind to have been found."

A Ware council official said that a number of cottages in Monkey-row were being inspected, but that their fate had not been decided.

Faced with the problem of finding a home when the war ended, Miss Savidge bought a small Thames steamer and converted it into a houseboat.

Mr Moodey also wrote something following his visit and Auntie May filed a copy of this, too:

EXTRACT FROM –

EAST HERTS ARCHAEOLOGICAL
SOCIETY

President: Sir Henry Maunsell Richards, C.B.
Hon. Secretary: Gordon E. Moodey, 27, West Street, Hertford.

No. 4 NEWSLETTER 1954

WARE: A Threatened Hall-House. No. 36 Baldock Street gives an instance of the surprises concealed by commonplace housefronts in our older towns. A long low range at right angles to the street, to which it presents a plastered cottage gable end above a baker's shop, No. 36 has on its south side an open court, charmingly designated Monkey Row. The end of the building farthest from the street is divided off to form a separate dwelling, numbered 1, Monkey Row, now owned by Miss Savidge, who, having had a hint that the whole structure might be condemned, prudently sought the advice of the Society for the Protection of Ancient Buildings. The report of their architect, Mr. Peter Locke, reveals that No. 36 Baldock Street is no less than a fifteenth century Hall-House, of which Miss Savidge occupies the solar wing. Her part of the premises shares the vast brick chimney stack, inserted in the sixteenth century at the solar end of the hall. High in the north wall is a six-light unglazed window, with square mullions diagonally set, and traces of an answering window survive in the opposite wall.

That this rare survival of early domestic architecture should be threatened with demolition is deplorable. A proposal to destroy the fifteenth century brasses in the parish church would cause an outcry, but a house of the same period has no less strong a claim to be preserved.

The battle to save Auntie May's house had begun.

CHAPTER NINE

Battling with Bureaucrats

In which Auntie May goes to great lengths to keep
her house exactly where it is

In a note she wrote before taking part in a television interview many years later, Auntie May described her fifteen-year battle with Ware Council as 'years of uncertainty – it was something like living with an unexploded bomb in the garden, which might go off at any time'. Her worries are reflected in a number of newspaper cuttings that she kept. She was by no means the only homeowner to have a metaphorical bomb dropped on them by a local authority. There are not many stories of such bombs being defused.

An article in the *Daily Mirror* of 9 July 1954 tells of how a Miss Kathleen Deering, 'a middle-aged spinster who hates making a fuss', had had her house compulsorily purchased by Wanstead and Woodford Borough Council. Her mother had paid £400 for it in 1948 and had spent a further £300 on improvements. The Ministry of Housing and Local Government ordered that she should be paid only £10 for it.

An article in the *Daily Express* of 14 September 1954 describes land-grabbing like this as a nationwide epidemic:

WHEN YOUR HOUSE IS WORTH NOTHING

Housing Reporter Edward Brett
plots the way of the grabber

PUZZLE: When is your land not your land?
Answer: As soon as a predatory local council casts
eyes on it.

Puzzle: When do you have to wait years to
receive payment for land seized from you?
Answer: When a predatory local council is the
land grabber.

Those two riddles are among hundreds that
emerge from one of the biggest postbags I have ever
had.

Daily Express readers were asked to tell
of land-grabbing by authorities who seem to
know more about the land than about human
beings.

As Housing Reporter I have been reading
hundreds of your letters every day. And a sad story
it is that many of you tell . . .

Waiting for her money . . . is Mrs Kathleen
Keane, of Acton, Middlesex. In 1947, she reports,
the borough council grabbed a house site belonging
to her and worth at that date £300. They offered
£10. For two years she carried on a legal fight until
the district valuer agreed she should receive £300.
So far, *seven years* since her land was grabbed, she
has received nothing.

You can go round the country with my postbag of letters from victims of planning and compulsory purchase and find sore heads and sad hearts all the way.

Intensified land-grabbing since the war has changed the face of Britain faster than people can alter their ways of thinking. Today the greater part of town areas are steadily becoming publicly owned . . .

Here in the post-bag is a letter from Mr. Harry Tanswell, the chairman of Billericay U.D.C. He forwards photo copies of two letters written within the last month.

One is from Billericay Council to the Minister of Housing and Local Government. It asks permission to pay more for land in cases where the price by the district valuer is manifestly unjust. The other letter is the reply from the Ministry. It says, in effect: NO.

Only one of the newspaper stories Auntie May read and kept offered a glimmer of hope. In the *Hertfordshire Mercury* of 28 May 1954, there is a report under the headline 'Demolition Order Quashed by Judge':

A successful appeal against a demolition order issued by Bishop's Stortford Urban Council in pursuance of their policy to improve the new town area was made at Bishop's Stortford County Court on Monday by Mr. John Henry Tawn, the owner of 79, New Town Road. Judge W. Lawson Campbell

quashed the order and awarded costs against the
council.

The first phase of Auntie May's battle to save her home was an
attempt to keep it out of the hands of the land-grabbers
altogether. Her files contain scores of letters to and from the
Society for the Protection of Ancient Buildings, the East
Hertfordshire Archaeological Association, Ware UDC and its
individual councillors, the Ministry of Housing and Local
Government, her solicitor, her MP and national and local
newspapers.

The arguments went back and forth until February 1959,
when Mrs Clarke, the owner of 36 Baldock Street, the other
half of the building, sold it to Ware UDC. The baker's shop that
had occupied the ground floor was closed, never to reopen –
though the tenants who lived upstairs were to stay for two more
years.

The sale came as a disappointment and a surprise to Auntie
May, who had thought that if Mrs Clarke did decide to sell, it would
be to her. Auntie May knew she couldn't save half a hall-house: it
didn't make any sense. But she didn't give up. She wrote to the
council to offer to buy or rent 36 Baldock Street, telling them that
she would repair it and then, if necessary, take it all down and re-
erect it on another site. They replied offering to buy her half,
instead.

Auntie May seems to have regarded this as some sort of turning
point, for in March 1959, she went through her files and records,
and made a list of all the telephone calls made, and all the letters
sent and received in her efforts to save her home since the bomb
had been dropped in December 1953. There are 220 items on it. At
the same time, she made a resolution. She wouldn't allow any more

decisions about her future to be taken behind her back. Henceforth, she would exercise her right to sit in the public gallery of meetings of the local authority. She would make her own record of everything that was said. She would keep one step ahead of the game – and make it obvious to every member of the Ware Urban District Council that she was determined not to let them demolish her house and home.

Auntie May wrote down what was said in shorthand and made a fair copy in a ruled exercise book. It covers all the relevant meetings of the Ware Urban District Council and its planning and finance sub-committees from 1959 to 1965. It shows quite extraordinary dedication. She must have spent hundreds of hours sitting in the public gallery, usually by herself. She was certainly the only member of the public present at the Ware UDC meeting held on 2 December 1959:

> *At the end of the public part of the meeting, the Chairman, Mr. Bowsher, wished everyone a Happy Christmas, including "the public". (Only M.A.S. *)*

Auntie May obviously wasn't allowed to participate in the debates – and it seems strange to read notes written in her handwriting referring to herself by her name in the third person. She frequently records the councillors' decisions to inform her of what she has just heard by writing to her solicitor. She could, however, put pressure on them outside their formal meetings, and she wrote to all new councillors upon their election to make sure they were aware of the facts of her case:

---

* May Alice Savidge!

1, Monkey Row,

Ware, Herts.

28th May, 1961.

Dr. J. E. Moore, New Road, Ware.

Councillor for Ware Urban District.

Dear Sir,

500 YEAR OLD HALL-HOUSE, COMPRISING

No. 1, Monkey Row and 36, Baldock St.,

Built as one residence and divided later.

In case the matter of my cottage or No. 36, Baldock Street comes up at a council meeting, I hope you will not mind my writing to give as brief history of the case so far, (as I have done in the past to other new Councillors), as I am naturally very anxious about it. No. 1, Monkey Row is the rear part of No. 36, Baldock Street, the little bakery, now closed and empty, next door to the Wagon & Horses Public House, which is on the corner of Coronation Road. No. 1, Monkey Row and 36, Baldock Street were built as one house and the timbers run right through, so that what affects one is likely to affect the other. They were built about 500 years ago, as a small Hall-House, and subsequently divided, probably when the chimney stack was put in, at about the time of the first Queen Elizabeth. Some members of the council do not like old buildings, and as well as that, the new Relief Road may come near here. Watton Road is opposite No. 28 and half of No. 30, Baldock St., so a continuation of it would be two-and-a-half houses away, but a really wide sweep of it could include No. 36 and mine, and leave the Waggon & Horses standing alone, with Coronation Road on the other side of it. If this little house is really in the way, I would rather move it and re-erect it, (including the front part, No. 36,) – preferably after I retire in 5 years time, – than see it destroyed. The Council knows this. To go back a little, – I bought this cottage in 1947, and the Council gave me a permit to have the roof thoroughly repaired. I have done a lot of other repairs as well. In 1953, the Council began to talk about Demolition, and it was only then that I found out how old the building is. A representative from the Society for the Preservation of Ancient Buildings came here, also one from the East Herts Archaeological Society, and one from the Hertfordshire Society, and they all agreed that the house had been built about 500 years ago, as a Hall-House, that is having a central hall with a fire in the middle of the floor, the smoke escaping through a hole in the roof. The large Tudor chimney stack had been inserted later.

In March, 1955, the Council accepted Undertakings not to re-let until improvements had been made and the Undertaking cancelled – though my part of it was not let, really, but owner-occupied. A year later, they accepted my plan for improvements to the kitchen, bathroom, etc., and the work was carried out at the end of the year, at a cost of £200, – rather more than the estimate. About six months later, they began talking again about pulling down my cottage and 36, Baldock St. This was after they had housed the family from No. 34. Several times in the past, I have tried to buy the front part of this house, (No. 36) and eventually the owner said she would come and talk it over, but instead she offered it to the Council, about two years ago, and they bought it. Then they asked me if I would sell them my part. I said I would rather re-erect the whole building; they wanted me to sign another paper, but it did not even mention the front part, so I did not sign it. The great interest of this little house is that it is complete, at present, though some of it needs uncovering.

About 5 years ago, I was asked to form a Nursing Division of the St. John Ambulance Brigade in the town; the Ambulance Division is the oldest in Hertfordshire, but they had never had a Division for the

93

women. Three of the Councillors were members of St. John, and I thought they would think very badly of me if I said I was too busy; of course, it has taken a lot of my spare time, and that, and the uncertainty here, have prevented me from doing as much as I could have done to the cottage. Even so, it is very comfortable, having a large living room, about 17 ft. by 11 ft.; a bedroom the same size; small bathroom opening off the bedroom; with electric water heater; kitchen with modern sink, etc., gas cooker, washing machine, indoor modern W.C., garden 40 ft. by 12 ft. and a small front garden; also a useful attic and cupboards.

Some very interesting original features of this house have come to light, as well as the Tudor chimney stack, with its large open hearth, downstairs, and four-centred arch upstairs; most important being the undamaged six-light unglazed medieval window, two lights of which now have Elizabethan diamond leaded glass. An eminent architect said that this window alone, put the building into the architecturally important class, as these windows have usually been cut out and something more modern put in; once cut away, they can never be replaced, as they are part of the building.

If this house does not have to come down, I would like to buy the front part, or rent it, and do it up, or even just do up the outside; it would look charming, if properly looked after.

Hoping for your support,

Yours truly,

May Savidge (Miss)

Looking through Auntie May's records of the sixteen years she spent with the fate of her home hanging in the balance, I wondered how she found the time and energy to carry on the fight. All those meetings, all those letters, all those phone calls, all that lobbying would have been enough to exhaust any normal individual. And

Auntie May had being making all these efforts in addition to leading what anyone would think a very full and busy life, holding down a full-time job, running a division of the St John Ambulance Brigade, visiting the old and the sick supported by the Ware Old People's Welfare Association, and meeting and corresponding with a wide circle of friends.

She had also found the energy to remember the man she had loved. Denis Elliot Watson had been dead and buried since 1938, but Auntie May's diaries record that she was still visiting and tending his grave. Among her papers were two bills from Chalker and Gamble Ltd, Monumental Masons and Funeral Directors, 're Grave No. D.7.41, Hammersmith Cemetery, Mortlake'. On 5 October 1956, Auntie May paid £2 10s for the earth that covered Denis's grave to be replaced by green stone chips, and on 30 October she paid £4 5s for a marble vase. I am still not sure why she chose to do this now – the date wasn't an anniversary as far as I knew. Or was it? Had they agreed to marry in October 1936? I have found no written record of the date of their engagement. The letters show that by that time, they were very much in love. Was Auntie May trying to draw a line under her grief? Or was it just that she realised that with all the time she was spending battling to save her house, she was too busy to visit Mortlake often enough to keep Denis's grave garden tidy?

And then I discovered two quite extraordinary letters. The first was from Edward Collins, whom Auntie May had met during the war, some fifteen years earlier. The folder that contains his correspondence is full. His letters all begin: 'Dear Miss Savidge'; they are friendly, but not intimate. Except for the last one, which is dated 2 February 1960.

Dear Miss Savidge,

I thought you might like to know how things are getting on with me. As you may guess, I have been very low indeed and did not have any inclination to write. I have, thanks to God, seen my dear cousin Iris in a new and wonderful light, besides her helping me in the things of this world, owing to her having given herself absolutely to the Lord Jesus many years ago, she has been able to show me the error of my ways and I see now that my past interest in spiritualism was nearly my complete downfall. I now have no doubt at all that it is ALL the business of the Devil. Once I turned my back on that it was not so hard to come to Jesus and ask his forgiveness for my sins. I had got to the state that even the smallest one looked so black that I was scared of it and the big ones brought tears to my eyes – this is absolutely the truth. With Iris's prayers and guidance . . . I experienced the wonderful thrill of being born again last Sunday. I did not expect it and doubted it could ever happen to me – I did not see Iris at all last week-end but despite that I experienced the most wonderful day in my life and it still continues. I can only thank the Lord Jesus for what he has done for such a sinner as I was. As you can tell from this I have changed a great deal. I would like to bring Iris over to Ware to see you when you feel like it, she is a very dear person and I know you, too, will love her – everybody does!

I for one cannot love her enough as she certainly saved my soul from eternal damnation by bringing me to the foot of the cross – the Lord then did the rest. However much I feel for her I love my Lord Jesus much, much more – words just fail to express how much or how I feel. I know this will hurt you as I know only too well how you feel towards me, believe me I do appreciate it and do pray to the Lord that you too may experience this most wonderful love. For my part and I am sure that I can write for Iris in this, I should like nothing better than that you be able to regard us as a new sister and brother. You can

BATTLING WITH BUREAUCRATS

rest assured that if there is anything that I or we can help you in either a spiritual or a worldly way we would be very happy indeed to do it.

Believe me, knowing what a comfort you were during the days just after the passing of my dear mother, this has been a difficult letter to write and in writing it I have prayed long and earnestly to the Lord. I do hope that poor Mrs Allen is still keeping in good health – no colds etc. though we know that her passing would be a blessing. I pray that she might find peace and rest. How are the animals, do hope Candy* is calming down a little or she will be too much for you. The "milk bottle tops" are mounting up again and will bring them over some time. I must end here as it's about bed time. I send you all my best wishes and may the Lord bless you and protect you with his most precious love.

Yours sincerely,

Edward A.C.

1, Monkey Row,
Ware, Herts.
18th February, 1960.

Dear Edward,

Please excuse the typing, but I cannot see to write. Thank you for your letter, explaining the situation more fully. I had, of course, realized what was happening, two or three weeks earlier, which was why I stopped 'phoning you.

Am very glad to hear that you have become a Christian. I did not know that you were not one, before; you sounded sincere when you joined in with the Lord's prayer, during the radio Watch Night Service. Your attitude towards Churches, years ago, always struck me as strange; you used to say that we would have to be married in a

---

* Candy was Auntie May's cat.

Registry Office, because you would not go into a Church as they made you feel queer; but then you had so many odd fears — I put them down to your sheltered upbringing. You seemed to have forgotten about it, at your Father's funeral, and your Mother's, and I thought it was probably due to an early recollection of too much incense, and that you had got over it.

Perhaps I took it for granted that you believed in God, because I do and always have done. I have lived without human company for the last twenty-five years, and at times before that, too; through more difficulties and dangers than average; this is a way at living that you know nothing about. I wonder what you think kept me going? I don't think I would be sane now, if I had not been able to talk and pray to God. It is true that I do not talk about it much, but I have been rebutted in the past, when trying to talk seriously to you; once when I had waited for days for a chance to say something, all you said was, "Look, there's one of the new Churchill tanks!"

I knew you had faults, (who has not?) I was not blind — some of them upset me a good deal, but because you had convinced me that you were fond of me and had need of me, I did not criticize unduly; I just hoped to be able to show you, gradually, that life can be lived differently, and I think I had made some progress. Now your Cousin, who you had only met twice in the past, has come along and changed you completely in a few hours. It surprises me, though, that anyone so dear and lovable as your Cousin Iris, should have thought it right to come between us, after seventeen years. It is not as though I am an evil spirit from whom you had to be parted before you could reform; I would not have tried to hold you back. I have not lived a gay life, nor an easy one, and among other things, surely twenty years of St. John Ambulance work is in keeping with the teaching of Jesus Christ, "Inasmuch as you did it unto the least of my brethren, ye did it unto Me". The Order of St. John has two mottoes: "For the Faith" and

"For the Service of Mankind" and our work is carried out without distinction of race, class or creed. But perhaps Iris did not think to ask, and you did not bother to tell her, about my existence. The world would be in a difficult state if all the converted fell in love with the converter, yet you seem to think that what you have done is right; one would think from the way you write that you had given up your girl friend and gone back to your wife.

In your letter you say you know "only too well" how I feel towards you, which rather implies that I made the advances, and that you had no feelings towards me. I wonder if you remember how this episode started? When we became acquainted seventeen years ago, I had been alone for nearly eight years;* Denis had been dead for nearly five years, and I had reached a state of peace – not happy, but cheerful and busy; and when you asked me to go out with you, after that car crash, I did not really want to break faith, but then agreed to go as long as it was only in a friendly way – nothing serious. That did not suit you, however; you said you were awake all night, crying, which made me change my mind, because it did not seem right to make you unhappy. Is it surprising that I thought you really cared? During the months that followed, you often spoke of our marriage, – once you said you were glad that I had not married Denis, because your parents would not like you marrying a widow. Then on 22nd August, 1943, you announced that you had remembered that before you met me, you had decided to stay single and look after your parents, and that you still intended to do so, but you did not want them to know why you were staying single. I remember I thought I would still have a friend to turn to, and said so, but soon found out that this was not necessarily so, and during the years that followed, single-handed and often in difficulties, and sometimes in danger, and you, the only one who knew

* That is, since her mother's death.

it, not bothering to come and offer a helping hand, I became convinced that you had finished with me completely, and were drifting quietly out of my life; I knew I would never have left you to face alone some of the situations that I had to deal with, and if I had never seen you again, then, I would not have been surprised. But later, you changed again, and became more like your old self, and you spoke as if we still belonged to each other – for instance, when you said you had bought a "Mayflower" car, you said, "Now I have two Mays". Your Mother also changed in the last few years, as if she knew at last, why we had not married; I did not know whether you had told her or whether she had guessed, but she was different, – more gentle and more affectionate, as if trying to say, "I know and I'm grateful".

And now that your Mother has gone and you are free to marry, you have suddenly transferred your affections to someone new, and would like me to be a sister to you and Iris. I am afraid I have had enough. Seventeen years is a long time, and I have put up with a great deal, but there is a limit. It is all right for you – you have had your parents all these years, and now you have Iris you have had me in the background, in case you needed me, and now you do not need me any longer. You have made your choice, and no doubt Iris is much more suitable, – but my heart is not made of stone, and I am not suffering from loss of memory; – in the small hours of the morning, when I am wide awake, I wish I could forget. Still I thank God that we were not married already, if you can change like this. No doubt it is better as it is; you might have wanted me to give up my St. John work, if you had married me, and I expect I can do more good this way. I hope you will be more faithful to Iris than you have been to me.

May God teach you to be patient, tolerant, kind and forgiving towards your fellow human beings who you meet in your everyday life, remembering that they are all His children, as well as you, and equal in His sight, and that any of them may be putting a brave face on a

*life of difficulty and tragedy, such as you have never known, and that
one more harsh word may be the breaking point. May He also teach
you not to be afraid, except of His displeasure, and to be faithful.*

*So I will close the book on our story, which has brought so much
more unhappiness than anything else, during its seventeen years.*

Good-bye.

*'The day returns and brings us the petty round of irritating concerns
and duties. Help us to play the man; help us to perform them with
laughter and kind faces, let cheerfulness abound with industry. Give
us to go blithely on our business all this day, bring us to our resting
beds weary and content and undishonoured, and grant us in the end the
gift of sleep. Amen.'*

*R.L.S.**

*The Commissionaires at the gatehouse of Murphy Radio,
Bessemer Road, Welwyn Garden City, will gladly accept silver paper
and milk bottle tops in aid of the Guide Dogs for the Blind; the
collector's name is Mr. Lawrence.*

How could I have missed it? Auntie May had had a boyfriend – of
sorts – for seventeen years, and I hadn't noticed. I went back
through the papers and diaries again, but I still couldn't find any
signs of it. There were chatty letters, Christmas and birthday cards,
diary entries recording visits to this fellow and his parents, but
nothing to suggest anything more than friendship. Except one thing,
perhaps. In his file was an undated small piece of paper that must
have accompanied one of the birthday presents they exchanged. On
it, in his distinctive hand, is written *'May 24th 1958: With love and
best wishes'* followed by his initials. It is the only other time the word
'love' occurs in any correspondence between them.

---

* Robert Louis Stevenson.

Had they loved each other? I wonder. Auntie May doesn't seem to have found much to admire in Edward except his devotion. When that failed, she saw only faults. It seems that the only time there was any intensity in the relationship was when it ended. Her letter does not express the sorrow of a disappointed lover, but the anger of someone who feels she has been strung along and used. It is the only thing she ever wrote that contains even a trace of self-pity. It is the only time that she expresses any kind of bitterness. It is the only time she mentions the pain of loneliness. And it marks the moment when she realised that she would spend the rest of her life on her own.

CHAPTER TEN

Working Holidays

In which Auntie May prepares for the possibility that
ultimately, the house might have to be moved

By the early 1960s, 1 Monkey Row was becoming increasingly
isolated. Auntie May's home was surrounded by an ever-widening
area of empty, derelict buildings and the spaces where other
buildings had once been. In March and April 1963, numbers 32 and
34 Baldock Street were demolished. The wreckers were almost at
the gate. In June 1963, she received a letter from a Mr Doubleday
of Hertfordshire County Council, letting her know that the
Hertfordshire Buildings Preservation Trust would like to reuse
materials salvaged from 1 Monkey Row and 36 Baldock Street after
they had been demolished. The demolition was not an 'if', but a
'when'. Auntie May was having none of it. She told him what she
had already told the Ware Urban District Council countless times:
that if she was allowed to rent 36 Baldock Street and keep it when
both halves of the medieval hall-house had to be taken down, she
would save the whole building by re-erecting it elsewhere.

But the wheels of local government bureaucracy were turning
slowly. Eighteen months later, 1 Monkey Row was still standing
and Auntie May was still living in it. Some members of the council
now tried a different tack, arguing that the condition of 36 Baldock

Street was so poor as to make it a danger to the public. It had been empty and unmaintained since 1961. But other councillors stood up for Auntie May as her record of the Ware UDC meeting of 7 October 1964 shows.

Ware UDC Meeting   *8 pm, Wednesday, 7 October 1964*

M. Goldstone (chairman); Mr Avery (vice-chairman)
Mrs Cooper; Mr Davenport; Mr Beazley; Mr Murphy; Mr Green; Mr J Sutcliffe.
Absent – Mr Doyle and the surveyor (whose father had just died).

No. 335. 36 Baldock Street.
The condition of this building was discussed when certain members expressed the view that it was a possible danger to the public.

Clr Murphy reminded the members that Miss Savidge, of 1 Monkey Row had asked the council some years ago if she might keep 36 Baldock Street decorated until such time as she retired when she wished to demolish her cottage and 36 Baldock Street and to re-erect the cottage on another site. She was due to retire in 1966.

The building of which 1 Monkey Row formed part was a fifteenth-century hall-house preserving the greater part of an original structure with Elizabethan and later alterations.

It was stated that Miss Savidge had been informed in 1960 that there was a possibility of the relief road affecting her property and advised to arrange as soon as possible the demolition of the property.

It was decided that the Surveyor be asked to inspect the property and report whether in his view 36 Baldock Street was in a condition dangerous to the public, and that the County Council be asked whether in fact the relief road would affect this property.

...

Only one week before the General Election – some of the Labour councillors got carried away by party politics.

The meeting closed about 9.15pm.

Demolition day was approaching, but Auntie May still hadn't found a site on which to re-erect her house. I would have thought that with so many friends in and around Ware, with all her charitable work for the local old people's welfare association and the St John Ambulance Brigade, and with her sister living nearby, the obvious thing to do would be to rebuild the house locally, but Auntie May was never one to do the obvious. She saw it as an opportunity for a fresh start – and she had a hankering to find somewhere by the sea. It was in her blood. Her grandfather had been a Norwegian fisherman, and living on the boat had been a really adventurous part of her life. The two coastlines she knew and loved were those of the West Country and East Anglia, and she decided to explore the possibilities of both.

In October 1964, she took a fortnight's holiday in Wells-next-the-Sea, Norfolk, where she rented a small furnished flat for six guineas a week. It is clear from her papers, diaries and correspondence that she planned every aspect of the holiday with her usual attention to detail. I found the notebook she manufactured to contain the checklist of things she put in her luggage. She made it by stringing together pieces of lined paper that she had cut to form alphabetical index tabs. It contains everything you might expect anyone to take on holiday – and very much more. The first entry under 'A' is 'address books (3)', and down between the 'Alarum clock (green one)' and 'Anti-histamine cream' is 'Alkathene film or bag to sit on if damp (large)'. She takes her 'Christmas card list', an 'Enamel plate for steaming

fish',* a 'Face flannel' and a 'Foot flannel', a 'Shovel (for
D[inkie]'s bucket)', a 'Shoe horn', a 'Tea cosy' and 'Vaseline (for
hair) (and Dinkie)'. Under 'K', there is only 'Knitting'; I had half
expected to find 'Kitchen sink'.

In July, she had written to the Wells council to ask for a list of
places to stay, and had selected West House in Freeman Street,
run by a Mrs Groom. Mrs Groom wrote to explain that the last
leg of the train service to Wells would cease to operate on
3 October, so Auntie May sent a letter to the divisional manager
of British Railways Eastern at Norwich Station to ask how best
to complete her journey. He replied that she should travel as far
as Dereham and then get the Eastern Counties Omnibus
Company bus. Auntie May visited Ware station to find out the
cost of the journey, made a list of everything she needed to take
with her, arranged for Mrs Crisp at the Hope public house to keep
an eye on her cottage, and booked a taxi from Charvill's to take
her, her pets and her luggage to the station. On the morning of
Saturday, 10 October she cancelled her order for bread and took
her document box to the bank for safe keeping. On her way
home, she saw a reminder of the destruction that was edging its
way closer to her house:

*W.U.D.C. men . . . destroying the garden opposite – for 2 p[ai]rs
semi-det[ached] houses – Mr. G. had worked on it for 40 years –
began before house was finished.*

Despite all her careful preparations, Auntie May's holiday did not
begin as smoothly as she had planned. It rained heavily the night
before she left, so she didn't get her tickets in advance. There

* I've still got it!

would have been plenty of time to buy them on the day if the car from Charvill's turned up at noon, as agreed, but it didn't. It was nearly twenty minutes late. Her train was at 12.27, and she had a phenomenal quantity of luggage to get onto it. It had to be held up for her, while the porters heaved it all aboard. Much of it – too much, it would turn out – was piled onto her eccentrically designed pushchair, which had a T-bar for a handle, that made it difficult to steer when overloaded. She had her dog on a lead and her cat in a basket. She had to get all this off and on the train four times during the journey – she had to change at Broxbourne, Bishop's Stortford, Ely and Wymondham. She gave the porters that helped her a total of 7s in tips. When she got off at Dereham, the struggle continued:

Bus driver had no key to boot, so my stuff occupied front seat* *– bus left as soon as we were all on.*

Arr. Wells about 5.45 pm – no car to hire. Dumped us at Stn.: (later I heard there are 2 taxis if you know where to 'phone). My pushchair had lost one back tyre on the way, then the front one came off – pushing was very difficult – stuff kept slipping – pavement bad in places (buildings demolished.) A fisherman carried Dinkie as far as a public house. Pushchair made dreadful noise. I had to take Dinkie separately for a few yards, then come back for pushchair with luggage. A lady finally carried Dinkie to the Groom's gate – I would not have known – no name on it – no number. Arr. About 6.45 pm. (1 hour from Stn.!) There is also a drive which is easier than the steps in the garden path. Mr. & Mrs. Groom invited me in for a cup of tea . . . very nice flat – very large bed-sitting

---

* She thus had to buy a ticket for the pushchair. It cost 11d.

room – 20'6" x 16'4" + 2'8" x 7'3" inside fireplace, also kitchen 10'2" x 7'9", larder, etc.

There was 1 pt. of milk I had asked for. Slept till 7 am. (clock struck 3 – wondered why it was light!)

Auntie May appears to have thoroughly enjoyed her fortnight in Wells, though I don't suppose many of Mr and Mrs Groom's guests began their stay by measuring the dimensions of the flat. She explored the town, the harbour, the coastline and the countryside. But she wasn't just here for a holiday. She visited all the local estate agents, and called on the council's surveyor, Mr Rogers and the town clerk, Mr Poynter, to find out whether there would be any problem getting permission to re-erect her house. She got on well with them – 'they both seemed very nice', she writes – and Mr Rogers told her that 'they would give sympathetic consideration' to the idea. Auntie May then viewed several building plots – even though, as she told Mr Rogers, she still 'might not have to move' her house after all. She thought that there was still a chance that it might be spared. Just in case it wasn't, she asked the Wells estate agents to add her name to their mailing lists.

For more than a year after Auntie May returned from her holiday, Ware UDC's plans to demolish 1 Monkey Row and 36 Baldock Street seem to have been on the back burner. Then, in late November 1965, it transferred ownership of 36 Baldock Street to the Hertfordshire County Council. It was a move that brought a demolition order for both properties a step nearer. But Auntie May's retirement date was getting nearer, too. She would soon have the time needed to arrange for the house to be taken down and re-erected elsewhere, if it came to it.

WED. 18.5.66

10.30 am. Research Cnf. Room – my Retirement Presentation
(Dr. Child) Quite a number came – cheque for £9 (+ 7s 6d later) for
me to get binoculars (or telescope) – no time beforehand.

Dr C. said some very nice things – my mind went blank, when I
started, a glance at my notes reminded me – though I can't remember
exactly what I said at first.

The first thing Auntie May did in her retirement was to return to
Norfolk, where she revisited Wells and took another look at some
of the building plots she had first seen in 1964 – but none of them
seemed quite right for her, and in any case, she still felt there was
just a chance that she might not have to move. On her return, her
diary fills with references to SJAB meetings and events, including
a flag day, fundraising sales, fêtes, first aid demonstrations, training
sessions and inspections. But thoughts of moving were never far
away. A note made on Monday 4 July records that she heard on
the radio that a Mrs Topham Smith had 'moved a timber-framed
house 25 miles'.

On Saturday, 30 July 1966, Auntie May attended my wedding
to Tony in All Saints Church, Croxley Green, Hertfordshire.
Immediately afterwards, she started planning a site-hunting
trip to the West Country. Mindful of the trouble she had had
carrying all her luggage on her last holiday, she bought herself
a Portable Porter trolley, with two wheels and webbing straps,
for 7s 6d. On Thursday, 25 August, she went to the railway
station to buy her return ticket to Dartmouth, recording that
she paid £6 3s for it, and £3 2s for Candy, who travelled as
a 'child'. She also recorded the details on her seat reservation
from Paddington to Kingswear, the ticket for which I found

between the appropriate pages of that week's *Radio Times*:

N°. M.333406 – for 10.05 train
Coach H. Seat 24.
Facing Engine.

She tried to book a car to take her to Ware station in time for the
7.27 to London the following Saturday, but found that Charvill's
didn't start work until 8am, and Joan's Car Service didn't open
before 9am. She'd have to get to the station by bus.

At 7 o'clock in the morning on Saturday, 27 August, Auntie
May and Candy set out with her pushchair and Portable Porter,
carrying a small cabin trunk, a large blue polythene bag, a leather
bag, a zip handbag and a cat basket containing Dinkie. Miss
Stewart, a friend of hers, happened to be at the bus stop. She told
Auntie May that she wasn't sure that the 7.12 bus still ran – but it
did, and the driver/conductor, Mr Flood, helped Auntie May get
her luggage on board, while Miss Stewart held Candy's lead.
Unfortunately, the dog got overexcited and pulled so hard that the
collar clip broke. Auntie May did catch the 7.27, but when she
picked up her trunk in order to change at Broxbourne, the handle
came off in her hand, and she had to tie it up with the length of
rope she had brought to tie things to the pushchair. This turned
out to have been a fortunate accident, because when she went to
pick up the trunk at Liverpool Street, she saw that the hinge of the
lid, which was made only of fabric, had torn from end to end. At
Paddington she was told that she would have to buy a return ticket
for 11s 3d for the cat; and when she finally got all her stuff onto the
10.05, she found that 'both H.24s had been marked "facing engine"
(or had the other one been altered? It looked like it.)'

Once again, Auntie May had made a disastrous start to a

holiday, but once again, there was no mention of annoyance or frustration in the record she made. If I were given to writing diaries, I would certainly have mentioned my anger at a taxi firm that sent a car so late that I nearly missed my train, or at a fellow passenger who had forged a ticket reservation so as to occupy the seat I had booked. I would have been furious to be told half-way through a journey that I had to pay extra for a cat carried in a basket, and I would have made my fury a matter of record. I would have been thoroughly fed up if the handle had come off a piece of luggage, and the lid had all but come off, too, and I would have written up my annoyance as part of my memory of the day. But Auntie May does no such thing. Her records are meticulous to the point of obsessiveness, but there is never any mention of resentment when things went wrong.

Why, I wonder? Is it that she was only interested in recording facts, not feelings? I don't think so. Those 440 diaries contain hundreds of references to how she felt when she was unwell, when she had 'no energy' in hot or humid weather, or when she was 'tired' or 'exhausted' after overdoing it – though her interest was in the fact that she was tired rather than what feeling tired was like. She does, at least occasionally, write up her feelings about people she met or dealt with. She writes of Mr Poynter and Mr Rogers in Wells that they 'both seemed very nice'. She also records sights that she found moving, including this, on her West Country holiday:

> *TUES 30.8.66 . . . _Full moon was rising_ (from bank of cloud just above the sea horizon) – golden colour – reflected right across to the beach – beautiful sight.*

Such glimpses of Auntie May's emotions are rare, but when they do appear, they are nearly always positive. One uncharacteristic expression of annoyance is in an entry for Monday, 12 December 1966, when she describes how another dog savaged Candy in the street while her owner did nothing to intervene:

Fancy bringing out a dog like that, without a lead. She must have known what he was like, by the way she called him in the first place. A dog is supposed to be 'under control'.

I think that one reason Auntie May records so few negative thoughts in her diaries is that she didn't have many. I can honestly say that in all the years I knew her, I never heard her utter a complaint – not even in her awful final illness. She simply accepted her lot and made the best of it. She didn't write up those disasters with the taxis and the luggage and the tickets because they had annoyed her, but because they had happened.

As to why she should want to record her life in such detail at all – well, that's another question. I've spoken to lots of people about her in the years since she died, and I've given lots of talks about her to groups of people, some of whom had known her. Some think she wrote up everything simply because she had a compulsive personality. They give the same explanation for her hoarding. I am sure this must be true, but I don't think it's the whole truth. It doesn't explain why this compulsiveness should show itself in keeping a running record of one's life, or in hanging on to everything that comes into one's hands. Somebody suggested that Auntie May suffered from a condition known as Obsessive Compulsive Disorder, but I am not convinced. Some OCD sufferers are indeed compulsive hoarders, but what I have read about them suggests that their hoarding gets between them and their ability to cope with the world. Auntie May was able to cope with anything. Her diaries are the proof of it. OCD hoarders tend to be loners. Auntie May certainly lived alone, but she had scores of friends and acquaintances – her diaries are full of references to them. No, I don't think she suffered from a mental illness.

I am not a psychiatrist or a psychologist. I can't offer a professional opinion on why Auntie May kept all those things and all those diaries. But I have an idea, for what it's worth. I think it all started with the death of her father. Ten must be a terrible age for a girl to lose her dad. Then there was the poverty, the constant house moving, the sense of instability – and then the death of her mother, too. I think she clung on to things for the sense of security that they gave her. I am sure she clung on to Denis's things because it was the nearest she could do to clinging on to Denis. I think it was a way of coping with mortality. I think she wrote down every detail of her life so that she could hang on to time itself, and not let it slip through her fingers. She wasn't frightened of death, but she found living with loss almost unbearable.

I think she was odd, unusual, eccentric, yes . . . but I think that she was oddly, unusually and eccentrically virtuous. These days, we think little of old-fashioned virtues like thrift and fortitude, but Auntie May embraced them absolutely. She didn't keep accounts of everything she ever spent and received because she was tight-fisted, but because she was thrifty. She was determined to live within her means so that she wouldn't be a burden to others. Her thriftiness allowed her to be generous – her accounts record countless payments made to any number of charities.

As for fortitude, I can't think of anyone else who would put up with the discomforts that she tolerated without complaint and as a matter of course. The years on a cramped boat, getting up several times a night to pump it out to keep it afloat; the months in the shell of 1 Monkey Row and 36 Baldock Street, with the roof off and rain running down the walls of the sitting room; the years in the Blue Lady caravan, in which the temperatures that she recorded got down as far as 20°F; the many more years in the house that she never got as far as making weatherproof, that got even colder than the caravan and was infested with rats; Auntie May put up with all this, alone and in poor health.

•

During her 1966 holiday Auntie May visited several estate agents and travelled the Devon coastline, looking at building plots. She also did some running repairs on her damaged luggage:

FRI. 2.9.66:

Fishing tackle etc. shop – Father also does leather repairs like stitching handles onto cases –

2 – 6 ft. webbing straps @ 4/-
1 handle (to use with them) 1/9d } *9.9d*
(for small cabin trunk, which is shaky.)

Kingsbridge Gazette   *3d*

She kept and filed the *Kingsbridge Gazette*, of course – I have it on my desk right now. And the trunk, the straps and the carrying handle she bought that day are even now upstairs in the attic of Ware Hall-House.

The following year, Auntie May headed further west, taking a holiday in a caravan in Cornwall. She visited several estate agents, and from the correspondence that she kept, it would seem that one of them, a Mr Braun, of Barnes, Cooke & Company of Hale, managed to interest her in the idea of buying a property rather than moving her house. He must have been a good salesman, because he persuaded her to view several cottages. He even wrote to her on her return to advise her against attempting a rebuild, but when she got back home, there was another letter waiting for her on the mat. It came from the Wells estate agents Andrews & Dewing. It contained the firm's September 1967 Property List. Auntie May immediately underlined one of the entries under 'Building Land' in red ink:

WELLS-NEXT-THE-SEA: Plummers Hill. Outline permission for one dwelling. £500.

She telephoned the agents, who were so confident that the site would suit her that they said they'd give her first refusal. She travelled up to Norfolk on Wednesday, 4 October, and was taken to see the plot. She liked it. She wrote a full description of it in her diary, noting that it was 'Quite secluded from onlookers', and that it was in 'a nice part of town, though no view of sea – near shops, though'. She went and sat on a bench down by the harbour and had a think. Then she went to the council offices in Mill Road, and got the planning permission forms from Mr Rogers. By the time she got home at 10.15 that night, she had filled most of them in.

On Tuesday, 28 November, Auntie May had two surprises. The first was the arrival of a freelance photographer sent by a Norfolk newspaper. She told him she didn't want any press attention as nothing had yet been settled, but he said that the paper would publish the story with or without the pictures, so she let him take some. Then, a telegram arrived, asking her to telephone a Fakenham number reversing the charges. It was from a Mr Fletcher from the Wells Urban District Council. He told her that the local planning committee had approved her application, though the case had to be passed by the county council, too. There had been three reporters present at the meeting, and news of her plans was out. The story appeared in the *Daily Mirror* on Friday, 1 December, and the next day, she found another telegram in her letterbox. This one was from the BBC *Today* programme, asking if she was available to record an interview on Sunday. She sent back a telegram saying she wasn't, and followed it up with a letter explaining that things were still up in the air. 'When matters have sorted themselves out,' she wrote, 'perhaps this will make a better story for you.'

But media interest in Auntie May's story was growing. She came back home on Thursday, 7 December to find 'two young men from the *Daily Telegraph* in the front garden, one of them with a camera'. Pieces and pictures also appeared in the *Times*, the *Eastern Daily Press* and the *London Evening News*. An *Evening Standard* reporter called, followed by photographers from different picture agencies. In the letter she had sent to the BBC on 4 December, she had written 'the whole matter is still in a very tentative state; you see, I do not know yet whether I shall have to move . . .' But the story of a little old lady defying a demolition order by moving her house and rebuilding it with her own hands was unstoppable – even if Auntie May was not quite as old as the published pictures made her look.

At the beginning of February 1967, Auntie May asked for access to next door, as she would need to make drawings of its interior if the building really was to be dismantled. On Friday, 8 February she was given the keys and took Candy into number 36 to see what state it was in. It was pretty derelict. 'The living room floor crumbles as it is walked on,' she wrote. 'The bakehouse floor has collapsed into cellar.' But there were more beams exposed than in her half of the building – and they were big, and in good condition.

From left to right, the Savidge family: Nelly [Cornelia], Henrietta, Frederick and May. Their father died soon after this picture was taken, when May was only 9 years old.

May's Dutch great-grandfather built this lighthouse on the dangerous island coastline of Texel, to stop wreckers from luring ships onto the sands and living off the spoils.

May's fiancé Denis Watson; a Shakespearian actor in London theatres and silent films, he was almost 30 years her senior. Sadly, like May's mother and father, he was to die prematurely.

May bought her first home, the Thames river bus *Formosa*, and lived on the river Lee for a number of years, by the Saracen's Head pub, famous for its 'Great Bed of Ware'.

Separated from the rubble of the previous demolitions by a paling fence, May's house in Ware, Hertfordshire awaits destruction, while she desperately negotiates the buying of the bakery next door.

May is rescued from one of her boats (in the background) at Westcliff-on-Sea, Essex; yet another adventure which made headline news in the national press. Sadly the boat sank in the storm that night.

Part of May's medieval house ready for transportation to the seaside a hundred miles away. There were eleven lorry loads and the rebuild would take her the rest of her life.

May in her old caravan where she lived for nearly twenty years during the rebuild. The 'bag lady' look hides her clear-thinking intellect and dogged determination.

All beams were labelled - here is part of the scullery framework. She treated these beams like wayward children that 'moved in the wind' and must be roped and pegged into their correct place.

May had no one to encourage her through the long days, so she used an alarm clock to set herself targets each day. Her diary notes how many nails she extracted each hour.

Thousands of hand-made Hertfordshire peg tiles, awaiting the rebuild. May even made an instrument for forming the oak pegs to hold those tiles onto the roof.

Treating timber against wood-worm and rot, May works by the old bakery door which once stood in busy Baldock Street in Ware. It's now a quiet pathway in the back garden, in Norfolk.

A proud photograph developed by May. Luckily, when the 1987 hurricane hit, only a few beams were dislodged. We feared the worst but May didn't even know it had occurred!

Perfecting an oak peg to secure a main beam. May made the old bakery her workshop as the large shop window offered maximum daylight. It was years before she had electricity on site.

Now well over seventy, May stands at the southwest corner of the hall house. Out of view, scaffolding is erected, ready for the tiles to be put in place - a triumphant picture of achievement.

What a strange concoction of possessions May left for us to find, from childhood bus tickets and piano accordions, to nine side-saddles in the overgrown garden! Every letter was written in duplicate, every sweet paper was filed on the day she ate it: vellum scrolls hidden in toilet roll middles. It was both wonderful and horrific.

Our first task was to make May's
scullery habitable - the only room with
four good walls. We emptied, cleaned
and plastered. How sad that she refused
to let us help while she was alive.

May's nephew, Tony, looks out of the
window while I chat to his cousin, Sandra.
The minstrel's gallery is now under
construction, tied up with string, in true
Auntie May fashion.

The first completed bedroom.
May's father, who was keen on cricket,
made the miniature bat for her when she
was six years old.

The Great Hall viewed from the cross passage near the front door.

I stand in the completed Great Hall with May's plans in my hand. At last the task is finished and I can live my own life again.

It was at this stage in the story that I first visited Auntie May in Monkey Row. I have already described my own memory of the event and Auntie May records hers in an entry in diary number 146:

> *SUN: 30.4.67* . . . *About 3pm? Chris & Tony arrived – first visit for Chris. TONY photographed the flowering cherry (in colour) – fully out today – and no wind – sun came out for second shot. Tea – (cakes & biscuits) – then they showed the best of their 450 coloured slides of their honeymoon. Marvellous – screen is made of cloth faced with tiny 'pastinilla-like' spheres – sort of luminous. Finished about 8.15pm? Supper – coffee, cheese, bread & butter, watercress, cake. They left about 9.30pm? (first time I've used the rose tea set.) Out late with Candy. (Lent Tony book for Nellie to read, Father Potter of Peckham.) Tony has left an adaptor behind – 2 pin 5 amp socket to bayonet. The lights blew and he replaced the fuses and fixed a wire that had slipped out.*

I find Auntie May's account of the visit fascinating. It brings my own memories instantly to life. In my mind's eye, I can see Tony photographing that tree as clearly as if he were doing it right now. It was so close to the house that you could hardly get through the front door. There were roses round the door but they had sagged and you had to duck to get past them. Yes, the sun did come out for a second shot, though if Auntie May hadn't written that down, I don't suppose I would ever have remembered: I suppose it reflects her own interest in photography. I certainly didn't consciously store a memory of what she gave us to eat for tea or supper, but seeing her record of it sets off a little film show in my head: there we all are, holding those pretty teacups . . . the roses on them are pink and Auntie May's has a little chip on the edge of the saucer. It makes me smile to think that she was more interested in describing the screen we projected the pictures on to than the pictures themselves – we were so proud of our adventures and our slides of them! And I can certainly remember the lights blowing.

I had, however, forgotten that she had given Tony a book to pass on to his mother. At the time it seemed to have no significance. Now, though, I think that it is very significant indeed. *Father Potter of Peckham* is the story of an Anglican priest who founded a community called the Brotherhood of the Holy Cross. It describes Father Potter's work in a slum parish, looking after boys and girls at the bottom of the heap. I still have the book, of course – Nellie must have returned it. It is listed in the catalogue of all her books that Auntie May drew up in 1969. The blurb on the cover describes the brotherhood's aim: 'to present the living, loving Christ to the people in a practical way – to poor people, because we love them'. Now that I have read Auntie May's diaries, I can see why she would have liked the book and wanted to share it with her sister. She was deeply, though modestly, religious. She regularly read the Bible – she took it with her on all her trips and holidays. She worshipped every Sunday morning at the chapel of Western House, the geriatric home that had once been the Ware poor house.* Her voluntary work for the Ware Old People's Welfare Association was a practical expression of her faith. There are frequent references in her diaries to visiting the needy: one of those whose names occur most frequently, a Mrs Peck, Auntie May seems to visit almost daily. I can't imagine Auntie May saying anything about presenting the love of Christ to the old and poor people of Ware. But that's what she did.

---

* She was often called upon to play the organ, but it seems she didn't play particularly well. (*SUN 4.8.68 . . . 'played hymns 165, 180 & 370 – but still not fast enough, so I had to miss about half the left hand.'*)

CHAPTER ELEVEN

Embracing the Inevitable

In which Auntie May prepares to move to Norfolk

When Wells Urban District Council approved Auntie May's application for planning permission, Auntie May suddenly became famous. In Hertfordshire, the *Mercury* ran the story on the front page; in Norfolk, the *Eastern Daily Press* and the *Dereham & Fakenham Times* published a photograph of her holding her pet cat, Dinkie, in front of her home at Monkey Row. Nationally, there were pieces and pictures in the *Daily Express*, the *Daily Mirror*, the *London Evening News*, the *Times* and the *Daily Telegraph*. On 8 December 1967, the *Daily Mirror* reported the facts in its own, excited style:

> **Miss May will move home . . . a bit at a time**
> FIFTY-SIX-YEAR-OLD spinster May Savidge is moving house – every 500-year-old oak beam and inglenook of it.
>
> She says she is going to knock down her pre-Tudor home and move it to a new site 100 miles away – ALL BY HERSELF.
>
> Then she is going to rebuild it – again all by herself.

Road

For otherwise her local council was to have demolished it to make way for a new relief road.

'It would be heart-breaking to see such a fine old building pulled down,' frail, grey-haired Miss Savidge said yesterday at the house in Ware, Herts.

'I don't see why it's such an impossible idea. I've got nothing to do all day, so I might as well do the job myself.'

Miss Savidge, who is a retired draughtswoman, plans to rebuild the house at Wells in Norfolk.

But there is one snag. The house is semi-detached, so she will have to buy the rest of the building, which has been vacant for three years.

The press reports all described the move as a certainty, but even at this late stage, Auntie May still hoped she would be allowed to stay. Not until the summer of 1968 – six months after her story had hit the press, and fifteen years after she had first heard of the council's plans to demolish her house – did she finally accept the inevitable. On Saturday, 8 June, when the estate agents phoned her to tell her another buyer was interested in the Plummers Hill plot, she made a formal offer of the asking price. The following Monday, she visited the office of her solicitors, Chalmers-Hunt & Bailey of Ware, and instructed them to represent her in the purchase. 'People had said don't buy it until all the drawings had passed,' she wrote, 'but I didn't want to lose it, so I said I would definitely have it, and trust to being able to agree the drawings with the authorities. Don't want to start a hunt for a site all over again.' On Thursday, 27 June 1968, she signed the contract. The die was cast.

Suddenly, the authorities began falling over themselves to help.

I guess that, until then, they must have wondered whether Auntie May would follow through with her plan when it came to it. In mid-September, a Mr Senior from the County Land Agent's department came to tell her that the Hertfordshire County Council would pay her the value of her part of the house as well as allowing her to keep it, provided she dismantled the whole building, took it away, and left the site clear. A month later, he called again, this time to offer some practical advice of his own. He told her that demolition work had started at the nearby pub, the Hope, and suggested she ask the workmen for a batch of tiles that she'd need for her own rebuild. She thanked him, bought £3 worth, and gave the men who delivered them an extra 5s as a tip.

You'd think that once Auntie May's project was under way at last, her diary entries for the summer of 1968 would have been dominated by it – but they are not. She is preoccupied with the problem of Mrs Peck. She isn't going to be around to look after her for much longer, and Mrs Peck is growing increasingly frail and needy. Being housebound, she couldn't collect her pension, so she has given her pension book to her daughter-in-law so that she can collect the money, use it to buy her weekly shopping, and give her the balance. She is also supposed to collect and deliver the heart tablets that Mrs Peck has to take daily. But she often can't manage it. So it falls to Auntie May to buy Mrs Peck's groceries and collect her weekly copy of the *Radio Times*, as well as to make sure she has the right change for the gas meter, to sort out her hearing aid, to get new batteries for her radio and to wind up her clocks – in addition to tending to her increasing nursing needs.

Another thing Mrs Peck couldn't do for herself was tend her children's grave. On Sunday, 21 July 1968, she asked Auntie May to put some flowers on it. She told May that one of the children had died in infancy, and the other, when he was older. Auntie May didn't think it right to ask for any more details, but when she visited the cemetery, she bumped into Mr Powell, the undertaker, who told her that the older Peck child – 'a dear little curly-haired chap, plump' – had drowned in the river. 'He said Mrs P. has never been the same since.'

But Auntie May couldn't spend all her time looking after Mrs Peck. She had a house to move. On Monday, 18 November she went up to Norfolk to take possession of the Plummers Hill plot. She stayed in a guesthouse for a fortnight, during which time she met her new neighbours, Mr and Mrs Hunn, and bought a second-hand caravan from a Mr Smith, 'a bait digger', which she arranged to have towed to the site. She returned on Saturday, 30 November, bringing two presents: a Norfolk tea towel and a stick of Wells rock. Both were for Mrs Peck.

Tony and I, meanwhile, had been rebuilding our own historic home – though we hadn't had to move it from where it had first been built, in Litlington, Cambridgeshire. The experience was later to prove invaluable, though we didn't know that at the time. We had been able to buy the place for a song because it had been due for demolition. It was not much more than a shell of a house, really, and Tony and I were spending all our spare time and energy on restoring and extending it. We were putting down roots. We loved that little cottage. It was called The Nook, and that's just what it was – a little corner of England into which we could retreat; a place of safety, our place. Every barrow-load of concrete, every bucket of plaster, every floorboard and door that we put into it, made it home. I was looking forward to bringing up children in it, launching them into the world from it and eventually, enjoying our retirement in it.

Busy as we were, we kept in touch with Auntie May. We visited her a couple of times a year and exchanged letters, birthday and

Christmas cards, and gifts. When our first child, Polly, was born in January 1969, Auntie May made her a beautifully embroidered pram cover and sent it with a hand-drawn copy of the family tree, tracing Polly's ancestry back to Johannes Kikkert.

Auntie May's diaries describe a quiet Christmas, followed by a period in which she spent a lot of time sorting out Mrs Peck's ear drops and heart pills. Then, in February, she made another trip to Wells to meet builders and planners, and to prepare the site. This time, she stayed in the caravan. It wasn't a very comfortable fortnight. When she arrived on 6 February, the weather was bitterly cold and the caravan door wouldn't close properly. She had to tie it shut with string. When she went to light the stove, she noticed that there was no glass in its door, so there was no way of controlling the draught. The fire burned far too fast, then went out. When it got dark, she turned on the gas to light the lamp, but found that the pipe leaked, so she had to turn it off again and manage with a candle. She lay down under the three blankets she had brought, but couldn't get warm. When she woke up the next morning, she found that the fumes had given her a blinding headache and the thermometer in the caravan was showing 32°F – freezing point. The next night was even worse. 'Awful night,' she wrote. 'Heavy snow, strong N. wind . . . caravan rocked a bit, & leans to the S., anyway. Fire would not light – too late to try any more – no gas – had a candle and the Beatrice stove in the evening.' When she woke up in the morning, the thermometer had dropped to 22°F.

But there were positive things to record, too. Her new neighbours, the Hunns, were friendly and helpful. They allowed her free access to their water, made her cups of tea, gave her a pint of milk and kindling for her stove, and when Mr Hunn went sea fishing, he brought back a fine cod as a present. She gave the head to the cat. Her meetings with Mr Terrington, who was to build the foundations, were all encouraging. She sorted out access to the sewers with Mr Rogers from the planning department. The Norfolk end of the project was starting to come together.

After a week back in Ware, she returned to Wells for a few days to get some important jobs done. She got the caravan levelled and stabilised, and mended the door. She made a start on putting up the garden fence. She drew a nameplate on a postcard and fixed it to the gate in the wall: 'Ware Hall-House Site'. She also met several other near neighbours, who invited her in for cups of tea. Mrs Hunn took her as a guest to a Women's Institute meeting, at which the speaker presented a slide show about Norfolk. Auntie May was beginning to feel at home.

What she hadn't yet done, though, was decide how she was going to get the house from Ware to Wells. One option she was considering was moving the frame by road – in one piece. The idea came in a letter from an admiring stranger in California:

> *King City, California, U.S.A.*
> *January 8, 1968*

Dear Miss Savidge:

In a Stockton, California, newspaper there appeared last month a short but interesting article about you and your 500-year-old home which the local council has marked down for demolishing to make way for a new road.

The article went on to say that in order to keep your home you are planning to knock it down piece by piece and rebuild it on a new plot of land 100 miles away as a 'do it yourself' exercise.

This interested me so much that I felt I wanted to take the liberty of writing to you to tell you how I admire your courage and 'spunk', as well as the ambition to undertake such an enormous job. I would be so interested in learning of your progress and final success. I have the highest praise for anyone wishing to preserve old buildings. Here in the western part of the United States, buildings only 50 years old are constantly being demolished to be replaced by more modern structures. However, many small homes, if they are of frame construction, that is wooden, are sold and moved to another location to make room for new freeways. I'm enclosing an amusing clipping of such a moving project recently nearby.

I am a widow of 68 and live in the frame house my father built over 80 years ago. He moved it at one time from one end of this 160 acre farm to the other end, but sawed it in two and moved each half separately on large rollers. I was born in this house, as no doubt you were in yours, and I understand only too well how you must love your home.

I wish you the best of luck in your re-building project. If ever you have time to spare to write to me how you are progressing with it, I would be most happy to hear from you.

Sincerely,

Mrs. Fred Koester.

The 'amusing clipping'* Mrs Koester enclosed described a journey on wheels made by a three-bedroom, 26ft-wide house up a narrow canyon: 'The first mile was uneventful except for swerving tracks cut by the heavy equipment. Beyond that point the road still looked this morning as if it had been visited by a capricious tornado.'

But Auntie May took the idea seriously, as I discovered when I was going through her correspondence files for the following year:

---

* The article is not dated and the newspaper is not named.

125

PICKFORDS LIMITED
HEAD OFFICE
HEAVY HAULAGE SERVICE
52 BEDFORD ROW
LONDON, W.C. 1

01-405-4399

Miss M. Savidge,
1, Monkey Row, Ware,
Herts.
28th March 1969

Dear Miss Savidge,

Thank you for your letter of the 26th March, from which I note that you hope to be able to move your cottage from Ware to a site in Norfolk.

Whilst it is true that we move a number of unusual loads I must say that we have no experience in the movement of cottages.

I cannot tell from your letter whether your hope is that the cottage should be moved fully erected or whether you wish it to be dismantled and erected on the site. If you are looking for a firm to carry out the dismantling and re-erection then I am afraid we cannot assist you.

However, if a fully erected move is envisaged then I would be happy to discuss the problems with you at my office at 11.0 a.m. on Wednesday the 26th March. In order that the matter can be discussed it will be necessary for you to provide the dimensions, i.e. length, breadth and height.

I must say that I feel that it is highly improbable that a fully erected move will be possible due to the age of the cottage and the restrictions on the route in the form of overhead bridges and narrow roads.

However, I will be available on 26th March if you wish to see me
at the address shown at the head of this letter.

Yours sincerely

E.G. Milne

Asst. Chief Heavy Haulage Manager.

Auntie May did meet the man from Pickfords, and it was immediately clear that moving the house in one piece by road was a non-starter. But then she had another idea:

1, Monkey Row,
Ware,
Herts.

5th May, 1969

The Officer in Charge,
Coltishall Helicopter Airfield
Near Norwich
Norfolk.

Dear Sir,

For several years Herts. County Council has been planning to build a new road in Ware, and it will come right through my little house. This is a very interesting timber-framed building, about 500 years old, having a central hall with rooms above it, and originally, a fire in the middle of the floor, the smoke finding its own way out. Later, a Tudor chimney stack was inserted, also two more bedrooms, and the building divided into two little residences. The building is on the list of Ancient Monuments and Historic Buildings, but this does not seem to count when a road is proposed, so I wrote to Herts. County Council in 1963, stating that I wished to re-erect the house if it was in the way of the road.

Since then, I have bought a piece of land in Wells-next-the-Sea, and obtained permission from the U.D.C. and Norfolk County Council to use it for this purpose. So many old houses have been destroyed already, and I feel that we have no right to keep destroying the things of the past.

It was my intention to take the timber frames to pieces and put them together again on the site. The joints are fixed with tapered wooden pegs, which can be very difficult to get out. Six months ago, I was informed that I had until April, 1970, at the earliest, to do the job, but now suddenly I hear that the round-about may be built first, and that I may have to clear the site by the end of August, 1969, – an extremely difficult job.

Therefore I am wondering if it would be possible to lift the framework by helicopter, to save the time in taking it to pieces. It is oak, and I worked out the weight to about eight tons. Am told that British helicopters will only carry about four to five tons, and if this is so, I wonder if you would be so kind as to let me know whether there is a U.S.A. helicopter that could tackle it please? – and if so, who I should write to. The roof timbers weigh about three tons, and could be separated from the rest of the structure if necessary, which would then be reduced to about five tons, but it would be much quicker to have the framework moved complete, and lowered on to the new foundations.

I would, of course, wish to pay towards the expenses, but hope they would not be too heavy, as I am not a wealthy person.

Anything which you can suggest towards getting this framework moved from Ware to Wells-next-the-Sea, will be greatly appreciated. Most Hall-houses are very much larger, and were either Manor houses or farm houses, where the employees lived in; this is one of the smallest to have been found, and I do want to save it for future generations.

Hoping very much that you can help in some way,

Yours truly,

May Savidge

Encl. S.A.E. 5ᵈ

•

202 Squadron Detachment Royal Air Force

Coltishall

Norwich

Norfolk

NOR 64Y

Coltishall 361 Ext 491

13th May 1969

COLT/202D/6/2/Air

Miss M. Savidge

1, Monkey Row

Ware

Herts

Dear Miss Savidge

Thank you for your letter of 5th May 1969 relating to the prospect of providing an air lift for the framework of your house at Ware.

As the officer responsible for the Rescue Helicopter Unit at Coltishall, the Station Commander has instructed me to investigate the problem and write to you direct.

We, of course, act under the orders of the Ministry of Defence, and I regret that it is highly unlikely that the use of service helicopters would be authorised for this purpose. There is however, a further

129

consideration. The heaviest vertical lifting capacity within the Royal Air Force was achieved with the Belvedere Helicopter. These machines, based in the Far East could lift a maximum of six thousand pounds (under three tons). Unfortunately, the Belvedere has recently been withdrawn from service. Other machines currently in use in this country have a capacity of under two tons and at this weight their cross-country range is severely limited.

With these unhelpful facts in mind I made contact with the Senior Pilot of Bristow's Helicopters Ltd at Gt Yarmouth to see what non-military lifting capacity is available in this country. It seems that apart from the big amphibious S61 Helicopter (which has no underslinging facility), there would appear to be no machine in current use that could take on such a large task.

Concerning the very last resort in your suggestion of the USAF based in this country, I have no specific information, but I am almost certain their machines are the smaller types, such as our own, established for Search and Rescue purposes.

I trust these details answer your questions on the matter and though unable to offer any physical assistance, I wish you well with this most interesting project.

Sincerely,

(R. J. LAWRENCE)
Flight Lieutenant
Officer Commanding

•

May decided to check with the Americans anyway and wrote on 25 May to the US Embassy in Grosvenor Square, enclosing a 5d stamp to cover the cost of their reply, and asking if they might be able to help.

EMBASSY OF THE UNITED STATES OF AMERICA
OFFICE OF THE AIR ATTACHE
24 Grosvenor Square London, W.1

Miss Mary [sic] Savidge
1, Monkey Row
Ware, Herts.

Reference is made to your letter of 25 May 1969 requesting assistance for the re-erection of Ware Hall-House at Wells-next-the-Sea, Norfolk.

While the United States Military Services have often helped people in their host country as a good-neighbor policy, we are, unfortunately, unable to help you with your request. Neither the United States Air Force nor the United States Army has helicopters available in Britain which could perform the task you desire.

You may wish, however, to contact a local contractor who would know where helicopters of the size and lifting power required to move your house are available.

Sincerely,
JAMES V. REGAN
Major, USAF Assistant Air Attache

So, that was that. The idea of flying the house to Wells was a nonstarter.

Meanwhile, Auntie May's diaries show that she was still worrying about who would look after Mrs Peck. She brought the subject up at a meeting of the executive committee of the Ware Old People's Welfare Association on 10 April. The committee undertook to make sure that care for Mrs Peck would continue.

Mrs Peck was worrying, too. On 13 April, Auntie May got a lift up to Norfolk, where she spent another fortnight.

*13.4.69: Called on <u>Mrs. Peck</u> (didn't have time, before.) She cried –
I wish someone else would visit her in my place before I really have to
go. Gave her Radio Times and swapped 6/- for gas.* She came to the
door suddenly and put her arms round me and kissed me – poor old
soul – I'm not going for long.*

Auntie May spent the following two weeks preparing the site for
the arrival of lorries, and planning the foundations and drains with
Mr Terrington.

*MON 14.4.69: . . . <u>Mrs. Terrington</u> is quite sure I will never re-erect
the house – her grandfather was a builder and she has spent her life
connected with it all. It was difficult to finish a sentence to Mr.
Terrington or to both – he was looking at the drawing – she said I
wouldn't get any help as everyone was busy (builders, that is) – I only
wanted an estimate for the foundations and drains – Mr. T. said they
would take about a month from date of starting – Mrs. T. asked if I
had ever re-erected a house before – also what figures I had – I said
no-one had quoted any figures – . . . she thought would take 10 months
– with men, I think – don't know how many.*

When Auntie May got back to Ware, she found a letter from the
county council requiring her to clear the Monkey Row site by the
end of August. Things were hotting up. Meanwhile, Mrs Peck was
getting increasingly ill and confused:

*MON 2.6.69: Out again just before 6.45 to Mrs. Peck – she was
awake, still looking very groggy – pain in L. side when she breathes,
pain in region of waist line (front) – pain in middle of chest. Still*

---

* That is, she gave Mrs Peck the right coins for her gas meter.

vomiting – including a lot of phlegm! She had a bit of jelly, which seemed to have stayed down, but doesn't want food. She is still climbing up to close heavy curtain, in case she gets into trouble for showing a light – she still doesn't realise that that's only a wartime offence. She knows that the street lights are on. Said I'd let the Dr. know – she kept saying 'I don't want to go away'.

Auntie May visited her daily. She fetched her small bottles of stout, essence of peppermint and home-made jellies. She sorted out her lamps and clocks, filled her hot-water bottle, made up her bed, emptied her chamber pot, made sure she took her pills, and rubbed her back with camphorated oil to ease the pain. Another Old People's Welfare worker, Mrs Brogden, was also visiting and bringing food, but Mrs Peck ate and drank little. Auntie May got the Salvation Army to call, too, and Mrs Peck's daughter-in-law made more frequent appearances. The doctor called several times:

MON 16.6.69: Dr. confirmed nothing organically wrong – he said he had thought there was, but the C. Hospital had said not. He thinks it must be wind & worry.

The following Friday evening, when Auntie May called on Mrs Peck, she found the door fastened, which was not usual, and she could see through the window that the bed was empty and the covers had been thrown back. She knelt on the window ledge so that she could see if Mrs Peck had fallen onto the floor, but she hadn't. She called on Mrs Cakebread next door, who told her that Mrs Peck's daughter-in-law had visited that morning and had been so alarmed by the state of her that she had called the doctor, who had suspected an internal haemorrhage and sent for an ambulance. Mrs Peck had been taken to Bishop's Stortford Hospital. The following morning, Mrs Brogden called at Monkey Row to ask Auntie May if she wanted to accompany her to the hospital. 'I would have been glad,' writes Auntie May, 'but really must get on with moving job – 3 weeks delay, now, over Mrs P.'s illness'.

Just how much had to be done is reflected in the length of entries in Auntie May's diaries. At this point, they get longer and longer. There are lots of St John Ambulance loose ends to tie up, and the letters from Pickfords, the RAF and the American Embassy have convinced her that the only way to move the house is to take it apart first. She spends a great deal of time trying to hunt down a builder with suitable lorries for the job, and makes arrangements to spend some more time in Norfolk to make sure that the foundations and drainage arrangements are precisely right before the dismantled house arrives. She keeps daily tabs on Mrs Peck by telephoning the hospital and Mrs Brogden. She learns that she is going to be in hospital for at least six weeks.

In Norfolk, Auntie May was shocked to find how overgrown the garden had become since she had last seen it. (I know just how she must have felt!) The grass was seeding, and there were brambles and nettles everywhere. She had to clear it all so that the precise position of the foundation slab could be pegged out. On most days, she was up before 4.30am so that she could work before it got too hot. She returned on 2 July. The following morning, she learned that Mrs Peck had died the previous day.

On Saturday, 5 July Auntie May went to see the undertaker, Mr Powell, to ask about the funeral. 'He spoke about her life – she was about eighteen when they took her little son home in his coffin, & he's never forgotten her distress, in all these years of funerals.' The service was held the following Tuesday at the Salvation Army hall in Ware. Auntie May brought a 'spray of yellow and red flowers (roses, carnations, chrysanthemums and laurels)'. A week later, she met the health visitor, who told her the cause of Mrs Peck's death. She had been suffering from cancer of the stomach.

Having discharged her final duty to Mrs Peck, Auntie May threw herself into the urgent task of stripping out both halves of the house. She got hold of an old oil drum, chained it to a post in the garden, and started a bonfire in it that was to burn more or less constantly for the next eleven months. She knocked through into number 36 and found it in a very poor state, though she was impressed by the size of the ancient beams that had never been covered up. It was hard and dangerous work:

TUE: 15.7.69: . . . Into 36 again . . . Fixed rope around counter, and myself, and went down into cellar – brought some more rotten wood up and put some on incinerator – not much – burning very slowly . . .

In the autumn of that year, Auntie May was back in the papers again. She had cut a deal with the local authority in which she was to be given the other half of the house in return for demolishing the whole building and taking it away. The *Daily Telegraph* of Saturday, 20 September reported that: 'Every brick, beam and timber of the house will be numbered by Miss Savidge, who will reconstruct it like a giant jigsaw puzzle. "It will take a long time to complete and I will live in a caravan while I am working on the site. I just won't have such a marvellous old house bulldozed into the ground," she said.'

Tony and I offered to help, but Auntie May wasn't having any of it. She was determined to do as much work as possible herself. She prepared for the move meticulously. First, she made a set of detailed drawings of the house. This was a particularly challenging task, as the shape of it had been dictated by the irregular hand-hewn timbers used to make its framework. There were no right angles in the building and the parallel walls were not quite of equal

135

length. She joked that she had been well prepared for this by her wartime work in the drawing office of De Havilland, for there were no right angles in a Mosquito, either! Then she painted a number on each individual timber – so that it could be identified when the time came to reassemble the framework – and marked the numbers on her plans. Press reports that she numbered the bricks, too, were an exaggeration. Auntie May knew that the brick infilling had been done long after the house had originally been built, and the order in which they were put back didn't matter. However, on one visit, I did find her using greaseproof paper and a crayon to make a rubbing of the brickwork in one of the fireplaces. I wondered whether she was losing her marbles, but she had a perfectly logical explanation. 'I have never laid a brick in my life,' she said. 'I am not quite sure which bond this is. It might be Flemish, or perhaps Old English. I have got to reproduce it and I want to get it right. Besides, I need to know how thick to lay the mortar, because if it is too thin, I am going to have to buy more Elizabethan bricks, and I can't afford that on my pension.'

The demolition was just as painstakingly methodical. First, she had the house surrounded by scaffolding, and then she supervised a team of local demolition contractors as they took the place carefully apart, tile by tile, beam by beam, and brick by brick. To prevent anyone stealing anything from the site, she continued to live in the house while they worked, only moving into the workshop at the bottom of the garden when the outside walls were finally taken down. Then she oversaw the loading of the parts of the house on to a Bedford lorry, which made the 200-mile round trip to Norfolk eleven times.

But it was obvious that she would never be able to get the site cleared by the original deadline and, on 25 August, the authorities sent her a letter extending it to 31 December. Auntie May received it with relief, but she could see that even that leeway was scarcely enough. Still – at least she now had a firm idea of how she would move the building. A piece of paper I found in her filing cabinet describes the plan in detail:

CONTRACT

I, William Robert Smith, of 1, Cundalls Road, Proprietor of Ware Demolition Co., undertake, for the sum of Three hundred pounds (£300), to demolish carefully the oak-framed house known as 36, Baldock Street and 1, Monkey Row, measuring 47'6" by about 18'6", but excluding the more modern extension used as a kitchen and W.C., and also excluding the workshop known as 9, Monkey Row. The materials and fittings are for re-use by the owner, May Alice Savidge, for the re-erection of the whole house in Norfolk. The bricks will be cleaned and the half-bricks saved, also the half tiles. If the re-use of the mortar, hair plaster, and mud and chaff is advised,* these will be kept separate from each other and bagged up. The owner will number the timbers as they are uncovered, and draw them on the plan and elevations. Unwanted rubble, etc., will be put in the cellar, to help fill it in, as Herts. County Council requires the site to be left tidy, and to be cleared by 31st December, 1969, at the latest. Public Liability Insurance has been taken out by the owner, but not Insurance for any personal injury, and no claim will be made on her should an accident occur.

W.R. Smith, WARE DEM. Co.

M. Savidge

Witnessed by

L.W. Gilling

---

* It wasn't. Auntie May wrote to the Society for the Protection of Ancient Buildings, and they advised against it.

What that contract doesn't mention is that Auntie May would continue to live in the house while they took it down. The conditions she put up with were unimaginable, as Tony and I saw when we visited later that year – the last time we saw her in Hertfordshire. Outside, the temperature was freezing, and inside it wasn't any higher, for the demolition men had taken off the roof. She was living in the downstairs sitting room, and there was nothing between her and the sky but the plaster of its ceiling and the floorboards of the room above. There was so little of the building left standing that Auntie May had to sleep in a little office room in the workshop that she called her 'shed'. She was wearing several coats, one over the other, and a woollen hat was tied to her head with a scarf. There was no electricity supply on the site. At night, the only light came from a hurricane lamp and she boiled the water for a pot of tea on a Victorian paraffin stove that she lit with mittened hands. She apologised for having already packed the best china, and poured my tea into a cup that was so badly cracked I had to pour what leaked into the saucer back into the cup as fast as I could drink it. We were horrified at the squalor of it all, but Auntie May just didn't seem to notice.

Tony told her that snow had been forecast and that when it melted, it would bring down her ceiling. She dismissed this as nonsense and said that in any case, it didn't matter – the worst that could happen would be that the plaster would fall down and she was going to have to knock it down soon, anyway. We said our goodbyes, but when we got to the car, we decided that we just couldn't leave her exposed to the elements like that. We went to the nearest builders' merchant and bought a huge sheet of polythene. Then we drove back to what was left of the house, climbed up the scaffolding, and covered the first-floor floorboards with the polythene, weighing it down with bricks. Auntie May politely thanked us for our efforts, but assured us that they really hadn't been necessary. But the next day, it did snow – and heavily. Heaven only knows what would have happened if we hadn't put down that plastic sheet.

In early December, Auntie May received a surprise in the post. It was a letter from the BBC offering her a 'Charlie Chester Award', which would be presented on the radio programme to be aired on New Year's Day. It was a significant accolade: Charlie Chester's weekly *Sunday Soapbox* show on the *Light Programme* drew an audience of millions. May wrote back immediately to accept. She had no interest in personal fame or recognition; she saw it as a chance to draw attention to the wider threat to historic buildings throughout the land.

But there was a problem. She was nervous about leaving the site. To the outside world, it no longer looked like any kind of home – and local youngsters had started to use the surrounding area as a kind of adventure playground. Her diaries recorded numerous close encounters with unsavoury youths. One of her friends, Miss Virgo – 'I don't know how I would manage without her' – came to the rescue. She offered to house-sit while Auntie May took part in the programme.

Before that, though, there was Christmas – the last that Auntie May would spend in what was left of her Hertfordshire home. She celebrated it alone. She could hardly invite anyone to a meal on a demolition site and she couldn't accept an invitation to go elsewhere, because she felt she had to stay and guard the dismantled elements of her house. Her Christmas dinner was not quite the traditional feast:

THURS: CHRISTMAS DAY – 1969.
Midnight Service on Radio 4 – till 1.15 a.m.

139

Dull, damp – drips stopped during day . . .

Opened some things from larder (now gone) –
1966 Luncheon meat (tin)
1959 tomatoes (small tin)
19—? Stewed apples (Kilner jar)
19—? Robertson's mincemeat (1lb jar)
Simmered the last 2 together, with sugar – something like Christmas
pudding! – eaten with bread and marg. – could have mixed the bread
in, too.

On New Year's Eve she 'took coffee etc. to shed office to hear
Charlie Chester show'. It must have been a strange way to end the
year. I doubt that she recognised the irony of it. All over the nation,
people were sitting comfortably before their fires, their families
around them, listening to a programme that celebrated her spirit
and determination; she was listening to the same programme alone,
in a freezing shed on what looked like a bomb site, wondering
whether her determination would achieve anything at all. The
project was taking far longer than she had estimated. The church
bells that marked the ending of the year also marked the passing of
the authorities' latest deadline for clearing the site, even if they had
made no threats to enforce it.

CHAPTER TWELVE

'This Is Our Home Now!'

In which Auntie May, Candy and Dinkie
move to Wells

A week later, May made a diary entry in capital letters, and underlined it twice:

WEDS: 7.1.70 – LETTER FROM MR TERRINGTON – SITE READY!

On 12 January '2 young men from County Hall came . . . they said they hadn't come to harry me, just to see how I was getting on. I was glad – the date has been worrying me'. In fact, Auntie May was getting on quite well. Mr Smith and his team were now taking apart the main beams of the house, and she was marking those beams with numbers and recording their position on the plan she had drawn of the house. She was also listing the order in which the timbers were taken down in her diary. I can't say it makes interesting reading, but I do find it remarkable that she should have decided to record every act in the process in such extraordinary detail:

FRI: 16.1.70 . . . Scraped muck from top of S.21 (to dry off, for

marking) & from front of B1.J.26 – (very wet). Cleared up the mess.
Quick lunch in shed, then painted numbers on S.21 & E.1 . . .

Despite the rain and the snow, things were going well, and Auntie
May was able to arrange for the first lorry load of building parts to
be moved to Wells at the end of the month.

SAT: 31.1.70 . . . Monk & Hawkins lorry had arrived by 8.20 am. –
3 men and a boy. Loaded up first Tudor bricks and left at mid-day.
Mr S. stays helping demolishing.

The move had begun, and Auntie May was clearly looking forward
to getting to Wells; but she was also looking forward to getting
away from the demolition site:

SUN: 1.2.70 – gang of long haired youths with sacks hanging around
– I shall be glad to get away from here – it was bad enough when it
was a car park, but it is worse now. There should be some privacy from
public & some peace in the Norfolk garden. Candy has barked herself
hoarse again . . .

On Monday, 2 February, Miss Virgo came to stand guard while
Auntie May went off to Wells on one of the lorry trips. Her diary
shows a rare glimpse of excitement. She had a 'lovely windscreen
view' of the sunrise and noticed 'just a sweep of clouds across the
sky' – but she didn't think much of the musical taste of the lorry's
driver: 'deafening Radio One, etc. – don't know how anyone could
drive with such a noise'.

When the lorry reached Norfolk, Auntie May went to see Mr
Terrington and paid him for his work on the foundations. She then
returned to Ware to supervise the loading of the rest of the

building. The lorry made two trips on Wednesday, and on Thursday a reporter and photographer from the *Daily Sketch* turned up. Much of the main structure of the house was now down, but the shell of the kitchen extension of the Monkey Row half was still there and Auntie May was still occupying it. The workshop that housed her stored furniture was still standing, too, and Auntie May was still sleeping in it.

That February, heavy snow was followed by freezing fog and hard frosts. In March, what Auntie May describes as 'the worst snow in the SE in living memory' started to fall:

SUN: 8.3.70 . . . Shed office 30 deg F – Very sharp frost – had left tap dripping into kettle in sink and there was a large icicle between tap and kettle with lots of additions at the lower end: ice outside spout, kettle frozen to sink: sink outlet frozen, but tap still dripping! Sun out about 8 am. Breakfast – kitchen – milk frozen.

Outside, the smoke from her incinerator mingled with the smoke from the bonfire that was once the Hope pub, and drifted across a frozen snowscape. But the big move wouldn't be long now. She would soon be in Wells, and starting the next phase of the project – and she was looking forward to it. When she phoned HC Lewis of Fakenham to arrange storage of all her boxes, she wrote 'Norfolk accents sounded quite homely'. On Monday, 16 March, she accompanied the van that took her furniture to Norfolk for storage. Candy and Dinkie came too, so Miss Virgo didn't have to stay. The following day, May's sister Nellie and her husband Bern came to visit, bringing some cakes and a trifle. Their visit coincided with the removal of the last beam of the framework – number S.21 – and they all had a piece of cake to celebrate.

There was still a lot of clearing and sorting to do, of course, and this was made more difficult by several days of rain. The kitchen and WC extension were still standing and, though the wall between the kitchen and the rest of the building was gone, Auntie May got Mr Smith to nail one of the doors over the gap. She also got him to put some old planks down on the floor as duckboards, for the whole site was now covered in slimy mud. The place must have looked like a First World War battlefield but, among all the wreckage, Auntie May managed to turn a corner of her half-demolished kitchen into a darkroom for developing the photographs she was taking of the work. On Tuesday, 20 January another newspaper reporter visited, and a woman whom Auntie May did not know called at the site to say that she had heard the story on the radio and would like to offer her a bed. Auntie May refused – 'I said I had to keep an eye on things here.'

Tony and I had seen Auntie May's living conditions at this time, and had done what little we could to improve them, but when I read her record of them many years later, I felt painfully guilty. If a complete stranger could offer to take her in and look after her, surely we, her family, could have done more? Why hadn't we offered to stand guard over the site for a day or two, so that she could take a break, and be warm and comfortable even if only for a short time? I suppose the answer is that we knew that she would refuse any help – though I still feel bad about it. But I also feel curious. By any imaginable standards, Auntie May's circumstances were intolerable. Why did she put up with them without complaint? Why didn't she make things at least a little easier for herself?

I think the simple answer is that she just didn't notice. She seems to have been utterly single-minded. Having decided on the great task she was to perform, she concentrated on it, seeing any inconveniences encountered along the way as incidental. She didn't

THIS IS OUR HOME NOW!'

dwell upon them any more than she ever dwelt upon herself. Others might see her as a stoic, but she didn't seem to think of herself as enduring anything; she was just getting on with what she had to do, dealing with things as they turned up. It was an attitude that left strangers amazed, and those of us that cared for her wringing our hands in horror. Nellie found it particularly trying: as her elder sister, she felt it was her duty to save May from herself – but she never succeeded and her offers of help or guidance were always rebuffed.

On Monday, 16 March, Auntie May made another day trip to Wells – this time in the cab of the van from Ware Furnishing that she had hired to take her furniture to Fakenham. She took Candy and Dinkie with her, and was pleased to see that Dinkie seemed quite at home, prowling confidently about the garden and caravan. When Auntie May got back at the end of the day, she was too tired to move the things heaped up on her armchair in the shed 'office', so she slept sitting on a box, leaning against the wall.

The weather improved in April and Auntie May took advantage of it. She used her pushchair to move a lot of the boxes of her possessions to Place House, the home of a 'Mr. W.' who had invited her to store her things there so that Mr Smith could knock down the workshop in which she had been keeping them. The end of the project was in sight. One of the last loose ends to tie up was the beautiful, double-flowering cherry tree that had stood outside the front door. Auntie May wanted to dig it up and take it with her, but wasn't sure if it would be possible. On Wednesday, 29 April she went to the nearby telephone box and called the Hertfordshire Training School – '(Ware 3666)' – to ask for advice. They told her she needed to ask a tree specialist, but Auntie May's record of the phone call is interesting – not because of what was said, but because of something that happened while she was making it:

2 young policemen opened door of 'phone box & one said 'Are you all right?' – they'd had a call that I had a handkerchief over the 'phone – I said I always do use a Dettol hanky over the mouthpiece – have done for years – said I once got an awful cold, after using a 'phone that looked as if someone had been breathing heavily onto it. I keep one special hanky – one policeman smelt it, to check – they also took my name and address – they said they get a lot of queer calls around this way – I suppose someone thought I was muffling my voice, but a single layer of Dettol hanky doesn't do that. I said that at work the 'phones were cleaned & disinfected regularly – but public ones are very germy things.

Auntie May was happy to live in the roofless shell of a house in mid-winter and sleep in a caravan that was ten degrees below freezing, but she wouldn't pick up a public phone without wrapping it in a disinfectant-soaked hanky for fear of catching a cold. When I read that, I couldn't suppress a laugh!

During May, Auntie May made several more trips accompanying bricks, beams and tiles on the Monk & Hawkins lorry. She planned to make the big move on 1 June, but there was one more problem to be dealt with. The possessions she had stored in the shed/workshop and its outside toilet were all gone: it was time for those outbuildings to be pulled down, along with what little was left of the kitchen. Where would she sleep while that was happening? Miss Virgo couldn't offer to help – she was in hospital – but when Auntie May telephoned to ask after her on Thursday, 28 May, Miss Virgo's companion, Miss Page, invited Auntie May to spend her last two nights in Hertfordshire at 121 Watton Road, where they lived with their chickens and goats. Miss Virgo's sister, Dorothy, was also staying, so that she could be near to the hospital.

Saturday, 30 May was a fine day, but the move didn't get off to a very good start. Soon after the lorry and three men turned up at 7.30am, they all realised that there was too much stuff to go in the last trip planned for the following Monday. By noon, they could fit nothing more on, so they set off to Wells with what they had. There was talk of making another trip the next day, but nothing could be confirmed until they got back to the office.

> *About 4.30 pm. Miss Page & Miss D. Virgo called on way back from hospital, but I was still very busy clearing up and covering up, in case stuff has to stay until next Sat. – with no one to look after it.*
>
> *Miss Page came back for me after milking goats etc. – about 8.30 pm. – we put several things in her car – some coats, etc., clean clothes, bread bin of food, towels, barometer, zither in blue washing bag – etc. – & Candy and Dinkie and myself – and she took me home to 121 W. Rd. Lovely refreshing evening meal (vegetarian) – & grape juice & soda water – also lovely bath – first one since Sept. – slept on camp bed in front room, downstairs, with Candy & Dinkie – such a joy to be where folks treat animals as important. Tried to 'phone Monk & H about 10 pm, as they had not 'phoned – no answer.*

Auntie May phoned them again at 8.30am the following morning, but she needn't have worried, for by the time she got to the site, the men were already there and at work. They were ready to go at noon. Auntie May stayed behind for a final tidy up, turned off the water at the mains stopcock, and picked up the thrift plant that she had dug up and the men had left behind. She carried it back to 121 Watton Road in a washing-up bowl.

She was up at 5.30am the following morning, ready to make her very last trip to the Monkey Row site. Dorothy Virgo made her breakfast; Miss Page refused to accept anything in return for her stay. The two of them helped her carry her things to the lorry. The driver loaded up the last things to go, including a pair of cast-iron bed ends and a tea chest, and Auntie May, Candy and Dinkie joined him in the cab. They got to Wells at 10.30am. Auntie May telephoned Mr Smith, the bait digger, to let him know that she had arrived and was ready for his help – and he and his brother came immediately. By 3.30pm, the job was done. The Smiths left to deliver the bait they had dug earlier that morning. The driver had a wash at the tap, and returned to Hertfordshire. Auntie May gave him a pound note as a tip.

Auntie May did some more clearing up, in case it rained – but it didn't. Then she looked around the garden in which she was to rebuild her house. The apple blossom was over, but the clematis and the lily of the valley and the strawberry plants were in flower. When she picked up the boots she had left in the Blue Lady caravan, a florin dropped out of one of them. She wrote the extra 2s in the accounts column of her diary, bringing the running total to £15 3s 5d. Just above it, she had already written in blue biro: 'Candy & Dinkie & I stayed – this is our home now.' She picked up a red pen, underlined it again, and drew a box round it. The second phase of her project had finally begun. She had celebrated her fifty-ninth birthday at the beginning of the week. She was five days into the sixtieth year of her life.

CHAPTER THIRTEEN

Rebuilding Begins

In which Auntie May makes a slow start and
encounters some unexpected difficulties

Auntie May recorded the big move in diary number 190. Two
hundred and fifty diaries and twenty-three years later, she still
hadn't finished rebuilding the house. The diaries in which she
recorded every detail of the reconstruction are a catalogue of
patiently borne difficulties. Looking back on it now, it is easy to see
why it all took so long. Anybody who has ever built a house from
scratch will know how hard it is to coordinate the stages of the
operation. A large building firm that employs tradesmen directly
can order them to turn up at the appropriate time. A small builder
who sub-contracts work to others has some sort of hold on them –
they know that if they let him down, he won't offer them further
work. Auntie May was her own project manager on a one-off
project, and thus completely at the mercy of all the tradesmen and
labourers she had to employ. Some of them were loyal and reliable;
others were not. I started to count the number of times Auntie May
wrote 'Mr X did not turn up again' or 'Mr Y <u>still</u> hasn't come, as
promised', but I gave up. The diaries are peppered with phrases
like that.

Another thing that slowed everything down was Auntie May's

decision not to employ anyone to do anything she could do herself. She believed that her tough upbringing had prepared her for nearly all the practical challenges she now faced. She said as much in an address to the Fakenham Ladies Circle Club in the spring of 1971. She called her talk *Dismantling & Re-erection of Ware Hall-House*:

> Looking through my notes, and trying to collect my thoughts on this move, it really seems as if everything has led up to it. For instance, my mother more or less brought us up on the maxim that 'there is no such word as "can't"', and I think this had a marked effect on my life. Another favourite saying was 'worse troubles at sea' – and she had reason to know what she was talking about.
>
> My father was an engineer, and I was always attracted to engineering, and to practical things like 'what makes the wheels go round'. But although women had worked on munitions during the First World War, engineering was still not considered to be suitable for girls when I was young, and my father had died just before I was ten, so we had rather lost touch with the engineering world.
>
> I started work as assistant to a wallpaper designer, and later became designer to a small silk printing firm. During the slump, I was lucky to get a job in an office, and in the evenings I learnt shorthand and typing, which came in very useful, later.[*] Fairly early in the Hitler War, I had the chance to go back to drawing – either on maps for the Admiralty, or on an engineering draughtsmanship course, which was the one I chose. We did some practical work, as well as drawing, as one should know how to <u>make</u> anything that one <u>draws</u>.[†]

[*] In the margin at this point, Auntie May has written 'Indicate pile of letters'. She certainly had plenty to choose from!

[†] Alas, I have only been able to find the first two pages of her typed draft of this talk. The rest has gone adrift.

May's combination of determination, inexperience and perfectionism meant that everything she did was done slowly. On my first visit to Ware Hall-House after her death, I heard a story that showed just how slowly that could be.

I was told it by the coalman, who turned up to make his usual delivery, not knowing that Auntie May had died. We told him to leave the fuel anyway and, after he had tipped it into the bunker, he stopped and smiled.

'I must tell you this tale about Miss Savidge,' he said. 'Once, when I came a few years ago, I saw her bent over a huge oak beam – it must have been an eight by eight – and she was trying to cut through it with a bow saw. She was really struggling. I told her I knew someone with a chainsaw that would cut it like a knife through butter; I could ask him to pop round, if she'd like. She said she'd rather do it the old-fashioned way, thanks – the way they did it in the old days, when the house was first built. When I came a fortnight later, she was still cutting it. The fortnight after that, the beam was still on the bench, and when I came through the gate, she picked up her saw and made the final cut. I reckon she timed it so I would see it!'

Our first sight of Auntie May in Wells was almost as dispiriting as our last visit to her in Ware. The new setting she had chosen for her house was beautiful. Wells is a pretty little seaside town with a working quayside and Auntie May's building plot was tucked behind The Buttlands, an elegant village green framed by Georgian merchants' and sea captains' houses and a couple of historic pubs. But when we opened the gate in the wall, the contrast with the rest of Wells was dramatic. There was Auntie May, surrounded by heaps of beams, bricks, doors, windows, floorboards, peg tiles, piles of lead piping, bits of old furniture and other oddities that she hadn't been able to bring herself to throw away. Try as I might, I just couldn't imagine that Humpty Dumpty of a house ever being put back together again – and Auntie May didn't have all the king's horses or all the king's men to help her. I tried to look enthusiastic and optimistic but, inside, my heart sank. The task looked overwhelming. She had got a local builder to lay the foundations and drains before she had arrived; she had recruited a few local fishermen who had agreed to help her move the bigger beams when they needed moving. Apart from that, she was determined to do it all by herself. Tony spoke for both of us when he said we would be happy to give whatever help we could, but Auntie May politely made it clear that she didn't want it.

Still – at least she had somewhere weatherproof to live: the old caravan, with the words 'Blue Lady' painted on the side. She didn't invite us in, but Tony and I stole a glance through the windows. It was so crammed with boxes of her possessions that we wondered how she managed to move about. But we could also see a little cast iron stove, and a glass-domed oil lamp, and a sink, and a table with a typewriter on it and a bed that served as a sofa . . . and Tony spotted an old Elsan chemical toilet in the tumble-down flint outhouse at the far side of the site, so we knew that Auntie May had everything she needed to survive – apart from comfort. It seemed terrible to leave her alone in such circumstances, but that's how she wanted it and there was no arguing with her.

The rebuild was also slowed down by the size and position of the site. The plot was big enough for the house and a small garden, but there wasn't enough space to lay out and sort out all the building materials – most of which had to be on-site from the start. Auntie May had to spend a whole year organising and pulling the nails out of the beams of the frame, moving them from one pile to another, and then moving those piles so that she had space to lay out the next. This was further delayed by the need to have help lifting the heavier beams, and the people she called upon (and paid) to help weren't always able to come when she needed them. The sorting was made even more difficult by the rest of the salvaged materials that were stored there. Auntie May (and her occasional helpers) had to work round stacks of tiles, bricks, doors and windows, door frames and window frames, fireplaces, floorboards and glass. In a normal building project, these things are delivered as they are needed, not all at once. A further complication was that access to the site was narrow and limited. Hemmed in on three-and-three-quarter sides by other gardens, the only way in was by a 4ft-wide gate – and to get to it, you had to go down a narrow lane and then up a narrower alley. (You still do.) When the time came for new building materials to be delivered, they had to be dumped well beyond the boundary and carried up a steep slope.

As if all these obstacles weren't enough, May was also hampered by her conscientiousness as a correspondent. She never left a letter unanswered, and she received lots – many of them from complete strangers. Every time her story appeared in a newspaper, a magazine or on television, more would arrive. Most writers didn't know her postal address, so they made a stab at it, assuming that the post office would know who they meant and where she lived: 'Miss May Savidge, The Blue Lady Caravan, Wells, Norfolk'; 'Miss M. Savidge (who is rebuilding her house), Norfolk'; 'Miss M. Savidge, Mediaeval Hall-House, Wells-next-the-Sea, Norfolk'. They all got there – even one in an envelope that shows that it went to Norfolk Island first.

Strangers wrote to express admiration and gratitude – they congratulated her on her spirit, wished her good luck and thanked her for making a stand against 'progress'. Several sent money. Many offered help. Some asked for it. She got a fair few letters from people who clearly weren't quite right in the head. She answered them all, though sometimes her replies were several months late. As I came upon these letters when I was going through her papers, I found myself wondering what it was about Auntie May that made people feel able to reach out to her with such warmth and trust. As I read her replies to them, I could see that their instinctive affection for her was well placed.

May 14th 1970

Dear Miss Savidge

I must first beg of you to forgive the liberty taken in writing this letter to you, but your spirit has amazed me <u>with admiration, to have your home moved</u>.

I give thanks to my God for being able to offer good References re business and private character. For serious reasons over the loss of my mother (a London nurse) when I was very young – 6 years old – I never married. <u>My mother died</u> in the service of the sick, in London hospitals.

Well, to cut a long story short, I decided some years ago to buy a form of modern living caravan, but <u>I now have to move it</u> – after it has been in the area for 7 years.

I just wondered if you would have a bit of land (at the back of your new home) <u>to offer at a Rental</u>.

However, whatever you think at receiving this letter, would you very kindly forgive me for the liberty taken in directing it to you . . .

Yours sincerely

*B— D—**

---

* I have changed this name and that of other people who wrote to her when they were down on their luck.

Ware Hall-House
Water Pit Lane
Plummers Hill,
Wells-next-the-Sea
Norfolk.

25th August 1970.

Dear Mr. D——,

Thank you very much for your letter of 14th May; I would have answered sooner, but have been so terribly busy getting things under cover from the rain, and trying to find things, after the removal of all the bits and pieces of my little house from Ware, to make way for a roundabout and new road. We overran the date, so it was all a rush.

Was sorry to hear that you have to move your caravan, which you have made your home, after seven years. Unfortunately, there is not enough space on this site for a caravan, and the Council would not allow it anyway; they have given me permission to live in one in my garden while I am re-erecting the house, but the permission is on a one year basis, and is for myself and my dependants – my cat and dog.

There is a privately owned caravan site just near here, in Burnt Street, Wells-next-the-Sea, where some people seem to live all the year round, and others come for summer holidays. The other site, which is run by the Council, is just near the beach, and is for holidays only; all the caravans have to be brought away and stored for the winter. I do not know if it is possible to get a single site anywhere around here, but you could write to the Wells Urban District Council and enquire, if you are interested in this area as a place to live.

Hoping you will soon be successful, and thanking you for your good wishes,
  Yours sincerely
  May Savidge
  Formerly of Monkey Row, Ware, Herts.

I found one exchange of letters particularly moving. It shows the quite extraordinary lengths Auntie May was prepared to go to in order to help total strangers, even at the most critical time of her project:

                                          The Daily Telegraph and
                                                    Morning Post
                                                      Fleet Street
                                                 London E.C. 4

Mrs. Savidge,
Monkey Terrace,
Wells,
Next-to-Sea,
Norfolk.

                                              July 13th, 1970.
Dear Mrs. [sic] Savidge,
    I have received the enclosed rather pathetic letter, from a man who is at present a prisoner in Wandsworth Jail. I also enclose a copy of my reply to him, from which you will see that I have been most careful not to give him the slightest impression that you would look favourably on his application.
    I hope however that you may agree with me that it would have been extremely unkind on my part to neglect his letter entirely.
    Yours faithfully,
    T. F. Lindsay,
    Assistant Editor.

Peter Clark, Esq.,	*The Dailing Telegraph and*
H.M. Prison,	*Morning Post*
Heathfield Road,	*Fleet Street*
Wandsworth,	*London E.C.4*
London S.W.18.	*July 13th, 1970.*

Dear Mr. Clark,

Thank you for your letter received here on 9th July.

I have been glad to send this on to Mrs. Savidge on your behalf, but of course you will understand that I have no idea whether she would be able to use your help – or indeed whether she needs any help at all.

    Yours faithfully

    T.F. Lindsay,

    Assistant Editor.

The letter that the *Telegraph* forwarded was handwritten on prison issue paper:

        H.M. Prison,

        Heathfield Road,

        Wandsworth,

        London S.W.18.

        [undated]

Dear Sir, This is a letter From The above name, And No. mentioned. So my name is Peter Clark. You will wonder, why I am writing to you, well I'll explain my reasons for it. I was reading your Paper, the daily Telegraph dated Tuesday July 7th – 1970. And I seen a Photograph of a woman her name is Miss May Savidge And that she is going to start re-assembling her 500-year-old home in wells Norfolk. So Sir I write to you And ask you if you would be kind enough to send this letter on to Miss Savidge at her Address as I would like to give her a help to build up her house. As you can see by this letter that I am in prison, but I am due for discharge this month July 27th.

So Dear Miss Savidge I write this letter to you in the hopes that you will let me help and work for you in building your house. I can do all building jobs, So when I saw your photo in the paper, I thought I would better ask if you would kindly let me help, And work for you, that's if you want me. I am a good worker Miss Savidge, And I am sure that you will be pleased at me. I have also worked on farms, And done all other kind of work. I know I am in Prison for a little silly mistake I made, But now I have Payed for the mistake And I will soon be coming out, so I want to start life again, I am not to old I am only 49 years old, I know that it is very hard for me, when I come out of Prison As a great many firms will not give me a job or work for them, when they know where I have been, so I ask you miss Savidge, would you really like me to work and give you all the help with building your new home. I do hope you will say yes to me And miss Savidge if you think that you can spare a few little minutes of your time, will you Please write me a little letter, I don't know if you will be angry at me writing this letter to you, But I hope you wont be miss Savidge, But I think you are a kind woman, And understand. Also will you write to me here miss Savidge my name And number And address is at the top of the page. I see by the photo in the paper that there is plenty of work to do on building your house up again, But as I have stated Id be only too pleased And willing to help And work for you.

So will you Please be ever so kind and write letting me know miss Savidge.

Yours faithfully
Peter Clark

Ware Hall-House
Water Pit Lane
Plummers Hill
Wells-next-the-Sea
Norfolk

18th July, 1970

T.F. Lindsay, Esq.,
Asst. Editor,
The Daily Telegraph and Morning Post,
Fleet St., London, E.C.4.

Dear Mr. Lindsay,
Thank you for your letter of 13th July, ref. TL/R, enclosing one from Mr. Clark, and a copy of your reply. I have written to him, explaining that I cannot afford help, which is why I am doing practically all the work myself. Have also enclosed the "Situations Vacant" pages from our two local papers; as he has done farm work, and will be free in time for the harvest, he may be lucky. Am glad he is trying to find work, and would certainly not ignore his letter. If he cannot get a start somewhere, he may drift again.

Perhaps you would like to make a note of my address, in case you ever need it again.

Yours truly
May Savidge, (Miss not Mrs.)

Ware Hall-House
Water Pit Lane
Plummers Hill
Wells-next-the-Sea
Norfolk

18th July, 1970

Dear Mr Clark,

Thank you for your letter of 7th or 8th July, which reached me, via the Daily Telegraph, on Thursday, 16th. I am glad to hear that you will soon be leaving Wandsworth, and looking for work. My difficulty is that I cannot afford help: that is why I am doing practically everything myself. By this method, I reckon I can re-erect this little house more cheaply than buying another one, as well as saving a very interesting old house.

The foundations, water and drainage were done by a small local firm, and were finished before I arrived here, with all the timbers and tiles, etc. Two fishermen, who helped to unload one of the lorries, have already agreed to come along for an hour or so, if any of the timbers are too heavy for me to move. There is not a great deal of work for people in this area, and some of them go to King's Lynn or to Norwich, and come home at week-ends. Even before I came here, I had received a letter from an elderly carpenter and joiner, asking for work, but I have not been able to do anything for him, either. If I had plenty of money, it would be different, but having to move at all is a great expense, whether I bought another cottage, or re-erected this one. I've never had much money, as my father died in 1921, just before I was 10 years old, and there were no pensions in those days, except for war widows and orphans. My Mother's Father had been killed when she was three years old, so there was no help *from that side of the family. No doubt, it was this background that first made me tackle the odd jobs at home, like carpentry, that a father usually does, and I have learned a good deal since those early days.*

As you have done farm work, and will be free in time for the harvest, I wondered if you would be able to get work in that line, for a start. The fruit growers seem to need pickers. Am enclosing the 'Situations Vacant' pages from our two local papers, the Lynn News and Advertiser, and the Dereham & Fakenham Times, known as the Journal.

Another possibility is a job where week-end work is necessary, as I understand that many people refuse jobs where they cannot get Saturdays and Sundays off, every week. Perhaps you would let me have an address that will find you in the future, in case I hear of anything.

Good luck in your efforts, and don't let the difficulties get you down; as my Mother always used to say, "Worse troubles at sea".

Yours truly,
May Savidge (Miss)

Ware Hall-House
Water Pit Lane
Plummers Hill
Wells-next-the-Sea
Norfolk

16th August, 1970

The Governor,
H.M. Prison,
Heathfield Road,
Wandsworth,
London S.W.18.

Dear Sir,

On or about 8th July, 1970, a prisoner, Mr. Clark, having read an article in the Daily Telegraph, 7th July, about the re-erection of my little house to make way for a roundabout and new road, wrote to me, via the Daily Telegraph, asking if I could employ him, as he was due for release on 27th July.

In reply, I explained that I could not afford to employ anyone, but said that I would let him know if I heard of anyone who could offer him work.

A faint possibility has now come to mind, but as I do not know why Mr. Clark was in prison, or what sort of man he is, I wondered if you would be so kind as to let me know, in strict confidence, something about him, please; what he is like, and especially if he has any tendency to violence, as the person of whom I am thinking, who needs someone to do some work, is older than I am, and lives alone, but is better off financially.

Am enclosing a stamped addressed envelope, and would be very glad of your advice.

Yours truly,

May Savidge, (Miss).

•

H.M. Prison,

Heathfield Road,

Wandsworth,

London S.W.18.

Please address any reply to THE GOVERNOR and quote JDW/LH

17 August 1970

Miss M Savidge

Ware Hall-House

Water Pit Lane

Plummers Hill

Wells-next-the-Sea

Norfolk

Dear Madam

Thank you for your letter of 16th August. I regret that I cannot be of any assistance as Clark was discharged from prison on 27th July and his whereabouts are not known to me. I would add that, in my opinion, Clark would not be suitable to work for the person you mention.

Yours faithfully

Governor

•

I spent countless hours reading through the letters May sent and received. Sometimes, I would decide to take just a quick look in one of her correspondence boxes, only to find that the next time I looked at the clock, a whole morning or afternoon had passed. Unlike her diaries, in which she recorded every detail of her project in tightly written notes, her letters were open and chatty – even when written to complete strangers. She wrote as she spoke: as I sat at her desk in the great hall, I could hear her telling her story in her own voice.

Ware Hall-House
Water Pit Lane
Plummers Hill
Wells-next-the-Sea
Norfolk.

18.11.71

*Dear Mr. Purdy,**
   Thank you for your letter of 12th Nov., regarding the re-erection of my little medieval hall-house from Ware, Herts. I was very interested to hear that you are preparing a thesis on the Restoration and Preservation of Buildings, as one of my reasons for tackling this job was the thought of all the buildings which have been destroyed unnecessarily in the past, and those which are likely to be in the future, if people do not __do__ something about it. One fact that the destroyers forget is that overseas visitors expect to see some old buildings, when they bring their much-needed currency to our country.

* Mr Purdy was a student at the Leicester School of Architecture, who had read an article about her in *The Architect & Building News*.

164

The article in the "Architect and Building News" was more correct than most reports of this move, though I do know of at least two <u>older</u> buildings in Ware, though they are both larger. Since the article was written, I have spent a year sorting all the timbers, etc., after spreading bricks over about half the garden for the purpose; I also had to remove thousands of nails before I could make safe piles of joists, etc. There was no time to remove nails before I came, which was a pity, as it would have been easier to load the lorries. I had some help to move the heavy timbers, and also a carpenter for 4 or 5 weeks, to get the base plate in position. This is a replacement; as you will know, base plates were laid on the earth, with no foundations, so we found only short lengths of the original one. Am now busy doing up some of the lower joists, before erection, and am <u>trying</u> to get some wooden pegs or dowels, which should be made from riven oak, not sawn oak, (for fixing the joints) – hope I do not have to make them by hand, as it would take so long.

You probably know that other houses have been moved, but by groups of people I think. Various friends said that I ought to write up this move, so I have kept notes, and there are endless letters, also photographs etc., but I am not sure what sort of details would best suit your purpose. You are welcome to come here, if it will help you, though the house is no higher than the base plate at present. Water Pit Lane is an old walled footpath, without a name-plate, off Plummers Hill, which is off the S.W. corner of The Buttlands, – a green, (with large trees around it) where by Henry VIII's orders, the local men and boys practised archery, for the defence of the realm. I usually go shopping on Tuesday and Friday mornings, and seldom go out otherwise, except to take my dog for a walk, as I am too busy.

Good luck with your work, anyway.

Yours sincerely,

May Savidge, (Miss).

After our first, discouraging visit to see May in Wells we had talked about her often over the next few months, and although we didn't speak to her – she had no telephone then – we exchanged several letters. Meanwhile, we had plenty to think about in our own lives. We were a long way from finishing the renovations to The Nook and I was pregnant with our second child. We, too, had four walls to rebuild. Auntie May had been to see our cottage during the renovations some years before – and much later it struck me that maybe watching our amateur building had given her the idea that one doesn't need to be a professional builder to renovate a house. When Daniel was born in October 1970, Auntie May sent a letter of congratulations and a gift. We wondered how she was getting on, but with another new baby to look after, the thought wasn't foremost in our minds. She wrote that she would have loved to come and see us, but she felt unable to leave the building site unattended until the house was up and could be secured. We resolved to visit her there as soon as we could.

In the event, our second visit to Auntie May's new home took place in the spring of 1973, nearly two years after she had first moved in. I remember the occasion well. We were looking forward to showing off our little family and seeing how near Auntie May was to finishing her project. She met us at the gate and led us up the steep path to the level part of the plot on which the foundations had been laid. 'As you can see, I have made a lot of progress,' she told us. But we couldn't see any at all. To us, the site looked exactly as when we'd last seen it. The progress, Auntie May explained, was in sorting out the piles of materials that the delivery men had offloaded willy-nilly. She had removed all the thousands of nails that had been left in the beams, and then restacked them according to the numbers that she had painted on them before they had been taken apart. The north, south, east and west timbers were now in their respective positions. The next job was for the base plates to be remade and fixed to the foundations. She had found a local carpenter who had agreed to do this, and he was going to start work 'very soon'.

So, the project had moved on a little, even if it didn't look like it. But at this rate, May would never get the house finished. Once more, we offered to come up and help; once more, she refused. Then events overtook us, as Tony's job took us to Scotland. We didn't want to go. We'd only just finished renovating The Nook and we wanted to enjoy it. Tony was an engineer and was then working for a vehicle instrumentation company. He was a gifted designer and his employers wanted to loan him to a tachograph firm in Dundee – to make the first British 'spy-in-the-cab' devices that a new European law required to be fitted in lorries and coaches. At first he refused to relocate, but they kept coming back with promises of higher pay and bigger incentives until we finally gave in. We moved to Dundee in 1974 and we didn't see Auntie May until we came back south two years later.

By then, Auntie May had – with the help of a couple of casual labourers – got the scaffolding up and the main frame of the building erected, and she had found a man who had agreed to do the infilling with brickwork. But he disappeared after a fortnight, so she had started to do the bricklaying herself. This would have been a difficult enough task for a professional bricklayer, for the spaces between the beams were irregular. Auntie May had no experience of bricklaying, but was determined to lay every single brick absolutely perfectly, so progress was pitifully slow.

Over the next few years, we made a point of visiting Auntie May with the children during their summer holidays. Each time, we would set off hoping to find the house nearly finished; but each time, we arrived to find that little had changed since our last visit.

There was always a hand-printed sign on the gate that said 'IF DOG IS IN GARDEN, PLEASE WAIT OUTSIDE UNTIL I COME'. The dog always was in the garden, but we would go in anyway. Whether the dog barked or not, Auntie May would know that someone had arrived, because she had rigged up a Heath Robinson arrangement of strings, wires and pulleys that connected the gate to a home-made bell hung on one of the beams of the house that would clank away when the gate was opened. She was always pleased to see us, but would never let us do anything to help. 'Why is it all taking so long?' our children would ask.

It seemed to us that going through Auntie May's garden gate was like entering CS Lewis's wardrobe: the world behind the gate didn't have lions and witches and fauns, but it did seem to have clocks and calendars that worked at a different pace. Every time we saw her, she would tell us how she had been waiting for months for one tradesman or another to turn up to do something without which the project couldn't move on. She pottered quietly along doing such tasks as an increasingly frail and elderly woman could manage. Meanwhile, nature began to hide those carefully arranged piles of beams, pushing nettles between them, and winding the floorboards in ivy.

CHAPTER FOURTEEN

Onwards and Upwards

In which Auntie May describes her progress in letters
to her numerous friends and admirers

Then, when we visited Auntie May in the summer of 1977, we saw
some real progress. The roof timbers were in place, and were
covered in felt and battens. The ground-floor brickwork was
finished. The window frames were all in place, even if they were
not yet glazed. At last, it seemed possible that all the bits and pieces
she had brought from Hertfordshire might one day, once more, be
put back together to make a house. But it was to be two more years
before the tiles were on the roof.

But though progress was slow, the tone of the letters May wrote
in the 1970s was breezy and optimistic:

Ware Hall-House
Water Pit Lane
Plummers Hill,
Wells-next-the-Sea
Norfolk.
16.6.74

*Dear Pauline**,*

Thank you very much for your letter of 11th: was glad to hear that you are coming up this way on holiday, and shall be very pleased to see you both . . .

Only the frame of the house is up so far, – it took me over a year to sort out all the bits, and put them in different heaps in the garden, with bricks underneath to keep them off the ground; also had to remove thousands of nails, which were in the way. Then I got a bit of help, to get the base-plate (a replacement) down on the foundations, which were done before I arrived. After that, I started on repairs to the timbers; the lower ends of all the vertical ones had suffered from having no damp-proof course, – no foundations, either, – so I have had to join pieces onto them. Nothing about this house is rectangular, either horizontally or vertically, so every join takes a bit of working out; it is fortunate that I was on aircraft jig-and-tool drawing during the war, there are very few right-angles on an airplane, either. Last September, two strong young local men came in their spare time and got the frame up – the main timbers, anyway, – the ones that have tenons at both ends, so cannot go in afterwards; there are still several smaller ones to go up, and some replacements. I did start bricklaying in November, until the frost made it awkward, then I did a lot to the hedge, as my new dog kept getting through it; it took me a great deal of time. The land drops away steeply on the other side, so I managed to get enough pipe to go all the way round, and wired wire-netting on to it, and filled in the gaps below. Some of the pipe came from a malting demolition here, and there were a lot of bricks there, so I had a load, which of course included a lot of rubble, but bricks are quite difficult to get now, and very expensive, and I am likely to need extra ones. As one cannot drive to my gate, the load was tipped up in Plummers Hill, and it took me over three weeks

---

* I have not been able to trace Pauline's surname. She appears to have been an old ICI colleague.

to get it all in by hand. However, I'm now dealing with windows, so as
to be able to get on with the bricklaying again . . .

She sent a letter around this time to a Mr and Mrs Huttlestone, who
– I guess – were among the many strangers who heard or read
about her, called at the site to wish her well and became life-long
friends and correspondents:

> *Ware Hall-House*
> *Water Pit Lane*
> *Plummers Hill,*
> *Wells-next-the-Sea*
> *Norfolk.*
> *17.11.74.*

Dear Mr. and Mrs. Huttlestone,

Thank you for your letter and the lovely photos; I think they are
very good indeed, and was surprised to see the one of Sasha* standing
there so quietly, after the way she had been barking . . .

Am very sorry indeed to have been so long in writing, but there are
so many letters in the queue, and I try to spend the daylight hours
outside on the re-erection job. Having no electricity makes writing etc
more difficult in the evenings; I've fixed up a small mirror to reflect
the light onto the paper – sometimes I have to use the front lamp off
the bicycle to help out. The Calor gas is all right over the sink, but
gives a poor light in this part of the caravan, so I use an Aladdin lamp,
but the only safe place for it is at the opposite side of the cabin. The
Calor gas is on that side, too.

It was so nice to see you both, and I was so glad that the weather
stayed fine for you and that you enjoyed the scenery, etc. There are

---

* Candy had died and been replaced by an Alsatian bitch, Sasha.

some miles of coast and country around here, where wild birds can be seen; about 30 miles of the coast is protected by the National Trust etc. I've had quite a lot of visitors, including BBC-tv, but it rained all that day; they were not after a news item, but are doing a series about people who have done something entirely different after retiring or having to give up work for some other reason. They did a bit of recording here and said they would come again later on. As well as the rain, the Water people were using a pneumatic drill nearby, so the BBC could not have done a proper 'take' anyway. The idea of the series seems to be to encourage people not to sit down and get bored and miserable, but to find out ways of doing whatever they have in mind, including learning new skills. Some folks get really despondent when they give up work. Incidentally, the pneumatic drill cut through my neighbour's gas pipe; she had a meal in the oven, and was resting – not feeling very fit after a car crash – and later on she found the meal still uncooked; the Water people had not found out whose pipe it was.

The rain has been pretty bad this Autumn, hasn't it? I keep covering up parts of the job with polythene, but the strong winds drive the rain in underneath at times. However, I'm progressing bit by bit, and hope we don't get too much snow.

Hope you are both keeping well; kindest regards to all, and I look forward to seeing you again next year, I hope. Thank you again for the photos . . .

Yours sincerely,
May Savidge

I came across another reference to May's lighting problems in a charming exchange of letters with the company that had manufactured her ancient paraffin lamp:

Ware Hall-House
Water Pit Lane
Plummers Hill,
Wells-next-the-Sea
Norfolk.
25th Nov. 1974.

Aladdin Industries Ltd.,
Aladdin Building,
Greenford,
Middlesex.

Dear Sir or Madam

No. 11 Mantles.

For some time, I have been trying to buy some Kone-Kap mantles, Ref. No. L.146, for use on my No. 11 Aladdin Lamp, and am getting worried as I am now using the last one of my little stock.

Will you kindly let me know where I can obtain some more, please?

Please find enclosed a s.a.e. for reply,

Yours truly,

May Savidge (Miss).

Ware Hall-House
Water Pit Lane
Plummers Hill,
Wells-next-the-Sea
Norfolk.
19.1.75.

Mr. J. N. Thurgood,
Chairman & Managing Director,
Aladdin Industries Ltd.,
Wester Avenue,
Greenford,
Middlesex / UB6 8UJ

Dear Sir,
    Thank you very much for your letter of 11th December, ref.
JNT.ME.336, regarding the supply of mantles, etc. I was surprised to
hear that the last No. 11 was sold in 1929; it says a lot for its quality,
though this one was not in daily use between 1949 and 1969: even so,
at 45 years or more, it is almost half-way to becoming an antique, and
still working perfectly. I first came into contact with Alladin lamps in
a country house in 1923, but I do not know when they were made. Have
now bought a new one, to use when my No. 11 Mantle collapses.
    Yours truly,
    May Savidge (Miss)

Another letter that caught my attention was to Rusty and
Nargesh Rustomji, who lived in Bombay, India. I recognised the
name from one of the calendars May had kept. Rusty had given
it to her as a present in 1923 – she had known him since she was
twelve.

Ware Hall-House
Water Pit Lane
Plummers Hill,
Wells-next-the-Sea
Norfolk,
England.
NR23 1ES
16.3.75.

Dear Rusty and Nargesh,

This was meant to be a Christmas letter, but I get so "snowed under" with letters and form-filling; I sent off the cards, etc., and hoped the air-letters would overtake the ones going abroad, but I am still floundering, partly because it is difficult to see, with the oil lamp in the only safe place . . .

Re-erecting this house still takes all my daylight hours; except for shopping, etc. Usually in the winter, snow or hard frost would drive me indoors, to get on with letters or other indoor jobs, but this year has been exceptionally mild, so far; there were summer flowers out in January – the wild plum hedge started to bloom, too, but I don't suppose we shall get any wild plums from those flowers. I feel obliged to get on with the house as fast as possible, partly because I have only temporary permission to live in the caravan in the garden, and have to apply each year for a continuation: another reason is that the timbers will deteriorate if left lying in the open too long. I don't think that I am being unnecessarily careful with my repairs to the timbers – you see, the frame has to stand up by itself; there was no brickwork, originally, – that went in at various times afterwards, and if the timbers rotted at all, or were cut away, the brick walls held the place up. But having taken it all apart, for transport, one cannot do the brickwork first, because one cannot tell where it has to go until the frame is in position. It isn't as if the frame were rectangular, or even straight – and it fits

together so tightly, with mortises, tenons and oak pegs, that it can't be
persuaded to go anywhere except in the right place.

With so many upright timbers to be avoided, I suppose any proper
bricklayer would think that the job was too fiddly; I did mention it to
four or five, but no one came, so I started trying the bricklaying myself;
I had done a bit before. However, a good deal of last winter and spring
went in doing jobs to the hedge, as my dog would keep going through
it, which could be very dangerous, if she reached the road. The ground
beyond the hedge falls away steeply, so it is difficult to block the base,
as the earth between the actual bushes slides down the bank, too: it
was a long job.

Am bricklaying again now between the showers; the bricks are not
all the same size, and are various colours, – both due to having been
added at different dates. Shall be very glad when the job is finished
and the furniture out of storage again, but it is an interesting job to do,
and is one little effort against the destruction of so many old buildings,
which people do like to see: also, with such a housing shortage, it seems
silly to destroy this one and occupy one that someone else could live
in . . .

Very best wishes to you both,
Yours sincerely,
May Savidge

May always replied to the letters she received, but her in-tray was
always piled high and her reply to Rusty and Nargesh was by no
means the only one to be sent a year late. Many of the letters she
wrote begin with apologies for the delay, followed by a detailed
explanation of why she hasn't been able to write sooner – as in her
Christmas 1977 letter to Gordon Moodey, secretary of the East
Hertfordshire Archaeological Society, whom she had known since
1954:

Ware Hall-House
Water Pit Lane
Plummers Hill,
Wells-next-the-Sea
Norfolk NR23 1ES

Christmas, 1977.

Dear Mr Moodey,

Thank you so much for your letters of last December, April and November, and for the Newsletters – 40, 41, 42 & 43, which I was very pleased to receive. Am extremely sorry that this letter is so late – have only just written letters to Australia and India, which should have been there by Christmas. All the year I thought the roof would be on by Christmas; earlier in the year I thought I would have moved in by then, – so Christmas arrived and I was prepared for it. During April, two young builders did a bit of work here, but disappeared – three times – by then it was the middle of June. They had talked about getting the roof on "now", but it seems I was only a stop-gap – I suppose they found other work nearer home, in a nearby town. I began enquiries for a little help to get those 24 joists in my bedroom ceiling/attic floor into place; they are tenoned into two tie-beams, which have to be lifted out, the tenons put in, and then replaced, so the job <u>had</u> to be done before the roof was started, as the principle rafters are tenoned into the tie-beams. At the end of October two local young [men] came and did the job, in one day – we used a little chain pulley to lift the tie-beams. Later, they put up four pairs of principle rafters, collar beams, etc., on odd days, but they both have other jobs – one of them goes to sea, fishing – so they cannot spare much time. Meanwhile my efforts to find someone to help with the roof have come to nothing, but I think someone is coming in January! – not the best time to be doing roof work – hope we finish before the March winds arrive – we

177

have had at least three gales since this part of the roof went up,
already.

Was very interested indeed in the change of attitude of the planners
regarding old buildings. I'm sure the elected Council people – and
others – would have been surprised if they had known the number of
people who used to express regret at the demolition that was going on;
but these people only speak to people like me, and not to the powers
that be – they have the idea that nothing can be done about it – it just
has to be, because somebody or other says so . . .

    Yours sincerely,

    May Savidge

I found it heartbreaking to read that May had thought she
would have been able to move into the house by the end of 1977.
More than seven more years would pass before she could finally
do so.

Meanwhile, she received a constant stream of visitors, many of
whom turned up unannounced. They all found the note on her
gate about the dog. When the postcard the note was written on
became worn and faded, Auntie May wrote out another. I found
five copies among her papers. I expect there were more. I also
found a note from a Mrs Fellows, whom May knew from their
days in the Ware St John Ambulance Brigade. It was dated 14
September 1978 and written in pencil on the back of a raffle ticket,
the only paper Mrs Fellows had in her handbag at the time. It
offers good wishes, tells May she has had a hip replacement and
says that she recently 'caught a glimpse' of Auntie May on TV –
when the BBC regional news programme *Look East* had come to
report on her progress.

Ware Hall-House
Water Pit Lane
Plummers Hill,
Wells-next-the-Sea
Norfolk NR23 1ES
17.9.78

Dear Mrs. Fellows,

Thank you so much for your little letter; I was very disappointed indeed not to have seen you on Thursday. I was there somewhere, and expect I was inside the unfinished house – my work bench is there.

There is a wire attached to the gate, which rings a bell close to the bench; my dog barks at nearly everyone who goes by along the footpath, so I only go to the gate if the bell rings. The path is a handy route to the Orchard Caravan Site in Burnt Street, so most of the people who go by are holiday-makers, and if the children find out that I have a bell, they keep ringing it and running away, – so I dare not mention the bell on the note on the gate. I tried to word the note so that people who wanted to come in would open the gate, but be prepared to close it again if the dog rushed towards it. There is an extension wire from the bell to my caravan at the far end of the garden, as I cannot hear the bell in there, but it requires the gate to be moved a foot at least, as the wire is rather long, so sags a little.

It was good to know that you are getting about again, after that hip operation, but I was very sorry to think of the pain you must have suffered before you had it. There are some wonderful things done to joints now-a-days, – I seem to remember drawing some of the plastic 'bones' when I first went to I.C.I.; I think the idea was fairly new, then.

If you are in this area again, I would be ever so pleased to see you. Just at present, I do all my shopping on Saturdays, as I am expecting someone to come to do the outside plaster around the upper half of the

179

house for me. I shall do the inside later; it will be a more fiddly job, as I want to show all the timbers on the inside. Someone else is going to put the tiles on the roof – I shall help. After they have both finished here, I shall revert to my old shopping days – Tuesday and Friday mornings; I have a padlock and chain inside the gate, but leave a note on it if I have to pop out; I also lock the gate at night, with all those clay tiles and other things piled up on the site.

. . . I am now making a window for the gable end, facing the gate – you may have seen a tower of light-weight scaffolding there. The original window had three oak mullions mortised into the collar-beam halfway up the roof, so was not intended to open; the replacement did not open either, but I felt that it ought to, at that height, in case it is ever needed as a fire escape, so I am copying the original window, but in an oak frame, with hinges. Working on old oak takes me a long time, as it is so hard; I must finish this window and some other pieces before the plasterer can do this south wall, but the other three walls are ready for him, so I hope he comes soon; he was coming in August . . .

Kindest regards to you all, and hoping you will soon be quite fit again,

Yours sincerely,

May Savidge

In December 1978 the publisher Jay Landesman Ltd wrote to suggest that Auntie May's story might make a book, to be written by a ghost writer. They had in mind 'a light-hearted account of the difficulties and the way you overcame them – an entertaining book based on your illustrations'.

Ware Hall-House
Water Pit Lane
Plummers Hill,
Wells-next-the-Sea
Norfolk,
NR23 1ES

12.1.79

M/s Jenny Wright,
Jay Landesman Ltd.,
159, Wardour St.,
London, W. 1.

Dear M/s. Wright,

Re-erection of Small Medieval Hall House.

Thank you for your letter of 6th Dec., suggesting a book about the re-erection of this little hall house, which was in the way of a new traffic roundabout at Ware, Herts., and which you read about in the Evening Standard of 1st Dec.: Christmas and other happenings have delayed my reply, I'm afraid.

First, I must say that there were several mistakes in the article, and that I have not yet moved into the house. I had some help with the roof, and the man has promised to come back and put the tiles on; I shall help. Another man is going to plaster the outside of the upper part of the house; I shall do the inside later, as it will be a fiddly job, making dozens of separate panels, so as to show all the timbers on the inside. At present, I am working on the outside doors, and a few windows, etc.; neither of these men is likely to come until the weather is good.

This house had been threatened since 1953, just because it was old,

181

so I had plenty of time to decide that I wanted to keep it, long before the roundabout was even thought of. Ever since the dismantling began, (in Sep. 1969) people have asked me to write about the whole job, so I made notes each evening about what we had done: after I arrived here (in June, 1970) I even typed out some of these notes, as I had been asked to give a talk about the move. Have also taken a lot of photos, and these and notes have come in handy at times, during the re-erection, quite apart from being a basis towards a book.

When I have moved into the house, I shall finish the typing and proceed from there. I have always been fond of writing and never thought of a "ghost" writer. During the years, many visitors have asked questions, so I have a good idea of what interests them and what they want to know. My writing would not be quite the approach you suggest, as that would disappoint people — they want to know much more than that — but it would certainly be light-hearted and with illustrations.

Am sorry for the delay — there is so much to cope with,

Yours sincerely

May Savidge.

If Miss Wright wrote a reply to this letter, I have not found it. I did, however, find a large number of letters written to May by people who had read about her continuing efforts in articles published in the national press. A Mrs Hillsdon wrote to share her memories of the baker's shop that had occupied one half of the building when it had been in Ware.

Buckinghamshire
May 24th 1979

Dear Miss Savidge,
I was fascinated to read the article in Woman magazine about the

removal of your cottage from Ware to Norfolk, as many years ago I was very familiar with the building.

As a child I spent many happy holidays staying at the bakehouse in Baldock Street . . . I remember the building well, especially standing in the old bakehouse watching the bread come out of the oven. My bedroom was the one with the window looking out over the yard of the public house next door and the floor was always warm from the oven beneath. The floor of the landing upstairs was most uneven . . .

I can see the shop now – with the sponge cakes in a glass case, the cottage loaves, the doughnuts, the varying sizes of fruit cakes and above all the sticky buns – two of which I was given each morning for lunch. It was a great privilege for me to be able to serve in the shop on occasions . . .

I hope your venture will soon be completed and I wish you many happy years in your cottage in Wells-next-the-Sea.

Yours sincerely,

G.N. Hillsdon (Mrs.)

One of many strangers to write to congratulate May for her efforts was a man who had been kept going through a family crisis by her example:

London,

3rd October 1979

Dear Ms. Savidge,

Some weeks ago my son became very ill, and during the long hard struggle before he died last Spring, the story of your courage and determination was one of the things that helped sustain us. The newspaper cutting telling of your tremendous achievement in rebuilding your house has been on my bedroom wall all these months; many times I intended to write to you, but somehow I never seemed to find the

time, the peace & writing materials all in the same space. But now I
have time to thank you for the inspiration you gave the children and
myself when we most needed it . . .

As May approached the tenth anniversary of her move to Wells,
the tone of her letters became noticeably less optimistic. There is
an air of resignation about them – though she is still cheerful
enough in herself, despite all the difficulties and delays. On 17
February 1980, she wrote to her old school-friend Peggie Hutton:

> *Ware Hall-House*
> *Water Pit Lane*
> *Plummers Hill,*
> *Wells-next-the-Sea*
> *Norfolk NR23 1ES*
> *17.2.80 for*
> *Christmas, 1979.*

My dear Peggie,

    This was supposed to arrive for Christmas; am so sorry it is so late,
but my lamp keeps going dim – too dim for writing by – so I am more
snowed under with letters than ever; shall be glad when I get electric
light again. The man who was going to put the tiles on the roof of the
house has not been here for almost two years; the man who was going
to plaster the upper part of the outside has not done any work here since
Dec. 1978, though he did call recently, after I had 'phoned. He does
have back trouble, having injured his back years ago, and they all
seem to be very busy. So I plod on alone, with the jobs.

    Yours affectionately,

    May Savidge

CHAPTER FIFTEEN

Becoming a Celebrity

In which Auntie May appears on television and receives –
and replies to – more and more fan letters

Stories of Auntie May's progress continued to be published in
newspapers and magazines at home and abroad, and in the spring
of 1980, national television came knocking, as a BBC television
crew arrived to make a short film for the evening news programme
Nationwide. I've got a tape of it. It's a little work of art. It paints a
subtle picture of Auntie May's gentle but determined character and
records exactly what she had so far achieved. Looking at it now, I
am struck by how derelict the Blue Lady appears. It had been pretty
tatty when she first bought it, but now, after she has lived in it for
more than ten years, the paint is peeling off and the weeds are
growing right up to it. May looks old and tired. She says very little
and speaks very softly in reply to Sue Cook's questions.

'May is a gentle, solitary soul; she spends her every waking hour
working,' says Miss Cook. That was true enough.

'How long did you think it would take?' asks Miss Cook.

'Well nothing like as long as this, but it's difficult to get help,'
Auntie May replies.

'Wouldn't you prefer to live in a nice warm modern house?'

'No, not really, not when you can live in an interesting old house. I don't want something silly and modern – that doesn't strike me as nice at all!'

'Isn't it a bit cold and lonely here?'

'No! I've got the dog and the cats. I'm used to being on my own – I've been on my own for donkey's years.'

'Have you ever thought about giving up?'

'No! Not likely!'

The camera watches her climbing a scaffold tower and slipping in some fillets of brickwork. She moves slowly, but purposefully. There is a strange little scene in a local pub, in which half a dozen cheerful regulars are shown chatting to Miss Cook. We don't hear what they say, but in a voice-over, Miss Cook says that there are mixed feelings about Miss Savidge in the town. The scene gives the impression that Auntie May is somehow not connected to the people of Wells – she is an outsider. There is an interview with Mr Terrington, the builder who put down the foundation slab for her. He is obviously full of admiration for Auntie May, but he does gently point out that he has never been convinced of the wisdom of the project. He says he suggested that he could have had a nice new house built for Auntie May to move straight into back in 1970, but that wasn't what she wanted at all. He says that her first idea had been to bring the frame of the house up in one piece, slung under a helicopter, but that was obviously never going to happen. Auntie May is asked how long she thinks it will be before she has finished work and can move in. She says she doesn't know, but that once the roof is on, and there are no more drips coming through, it should be quite soon. Mr Terrington is asked the same question and he says that, if she doesn't get help, he really doesn't see how the project can ever be finished during her lifetime.

In 1981, more publicity – an article in the *Guardian* and a news item on national television – moved a number of strangers to write to May. The *Guardian* piece, published on 5 January 1981, was accompanied by a photograph of Auntie May at her most bag-lady-like, wearing a woollen hat under a headscarf, and clutching an overcoat to herself with mittened hands. The text misspells her surname and rechristens her 'Edna'. Nellie thought this might be on account of an Edwardian actress of that name, but I suspect that the writer had subconsciously likened Auntie May to the scruffy and lonely misfit played by Patricia Hayes in the TV play *Edna, the Inebriate Woman*. In the photo in the *Guardian*, Auntie May stands by a tumble of brambles and old timbers in front of the house, which looks decrepit and tatty – more like a building falling down than one being rebuilt.

> Although now aged 69, she insists that the time she takes is immaterial. 'It is only a fraction of the life of the house, which is how I like to see it,' she said. 'I want to live here, of course, but I want others to be able to live here after me. That is what is important.' There are some who feel she will never finish her tasks. Miss Savage [*sic*] has no date in mind but is sure that one day the construction will be complete.

It is clear that the author of the piece is not quite so confident.

One of many to send in money was a woman in London, who enclosed a cheque for £100:

January 7th 1981

Dear Miss Savage,
*   In front of me I have a cutting from The Guardian with your*
photograph and story and I cannot let another day pass without

telling you of the happiness and humility with which I read and re-read it.

Thank you for showing us, in these sad, bewildering times, what courage and quiet determination to achieve a selfless vision can do.

Please accept the enclosed cheque towards the re-building of Ware House – if it advances by only half an hour the completion of your task, I will be very proud . . .

PS Please do not give up a moment of your precious time to answer this; it needs no reply.

Poor people sent in offerings, too. In March, a woman from Colchester wrote May a letter of support that began: 'Please find enclosed one antique nail. My husband got it when he was in the building trade, now retired in ill health. I admire your guts immensely, it spurs me to get jobs done myself around my modern bungalow . . . ' Another letter received about this time came from a Belfast student, who enclosed a £5 note, and apologised for not being able to afford to send more.

Many of the letters May received thanked her for saving her ancient house for the nation:

Yorkshire.
April 28th 1981.

Have just seen on TV the programme about your 'moving house' to Wells-on-Sea. I think you're marvellous. Yours is the spirit of independence and creative imagination that once made Britain great. I pray that the programme may result in really useful offers of help, so that the beautiful house for which you care so much may be completed this year, and you may enjoy many years of living in it. You are building part of the nation's heritage, not just a place for you

to live. I'm the same age as you were when you started the project,
and can imagine just a little of what you must have felt . . .

I read these letters in the dusty, cluttered house after May's death,
squashed between upturned chairs and bedsprings. It was a
compulsion. To peek into those cream-coloured folders made me
feel part of May's life – and often moved me to tears.
May received hundreds of unsolicited letters like these and
replying to them took time. A huge backlog built up, in which
letters to her family and friends got caught up. In July of the
previous year, she received a tear-smudged aerogramme letter
from Nargesh in Bombay, telling her that Rusty had died. She
finally got round to replying to it just over a year later.

Ware Hall-House
Water Pit Lane
Plummers Hill,
Wells-next-the-Sea
Norfolk,
NR23 1ES
England.

21st June, 1981.

My Dear Nargesh
    Thank you very much for your letter of last year; I was so very,
very sorry to hear your sad news – it must have been a terrible
shock to you, being so very sudden, although a wonderfully peaceful
way to leave this life. I hope you are getting used to loneliness a
bit now, although I know only too well that nothing fills the gaps:
keep[ing] busy, and keep[ing] your mind occupied helps, I
find, and also one gets tired enough to sleep . . .

Am very sorry indeed that this letter is so very late; it is not due to heartlessness – I owe hundreds of letters, some of them official ones – electric light would help a great deal – I get so tired, especially in a dim light. My paraffin lamp went wrong for about a year, and I have never managed to catch up since. There are boxes of letters piled up in the caravan which is so full that it is difficult to find anything. Last year I had more visitors than ever, mostly complete strangers, and as the caravan is so far from the gate, I took the typewriter into the unfinished house; had to fix a polythene tent over it, as the roof dripped rain: I tried to type with a hurricane lamp hanging up . . .

Recently, a good builder has been helping here, and the roof tiles are now on, so at last, there are no drips: he has done some other work here, and has promised to come back and do the downstairs floor, so I hope to be able to get my furniture out of storage soon. Meanwhile I am doing various jobs, mainly carpentry – repairing windows, etc., and cutting down the growth in the garden, before the weed seeds blow into other people's gardens. Before Christmas, I bought cards and stamps, but that is about as far as I managed to get – I was just too tired to get them written and posted, so must try to make amends now, while there is more daylight, and before the builder comes back; I get very tired trying to keep up with him, as he is much stronger and younger than I am, but a marvellous help: I often fall asleep over my evening meal . . .

I do hope you are keeping well, and hope to hear from you when you can manage it; there is a lot to see to, when living alone.

All my good wishes and deepest sympathy,

Love from,

May

Please forgive the long delay.

Things took another significant turn in 1982, but unfortunately, it wasn't a turn for the better. The firm that had stored Auntie May's possessions for the past eleven years ceased trading and she decided to have all her stuff delivered to the house. Thereafter, the house was jam-packed with clutter. Nellie had told me that May had always been a compulsive hoarder, but only now did I realise quite how much she had accumulated over the years. When she had lived in Monkey Row, most of it had filled the neighbouring two-storey workshop, which had been as big as a family house. Now, it filled Ware Hall-House to bursting.

When we visited her in the summer of 1982, we found the Blue Lady caravan crammed with boxes. Cardboard cartons covered the bed, stacked right up to the ceiling. There was no room for anyone to get in, let alone live in it, and Auntie May had moved into the house. But things were almost as bad there – there were only three small spaces in which she could stand or sit. One was in the front room, where she typed her letters on a tatty antique desk; the second was an old chair and table in the great hall, in which she slept and ate. There was a small area in front of the butler's sink in the room that had originally been the bakery. The only other space not covered by ceiling-high packing cases was occupied by the dog basket – which visitors had to stand in.

And yet Auntie May had made some progress since we'd last seen her. She had put down floorboards upstairs and in the attic. But she had immediately covered them – again, ceiling-high – with her possessions. The ground floor wasn't quite so full, but only because Auntie May had left narrow passageways between the vast piles of boxes and clutter. There was no way much internal rebuilding work could be done while all that stuff was there – but then, for the time being, that didn't matter, for there was still much to be done outside.

In December 1982, a BBC *Look East* producer wrote to Auntie

May to ask if he could bring a TV crew to film an update on her progress since his last visit in 1978.

Ware Hall-House
Water Pit Lane
Plummers Hill,
Wells-next-the-Sea
Norfolk,
NR23 1ES
9.12.82

Mr. Ian Masters, BBCtv Look East,
St. Catherine's Close,
All Saints Green,
Norwich,
Norfolk, NR1 3ND

Dear Mr. Masters,

Thank you for your letter of 6th December. I was surprised to hear that some of your viewers had written to ask how this job is going.

When you came in 1978, I think that the roof and the upper part of the outside of this house would have been covered with roofing felt; the man who was going to do the plaster on that upper part did not come back, nor did the man who was going to finish the roof; I did not think I would be safe on the tile battens at my time of life. *Other men said they would come, but did not; at the beginning of 1981, however, a different man came and did the outside plastering, and put the tiles on the roof, and did a few other jobs as well. He is very good and very busy, but he had a bit of time to spare last Christmas, and came and did a bit to the downstairs floor – (2″ cement screed on the concrete),*

---

* Auntie May was 71.

and more of it on some Saturdays. Before he had finished, however, the firm where my furniture was in storage closed down, so as the roof is watertight, the furniture, etc., is here now. It is good to see it again, and better for it to have some air, but it is rather in the way.

The same man says he will come again some Saturday mornings, and do a bit more to the floor, – then the plumber could come – so now I do all my shopping for the week on Fridays; therefore, Mondays to Thursdays would be the best time, if you wish to come; I am here all day, usually doing the woodwork jobs, as cement work is a bit heavy for me . . .

> *Yours sincerely,*
> *May Savidge (Miss).*

A letter to May's cousin, Alan, and his wife, Joan, describes the progress that was made on the house in the spring and summer of 1983:

> *Ware Hall-House*
> *Water Pit Lane*
> *Plummers Hill,*
> *Wells-next-the-Sea*
> *Norfolk,*
> *NR23 1ES*
> *4.9.83*

Dear Alan and Joan,

Thank you so much for your letter of 1st August, and for the cheque which you very kindly enclosed: it is very good of you and is much appreciated. Yes, I am still very busy on this job – the fine weather helps sometimes, but is rather overpowering – I see that you are not keen on the heat, either. Fortunately, there is usually a bit of breeze on this coast . . .

*In May the plumber came and fitted the kitchen sink; there is one in the caravan, but I have to carry the water there, so having my old sink and a proper tap is a real treat. He is coming back to finish the bath, etc. Just when he was able to come, I started having trouble with one leg, which I had knocked, and had to rest it a lot, but it has just cleared up, at last, so I am getting on with windows, etc. Have also got some floorboards for the attics — only one had a floor, before; I want to take some things up there, as, since the furniture came out of storage last year, there is a bit of clutter on the downstairs floors.**

Am enclosing a plan of this house, as you suggested — am not re-erecting the Tudor chimney stack, as it was not there in the first place, and blocked the cross-passage completely, as you can see from the two shallow hearths which used to be of the inglenook type and were back to back, with two more hearths upstairs, with brick four-centre Tudor arch fireplaces. The upstairs bathroom will be where the huge chimney stack was (ventilation in the roof) so that the landing can run full length. The extra bathroom, downstairs, is in most of the former pantry. Am still using ladders indoors, but can do the stairs in the winter, being an indoor job; I have to barricade the first ladder, as my dog can get up it, but can't get down again . . .†

Love to all,

May

It was about this time that another film crew arrived. This one was led by the young Polish director, Witold Stok, accompanied by his wife, Danuta. They had picked up the story in the article published in the *Guardian*. Something about that article fired the Stoks'

---

* This is something of an understatement!

† There were three ladders in the house at this time. One was riddled with woodworm and carried a notice: 'Warning: for cats only'. When I saw this on our visit in the summer of 1982, I had to suppress a childish giggle.

imagination and Witold wrote to Auntie May asking if he could come and talk about making a film. She agreed. She never sought publicity, but she never turned it down. She felt that it was just plain wrong to destroy our architectural heritage, and the more people that were shown it could be saved, the better.

Auntie May mentioned the Stoks' visits in the letters she wrote to thank us for the Christmas presents we had sent her in 1981. We realised she must have been having difficulties completing the project, because she didn't find time to write it until the end of the following October:

Ware Hall-House,
Water Pit Lane,
Plummers Hill,
Wells-next-the-Sea,
Norfolk NR23 1ES

26.10.82

Dear Tony & Christine, Polly & Danny,
Ever so sorry this is so late for Christmas, again; I was just getting on with letters etc., last winter, when Mr. S., who had put the tiles on the roof, had a bit of spare time so came back and did some of the downstairs floor – putting the 2″ screed on top of the concrete base. It is a heavy job for me, especially as the sand has to come into my garden in wheelbarrow-loads up from Plummers Hill; he has a youth helping him now, and one pushes, and the other pulls a rope tied to the front of the wheelbarrow. I had to keep moving things out of the way, indoors, so that he could do a bit and let it dry and set properly; also had to keep my dog off – the cat's paws did not make much of an impression.
Before Mr. S. had finished, however, the firm where my furniture

was in storage decided to close down, so as the roof is now watertight, I have all the furniture here. It is nice to have it, and better for it, too, as warehouses do get damp, but it is rather in the way; there are so many boxes of things piled up everywhere. Mr. S. is coming back sometime, to do more of the floor, then the plumber would come – he has been to see the job – a different man, as the other plumber never came.

Meanwhile, I'm very busy indeed with woodwork, etc., also moving things to make more space, – and now, to add to the chaos, I've mislaid my address books, – a real problem – I can remember <u>some</u> addresses, but not all, and the postal codes.

Thank you very much indeed for your lovely presents and cards; I am so sorry not to have written sooner – I do wish I could keep up with letters, etc., but I owe so many, and I am trying so hard to get this house finished enough to be able to invite people to stay – there are enough bedrooms – at present, two beds are covered with apples! – a good crop, but a lot of maggots.

Must get this posted; love to all, and I do hope you are all keeping well,

> *Yours affectionately,*
> *Auntie May*
> *XXXX*

P.S. More delays – before I'd managed to wrap up the parcel, the members of the little Polish group have been again, doing a bit more to add to their film – there wasn't much space for our feet among all the boxes, etc. We were looking through my photos of this job at various stages, and came to the photo of you all: they may wish to include one of them – I hope you wouldn't mind.

> *Love from*
> *Auntie May*

•

The final cut of the Stoks' film was 25 minutes long, and it was first shown at a conference held at Ruskin College, Oxford, on 10 March 1984. Auntie May didn't see it until its second screening, at the Wells Centre on the following 5 May. I wish she had told me about it: I'd have loved to be there with her. But I only heard about it in a letter she sent me some months later, and I didn't get to see the film until after she had died. I found a copy of the programme of the Wells showing among Auntie May's papers and what I read made me want to get a copy of the film:

> *This creative documentary captures the rhythm of the woman's lonely and endless task. She saws, chisels, hammers, builds, survives Spartan conditions yet, as her voice-over discloses, she never loses hope. But twelve years after its dismantling, the house still remains unfinished . . .*

I wrote to Witold Stok and he sent a charming reply along with the videotape. It is a curiously affecting little film, in which Auntie May is shown pottering about at all sorts of tasks amongst her clutter, while her old clock ticks slowly in the background and her radio carries the BBC news. One item is a report of the death of the one-time Soviet president Leonid Brezhnev. Another describes the wedding of the Prince and Princess of Wales. Auntie May doesn't seem to be listening – the point seems to be that these events are happening in a world in which Auntie May plays no part. While the commentator rattles on about the glamour of Lady Diana's wedding gown, Auntie May pulls on a battered overcoat as she prepares to go out. The contrast is pointed, but not patronising. She is presented with admiration and respect.

I later learned that not everyone in the audience at the Wells Centre screening had responded positively. It must have been a strange evening. Years later, Witold and Danuta described it to me and I read about it in a book I found among Auntie May's possessions. Its author, Patrick Wright,[*] devoted a whole chapter of *On Living in an Old Country*[†] to the story of Auntie May. He describes seeing Auntie May sitting at the front of the audience, dressed in her all-weather topcoat, woollen hat and scarf – even though it was a mild, spring day. She had brought a bunch of honesty from her garden to give to the Stoks. (Wright wondered whether it was her way of saying that she hoped their film would be an honest account.) Most people in the audience treated her protectively – someone took her by the arm to help her to her seat, which was quite unnecessary, as she was still capable of climbing ladders and scaffolding unaided; but then, she was in her seventies and she looked frailer than she was.

After the film, the audience was invited to discuss what they had seen. One or two of them addressed a question to Auntie May, but most people talked about her as if she wasn't there. A rather snooty woman said that one Miss Savidge in Wells was enough, thank you; any more, and the value of local property would be dragged down. A couple of women argued that the film wasn't feminist enough: why was it called *Miss Savidge* – what had her marital status got to do with anything? One man said to his neighbour that Auntie May was a fly old bird who had been milking public sympathy for years. Someone else said that if everybody in the room were to give up just one afternoon a week

[*] Patrick Wright is one of the hundreds of names recorded in Auntie May's loose-leaf visitors' book. He came on 6 May 1984. The Stoks had last signed it in March 1983, leaving notes of farewell and thanks on 24 May.

[†] A new edition of this book has just been published by Oxford University Press.

to help her, the house would soon be finished and she could be comfortable at last. There was a murmur of general approval and several people shouted: 'Hear, hear!'

I don't think any of these people understood Auntie May at all – not even the kindliest of them. I wondered how many of them really understood the film. I think it's beautiful. It shows Auntie May as someone detached from the concerns of modern society – and though the audience didn't realise it, the comments they made confirmed the view of the Stoks.

Another interesting point that Patrick Wright makes is that the conference at which the film was first shown had been about patriotism. Later, when I delved into the records that Auntie May left behind her, I could see what the Stoks must have seen: that Auntie May's determination to save her house sprang from her love of her country, of the history that had made it what it was and the inheritance that she wanted to pass on to later generations. Early in the film, Auntie May says something particularly revealing: 'I was a bit fed up. They keep destroying everything.' She speaks of the enemies of those values as 'they'. I think that's why the Stoks called their film *Miss Savidge*. The title suggests the contrast between the faceless, soulless and unseen authorities that have taken over England, and an individual who has sacrificed everything to stand in their way. That individual has a name. It is Miss Savidge. It's Auntie May.

CHAPTER SIXTEEN

'Getting a Bit Old Now . . .'

In which Auntie May finds the going
increasingly difficult

On 30 August 1985, the *Dereham & Fakenham Times* revisited
May's story under the headline 'May, 74, works on at rebuilding old
house'. It reports that 'the major building work has been finished
for some time', but that 'Miss Savidge has not yet moved out of the
caravan that has been her home since 1970'. What the reader isn't
told is that apart from the fact that 'brick floors are being laid',
the project is not much further on than it was two years earlier:
'Miss May Savidge, now 74, continues to climb up ladders and
scaffolding with great agility while she continues to tackle her
present task of replacing windows.' She is still having problems
'finding someone to replace leaded glass'.

The upbeat tone of the report did not reflect reality. The project
had stalled. Much of Auntie May's energy was now being spent on
patching up jobs that had been finished earlier. Days fill with trivial
tasks, like repairing mop handles, mixing tiny quantities of mortar
to plug gaps in the walls, or struggling to remove rusted-in screws.
Her diaries contain increasing references to time spent repairing
rips in the PVC sheeting that covered the window frames, none of
which yet contained glass. On the day that she had made her final

move to Wells, she recorded the occasion triumphantly in her diary; I expected to find a similarly upbeat note of her final move from the caravan to the house. There isn't one.

I scoured and rescoured the 1985 and 1986 diaries, but there is no record of her moving into the house. She does refer to taking her meals there, and it is clear that, from the autumn of 1985, she and the animals are spending their nights there, too, because the first entry of the day is often a note that she has had to clear up the 'puddles' and worse that her Alsatian, Lorraine, has left in the cross-passage of the house.

I puzzled about this. It didn't seem to make sense. When we visited Auntie May in the summer of 1985, she was obviously living in the house, where there was now a working WC and bath – though it was also clear that she was sleeping in her chair in the great hall downstairs and not in a bed. There were tiles on the roof. She told us that she had found a very helpful local plumber, Mr Jarvis, who had renovated and refitted the old taps, water heater, bath and basin she had brought from Ware, and had built the walls of the bathroom itself. Then I read that *Dereham & Fakenham Times* article again:

'I have started eating meals in the house because I am worried about the dog knocking over the gas lamp in the caravan,' said Miss Savidge. 'I can't get permission to move in until the windows are fixed.'

Maybe that's why she didn't mark the move in her diary – in one sense, she never actually made it. I think she believed she wasn't allowed to and was worried someone in authority would turn up and condemn the place as unfit for human habitation and force her to live in a 'council bungalow'. I am sure that was the main reason she didn't want anyone from the surgery to enter the house. I wonder whether to begin with, at least, she persuaded herself that she hadn't actually moved in, as she wasn't sleeping in her bed. From this time on, the first diary entry of the day notes which chair she had dozed in the previous night – and the stool or stools on which she rested her legs. After a while, each entry is the same: 'Old chair, corded stool, canvas stool.'

Our visit that summer wasn't a happy one. When Tony rang the bell at the garden gate, Auntie May didn't appear for ages, so we let ourselves in. This was a mistake: her Alsatian, Lorraine, was loose and ran at Tony, who was holding a present that we had brought. I can't now remember what it was, but he needed two hands to carry it, which meant that when the dog went for him, he couldn't fend it off. It bit him in the leg, and wouldn't let go. May was mortified, but she did point out that the note on the gate said visitors should wait to be let in. The atmosphere remained tense for the rest of the day.

We could see that the project was drifting. It was as if Auntie May had lost sight of the bigger picture and had her head down to concentrate on the minor tasks that were arising day by day. Not all of these related to the building. It seemed to us that much of her energy was expended on looking after the dog, which seemed to be like a cuckoo in the nest, demanding attention that was needed elsewhere. In the car on the way home, we agreed that if things went on like this, Ware Hall-House would never be finished – and, worse, it might even begin to fall down.

Years later, when I read Auntie May's diaries, I realised that her problems had been even worse than we had imagined – though she records them with no trace of self-pity or complaint. We had been right about the dog – but we hadn't known the half of it. The 1985–1988 diaries are dominated not by difficulties with the house, but by difficulties with Lorraine, the Alsatian bitch she had adopted after it had been found wandering in King's Lynn. May's hope that she would eventually become biddable were not realised. She was never even properly house-trained. For month after month, May records clearing up 'puddles' and fouling in the cross-passage leading to the front door – she had a carpet she would have liked to put down there, but knew that if she laid it, it would only be ruined. Sometimes she had to clear up three or four times a day, even immediately after exercising the dog in the garden. As if this weren't trouble enough, Lorraine wouldn't walk to heel, leapt up at other dogs and several times pulled Auntie May to the ground. People noticed. The kindly Mrs Leftley at the grocer's recommended that she got a 'Halti' leash – a lead and muzzle combined. Auntie May got one, but she still couldn't control the dog. Every time she opened the gate to take her for a walk, there was 'the usual battle' over who was in charge, and Auntie May never won.

In November 1985 Auntie May was on television again. This time, it was BBC1's regional news programme *Look East*. The programme celebrated her move into the house and gave the impression that the project was nearly finished. But this was far from true. There was still no staircase – the first and attic floors were reached by ladder. There was still only a 'builder's supply' of electricity – four sockets on a board in the hallway served the whole house. A single, bare bulb hung over Auntie May's table and chair in the middle of the great hall – which, like the rest of the house, was still packed, floor to ceiling, with all those boxes of Auntie May's stuff. Auntie May cooked and heated water on a veteran Beatrice paraffin stove in a tiny space cleared in the room that was nominally the kitchen.

Auntie May was in, but she still didn't have a telephone. Anyone wanting to contact her had to call in, write – or, as many journalists had done over the years, send a telegram. Tony and I were worried about her health. She had never really been well in all the time I had known her. She suffered constantly from indigestion. Even a cup of tea could upset her stomach: she had to drink it very weak. Over the years, she had worked out which foods troubled her least and stuck to them. There weren't very many of them. She seemed to live on a diet of bananas, carrots, prunes, cheese, biscuits and Kit Kats. On one of our visits, Tony and I battled past the nettles and brambles, and took a walk around the overgrown garden. We found a 5ft pile of what looked like little jet-black twisted sticks – it turned out they were hundreds of desiccated banana skins. Heaven only knows how many bananas she must have eaten in her lifetime. I guess that she liked them because they were easy to chew – she had terrible trouble with her teeth. She also suffered terribly from ulcers on her ankles and legs. She never complained of them, but we knew they were there because we could see the bandages. Sometimes she was in so much pain that she could hardly walk.

The cold can't have helped. The winter of 1985–1986 was bitterly cold. We knew the temperature in the house must have fallen well below freezing, because when we visited in the summer of 1986, Mr Jarvis told us that Auntie May had called him out three times in February and March to mend her frost-blown pipes. The only heating in the house was an ancient electric fan heater that looked like a vintage aeroplane engine. It ran so constantly that its housing glowed red hot and Auntie May was frightened that it would catch fire.

MON: 17.2.86 – Fingers get so cold – otherwise O.K. . . .

FRI: 21.2.86 Up at 7am. Temp. in Great Hall 24°F. at 10am.
L[orraine] puddle & f[ouling] in x-passage . . .

The following Monday, the pipes in the house burst, and while she was waiting for Mr Jarvis, the plumber, she spent her time struggling to get a mattress into one of the bedrooms. There were no stairs in the house yet, so she tried to get it up the scaffolding tower and in through the window, despite the *'ICY E. WIND'*. She failed. A week later, she had another go: *'Tue 4.3.86 'managed to get 4 ft. mattress up to B[edroom]3 and onto bed.'*

In March, Auntie May spent even more time than usual cleaning up after Lorraine, who was suffering from vomiting and diarrhoea. Another way in which the dog – 'That damn dog!' I found myself thinking – was making Auntie May's life even more difficult was by driving away her cats. At this time, she had three: Shelley, Charlotte and Ginger. The only way she could feed them was to climb the ladder to the first floor and put their food in the bedrooms, where Lorraine couldn't get at it or them. For the rest of the time, the dog stayed by Auntie May's side, so the cats wouldn't approach her – and she was reduced to watching them from afar. She compensated for not being able to pet them by making detailed notes of her sightings of them in her diary. One day, the dog managed to follow her up the ladder – and, worse, couldn't get down again. After that, Auntie May had to keep a plank against the rungs when she wasn't climbing them herself.

On 13 June, she received a pleasant surprise in the post: an invitation to a Buckingham Palace garden party to be held on 17 July. Whoever drew up the invitation list must have read about her in the papers, or seen her on the television. The invitation was for Auntie May and a companion. She asked Nellie to accompany her. (Years later, Nellie told me that when May had telephoned her

205

from a callbox to invite her, she had begun by saying that she was calling to ask if she would like to come with her to see the Queen. Nellie, assuming that May had finally lost her marbles, told her to put the phone down, calm down and ring again when she was feeling better. Five minutes later, May telephoned again. Only then did Nellie take her seriously and agree to accompany her to the palace.)

May got herself a new outfit for the garden party: a handsome flower-print voile dress and a white hat with matching gloves. I suppose she only ever wore them once. After her death, I found them all carefully wrapped and stored in her wardrobe. They were like new. The day itself, alas, did not go well. Auntie May admired the gardens and the flamingos, and caught sight of a hat that she thought might have been on the head of the Queen; but then she was so overcome by the heat that she was physically sick and had to be helped to a seat to recover. She was sick again on the train on the way home. Later, she noticed 'patterned lights' before her eyes. Her health was beginning to break.

It was at about this time that we had a family conference and decided we would try to persuade Auntie May to get a telephone installed. Nellie and Bern, and Mies – her Dutch cousin – and Tony and I agreed that we would all slip the idea into a letter, as if it had occurred to us independently. Nellie and Bern would say they were getting old now and finding it increasingly difficult to get up to see her by car. Mies would write to say that it would be very useful for keeping in touch with her in Holland, given that letters take longer to arrive from overseas. I would just say that I thought a phone might be a good way of keeping in touch.

The real reason was that we were all terrified she would have a fall and have no way of calling for help. We all wrote as planned, but unfortunately, she had an answer for us and it was an answer that made perfect sense: a telephone would make her life more dangerous, because if it rang when she was up a ladder or on the scaffold tower, she might slip as she hurried to answer it. We had a rethink and Mies wrote to suggest a cordless telephone – one that she could carry with her. A few weeks later, when Tony and I visited, Auntie May told us that she was thinking of getting a telephone – one of those cordless ones. We bit our tongues and said: 'What a good idea!'

Needless to say, once she was connected, she logged every call she made and received – even the calls that she wasn't able to answer in time. Every time the phone rang or she made a call, she wrote 'phone' in the margin of the diary, beside an entry noting precisely what happened – even if the phone rang only once and she didn't manage to answer it. One of the first calls she received was from Mrs Terrington, who offered to do her daily shopping; and Mr Terrington 'said 'phone if I need help, even during the night! – very kind of them'.

Such offers of help were timely. Auntie May writes that she is frequently tired, and some of what she writes is confused. On the 1986 anniversary of her parents' wedding, she writes '*MOTHER & DAD – 60 years since Dad & Mother got married.*' But it can't be: in 1986, Auntie May was seventy-five years old. It must have been the eightieth anniversary.

During the autumn of 1986, there is little mention of building work in the diaries, but among the handful of telephone calls recorded there is an amusingly inappropriate one from a double-glazing saleswoman:

TU: 4.11.86 . . . 6.15 pm. – 'phone – young woman on double glazing
etc. – haven't fitted single glazing yet . . .

I laughed out loud when I read that.

The 1986–1987 winter was another ordeal by frost for Auntie May. In January, the temperature plummeted, outdoors and in. On the morning of 11 January, she woke to find the water in two milk bottles she had left on the draining board had turned to ice, cracking the glass, and that the hot-water bottles she had put in the cats' baskets upstairs had frozen solid. Mr Terrington telephoned to ask if she was OK – he had noticed there were no footsteps in the snow leading from her gate. She told him she hadn't been able to get down the path, so had exercised the dog in the back garden. He said that if she needed anything at all she should call him and he'd come immediately. But Auntie May didn't call, she battled on.

MON: 12.1.87 . . . Removed 4' to 6" snow . . . & put food for birds – G[inger] puss in B[edroom] 4 – took some food there too. Even pets' food in tins frozen after opening. After garden with L[orraine] I slipped over – had to crawl back to E. door, to get up . . . Later, up to B[edroom] 2 – on stool from bathroom, got 2 nails into top of window frame for a piece of wood in the gap – while doing this, L[orraine] barked – down – E. door – Mr. M. Owen to see if I needed anything – he wrote my 'phone number – gave him 2 g[allon] paraffin container . . . Too dark to finish window piece – hands so cold – down again – more HW bottles for Charlotte.

TU: 13.1.87: Mr M. Owen came with 2 g[allons] of paraffin: £3.20. Mr Leslie IRONS called (Priory Cottage) to ask if I wanted anything – left his card for 'phone no. – I said if he saw a loaf . . .

WED: 14.1.87 . . . SNOW up to top of gum boots – skirt wet . . . Pat Terrington 'phoned – I mentioned loaf – son will come this afternoon to clear path.
Mrs IRONS & daughter (no hat!) came with loaf – small cut loaf.

Abt. 1 pm. – Peter Walsingham – thinks he will run out of paraffin – lorry could not get here Monday so he brought some to regular customers – 1 gallon.

Kevin Terrington came with loaf (large white) . . .

Afterwards, B[edroom]2 – fixed 2 boards (wide T[ongue] & G[roove]) into space at top of window with orange 'Farmer's Glue' – icy wind – fingers very cold – put some wood props to hold boards from blowing in.

During the rest of 1987 there are many days in which she records nothing beyond the time she got up, the state of the weather, her sightings of the cats and the time she locked the gate at the end of the day. The last entry on many days is the word 'Dozed'. There are many nights in which she records things that happen in the small hours – sometimes she is woken by them, but more often she is awake anyway:

Th: 26.2.87 . . . 3.20 a.m. G[inger] Puss on bed B[edroom]1 – 3.50 a.m. Garden with Lorraine – no use – (4.10 a.m.) Shelley stayed in parlour. Hardly any sleep (R. leg) – kept having to change position.

She writes down the time whenever the bell rings, but the note is often followed by 'nobody there'. Sometimes children have rung it and run away; sometimes, she is just too slow to get to the gate. Her shopping lists all contain Savlon for her ulcerated legs, and paracetamol for all sorts of pain. She writes that she finds it difficult to walk: her ankles are so swollen that she cannot put on her 'top boots', which 'protect my legs from Lorraine's claws, when she jumps at other dogs'. She has a set of dentures made and fitted. She makes frequent references to tiredness. She notes the deaths of several friends. And on Thursday, 5 March, she gets some bad news:

After 5.30 p.m., 'phone – Mr. M. Owen – just got back from Fakenham and found G[inger] Puss dead in his garage – he wondered whose cat he was . . . I said I thought he'd been living wild for some years – he was so terrified of people – I said he might have got some food elsewhere, as he was only sleeping here – but I think he had given up eating really – plenty of food on landing, but he didn't even touch the milk. Poor puss – just when I thought he was getting used to me . . .

Ten days later, Auntie May heard Shelley making unusual miaowing noises. The next day, she found that she had burrowed under the blankets piled on one of the beds upstairs. She put a hot-water bottle beside her and offered her a little warm milk.

'She cried a few times during the night, but raised her head in response to stroking under the chin. I tried to sleep – (on edge of bed) (she was in the middle) – up after 6.30 a.m. – left her well covered up . . . – about 11 a.m. Shelley was dead. She had come out from under blankets.

TU: 17.3.87

Aft[ernoon]. Finished hole and buried my darling Shelley – such a loyal little puss – afraid of other people, so I had thought she was safe here – her twin brother was a friendly puss & he has disappeared & her mother, also friendly, has left me and prefers outside Homestead* kitchen window – Buried Shelley in cardboard box – lying on left side – head to the W. end, so facing the house – her coat looked beautiful – black with ginger mixed in it – white underneath, also lower part of

* The name of a nearby house.

face — black sleeves on left front paws — others white — put dark grey
tiles on top of grave — then planted the Cheerfulness bulb in the middle
— the one that she dug up from . . . near ash tree.

Locked gate — after 6.30 p.m.?

V. tired & R. ankle and leg hurting — Dozed.

Auntie May's legs and ankles continued to cause her pain and make it difficult to sleep. On 25 September, when she went to collect her pension in the Station Road post office, she fainted and had to be helped onto a chair; she recovered and went on to Leftley's in the High Street, where she fainted again. The Leftleys took her and her trolley home in their van. A few days later, her GP Dr Ebrill called at the house to see if she was OK. She left the chain on the door and assured him through the gap that she was able to cope. On 21 October, a health visitor called, and Auntie May spoke to her with the door on the chain, while Lorraine made a lot of noise and jumped up at her.

Auntie May wasn't giving up. She was determined not to spend another winter in a freezing house and started looking for a Rayburn cooker to install in the kitchen. That would keep one room in the place warm, at least. But solid fuel cookers need chimneys and the rebuilt Ware Hall-House didn't have one. Before a Rayburn could be fitted, the place needed a flue. Auntie May decided that the short-term solution was to get an electric cooker — but she was stymied here, too, because she hadn't yet plastered the kitchen wall against which the cooker would sit.

Meanwhile, everyone could see that Auntie May was running out of steam. We had seen how weak she was becoming when we had visited in the summer. Tony and I were terrified that she would have a fall and not be found. In the winter, that might mean freezing to death. But for all her medical experience and training, she kept the doctor at arm's length. On one visit, I called the surgery to give Dr Ebrill our phone number, and to let him know that we were doing our best to keep an eye on her. He told me that he understood the problem – he was in fact making regular calls to check that she was OK, though to begin with, she would only speak to him through the letterbox. In 1990, Dr Ebrill told me that it couldn't be long before she would have to accept medical help. 'We are just waiting for a minor catastrophe,' he said.

Tony and I decided we had to do something to help. We telephoned in October and told her that we would be coming up with some Perspex to fit in her windows. It wouldn't be as good as glass, but it would at least make them weathertight. In the event, Tony's work commitments prevented him from coming, but our son Daniel came in his place and we brought everything we needed for a day's work. We also brought up a little electric oven and cooked frozen pizzas in it. We left it behind as a present – though we later found that Auntie May hardly ever used it.

The little oven had been my mother's and I began to realise that my feelings for May were somehow daughterly. I'm sure many can relate to losing a mother – and how the subsequent opportunity to care and look after someone frail brings with it a certain comfort.

Despite all her difficulties with her house, her health and her animals, Auntie May's spirit was not broken. On 7 November, she attended a public meeting in the Community Centre, called by the Campaign to Save Wells Hospital. As soon as she got home afterwards, she typed a letter in support.

Ware Hall-House
Water Pit Lane
Plummers Hill,
Wells-next-the-Sea
Norfolk,
NR23 1ES

7th Nov. 1987

Mrs. E.M. Allen,
Chairman
East Anglia Regional Health Authority,
Union Lane,
Cambridge.

Dear Madam,
Please let me add my note of dismay at the idea of closing Wells Hospital. Has anyone thought of the <u>cost of all the extra transport to King's Lynn or Norwich — not only in money, but in lives?</u>
There is already a great deal too much traffic on the roads, and too many accidents, even in good weather: what about fog, ice and snow?
The delays and additional accidents should not be ignored; they all cost far too much.
Yours truly,
May Savidge (Miss).

Later that month, I made another visit to Wells. Horrified by how weak she had seemed on my last visit, I brought her a bottle of multi-vitamins.* Worried about her being scratched and knocked over by her dog, I brought a screw-in spike, set it in cement in the

---

* I found the bottle, unopened, after her death.

213

garden and attached a long chain to it. Frightened that she would knock over the ancient paraffin lamp in the kitchen, I got an extension lead and rigged up a light bulb there. Up until then, she had only been using electricity to run a single light, her radio and the fan heater, all of which were connected directly to the builder's supply that brought power to just behind the front door. Auntie May, who never did seem to get to grips with matters electrical, hadn't thought of using extension leads and was grateful for the suggestion.

Three days later, Auntie May had more bad news. She hadn't seen Charlotte for four weeks, and when she went into town on Friday, 20 November, she bumped into a Miss Danby, who told her that the cat had wandered into Mrs Pinder's house, where she had been allowed to sit in front of the gas fire. She had accepted a little milk and then curled up in the garden shed for the night. The following morning, Mrs Pinder had found her there, dead. Mr Abel had buried her in the garden. Neither of them had known that she was Auntie May's cat.

Nineteen eighty-seven came to a quiet end. Auntie May spent Christmas and New Year's Day alone, though she was invited in for a glass of sherry – the first alcoholic drink she had had for years – by a neighbour, Mrs Jones, who heard her struggling to post a Christmas card through her letter box.

The diaries for January, February and March 1988 are sparse and patchy. The handwriting wobbles and there is little to record except shopping lists, nosebleeds and polythene windows blowing in and being patched up.

But at the end of April, the diaries begin to fill up again and the handwriting is once again neat and purposeful. I am sure the spring weather must have helped. On 24 April, Auntie May wrote and underlined, twice: 'B2 WINDOW – AT LAST watertight.' That day, some old ICI friends made a surprise visit – one of them was staying in Holt, where, she said, the ironmongers, Bakers, had a display of new and second-hand cast-iron cookers. On Wednesday, 27 April, Auntie May got a lift to Holt and chose a solid-fuel Rayburn. She left a £400 cheque by way of deposit and asked to have it delivered later that summer. Things were looking up.

Over the next few months, Auntie May spent some time plastering in the kitchen, but progress was slow. Reading the diaries, one can see why – she was making up mixes using only a pint of water at a time. A professional plasterer would have used gallons – and, indeed, would have someone to do the mixing for him. She seems to have spent as much time cleaning splashes of plaster from the floor as putting it on the wall. She finished on 15 September and spent the next month moving furniture around so that there was room to get the Rayburn in. Then she telephoned Bakers and told them she was ready for it. They delivered it on 17 October. At the top of that day's page in the diary, she wrote 'RAYBURN at last' and underlined it in red.

But getting the Rayburn working involved rather more than just getting it in. That day, Auntie May telephoned a builder she had been recommended, to ask if he could build her a chimney – he said he was tied up for months. The next day she asked Mr Terrington if he knew anyone who could do it; he said he would ask around, but didn't think she had much chance of getting it started before Christmas. When he called round to take a look the next day, he pointed out that the floor wasn't strong enough to take a brick-built chimney of that height. A few days later, she got the man from Bakers out to ask if they could fit a steel flue instead. He said that they could supply one, but didn't have the men to put it up. Auntie May had her old problem again – finding a builder who could come and do some work.

The days were getting shorter and it looked like Auntie May was going to be spending another winter in an ice-bound house. Armistice Day came round again and she found herself remembering the original event:

FRI: 11.11.88. 70 YEARS. – I remember <u>Ellen Pritchard</u> telling <u>Mother</u> that morning that there was talk of an Armistice – I didn't know what an Armistice was, <u>but it happened</u>.

Christmas came and went. The weather over the New Year was mild. On 12 January Auntie May called another builder for help with the Rayburn. Towards the end of the month he came to size up the job and agreed to take it on.

But he didn't come back. The weather was mild, though, and as winter turned to spring, the Rayburn business became less urgent. On 27 April, Auntie May noted in her diary that it was exactly one year since she had paid her deposit to Bakers of Holt.

She spent a lot of time in the garden that summer, but found it difficult to move about on the uneven ground, even with her walking stick. When both hands were free, she tried keeping her balance by using two garden rakes 'like ski-poles'. It seems to have worked, but I don't think she can have been using them on the night of 29 June:

<u>10.30 p.m.</u> gdn. with L[orraine] – slipped over – took me an hour to get up – earth a little soft from rain – in 11.30 p.m., slightly muddy.

Rereading the diaries now, the words 'if only' echo through my mind. If only we had lived nearer – Tony and I are both such practical people and there was so much more we could have done to help. If only Auntie May had booked her builders in advance, instead of asking for them when she needed them and then politely waiting. If only Auntie May hadn't been so frightened that 'they', those in authority, might force her to move out if they saw the conditions she was living in, perhaps she would have allowed 'them' to help. If only Auntie May hadn't found her elder sister's concern for her so patronising, perhaps she would have let Nellie and Bern do more for her, too. If only she hadn't been determined to keep her family at arm's length; if only, when she said 'No thank you, I'm fine' to us, we had replied, 'No, Auntie May, you're not, and we are going to do something about it'; if only, if only . . . but it was not to be. She was determined to defend her independence at any cost.

The first anniversary of the Rayburn's arrival was on 17 October. Christmas came. The weather over the New Year was dull, with temperatures in the low 40s Fahrenheit. On Tuesday, 2 January 1990, Auntie May managed to get hold of the builder. He said he hadn't forgotten Auntie May's job; he had been busy. In fact, he had nearly called a few weeks ago when he had last been in Wells. He would look out those Rayburn leaflets and come and see her soon. He would ring first, in case she was out. A month later, he hadn't called. She wrote that she had meant to telephone him on Friday, 2 February, but had dozed off.

The weather turned windy. On 26 February, Auntie May noticed that the whole frame of the roof window had been blown out – she couldn't find it in the garden and put roofing felt on the floor of the attic to stop any rain that came in from running downstairs. March turned to April. The garden filled with hundreds of purple and white honesty flowers; the tulips and the white hyacinth came out – but there was no news from the builder. On Easter Monday, 16 April, the yellow marigold rose opened. By the end of the month, the flowering currant was almost over, but the laburnum, the hawthorn and the clematis were in bloom.

The builder did some measuring in early April and, when he had gone, Auntie May noticed that he had left behind his tape. He didn't return in April. He didn't return in May.

In June, Auntie May ordered a garden seat from Platten's DIY shop in Wells. She spent some time clearing a space for it, and otherwise pottering about the garden. She writes the word 'TIRED' after noting small garden tasks. The seat was delivered on Friday, 22 June.

SAT: 23.6.90.
F[ell] a[sleep] in old chair, corded stool, canvas stool.
   Sun & clouds – breezy, windy. 58°F.
   Cut off length of wire (16 SWG) – & bent it – gdn. – curled it around little tree trunk, then locked chain onto it & pulled chain around tree trunk & padlocked it to leg of seat – O.K. All the seats were chained at Platten's D.I.Y. forecourt – and this garden and gate are so hidden. Nice to be able to sit down for a minute out there – legs get so tired (& let me down at times). Better varnish it, or paint it, during a dry spell – Blackbird perching on its back already – better put a duster in polythene bag out there.

At the end of June, the builder reappeared, and told Auntie May that he feared a steel flue might end up costing more than a brick chimney, even with all the necessary foundation work. He would find out more and come back to her.

At 3pm on Wednesday, 12 September, he turned up with his tools and set to work. He cut some holes in the upstairs floorboards and measured the gap where the roof window had been. He said he would make a replacement at home and fit it later. He appeared several times over the next few weeks. On Wednesday, 17

October, Auntie May wrote in capital letters in her diary: '2 YEARS SINCE RAYBURN CAME.'

On 30 November, Auntie May telephoned, and 'asked if there was any chance of getting the Rayburn installed by Christmas'. Christmas was exceptionally windy. One of the plastic windows blew in on Christmas Day. On 28 December, Auntie May's legs hurt so much that she went to the doctor, who prescribed an antibiotic. The winds got worse in January. The word 'tired' occurs frequently in the diary. Auntie May had another serious nosebleed – it lasted three hours, this time. On 1 February, she telephoned the builder. He said he had a couple of jobs to finish, some emergencies – and 'one of three years' waiting'. I can well believe it.

On 6 February, the temperature dropped to 36°F and it began to snow. Auntie May noticed that the kitchen tap was 'almost frozen' and that there was 'some ICE in kitchen'. She went into winter survival mode. She knew what to do.

Filled various water containers, including v. large saucepan – Turned off water at main & downstairs W.C. – up to other W.C. – emptied cistern – down again and turned on outlet to empty all pipes – gdn. To see if it was running O.K. – very slow – thought there would have been a good flow – perhaps pipes are already partly frozen – later, icicle from outlet – also from kitchen tap.

The following day, the temperature dropped to 28°F. Auntie May found that the mop she kept in the cross-passage to clear up after Lorraine had frozen solid. At 12.30pm, the electricity supply failed – and the only heater in the house was electric. She telephoned Seeley's, the electricians. They came, and decided it was an Eastern Electricity job. Eastern Electricity came, and decided that it wasn't.

Auntie May called Seeley's again, and they came straight back – to discover that the fuse in the extension lead had blown.

During the cold spell, various neighbours called to offer help; they brought water, and salt and grit for the path and steps. On Tuesday, 12 February, the temperature rose to 36°F and Auntie May noticed that the mop in the cross-passage had thawed. She had tried to thaw it in front of the fan heater, but it hadn't worked. By Sunday, 17 February, the temperature had risen to 37.5°F and the snow in the garden had gone. Auntie May turned on the mains water stopcock – but it leaked. She phoned Mr Jarvis, the plumber, who said he would come round the next day. He came at 3.15pm, and fixed the stopcock and several other leaks he found, too. He couldn't stop for a cup of tea – he had three more calls to make.

He left at 4.30 p.m. Lovely to have tap water again. V. tired.

Auntie May made some progress in 1991. Mr Jarvis pointed out that one reason the place got so cold was that the kitchen door fitted so badly. He fixed it for her.

Nineteen ninety-one was also the year in which Auntie May finally found someone prepared to make and fit windows with leaded lights. She had first started looking nine years earlier, but the urgency of the task had been overtaken by other priorities. In April, she saw an advertisement for the Thorpe St Andrew Glass Company in the *Yellow Pages* telephone directory. Anybody else would have phoned them up, but May didn't. She sent them a letter, in which she told them the history of her project and offered them salvage materials they might wish to use: 'I have some lead, if that would help, mostly old gas pipes and electrical coverings, also some glass; I also have sufficient "Bantam" scaffolding and some ladders.' I don't suppose many of the glass company's customers made offers like that. I don't imagine many of them felt the need to explain why they needed to ask for professional help, either: 'I do as much of the work here as I can myself, not being wealthy,' she wrote, 'but am getting a bit old now.' She was, in fact, not quite eighty.

The glass man came, measured up and gave May a price. She agreed and that summer, the job was done. By the time he left, all the windows that had originally had leaded lights were fitted and glazed – but there were still several other windows that were just frames covered by polythene. It was twenty-one years since Ware Hall-House had been moved to Wells.

CHAPTER SEVENTEEN

The Beginning of the End

In which despite her failing health, Auntie May
clings fiercely to her independence

Nineteen ninety-one was the year in which May's troubles with mischievous boys from the town reached an unpleasant peak. I had known that some of them used to tear off the name card from her gate, or ring the bell and run away. But I didn't know about the more serious incidents until I found her diaries. I found those passages very difficult to read. I still do. She recorded them with her usual attention to detail and with a directness that makes it seem the events have only just occurred. Reading them made me – still makes me – want to rush round to comfort her and to give her tormentors a good talking-to. But I can't. It's another 'if only' to add to my list.

On the afternoon of Friday, 7 June, a boy came to the door claiming that May's next-door neighbour had asked him to cut her side of the hedge. It was an obvious lie. She asked why the neighbour hadn't called round himself. At this, he changed the subject and asked her whether she could lend him £5 – or even £2 – he would bring it back tomorrow. Meanwhile a taller boy appeared, who made Auntie May feel even more physically threatened. She told them both to get out of her garden and shut the gate. They went. 'I have no witnesses,' she wrote. 'There were two of them – they could deny it.'

Auntie May rarely recorded her feelings in her diaries, but her unhappiness is obvious in an entry she made two days later:

SUN: 9.6.91 53 YEARS SINCE dear Denis died – *Thank God I've met some decent men in my life – can't think what Denis would have said to that stupid boy on Friday afternoon.*

Two other boys taunted her on 13 August.

Abt. 7.15 p.m. – 2 boys knocked at door – one looking through letter box (10 or 12 years old?)

'Do you want any help? Do you want any shopping?' (At 7.15 p.m.?)
'Have you got any fags?'
'Just one?'
'I don't smoke'
'You do smoke' – cheeky pair – kept saying 'You do smoke' and 'Can we come in?'
Would not say who they were – asked them to go – I wanted to hear 7.20 programme – I mentioned police and telephone –
'You haven't got a telephone – you haven't got a telephone.'

When I closed the door, they got hold of it and shook it as hard as they could – letter box and knocker, I suppose – I told them to go – trespassing – bolted door – parlour, to see what they might do next – they pulled bell wire as hard as they could – Down to gate with Lorraine (lead around rope) – gate wide open – bell wire broken . . . Not a pleasant pair.

That autumn, Auntie May was plagued by a number of other boys who turned up to ask her to sponsor them for charity walks; some brought genuine sponsorship forms, but others did not. On 20 October, one called to ask for sponsorship on a cycle ride 'in aid of the churches'; she gave him £1. When he had gone, Auntie May found a further £8 missing from her purse. Two days later, someone pushed a lighted banger through her letterbox. Two days after that, a bigger one was set off right outside her door. When she came out to investigate, she found a boy making 'red Indian' noises at her over the gate.

Auntie May's entry for Christmas Day is depressingly sparse:

_38°F. – No wind. Some sun._*

By January 1992, Auntie May had turned to Mr Jarvis the plumber to get the Rayburn installed. He was putting the finishing touches to it one day when a gang of boys broke the padlocks on her gate and forced their way into the old Blue Lady caravan. An antique teapot was stolen. In ordinary circumstances, Lorraine would have seen off any intruders, but she had fallen ill and wouldn't leave her basket. On 16 January Auntie May found the padlocks broken again and four boys in her garden. She telephoned the police. It was a bad day, followed by a worse night. She sat up, nursing the dog and worrying that the boys might come back under cover of darkness. Then, at 2.10am, 'Dear Lorraine died.'

It was all getting too much. In the diary for the rest of the month, Auntie May was frequently 'tired', 'very tired', or 'tired and hungry'. On Monday, 27 January, Nellie telephoned and

---

* When I read this, I remembered a very different Christmas May had recorded ten years earlier, when she climbed up the scaffolding at midnight on Christmas Eve to take photographs of the stars.

repeated a suggestion she had made several months earlier – that Auntie May should find a flat and move out of the house for the rest of the winter. Auntie May said that wouldn't be necessary.

On the afternoon of the following day, Tuesday, 1 February 1992, she wrote:

Mr J. lit the Rayburn fire!!!! Lovely. Wood and some 'Phurnacite' from small bunker by caravan.

It was three years and eight months since she had paid the deposit on the Rayburn at Bakers of Holt.

Things were looking up. The ever-helpful Leftleys found Auntie May a new dog and collected it from the RSPCA in Norwich. It was a mongrel, called Muttley.* The man from Thorpe St Andrews Glass came to fit the leaded windows. The stolen teapot was recovered from an antique shop. The boy that had taken it was given a police caution. The policeman dealing with the case said to Auntie May: 'That should get those boys out of your hair,' and, for a while at least, it did.

But Auntie May's health was failing. The handwriting in the diaries begins to deteriorate. At 10.30 on the morning of Friday, 24 April, she lost her balance, fell and cut her face. It took her over an hour to get back on her feet. She wasn't strong enough to take Muttley out for walks; indeed, she was 'too wobbly' to go out at all. She found it difficult to keep the Rayburn alight – the fire-box needed riddling and she hadn't the necessary strength. Friends and neighbours rallied round. The doctor called and the health visitor made regular visits. Pat Terrington suggested that one of her

---

* Auntie May couldn't have known that it had been named after the sniggering hound in an American children's cartoon series – she never owned a television.

employees, the ever-kindly Sylvia Yarham, might be prepared to help by taking the dog out a couple of times a week and, in the event, she came much more frequently. Sylvia and Pat also brought bits and pieces of shopping that Auntie May needed in addition to the order that Leftley's delivered. Pat agreed to be named as a contact on the form Auntie May filled in to get an 'emergency pendant' – an alarm worn on a necklace that sent a call for help when pressed. Heaven knows, she needed one. She didn't have a staircase in the house and was still getting upstairs by using a ladder:

> *SUN: 4.10.92.*
> *Aft[ernoon]*
> *Up to B[edroom] 1 etc. Very difficult at TOP of ladder – nothing to hold on to, & I have to crawl. V. difficult to get up. Tied rope around banister rail to hold when coming up . . .*

Tony and I kept in touch with Auntie May by telephone. We had been rather preoccupied with planning our daughter Polly's wedding that summer. We tried to persuade her to come, but she said she was too frail and bent, and reading her diaries later, I can see how true that was. But she did send a present: '2 pr. Pillow cases in wedding paper – & card of tide at W. end of Wells beach.'

Nellie was keeping in touch by phone, too. At 'about 8.40pm' on 23 October, Auntie May called her to thank her for the latest cheque she had sent to cover the cost of the telephone. She also thanked her for sending two wedding photographs and Nellie told her all about the event. But the call left Auntie May feeling downhearted. In the 439th of her 440 diaries, for the first time, a shadow of deep sadness falls across the page:

I've got <u>Emergency Pendant</u> (Nellie knows a man who has one) – it
is attached to phone –
    <u>Rayburn</u> *O.K. – & <u>dog</u>. –*
Yet she still wishes I would get a bed-sitting room somewhere –
Give all this up?
(I don't try to influence her life) So depressing – I would have to give
up – (she would like me to give up) – DOG, EMERGENCY
PENDANT, 'RAYBURN', HOUSE, GARDEN, FURNITURE,
ETC. – W.C. on both floors.
HOW WOULD I GET THERE? Have not been out shopping since
Easter –
I spent most of my <u>early life</u> in <u>other people's homes</u>; now I have
<u>freedom</u>, and I've <u>worked hard</u> for it.

She was clearly deeply upset by Nellie's suggestion, even though I am certain it was only meant for the best. The idea preyed on her mind. On 29 October, she wrote: 'Still trying to forget <u>Nellie's BED-SIT</u> wish (23rd OCT.)', and when Nellie telephoned on Friday, 6 November, Auntie May wrote 'she did not mention bed-sitting room this time'.

•

Auntie May's eyes were getting worse. She kept seeing coloured lights and patterns before them, and on 7 November it got so bad that she 'had to stop trying to write'. She was also having problems with her pendant alarm: she kept leaning against it and setting it off by mistake. On Sunday, 8 November, after she pressed it by accident for the seventh time, she made a protective cover for it out of 'A soup packet & a clothes peg'. On 21 November, she mislaid her keys and spent the next two days looking for them.

On the morning of 3 December, she pressed her emergency pendant button by accident again. At about 3.15pm, Sylvia came to walk the dog, bringing Auntie May a present — a pink and red scarf that her mother had knitted for her. Mr Jarvis, who had been working on the stairs, riddled the Rayburn before leaving at 5pm. Auntie May put her empty milk bottles on the doorstep at the east end of the house.

Diary number 440 ends half-way through the following day. Mr Jarvis is finishing off the stairs. She gives him a cup of coffee at 11am. She has lunch at 1.15. At about 1.30, she telephones Leftley's to place a shopping order. The entry is at the bottom of the last page of the book. For a few weeks, she carried on writing increasingly illegible notes on the back of dog tin labels, but if she copied them into a final diary, I haven't found it.

I do, however, have a good idea of what happened in the last few months of her life, because it was witnessed by many visitors to Ware Hall-House. Christine Abel and Sylvia Yarham continued to keep an eye on May and help her look after Muttley; the Terringtons called in to make sure that all was well; the Leftleys continued to make grocery deliveries and personal visits. On most days, Mr Jarvis was there, doing various building and repair jobs, and generally doing his best to make May comfortable. Having fitted the Rayburn, he had realised how much she had come to rely on him and had taken her under his generous wing. 'She reminded me of my old mum,' he told me later. But Auntie May, alas, continued to be a difficult person to help. Realising that she was sleeping in a chair, Mr Jarvis cleared a space upstairs and began to build and furnish a bedroom for her, but she wouldn't sleep in it. He told me that when he showed it to her, all she said was that the carpet he had put down didn't belong in that room and that she couldn't sleep there anyway, as it was the guest room.

In March 1993, Tony and I took Auntie May's Dutch cousin, Mies, to visit her. Mies was about the same age as Auntie May, but by then, Auntie May was looking very much older. I hadn't seen Auntie May since the previous summer, when she had been bright and cheerful, but now, she looked sad, listless and weak. The grey hair that peeped out from under her headscarf was matted. Her skin was dry and looked dirty. She moved slowly and was clearly in pain. She invited us into the kitchen, so that we could sit in front of the Rayburn.

I have a sad and vivid memory of the scene. I remember her opening the fire-box, picking up a fragment of a rotten oak beam from the wood basket and setting it on the feebly glowing ashes in the grate. We sat there, surrounded by coats, jackets and dresses on hangers suspended from nails in the beams of the ceiling: the headless ghosts of Auntie May's past. The room was impossibly cluttered, even by Auntie May's standards. Every surface was covered in piles of empty jars and cans. I got out my daughter's wedding photographs. As I passed the photos to her, one by one, she peered at them. I noticed that her glasses were filthy. I wondered whether to offer to clean them for her, but feared she might take offence. She looked at a dozen or so pictures and made a comment on them; then, as she paused over one of them, we realised she had fallen asleep.

I remember thinking that she looked as if she was dying. Her face, her hair, her eyes, the pain she couldn't conceal, the clutter over which she had finally lost control – everything about her said: 'This is the end.' In the car on the way home, none of us felt like speaking. Mies broke the silence. 'Don't cry, Christine,' she said. 'May's not unhappy.' But all three of us knew that wasn't true.

CHAPTER EIGHTEEN

The Final Catastrophe

In which I describe the events surrounding
Auntie May's death

The catastrophe the doctor had foretold several years earlier came the very next day, and it was not minor. Auntie May was trying to light the paraffin stove in the great hall. It was cold, and she had arthritis in her fingers: she dropped a match. The floorboards under the stove must have been soaked by countless paraffin spills over the years and they caught fire immediately. She tried to beat out the flames with a towel, but they quickly spread. I know exactly what happened, because as luck would have it, Mr Jarvis was working upstairs at the time. He told me he heard May shriek and saw the flames through the gaps in the floorboards. He rushed down, ushered her into the garden and dialled 999.

When the firemen arrived, they couldn't get through the door with all their gear on. They smashed a window and threw out as much junk as they could in order to get in. When they reached the kitchen, they put out the flames quite quickly. Auntie May, meanwhile, was looking lost at the bottom of her garden, surrounded by brambles and nettles, clutching the collar of Muttley, who was barking furiously.

Meanwhile, an ambulance appeared. There was a nurse on

board, who spent a long time persuading Auntie May that she really needed to go to hospital, 'just for a check-up'. Shocked, frightened and exhausted, Auntie May finally gave in. Mr Jarvis assured her he would make sure the house and dog were looked after, and off she went.

The hospital told Nellie, who was her next of kin, but they passed on her instruction that nobody else was to be told, so Tony and I knew nothing of all this for nearly two weeks. We had a long-standing arrangement with Mr Jarvis that he would let us know if Auntie May ever needed us, but on the day of the accident, she had made him promise not to tell anyone what had happened. But when he visited her in the Wells Cottage Hospital, he could see how quickly she had declined, and he telephoned Tony and me to let us know. Poor Mr Jarvis! He clearly felt awful about breaking his word to Auntie May, who had trusted him so totally. But I am very glad he did.

I drove up to Wells immediately. Auntie May looked better than I had feared – better, indeed, than when I had seen her the day before the accident. At last, somebody was looking after her. She was propped up in a bed with fresh, white sheets, her ulcerated legs under a protective cage. Her eyes seemed small and sunken, but her skin was moist and waxy – almost translucent. Her hair had been washed and cut. She pushed it from her face with the back of her hand as she spoke.

The doctors hadn't told me what was wrong with her – she had forbidden them. When I asked her directly, she said that she was 'fine' and just needed a bit of a rest. It was obvious that this wasn't true, but I allowed myself to hope. I booked myself into the Normans Hotel and visited Auntie May daily until the end of the week. She had never been an easy person to chat to, but now, she seemed to drop her defences and began to tell me little stories from her past. I remember how when I mentioned the name of Polly's Polish husband, which was Kossowicz, she corrected my pronunciation. 'No! Not "Kossowicks", "Kossoff-itch". Like David Kossoff, the actor. He worked with me in De Havilland's, you know. We were good friends. He used to draw little cartoons in the margins of my technical drawings,' she said. When I told her that Tony and I had been on holiday in Wales and had visited the fairytale seaside village built by a famous architect, I couldn't remember the name of the place – but Auntie May came straight out with it: 'Portmeirion,' she said. 'Built by Clough Williams Ellis.' However ill she might have been, her mind was still sharp.

The doctors said her condition was stable, so I felt it was OK to go home. It was just about the only time I ever did leave her knowing that she was comfortable and safe, but a couple of days later, the hospital telephoned to say that they thought I ought to come back, and come back quickly. They didn't say so, but when I got there, it was obvious: Auntie May was dying, and dying fast.

•

Auntie May's will told us precisely what to do with all her possessions, but said nothing at all about what she wanted done with her body. It seemed odd at the time, but I now see it as one of many signs of her selflessness. She was cremated locally and her ashes laid in her mother's grave in Pinner cemetery. Later, when I found that she had marked every anniversary of her mother's death in her diaries, I knew that we had done the right thing. Auntie May was at peace.

CHAPTER NINETEEN

Restored to Life

In which I describe what happened to the house – and
to me – after Auntie May's death

Tony and I spent the next six years working together on the house.
It wasn't easy. To begin with, we would leave our own cottage in
Cambridgeshire every Friday evening, spend the weekend in Wells
and return on Sunday night. Progress was slow. After we realised
that the project needed more time and more money spent on it, and
I gave up my teaching job and moved permanently into Ware Hall-
House, I became general gofer and dogsbody, preparer and
finisher. I plastered (not very flat, not very smooth, but with
mediaeval-looking results!). I cleared the tangled forest of the
garden. I ordered the building materials and made sure they were
ready for Tony when he turned up at the weekend to carry out the
heavier work. 'We didn't get the house,' he used to say. 'The house
got us.'

But it got us in different ways. I felt that I had to do more than
just finish the building – I had to carry on and complete Auntie
May's life. That was the meaning of the promise that I had made to
her on her deathbed, though I hadn't realised it at the time. For
me, it was a responsibility that became a joy. For Tony, though, it
was a burden that became increasingly irksome. Looking back, I

can see why. He still had a full-time job. We had spent most of our married life rebuilding and renovating our own house and, at a time when we should have been thinking about retirement, he had been saddled with another one to restore – one that he didn't own, one that he hadn't chosen and one that he had many times said he didn't want.

Then there was the expense. In 1997, Tony said we needed to sit down and think about things. It no longer made sense for us to run two houses at once. Apart from anything else, we couldn't afford to. He suggested selling The Nook and buying a bachelor flat, but I saw it as a chance to do something more romantic – to buy a boat that we could both enjoy together. Tony agreed, and we bought a handsome vintage Dutch barge in Holland, sailed it around the Ijsselmeer and then eventually moored it at the Fish and Duck, near Ely. Tony lived on it during the week and joined me most weekends.

Then, out of the blue, he was made redundant. I thought this was wonderful – now, we could be together full time in Wells and moor our boat in the harbour. But it didn't work out like that. Shortly after he rejoined me full time in Ware Hall-House, I found out that he had been leading another life – a simpler, easier life that didn't involve the complexities that had been thrust upon him. He had another woman. When I found out, my world fell apart. I had been faithful to him for nearly 40 years. He had been my only love – my only real boyfriend since the age of fifteen. I had a nervous breakdown.

The Savidge sisters saved my sanity. I went to live with dear Nellie, who was then a widow in her mid-nineties. Tony had left us both and we looked after each other, finding solace in our mutual loss. I was never really quite sure who was helping whom, but we muddled through our traumas together and shared many thoughts and memories of May. They were very different characters. May could never part with anything; Nellie pared her possessions down to an absolute minimum. There was nothing in the house that wasn't used. There were two knives, two forks, and two spoons in the kitchen drawer. There were two cups, two saucers and two plates in the sideboard. There were two sets of sheets for each bed – one for use and one for the wash. Every tabletop and cupboard surface was clear of clutter. Nellie and May were poles apart in character, but I came to realise that they were poles of the same planet. They were both obsessive about *things* – May couldn't part with them and Nellie wouldn't be burdened with them. Now, I wonder whether this reflects their damaged childhood – the poverty that followed the death of their father, the succession of lodging houses that were never their own home, the loss of the family furniture and possessions . . . does this explain their obsessiveness? I can only guess. I was with Nellie for just a year before she developed cancer and died. I was heartbroken. She was like a second mother to me.

I returned to Wells and began my task again in earnest, converting my anger at what had happened to me into energy that I used in hard work. Friends and family rallied round. They helped me to landscape the garden: it now has a parterre, with four tonnes of slate chippings surrounding a little fountain. I helped to fit new bathrooms. They helped to build an extension – an orangery. It wasn't part of May's original plan, but I would like to think she would be pleased by it – it's a little bit of me that I wanted to contribute to the house. When the time comes for the house to pass to my children, Daniel and Polly, no doubt they will add something of themselves, too. But the building will always be Auntie May's memorial and there are permanent reminders of her everywhere. The beams still have her marks upon them; her mends, where she cut out rotten wood and pegged in pieces she had cut with her own hands, still whisper her name.

The place is peaceful. Once, when people called at the front door, they were greeted by the snarling and growling of May's dog; now, they enter to the sound of an old-fashioned bell on a spring. They step into a corridor that is no longer crammed with jam jars, furniture and boxes, but is an airy passage some 30ft in height. Above it, they see a galleried landing with a ladder-stair to the attic floor, where I now store most of May's boxes and trunks.

Downstairs, two mahogany doors open onto the great hall, with heavy beams and an inglenook fireplace. Half the room is filled with a grand boardroom table. I am sitting at it now. Under it, my feet are touching more of May's boxes – the ones that contain the diaries and papers I have used in writing this book. On the far side of the room, a door leads to what used to be the bakery. The space is now a hall, utility room and bathroom, but the shop window is still there. It used to stand on the narrow pavement of the main road in Ware, with traffic rushing by, but now it overlooks an ancient apple tree in a sleepy garden, where the only sounds are birdsong and the buzzing of bees. The house has retired, and is quiet and contented at last.

A few years ago, an elderly lady and her son knocked on the front door and introduced themselves. She told me she had lived above the bakery when newly married. I invited them in for tea, and when we stood in what had been her old bedroom, she told me that the window had overlooked the cobbled courtyard of the pub next door. Now, you see a moss-covered folly that we built to look like the ruins of a mediaeval monastery. The son asked if Auntie May had found any marbles when she had dismantled the house. She had: a whole jarful. He and his brother had played marbles in their bedroom, he said, and had lost many between the floorboards and the ceiling below. 'Was there a red one?' he said. There was.

Past the inside balcony is my own bedroom, which was originally the 'solar', the sleeping area of the mediaeval house. It has a large, arched, leaded window that we found in the garden. Another bedroom is behind a secret door in a false bookcase. People say it contributes to the fairytale feel of the house. I suppose it does. The windows do, too. They are all of different shapes, sizes and ages. Sometimes, it seems as if the house hasn't been frozen in time, but has frozen time itself. There are mirrors everywhere – I wanted to bring in more light – and in many places it is difficult to tell what is real from what is reflected. A bed-and-breakfast guest making a return visit said she had half expected to follow the wall down the lane to find that there was no longer a gate in it and that her first stay had happened in a dream.

The house certainly has its own personality. It even has its own voice, but it is a voice that has mellowed. When the wind blew, the frame would rock and the oak joints would let out creaking, graunching squeaks; I haven't heard them since we stabilised it by building internal buttresses. One or two windows still leak, including the skylight that Auntie May made from old fish boxes. But I live with it. Auntie May's copper jugs and preserving pans catch the plinking, plonking drips. On wet days, soft music made by rainwater plays gently through the house.

Most visitors catch their breath as they come through the front door. When the BBC's *Antiques Roadshow* came to Norfolk in May 2006, I invited them to come and see a piece of her furniture, a desk with a connection to the American author Mark Twain. They sent antiques expert Paul Atterbury to look at it, but when I opened the door to him, he said: 'Never mind the desk, what about the house?' He was bowled over by what he saw and persuaded me to appear on the show to tell Auntie May's story. Later, he chose Ware Hall-House as his 'favourite find' in a *Roadshow* special broadcast in 2007.

On each occasion, letters from viewers flooded in. Some came from people who had known Auntie May when she lived in Ware, or had met her after her move to Wells – they were all proud to have met or known her and wanted to share their memories. Since then, as the programmes are shown in country after country, a stream of letters from overseas have been arriving. So many came that I wondered whether I should be replying to them all. I rang the programme's secretary for advice. 'What do people do when this happens?' I asked. 'Well,' she said, 'it doesn't, usually.'

But then Auntie May was an unusual character. Tony had been wrong when he had accused me of turning into her. I couldn't have endured what she had put up with – living through all those winters in the leaky shell of a house in which the temperature fell below freezing for weeks at a time; never getting a full night's sleep in a bed, but dozing fitfully in a chair; living on a diet of bread, bananas, packet soup and biscuits; suffering constant pain from ulcers that never healed, without complaining – no, I could never do that. I can't think of anyone who could. The only other people that I can think of who might have put up with such things were the ancient saints. The difference, I suppose, is that those saints went out of their way to find suffering; Auntie May just encountered it and coped. I think that makes her pretty saintly, too.

Now that I am at the end of telling her story, I find myself thinking of so many things that I haven't mentioned. Many of them would warrant a chapter in their own right. I haven't described the tin box containing snippets of the black and white films in which Denis Elliot Watson had acted. I haven't told the story of the 'Cupie' doll: Nellie had owned it when a child and had thrown it away after it had been broken. May rescued it and kept it, and Nellie next saw it ninety years later. I haven't said anything about the antique paraffin projector with a whole set of Victorian missionaries' slides illustrating the perils of the demon drink – where did that come from? I haven't described the four ancient typewriters, the collection of nineteenth-century Valentine's cards, the chocolate boxes filled with sets of cigarette cards, the silk-tied Chinese books of woodcuts of birds, animal and insects, or the suitcases filled with fragments of antique Dutch lace. I haven't written of Auntie May's friendship – was it more? – with Captain Ricketts, the sailor, who died of flu in 1953. I haven't mentioned finding and trying on a trunkful of beautiful nineteenth-century dresses and discovering that they fitted me perfectly. I haven't described my pleasure at finding the very dress worn by Auntie May's friend Emily, in the portrait that hangs in the cross-passage, or my delight when, years later, I came across the necklace that she wore in it, too. And there's something else I haven't said that I should have: I haven't said how much I owe to Auntie May. I'll say it now.

Auntie May: your building project gave me a real sense of purpose when I desperately needed one. Retracing the steps of your life rekindled mine. Reading your diaries and going through your possessions, there were times when what I found made me weep; but there were also times when I could almost feel you pulling at my sleeve, inviting me to look here, or there, and see the many fascinating things that you valued and stored away so long ago. It seems a lifetime ago that I was standing by your bedside, pledging to do whatever you had left to be done. Your house is calm now: it's warm, and it's comfortable. Your task is complete – and now, so is mine. Your last word to me was 'Sorry'. It shouldn't have been. I want my last words to you to be 'Thank you'.

Index

ARWYN
THOMAS

MWY NAG UN LLWYFAN

Yn gyflwynedig i Alun Jones a wnaeth
roi trefn ar y gyfrol, yn ogystal â rhoi sawl
cic i'r bwced cyn i'r anifail glywed.

ARWYN
THOMAS
MWY NAG UN LLWYFAN

Argraffiad cyntaf: 2021

Dymuna'r cyhoeddwyr gydnabod cymorth ariannol
Cyngor Llyfrau Cymru

Llun y clawr blaen: Rhianedd Fernando
Cynllun y clawr: Y Lolfa

Rhif Llyfr Rhyngwladol: 978 1 80099 116 3

Cyhoeddwyd, rhwymwyd ac argraffwyd yng Nghymru gan
Y Lolfa Cyf., Talybont, Ceredigion SY24 5HE
gwefan www.ylolfa.com
e-bost ylolfa@ylolfa.com
ffôn 01970 832 304
ffacs 832 782

Cynnwys

Cyflwyniad

Mae hunangofiant yn dibynnu cymaint ar yr hyn sy'n fyw yn y cof, neu wedi ei gadw ar glawr yn rhywle, felly rwy'n ymwybodol bod bylchau a bod llawer o hanesion ar goll. Felly, ymddiheuraf i chi'r darllenwyr sy'n cofio am hanesion eraill nad ydynt wedi eu cynnwys.

Diolch i Jim Parc Nest am y cywydd unigryw ac am bori drwy'r gyfrol. Hefyd i'm cyn-ddisgybl Nigel Owens am ei eiriau caredig di-garden. Mae angen diolch hefyd i Rhianedd, fy merch, am lwyddo i greu portread i'w osod ar glawr y gyfrol, un y gallaf fod yn falch ohono.

Hoffwn ddiolch i Lefi o wasg y Lolfa am ddangos hyder yn y gyfrol ac am benderfynu ei chyhoeddi. Diolch i bawb yn y wasg am eu gwaith manwl a gofalus a hefyd am fod mor ddiffwdan.

Yn olaf, diolch i'r Cyngor Llyfrau am eu nawdd.

Mwynhewch!

CYWYDD CYFLWYNIAD

Cof Arwyn y cyfarwydd,
yr actor a'r athro rhwydd
ei wers hiwmor, sy' yma.
Swydd ddi-dwyll hanesydd da
fu'i faes, ac fe safai e
dros ethos iach Y Pethe.

Mor enwog yw ym Mronwydd
am ddod yn Fotham ei ddydd;
o'i law, saetha'i bêl ar lain
griced yn fwled filain
heibio i'r bat, nes bo'r bêl
yn rheibio'r stwmps yn rwbel.

Ac yma, mae ef hefyd
wrth ei fodd gan rith o fyd
mewn dramâu'n ymwneud â'r myth
ddatgêl ddeutu gwehelyth,
ar oleddf o'r lleddf i'r llon,
rhwng hwyl a thorri 'nghalon.

Ei gamp oedd ei Estragon,
rhyw greadur â'i gredo'n
ei gynnal rhwng gwamalrwydd
rhoi'i drasi-gomig i'n gŵydd,
neu ildio'n gudd i faldod
â'i dduw, fydd o hyd ar ddod.

Jim Parc Nest

8

Cyflwyniad Nigel

Fel cyn-ddisgybl a chyn-aelod o'r staff ym Maes-yr-yrfa, rwy'n teimlo hi'n fraint cael ysgrifennu cyflwyniad i'r prifathro a oedd yno ar y pryd, Arwyn Thomas. Wedi i fi dreulio blwyddyn yn Ysgol Ramadeg y Gwendraeth symudes i Ysgol Gyfun Maes-yr-yrfa, a oedd yn cynnig addysg drwy gyfrwng y Gymraeg. Mynd gyda fy ffrindie wnes i, a dweud y gwir, ond wnes i ddim difaru dim achos i Ysgol Maes-yr-yrfa rwy'n ddyledus am beth bynnag rwy i 'di llwyddo i'w gyflawni yn y 'mywyd cyhoeddus hyd yn hyn. Fel disgybl, roedd 'da fi'r ddawn i wneud drygioni a chreu doniolwch, ond buodd Arwyn Thomas a gweddill y staff yn deg iawn wrth fy nhrin.

Wedi darllen y gyfrol hon sylweddolais fod un peth yn gyffredin iawn rhyngddo i a'r prifathro a hynny oedd mwynhau gallu dynwared. Dynwared 'y dyn sâl' fel y byddai Ifan Gruffydd yn ei wneud oedd fy arbenigedd i, yn ogystal â dynwared ambell athro yn yr ysgol! Ces i sioc wrth ddarllen y gyfrol hon bod Arwyn Thomas yntau hefyd yn dynwared pobol pan oedd e'n ifanc ac wrth ei fodd yn gwneud. Rwy'n ddiolchgar iawn i'r ysgol ac i'r adran Ddrama yn arbennig am greu a chynnal fy niddordeb yn y pwnc a rhoi cyfle i fi berfformio.

Pan es i 'nôl i'r ysgol ym mis Medi ar ôl sefyll fy arholiadau TGAU i ailsefyll rhai pynciau digwyddai'r prifathro fod mewn tipyn o drafferth ar y pryd, gan y byddai'r gofalwr yn mynd i'r ysbyty am driniaeth ac roedd yn rhaid cael gofalwr cyn gallu agor yr ysgol. Ces gynnig y swydd dros dro ganddo. Ymhen rhyw flwyddyn wedyn ces gynnig swydd arall yn yr ysgol fel technegydd, yn gyfrifol am y gwasanaeth llungopïo ac am yr adnoddau technegol. Wedi derbyn y swydd honno byddwn i wedyn yn hala athrawon i 'wherthin yn hytrach na'u hala nhw'n benwan! Ond, ddiflannodd mo'r elfen ddrygionus yna yndda i pan ddes i'n aelod o staff yr ysgol. Ie, rhaid cyfadde mai fi a'r gofalwr, Robert Sams oedd yn gyfrifol am gloi'r athrawon yn ystafell yr athrawon ar ôl ysgol un noson, ond wedyn buodd yn rhaid i fi dalu am hynny wrth gael fy nal ar ddiwrnod ffŵl Ebrill yn siop Leeks yn Cross Hands, fel y cewch ddarllen yn y gyfrol. Roedd y cyfnod hwnnw'n un hapus dros ben gan ei bod hi'n ysgol mor gartrefol, diolch yn rhannol i'r prifathro, Arwyn Thomas. Mae'n bosibl taw fan'na fyddwn i heddiw pe na bai dyfarnu wedi mynd â 'mryd.

Rwy'n siŵr y cewch chi wrth ddarllen y gyfrol hon, fel y ces i, gyfle i ddod i nabod y gwir Arwyn Thomas a dod i sylweddoli gymaint o ddoniau sydd ganddo. Cewch hefyd gyfle i werthfawrogi ei ffraethineb wrth iddo adrodd yr hanesion a digwyddiadau doniol y bu'n rhan ohonyn nhw yn ystod ei fywyd a mwynhau ei ddawn dweud wrth bortreadu rhai cymeriadau brith a gyfarfu.

Nigel Owens

Byd Mebyd

Pant-y-Fedwen, Nebo

Mae'n debyg mai gwanwyn 1942 oedd hi, ynghanol cyfnod yr Ail Ryfel Byd, pan symudon ni fel teulu o Bant-y-Fedwen yn Nebo i Bantglas. Bellach ro'n ni rhyw ddau gan troedfedd yn is o ran uchder, ac wedi cyfnewid hewl unffordd Rufeinig am hewl brysurach o'r Bronwydd i gyfeiriad Llanpumsaint. Rhyw frith gof sydd 'da fi o'r diwrnod mowr, hanesyddol hwnnw yn fy mywyd. O'n i'n eistedd yng nghanol pentwr o drugaredde mewn gambo'n cael ei thynnu gan geffyl, ar hewl fach yn arwain o gyfeiriad ffarm Penllwynuchel tua chapel Nebo. Cofiaf edrych dros y clawdd ar y chwith i'r cae, a thu hwnt iddo gan edrych yn ôl tua'r cartre cynta, lle ces fy ngeni, sef Pant-y-Fedwen. Tebyg iawn 'mod i'n ymwybodol felly, fod rhywbeth tyngedfennol ar droed. Rhaid 'mod i wedi cwmpo i gysgu'n weddol fuan wedyn, achos alla i ddim cofio cyrraedd sgwâr Nebo hyd yn oed, heb sôn am weld y capel, na'r siop, na'r hewl fowr. Does 'da fi ddim atgof chwaith am gyrraedd Pantglas, na dringo'r hewl fach, serth tua'r clos caregog. Chofia i ddim am gyrraedd y tŷ, y noson gynta, na thrannoeth chwaith. Ond 'na fe, rhaid 'mod i wedi blino'n lân ar ôl yr holl gynnwrf.

Er y bwlch hynny, erys rhai delweddau cadarn o'm pedair blynedd gyntaf yn y Pant, fel y gelwid Pant-y-Fedwen ar lafar gwlad. Anodd yw gosod trefn ar atgofion cynnar bywyd. Yn weddol ifanc, prin dwy flwydd oed falle, cofio sefyll i fyny

11

ar y sgiw yn y gegin fach a Mam yno yn gofalu amdanaf. Es yn ormod o foi, mae'n debyg, ac wrth i fi siglo 'nôl a mlân fe dipiodd cefen y sgiw drosodd a 'nhaflu'n un twmpath ar lawr. Mae'r sioc a'r sgrechen yn aros yn y cof!

Cofio'n dda am Mam yn gwneud menyn yn y gegin fach. Siglo wrth droi llond budde o hufen nes i'w breichiau wynegu o dan y pwysau, cyn i'r eiliad hirddisgwyliedig gyrraedd. Y fydde yn trymhau'n sydyn wrth i lwmpyn mawr o fenyn ffurfio a'r hufen, o'r diwedd wedi troi'n fenyn. Wedyn, clywed sŵn clatsio wrth i Mam dowlu'r menyn o'r naill law i'r llall, i'w waredu o bob diferyn o laeth enwyn, cyn ei lunio yn batrymau deniadol, sgwâr. Yna, byddai'n cyrraedd y ford o'r diwedd a chael ei daenu'n gyfoethog dros doc o fara. 'Na chi flas hyfryd! Un diwrnod, roedd hi'n fisi wrthi'n gwneud pancws ac fe ddyfeisies i gynllun bach eitha cyfrwys, os ca i ddweud. Pan o'dd hi wedi troi ei chefen ac yn wynebu'r tân, miwn â fi'n gloi i'r gegin yn nhraed 'yn sane a sgwlcan un bant o'r ford. Aeth un bancwsen yn ddwy, ac wedyn yn llawer mwy, ac yn ormod. Cymaint fu'r trachwant nes iddyn nhw droi ar 'yn stumog i, a digon cyfoglyd fu blas pancws am hanner fy oes wedyn. Erbyn heddi wy'n gallu mwynhau un neu ddwy, ond dim mwy. Dysgais fy ngwers.

O ymweld â'r Pant heddi, mae adfeilion yr hen Bant i'w gweld yn glir y tu draw i'r bont bren dros y nant fechan yno. Ar un adeg bu yna deuluoedd yn byw yn y ddau le, ond dw i ddim yn siŵr ai yn yr hen Bant y gwnaeth 'Nhad a Mam gychwyn eu bywyd priodasol, neu yn y Pant sy'n bodoli heddiw.

Roedd fy mrodyr, Jac a Donald yn eu harddegau bryd hynny, hwythau bedair blynedd ar ddeg yn hynach na fi. Cofio eu gwylio nhw'n cario gwair rhydd i'r boudy o'r sied wair ar waelod y clos mewn llywanen, sef sach agored wedi ei lapio o amgylch y porthiant. Un diwrnod, cafodd Donald gwt gwaedlyd ar ei goes wrth ddefnyddio'r gyllell dorri gwair, teclyn o'dd i fi'n edrych yn hynod o beryglus. O'dd dim angen fy siarsio i gadw draw yn ddigon pell oddi wrth honno wedyn.

Ar un diwrnod felly, wrth i fi wylio Donald yn croesi'r clos â llywanen ar i gefen yn y Pant, sylwais yn sydyn fod dieithriaid yn cyrraedd. Fe'u gweles yn agosáu ar y llwybr cyhoeddus ar draws y cae o gyfeiriad Ffosmaen. Fel arfer dim ond fy mrodyr yn dod gatre o bentre Llanpumsaint neu Tomos Bowen, y postman, ar i rownds, fydde'n ymddangos o'r cyfeiriad hwnnw. Cyrhaeddai bob cart a cheffyl ar yr hewl gefen o gyfeiriad yr hen ffordd Rufeinig, naill ai o Nebo, neu lan y rhiw heibio Bwlchyronnen o'r Cwpers. Roedd yna hefyd ffordd gart o Bantiouar, a honno oedd y ffordd droed agosa i fynd i gapel Nebo, neu'n bwysicach i ni, i'r siop fach yn Nebo, er nad oedd fawr o ddim ynddi ar werth adeg y rhyfel.

Ond pwy o'dd y bobol ddierth 'ma, yn cerdded yn ansicr dros y caeau o Ffosmaen? Er eu bod nhw'n cerdded miwn i'r gwynt, eto i gyd cyrhaeddodd eu lleisiau o'u blaen nhw. Wrth iddyn nhw nesáu at iet y clos, a'r lleisiau erbyn hyn dipyn yn gliriach, sylweddoles nad o'n i'n gallu deall gair o beth o'dd yn ca'l 'i weud. 'Germans!' medde Donald, fy mrawd yn gellweirus. Ond na, fe wyddwn yn syth mai celwydd o'dd hynny, oherwydd ro'dd rhain yn siarad yn yr un ffordd â'r dyn ar y set radio Marconi ar seld y gegin. Ac er nad o'wn i'n deall dim gair o'r hyn fydde'n ca'l ei ddweud ar y radio, gwyddwn yn iawn nad o'dd y dyn bach ynddi yn hoffi Germans o gwbwl. Er gwaethaf ymdrech fy mrawd i'm drysu, rown i wedi llwyddo i ddehongli'r sefyllfa'n gywir, ac felly yn cwrdd â phobl yn siarad Saesneg am y tro cynta. Yn camu'n bryderus i glos Pant-y-Fedwen ro'dd Mari Horn a'i mam – Ifaciwîs o swydd Caint yn Lloegr, ble bynnag oedd hynny.

Brith yw'r atgofion eraill yn ystod fy nghyfnod yn y Pant. Cymdogion yn cyrraedd am swper ac yn aros yn hwyr i siarad a chloncan, a finnau'n cael fy anfon i'r gwely. Fydden nhw ddim yn gadael tan ei bod hi'n ymddangos i fi'n berfeddion nos. Daeth rhywrai i ware darts gyda 'mrodyr ryw noson, a'r Bwrdd wedi ei osod i hongian ar ddrws y gegin fach. Des inne miwn yn sydyn a derbyn darten ar fy nhalcen, fodfedd uwchlaw fy llygad dde, ond yn wyrthiol rown i'n ddianaf a di-boen. Lwcus! Galle hi fod yn lot gwath, a dyna'r cynta o'r troeon lwcus yn ystod fy mywyd. Yn ddiweddar iawn, ces gopïau o hen luniau'n dyddio o'r tridegau wedi eu tynnu adeg cywain gwair yn y Pant. Mae llun o Modryb Bet a Mam-gu wrthi'n rhacano gwair yn gofnod o fywyd cefn gwlad hamddenol y cyfnod. Yno hefyd ro'dd llun pwysig arall o 'Nhad o flaen yr iet yng nghwmni'r ci a 'mrodyr y tu ôl iddo. Dyma'r unig lun a welais erioed o 'Nhad ac ynte'n ddyn ffit a chyhyrog. Mae'r holl atgofion amdano ar ffarm Pantglas yn un o ŵr tost a fu farw'n ifanc yn 1946.

Pantglas

Pan fu farw fy mrawd hynaf Jac daeth y cyfrifoldeb am y ffarm i'm dwylo i. Ar wahân i adnewyddu'r tŷ bron yn gyfan gwbwl, dyma fi'n creu llyn a pherllan i'r dde o'r ydlan. Atgofion plentyndod cynnar fu'r anogaeth i wneud hynny, oherwydd cofiaf yn glir iawn mor atyniadol oedd y llyn gwreiddiol i fachgen bach fel fi. I'r dde o'r ydlan roedd y llyn hwnnw ac arno hwyaid yn symud yn hamddenol ar ei draws gan fy nghyfareddu fel plentyn. O'r llyn llifai'r dŵr i lawr heibio cefen y storws i fwydo'r rhod ddŵr ger drws cefen y cartws. Y rhod fyddai'n creu'r pŵer i droi'r peiriannau yn y storws. Pan na fyddai digon o ddŵr i neud y gwaith bydde ceffyl yn cerdded mewn cylch i weithio'r peiriant tsaffo.

Ger mynedfa'r ydlan roedd dau dwlc mochyn. Ar ochor ogleddol y clos roedd y boudy godro – saif un wal o'r boudy o hyd yn gymorth i ddal y ffrwythau logan blasus sy'n tyfu yno. Yn y pedwardegau, oes y ceffyl oedd hi, a'r stabal i ddau ar waelod y boudy yn agos at fwlch y clos. Ond yna, daeth y Ffergi Fach yn y pumdegau, ac aeth y stabal yn rhan o'r boudy, a daeth rhan arall ohono'n gartref i'r peiriant cynhyrchu trydan. Cofiaf yn dda am drafferthion y peiriant hwnnw, a minnau'n adolygu neu yn darllen yn y gwely'n hwyr y nos, yn gorfod codi a mynd mas lawr i'r sied i droi'r peiriant bant. Gwellodd pethe pan ddaeth y peiriant nesa, gan y bydde hwnnw'n stopio ei hunan wrth i'r golau olaf ga'l ei ddiffodd. Ond hyd yn oed wedyn, ambell waith bydde rhywun wedi anghofio troi switsh y gole bant mewn rhyw gwt rhywle ar y clos. Gorfod codi wedyn i weld lle roedd y gole hwnnw cyn cael heddwch. O 'na nefoedd geson ni pan gyrhaeddodd y cyflenwad trydan canolog!

Rhedai'r cyflenwad dŵr bron chwarter milltir ar yr wyneb, o darddiant cryf allan o'r graig. Enw'r cae ar fap y degwm 1840 yw cae Ffynnon Teilo – ro'dd dŵr sanctaidd 'da ni siŵr o fod felly! Trefnwyd i'r dŵr redeg drwy'r boudy er mwyn hwyluso cadw'r gwartheg yn lân a chymen. Er, yn y dyddiau cynnar hynny, bydde Mam yn ein gorfodi i 'nôl ein dŵr yfed o bistyll yn yr allt islaw mynedfa Parce. O'dd hi'n dipyn o faich cario llond stên drom bob cam lan yr hewl fach i dŷ Pantglas.

Uwchben cefen y tŷ roedd yna ardd ffrwythlon sy'n dal fel 'ny hyd heddi. Wrth yr ardd roedd ardal yr ieir, y Rhode Island Reds a'r Brown Leghorns gan mwyaf, yn clwydo'n saff rhag y cadnoid mewn tair sied ffowls. Roedd yr hewl fach a'r clos yn garegog dros ben, gyda chraig yn amlwg rhwng y boudy a'r cartws. Ger mynedfa'r clos roedd coeden gastanwydden enfawr a phlannais un arall yn yr union fan ddeng mlynedd yn ôl.

Dyna'r hen Bantglas cyn i Mam brynu'r lle a chychwyn gwelliannau di-ri. Rhoddwyd tar ar yr hewl a'r clos ar ddechrau'r pumdegau a daeth yr adeiladwr Dai Llain a Handel y plastrwr drygionus i ail neud y tŷ. Yna, yn eu tro, daeth peirannau godro a nifer o welliannau eraill yn sgil y trydan canolog a ddaeth erbyn 1960.

Ysgol Llanpumsaint a chymdeithasu

Dwy filltir a thri chwarter oedd hi o Bantglas i ddrws ysgol Llanpumsaint. Shwd ydw i mor siŵr o hynny? Yn 1945 penderfynwyd cario pob disgybl oedd yn byw tair milltir neu fwy mewn tacsi yn rhad ac am ddim i'r ysgol. Er mesur fwy nag unwaith gwrthodai Pantglas fod yn fwy na dwy filltir a thri chwarter, felly ro'n i tu fas i'r cynllun mawr newydd. Bydde tacsi Dai Bedw yn paso fi ar y ffordd rhywle lan rhiw Graig ac Alfie Wern, oedd yn byw dair milltir a chwarter o'r ysgol, yn codi dau fys arna i drwy ffenest gwt y tacsi wrth baso bob bore, ac yn codi lot mwy o fysedd ychwanegol pan fydde hi'n bwrw glaw! Ond 'na fe, collodd e lot o sbri'r cerdded cymdeithasol yn ôl a mlân i'r ysgol.

Mae'r daith gynta 'na i'r ysgol yn dal yn gofiadwy glir. Cerdded 'da Mam ac wrth baso'r Hendy ger Cnwcypistyll daeth Mam-gu mas ac fe dorrodd y ddwy mas i lefen. Rhaid bod yr ysgol hyn yn beth ofnadw, meddylies i, ond wrth lwc a'th pethe'n iawn yno, ta beth. Gweld stôf fawr ar ganol ystafell ddysgu'r Babanod a Miss Defis yn ein trin a'n trafod mor neis. Ond, digwyddodd trychineb yn eitha cloi wedyn, wrth i bawb dorri mas i lefen pan wedon nhw wrthon ni bod Miss Defis yn symud lan i Bencader i ddysgu.

Bu cerdded i'r ysgol yn brofiad digon hapus. Lan y rhiw o Pantglas i gwrdd â Tomi Bryncene a chwarter milltir wedyn Dai Twm, Ffynnonfelen, dau o ffrindie bore oes. Cyrraedd gwastadedd Nebo wedyn ac ymuno â Marina a Dai Henry Lleine a wedyn Sulwen Ffynnon Newydd. Erbyn cyrraedd Bethoron, tŷ fy Anti Esther ac Is-Swyddfa Bost ardal Nebo, bydde criw ardal Nebo wedi cyrraedd wrth groesffordd Cnwcypistyll. Maen nhw'n rhy niferus i'w henwi i gyd, ond yn cynnwys Mair a Magi Bwlchtrap, Emlyn a Vernon, bois Penyrheol, merched a bois Llwyncroes, a rhagor o Penllwyniorwg a Phenllwynuchel. Rodd hi'n bleser wedyn mynd lawr y rhiw heibio Pant-y-Clun, a bydde merched erill, Beti Helfa Hall a Dilys Ffosmaen yn ymuno â ni.

Un nodwedd anghyffredin o bwysig wrth edrych yn ôl yw na fu yna erioed unrhyw elfen o fwlio, a wnaeth dim un o'r criw mawr 'ma godi ofon ar unrhyw un ohonon ni. Does 'da fi ddim cof am unrhyw ymladd drwy'r holl gyfnod. Ffaith a ategwyd gan Delme a symudodd i fyw i'r Pant wrth iddo sôn am y cyfarfodydd anffurfiol hapus ar nosweithiau Sadwrn neu Sul ar Sgwâr Cnwcypistyll. Gallaf gytuno wrth edrych yn ôl ar yr ymgynnull bach nosweithiol answyddogol ym mhentref Llanpumsaint yn ogystal, wrth y goeden fowr neu o dan bont y Railway. Ffaith bwysig iawn i'w chofnodi yn y dyddie hyn.

Fuon ni ddim yn cerdded bob cam yn hir. Er ei fod bellach yn byw yn y dre yng Nghaerfyrddin, magwyd John Williams, y postman, yn Llainwen, Banc Nebo, dyn teyrngar i'w ardal, ac yn haeddu bob clod 'da ni'r plant. Tua'r un amser ag y byddwn i'n cychwyn ar fy moreol daith, byddai'r fan goch yn dod heibio. Un bore a hithe'n pisho'r glaw, finne eitha gwlyb cyn cyrraedd Bryncene hyd yn oed, dyma John yn stopo a gweiddi 'Jwmpa miwn i'r gwt. Ti'n stecs, ond cofia, cadwa dy got bant oddi wrth bopeth rhag eu glwchu. Paid â glwchu'r llythyron na chwrdd yn yr un ohonyn nhw, er mwyn mowredd! A gofala bido symud un o'r parseli.' Whare teg, dw i'm yn credu i fi nag un o'r lleill dramgwyddo unwaith, cymaint ein parch at y gŵr caredig ac addfwyn hwn. Derbyniodd Tomi a Dai Twm yr un cyfarwyddiadau wrth iddynt hwythau ddringo miwn ata i. Aeth yn draddodiad wedyn, hyd yn oed mewn tywydd sych.

Bydde'r lifft yn cwpla ar sgwâr Nebo. Yno, godderbyn â'r blwch postio coch yn y clawdd, agorai drws y tŷ, a dyna ble byddai fy Anti Esther yn barod i dderbyn John miwn am i ddisgled o de boreol a bydde holl lythyron banc Nebo yn cael eu dadlwytho yno. Hi fyddai'n dosbarthu'r rhain i gyd wedyn ar i rownd wledig fydde'n cychwyn yn Bwlchtrap a gorffen ym Mhengraigyrystyn ac ambell lythyr hyd yn oed i Ddolgwm, yr ochor arall i'r hewl fowr yng Nghynwyl Elfed. Bydde'r fan fach goch yn rhy fach i lyncu holl blant Nebo, felly cerdded amdani. Ta beth, ro'dd hi'n rhwyddach mynd lawr rhiw am y pentre yng nghwmni criw mawr hapus o blant yr ardal. Plant heddychlon yn llawn sbri a drygioni iach.

Un bore Gwener, siarsiodd John y postmon ni na fydde fe'n dangos ei fod yn ein hadnabod ni o gwbwl ar fore Llun, oherwydd bydde'r Inspector gyda fe. Wrth i'r fan fynd hibo'r bore 'ny dyma Tomi a fi'n troi'n cefne at y cerbyd. Fel arfer bydde'r postman yn gadael llythyron y ffermydd mewn tshyrn wag ar y stondin lath, ond gan fod pethe'n swyddogol iawn y diwrnod hwnnw bu'n rhaid i'r fan fynd bob cam draw i glos Ffynnonfelen. Erbyn 'ny roedden ni ein dau wedi cwrdd â Dai Twm, a throiodd y tri ohonon ni ein cefne wrth i John a'r Inspector fynd heibio. Daeth hi'n gawod o law trwm yn sydyn a rhyw ganllath wedyn dyma'r cerbyd yn stopio gyda gwahoddiad i ni lithro miwn i'r gwt. Mae'n debyg i'r arolygydd craff ddarllen y sefyllfa a chyfarwyddo John. 'Stop! Let 'em in, otherwise they'll be sopping wet!'

Beics

Roedd y cyfarwyddiadau i ddyn post Ei Fawrhydi yn hollol glir o'r dechrau, ac wrth i lyged pobl y dre sbecian tua'r wlad, doth ymyrraeth yr awdurdodau yn 1945. Gwnaeth Post Brenhinol yn hollol glir nad oedd ei gerbydau i'w defnyddio at unrhyw ddefnydd arall heblaw am yr hyn a hysbyswyd yn fras mewn paent melyn ar goch ar eu hochrau, sef dosbarthu llythyron a pharseli. A dyna'r hoelen yn arch y liffts answyddogol. Bellach rhaid o'dd ffeindio ffyrdd ein hunain i Lanpumsaint ac felly bydde'n rhaid goddef 'to gweld cerbyd Dai Bedw yn ein pasio ddwywaith y dydd. Llawer gwath na 'ny o'dd gorfod byw 'da wynebau sbeitlyd a hunangyfiawn y plant oedd yn byw dros dair milltir o'r ysgol. Felly dyna pam ro'n i'n lot gwath fy myd yn 1945 nag o'n i cynt, a hynny i gyd er ein bod ni wedi ennill y rhyfel yn erbyn Hitler, yn ôl pob sôn.

Cyn hir trodd y gwynt drwg a fu'n hwthu mor gas arnon ni, yn fanteisiol ac ar ôl hir ymbil ar ein rhieni fe gethon ni'r plant a o'dd dros ddwy filltir o'r ysgol, bobo feic. Sicrhau bod y cynta yn ei ga'l o'dd bwysica, oherwydd yn ôl traddodiad cefn gwlad o efelychu ei gilydd, do'dd dim un rhiant am weld ei blentyn e heb feic pan o'dd pawb arall wedi ca'l un. Felly dyna gychwyn ar sawl blwyddyn o sbort a sbri ar gefen y beic. Daeth y daith o fynd a dod i Ysgol Llanpumsaint yn dipyn mwy anturus, lot o raso a chystadlu a herio ein gilydd. Ambell waith byddwn i'n cyrraedd gatre yn hwyrach na phan o'n i'n cerdded!

Y prif fan cyfarfod yn y bore ac ymwahanu yn y prynhawn o'dd sgwâr potsiar, sgwâr Cnwcypistyll, neu sgwâr Nebo, ger

Bethoron a'r Hendy. Fan'na bydde bois Nebo yn cyrraedd yr hewl fowr; Vernon ac Emlyn Tŷ Capel, John a Lewis Llwyncroes ac Arwyn Penllwynuchel. Gyda Dewi Brynawel, Dai Lleine, Dai Twm, Tomi a finne, yn llenwi'r sgwâr. A dweud y gwir o'dd hi'n debycach i'r *Tour de France* na gorllewin Cymru. Os bydde'r whant yn codi, neu os o'n ni'n rhedeg yn hwyr, bydde hi'n ras wyllt am filltir a hanner lawr y rhiw at Lanpumsaint, gyda'r uchafbwynt bob tro wrth i ni geisio cymryd y tro ar waelod rhiw Cwpers heb gyffwrdd yn y brêcs. Gan fod yn rhaid troi i'r dde yn siarp am yr ysgol ar waelod y rhiw serth a heb ddefnyddio'r brêcs, a'th llawer un i drybini. Ond gan fod y cloddie'n fwyn ac yn feddal wrth landio ar eu pennau ynddyn nhw, chath neb niwed mowr er y crafiadau a'r creithiau ar y pengliniau.

O fod yn berchen ar feic teimlem ein bod wedi sicrhau safle bwysig mewn cymdeithas o'r diwedd, fel tase'r beic yn rhywbeth byw fel ceffyl rasys. A dyma'r cyfrifoldeb mwya a'r drutaf a ddaeth i ran pob un ohonon ni wrth i ni orfod cymryd gofal drostynt. Flynyddoedd cyn hynny, ro'n ni i gyd wedi bod wrthi'n rhedeg cylch, yn llawn balchder ohono ac yn ymhyfrydu yn yr holl driciau ro'n ni wedi eu meistroli wrth eu rhedeg ar iard yr ysgol, neu ar yr hewl, neu ar y clos gartre. Ond peth bach pitw oedd cylch haearn o'i gymharu â beic oedd yn eiddo ac yn gyfrifoldeb ychwanegol i ni. Do'dd dim lot a alle fynd o'i le ar gylch o haearn a bachyn, ond gallai pethau di-ri fynd o'i le ar wahanol rannau o feic. Mawr o'dd y trafod gan feddygon doeth am anhwylderau corfforol beics ar sgwâr potsiar wrth i'r cyfnos ein hamgylchynu.

Dysgwyd nifer o driciau syrcasaidd a dyfeisgar, cario rhywun arall ar y bar, gosod un arall ar y sêt a woblo nôl a 'mlân. Dysgodd Dai Twm shwt i frecio gan wasgu darn o bren yn galed ar ben y teiar blaen; trïodd Tomi ei efelychu ond yn ei frwdfrydedd didoreth gwthiodd y pren yn rhy isiel ac i mewn i'r sbôcs. Aeth â'i din dros ei ben dros yr handlbars a lawr glatsh ar yr hewl, ond yn lwcus unwaith 'to, chafodd e ddim niwed mowr. A'th rhywun arall mor bell â throi sêt y beic rownd i wynebu am yn ôl, a cheisio ei farchogaeth sha mlân, rial boi syrcas! Do'dd dim diwedd ar ein dyfeisgarwch a'n stynts, reido drwy ddŵr glaw a thros afonydd ac ar hyd cwteri'n llond stecs a mwd.

Er i'r daith gatre, o ddringo 'nôl lan rhiw Cwpers, fod yn ddigon o her, penderfynwyd bod yn rhaid ei hymestyn ymhellach, unwaith. Ar ryw esgus gwanllyd o hebrwng Arwyn Waunyrhelfa gatre un prynhawn, dyma osgoi'r hewl arferol ac wynebu rhiw fwy serth o lawer, sef rhiw Llandre. Yn y dyddie hynny, un gêr yn unig o'dd 'da ni ar y beic ac felly gan fod rhiw Llandre mor serth, rhaid oedd cerdded a phwsio'r beic, gan bwyso arno'n drwm i ga'l anal. Wedi cyrraedd y gwastadedd ro'dd cyfle i reido drwy glos Penhill a chyrraedd Waunyrhelfa, cartref Arwyn. Wedyn, doedd dim hewl i'w dilyn i gyrraedd yn ôl at ein hewl arferol ni. Bu'n rhaid croesi'r caeau a chroesi afon Cerwyn cyn dod mas ar y ffordd fowr ger Ffosmaen er mwyn dilyn wedyn yr hewl arferol am gatre. Dyna un ffordd o gymhlethu bywyd wrth ddychwelid, ond nid dyna'r ffordd ore o ofalu am ein beics gwerthfawr!

Adeg y Rhyfel

A minnau yn oedolyn ac fel hanesydd yn canfod holl greulondeb a dioddefaint yr Ail Ryfel Byd, des i deimlo euogrwydd am i fi fod mor ddiniwed ynglŷn â'r hyn a ddigwyddai yn ystod fy mhlentyndod yn y blynyddoedd hynny. Rhywbeth pell oedd y Rhyfel wrth i fi glywed adroddiadau'n aml ar y radio yn Saesneg, heb eu deall. Yr unig brofiad anghyffyrddus fu cael ein gorfodi i wisgo'r gas masg yn yr ysgol un dydd a theimlo fy hunan yn mogi wrth wneud. Aeth yr hen beth yn syth i gefen y twll dan stâr gynted ag y cyrhaeddes i gatre ac yno cafodd e fod. Llawer hapusach oedd cael bathodyn am gasglu salfej. Wedyn gweld milwyr, Iancs, yn pwyso ar bont y pentre a'r bois hynna yn ein dysgu ni i weud, 'Any gum, Chum!' Pan ges gyfle ar daith gwylie, i sefyll ar yr union fan lle bu Hitler yn traddodi ei areithiau mawr yn Nuremburg, ro'dd y cylch yn grwn o'r diwedd. Ond ro'dd y gas masg wedi hen ddiflannu erbyn hynny.

Flynyddoedd wedyn bydde pobol yn cydymdeimlo â ni am na chawson ni deganau na ffrwythau yn blant. Do'dd dim sôn am fananas adeg y Rhyfel, ond os nad oeddech chi wedi eu gweld nhw erioed, yna doeddech chi ddim yn gweld eu hishe nhw wedyn. Do'dd 'na fyth brinder bwyd ar ein ffermydd gyda phawb yn cadw mochyn a ieir, a bydde digon o la'th gan y gwartheg i'w yfed ac i wneud menyn. Wrth gwrs bydde Mam yn crasu bara ac yn gwneud cacenne. Rhaid peidio anghofio bod yr ardd yn bwysig hefyd a bydde ynddi ddigon o lysie gogyfer ag amser cinio. Miwn yn y boudy yn gynnar un noson a'r teulu wrthi'n godro ymysg rhyw fân siarad y clywes i'r geirie pwysig: 'Ma nhw'n gweud bod y rhyfel drosto!' Felly, rhaid mai 1945 oedd hi.

Os nad o'wn i wedi teimlo'n ddifreintiedig adeg y Rhyfel fe ges i'r teimlad ychydig ar ôl hynny wrth i'r siarad fynd ar led fod bananas ac orennau ar eu ffordd. Disgrifiwyd sut y dylech chi flingo'r croen hir a melyn ac yna bydde cyfle i chi flasu'r peth hyfryd y tu fiwn. Wrth gwrs, bydde trafod mowr am ragoriaethau'r oren hefyd. Nawr, do'n i ddim wedi cael y profiad o flasu'r naill na'r llall a dyma ddechre teimlo'n ddifreintiedig. Ar fws Beehive, Pencader i'r dre un dydd Mercher, dyna i gyd o'dd y glonc. O'dd swae mas y bydde Taylor, dyn y ffrwythe yn y farced, yn derbyn cyflenwad o fananas. 'O, ma nhw mor ffein. Ond pidwch byta gormod,

neu ewch chi'n rhwym!' dyna oedd cyngor Jones wrth stopo
yn Halt Abergwili a bod hi'n well dag e flas oren. Anghytunai
Jennie Graig gan bledio achos y fanana.

Ymunon ni â'r ciw anferth rownd dau gornel y tu fas
i'r farced gyda Mam yn llawn gobaith y gwelai ei chrwt
bach hi fanana cyn diwedd y dydd. Heibio un cornel a nawr
yr hyder yn codi, ond arafu wnaeth y ciw cyn ail ddechre
symud wedyn. Rownd y cornel ola ac o fewn cyrraedd y
drws dyma stop sydyn a sibrwd anniddig ymhlith y rhai
o'n blân ni. Ro'dd 'na dwll bach yn un o'r hestyll, un digon
mowr i fi aller pipo drwyddo, a gallwn weld dyn y tu ôl i'r
cownter yn gweiddi a chwifio'i freichiau ar y bobol. Mae'n
debyg mai Mr Taylor o'dd yn datgan *All gone! Sold out!*'
'Nôl am y bws yn Sgwâr Potsiar (Elyston Square) a miwn
i ganol y tawelwch a'r siom. 'Falle bydde rhagor ar gael yr
wythnos nesa neu cyn pen y mis!' Dyna beth o'dd e wedi
ei weud. Dibynnu pryd dethe'r llong miwn i'r Barri. Pawb
â'u penne i lawr ar wahân i Marged Parce. O'dd 'na hanner
gwên ar ei hwyneb hi wrth iddi ddal yn dynn, dynn yn ei
basged siopa?

Cwningod

'Cer lan i Ca Cnwc a dere 'nôl â dwy lefret fach neis. Fi'n neud
cawl 'fory!' Cyfarwyddid a ddeuai'n amal o enau Mam yn
niwedd y pedwar a'r pumdegau. Cydio yn y dryll twelf bor a
bant â fi. Ymlusgo'n araf ac ysgafn i'r twll yng nghlawdd Cae
Gwair ger yr allt ac o blith y dorf o gwningod fydde'n pori
ar Cae Cnwc, ceisio dewis un fach ifanc, lefret. Os bydde'r
ergyd gynta'n creu môr o gynffonau gwyn yn diflannu tua
diogelwch yr allt, bydde'n rhaid bod yn gloi iawn i lwyddo
taro un ar yr ail ergyd. O fethu yr eildro bydde 'na hanner
awr i dri chwarter o aros yn llonydd cyn iddyn nhw ail
ymddangos am eu swper.

Dychwelodd fy ewythr o'r Rhyfel gyda reiffl Point 2/2 o'r Almaen a derbyniais gyfarwyddiadau manwl iawn a gofalus ganddo, oherwydd gallai'r bwledi pwerus deithio cryn bellter. Byddai'n rhaid edrych ymhell tu hwnt i'r targed i wybod ble gallai'r ergyd orffen ei thaith. Oherwydd bod ei sŵn dipyn yn dawelach nag ergyd stwrllyd dryll, bu hynny'n gymorth mawr wrth saethu cwningod, Codi eu clustie heb redeg bant wnâi rhai, felly cyfle gwych i ddewis y nesa. Un noson, wedi saethu cwningen yn llwyddiannus, o gerdded lan i'w chasglu beth weles i ond tair yn gorwedd yn farw ar y borfa – roedd y bwled wedi mynd trwy gorff y gynta a'r ail nes lladd y drydydd. Digwyddiad hollol anarferol, ond hefyd yn datgelu pa mor bwerus o'dd y dryll a pha mor niferus oedd y cwningod bryd hynny ar dir Pantglas.

Dyna'r rheswm dros y weithred fwyaf erchyll ac anfaddeuol wnaeth dynoliaeth ei chyflwyno i natur erioed. Dynion drosglwyddodd a lledaenu'r clefyd Myxamatosis ar draws gwledydd Prydain am fod cwningod yn rhy niferus. Anghofia i byth 1954 pan gyrhaeddodd y pla ein hardal ni. Haint oedd hwn a fydde'n peri i'r llygaid, y trwynau, y clustiau, yn wir holl bennau a chyrff cwningod chwyddo'n llidus. Bydden nhw'n diodde ac yn sgrechen mewn poen am ddyddiau, yn wir cymerai hyd at wythnos iddyn nhw farw. Creaduriaid gwyllt a gadwai eu pellter oedd cwningod erioed, ond wedi iddyn nhw ddal yr haint byddent yn tyrru i'r heolydd yn araf a phoenus, fel tasen nhw'n gofyn i ddyn am help. Wn i ddim sawl cwningen a laddes i drwy roi cnoc iddi ar ei phen, er mwyn ei rhyddhau rhag yr holl boen.

Wedi hynny, saethes i ddim yr un gwningen wedyn, na'r un anifail arall chwaith. Cafodd yr hen ddryll ymddeoliad cynnar yn y twll dan stâr. Wedi gweld y fath ddioddefaint, daeth terfyn ar gawl cig cwningen, a oedd mor flasus. Cyn hynny bydde pawb yn yr ardal yn trapo cwningod, a bydde trapwr ym mhob ardal a âi o ffarm i ffarm yn dal cwningod. Roedd trapo cwningod hefyd yn hynod o greulon, er nad oedd yr oes honno'n dewis cydnabod hynny. Adeg y Rhyfel bu cwtogi mawr ar fwydydd a daeth trapwyr gorllewin Cymru'n arwyr mawr i bobol dinasoedd fel Bryste a Birmingham, gan mai cig cwningen oedd yr unig gig ar gael iddyn nhw. Erbyn heddiw caiff unrhyw un sy'n defnyddio trape ei erlyn mewn Llys Barn – hyn yn dangos fod safonau yn newid o oes i oes!

Byddai trapwyr fel Dan Mani, Bronwydd yn cyrraedd ffarm ac yn aros yno am ryw wythnos neu ddwy i ddal cannoedd, gan eu hongian lan yn y Cartws tan i lori Jac Blaenparsel gyrraedd i'w hanfon bant i'r trefi mawr. Byddai'r holl fenter yn werth rai cannoedd o bunnoedd i'r ffermwr ac yn dâl dyledus i wneud iawn am yr holl borfa a gollwyd. Bydde trapwr medrus fel Dan Mani yn gallu gosod trap yn yr union fan yn y rhediad fel y gallai ddal y gwningen yn ei thraed blaen, yn sownd yno tan iddo gyrraedd fore trannoeth. Creulon? Oedd, wrth gwrs. Ond ddim hanner mor greulon â'r Micso melltigedig wnaeth i'r anifail bach ddiodde am wythnos neu fwy.

Y Cynhaeaf Gwair

Gorchwyl bryderus ac ansicr iawn oedd ceisio cynaeafu a chywen gwair yn hinsawdd anwadal Gorllewin Cymru. Ar adegau, caed y gwair yn aeddfedu'n rhy gyflym mewn tywydd crasboeth, fel torth mewn ffwrn, a hwnnw'n mynd yn gyngras oherwydd nad oedd digon o ddwylo ar gael i'w gario i'r sied cyn iddo sychu gormod. Ond fel rheol, fel arall fyddai hi. Mor aml y gwelwyd y gwair yn araf bydru ar gaeau gwlyb dan wasgedd diwrnodau di-ben-draw o gymylau llwyd a glaw mân rhwystredig. Doedd dim y gallai'r ffermwr druan ei wneud ar ddiwrnode fel hynny.

Pwy ddewisai fod yn ffermwr, dwedwch! O ganlyniad bydden nhw'n barhaol yn byw mewn stad besimistaidd. Hyd yn oed pan fyddai mis Mai wedi esgor ar dyfiant ffrwythlon, yr adwaith fyddai, 'Mynd yn wastraff wneith e. Chewn ni'm tywydd ffafriol i ga'l e miwn.' Ac oedd, roedd peth gwir yn hynny Ni ellid disgwyl, fel arfer, mwy na rhyw ddau ddiwrnod braf o heulwen a gwynt cyn i'r cymylau fygwth y gwair ar lawr unwaith eto. Pan gaen nhw ddiwrnod perffaith i gywain gwair, disgyn ar y Dydd Sul a wnâi'r diwrnod hwnnw. Ie, y diwrnod gwaharddedig rhag gwneud unrhyw waith. Gwelais Wili Parce yn colli'r cyfle i gywen mwy nag un cae a hwnnw'n berffaith barod, am ei fod e'n warden yn eglwys Sant Celynin, lawr hewl a llai na hanner milltir bant. Er hynny, fe weles i fe un nos Sul braf, yn gyfrinachol yn cario sawl picwarched o'r cae dan tŷ o dan gysgod y clawdd yn y cyfnos, i loches yr ydlan ac ynte'n gwbod iddyn nhw broffwydo glaw y bore wedyn. Wedes i ddim wrth neb tan nawr!

Oherwydd yr holl ansicrwydd gellid sylweddoli fod yna lawer iawn o draddodiad, ofergoeledd a thrafod yn gysylltiedig â lladd gwair. Pryd i ddechrau lladd gwair? Pa arwyddion tywydd i'w credu neu eu hanwybyddu. Pwy o'dd wedi lladd yn barod, a phwy o'dd heb fentro? Do'dd dim rhaid trafod rhai pethau, gan mai John Bryncene fydde'n cwympo'r caeau cynta bob blwyddyn ac felly, fe fydde'r cynta i orffen ei gynhaea. Yr ochr draw i'r hewl ar dir Ffynnonfelen, bydde'r byd yn troi yn llawer iawn mwy jicôs.

Ail neu drydydd fyddai Pantglas yn y rota ddigyfnewid hon. Digyfnewid hefyd oedd y drefen o ba gaeau fyddai'r cynta i wynebu'r peiriant lladd gwair. Rhaid i gae Fflat fod yn gynta bob tro oherwydd byddai'n rhaid trafeili drwyddo at y rhan fwya o'r caeau gwair eraill. Petai'r tywydd yn anwadal, yna tro Cae Bach ddeuai nesa. 'Dyw e dim yn ormod i golli,' chwedl Mam. Gan fod y caeau hynny yn rhyw chwech i wyth erw yr un, rhaid fydde bod yn ofalus iawn gyda Rhenbant Penrhiw a Rhenbant Troedyrhiw, a hyd yn oed mewn cyfnod o wasgedd uchel ac arwyddion am sbelen o dywydd braf, anaml iawn y gwelwyd Donald, fy mrawd, yn barod i fentro cwympo dau gae gada'i gilydd. Fe wyddai'r ehedydd, y petris, y llygod bach, y cwningod di-ri a'r cadno ysglyfaethus, mai Cae Warallt a Chae Ffynnonfelen fyddai'r ola i gwympo. Bydde hynny yn rhoi digon o amser i'r holl adar a'r anifeiliaid bach symud a newid eu harferion dyddiol. Adeg y Rhyfel, tyfwyd llafur ar y ddau gae sy'n ffinio â Ffynnonfelen, ac erys y cof yn fyw am yr ysgubau, am eu stacano, cyn creu wedyn sawl helem fach yn batrwm dros y cae, a'r dwylo o ganlyniad yn llawn pigau'r ysgall dieflig. Yn fuan wedi i ni roi'r gorau i dyfu llafur diflannodd y petris o'r tir.

Yn ystod y pumdegau, cyn oes y beler, roedd llwytho gwair rhydd yn dal i fod yn grefft ac yn ddawn gynhenid wnâi ddenu edmygedd yng nghefn gwlad. Gwaith y llwythwr oedd dosbarthu haenau o wair rhydd fyddai'n cyrraedd ei freichiau ar ben y treiler, o bicwerchi'r pitswyr. Y grefft oedd ei osod a'i gadw yn wastad ac yn sgwâr, wrth i'r llwyth godi o bicwarched i bicwarched.

Ar y dechrau, bydde hi'n weddol hawdd cadw trefen ar bethe, ond fel y codai'r llwyth, anoddach fyddai cadw'r ochrau'n syth. Wedi i ben y llwyth godi rhyw wyth troedfedd o'r ddaear, doedd dim modd gweld a oedd yr ochrau yn tynnu i mewn yn ormod, neu'n gorlifo drosto, neu gyda'r llwythwr dibrofiad, yn cornwydo mas dros yr ochor ac yn edrych yn ddigon salw. Ond, do'dd dim amdani felly, ond palu mlân a dal i lwytho mewn gobaith y daliai'r llwyth nes cyrraedd yr ydlan!

Doedd y perfformiad ddim ar ben, waeth pa mor daclus yr olwg arno, nes i'r llwyth gyrraedd pen y daith yn ddiogel yn yr ydlan. Ar ffarm weddol wastad prin iawn y bydde hyn yn destun llawer o bryder, ond ar lefydd llethrog, troellog, ac ar heolydd ffarm caregog fel Pantglas, mawr fu'r gofid am y daith i'r ydlan. Wrth ddisgyn y tri chan troedfedd o fanc Pantglas i'r clos islaw, gallai olwyn daro carreg neu welten, neu lithro i mewn i dwll, a gallai fod yn ddigon i ddymchwel unrhyw lwyth nad oedd wedi ei lunio'n gytbwys. Er na wydden nhw ddim am y grefft o lwytho, synhwyrai bois y sied wair, a hyd yn oed wragedd y tŷ o bellter, os oedd rhywbeth o'i le ar lwyth.

"Na lwyth da! Ma hwnna'n iawn,' medde Tom Graig.

'Sa' i'n lico'i gefen e. All e fynd unrhyw funed.' Roedd Dan Clifford House, drws nesa, ychydig yn fwy o sinig.

Tueddai Wncwl Dai Bethoron weld y du bron bob tro. 'Falle 'i fod e'n iawn nawr, ond arhoswch nes iddo gyrraedd y tro. Gewn ni weld wedyn os yw'r pwyse'n gyson'.

Anaml y deuai cyfraniad o enau Wili Parce, bos y sied wair, gwell ganddo fe gymhennu, gwastodu a pharatoi yn y sied gan wbod bod y llwyth nesa'n mynd i gyrradd wap. Bod yn barod i'w dderbyn o'dd yn bwysig iddo fe.

Ar waelod y ddau lether ac i'r dde wrth ben y tŷ, troi am yn ôl wnâi'r hewl, fel penelin braich. Fanna bydde llwyth yn moelyd gan amla. Pe bai gwendid yn y llwyth bydde pawb yn dal eu hanadl a dilyn ei hynt dros bob siglad ar y daith i lawr. Er na allaf gofio mwy na rhyw dri llwyth yn dymchwel yn llwyr dros gyfnod helaeth o flynyddoedd, ond bob cynhaeaf collwyd mwdwl neu ddau wrth iddyn nhw lithro bant o'r llwyth, dan lygaid beirniadol y gynulleidfa islaw.

Er i fi gael 'y magu yn Pantglas, wedi dechrau dreifio Fordson Major Bryncene yn chwech blwydd oed, ac er 'mod i'n hen gyfarwydd â phob troedfedd o'r hewl i gaeau'r Banc, yn adnabod pob twll arni bron ac wedi aeddfedu'n yrrwr digon pwyllog, aeth blynyddoedd heibio cyn i fi dderbyn y fraint o gael llywio un o'r llwythi mawr lawr i'r clos. Y llwythwr fyddai'r cynta i ddod dan y lach pan lithrai'r gwair oddi ar lwyth, ond doedd hi ddim yn bosib i'r gyrrwr ddianc chwaith. 'Beth o'dd yn bod ar y twpsyn? Ma' llwythi lot mwy o seis na 'na wedi cyrradd lawr yn saff!' Gallai gyrrwr da wneud byd o wahaniaeth, wrth warchod, ac araf dwyllo llwyth gwael i ben y daith. Wedi sylweddoli bod yna lwyth sigledig ar ei ffordd, gwelid y gwragedd yn y tŷ yn rhoi stop ar dorri bara a thaenu'r menyn i wylio'r ddrama.

'Pwy sy'n dreifio?'

'Dai Parce.'

'O! Bydd e'n olreit te.'

Yn ôl traddodiad fe fyddai yna ymgais i dowlu'r holl wair ar y llwyth ola a chlirio'r cae'n gyfan gwbwl, er mwyn osgoi anfon gambo neu dreiler arall yr holl ffordd yn ôl i'r Banc gyda'r cyfnos, i gasglu'r cetyn llwyth ola. Roedd John Bryncene yn gamster ar allu rhoi'r cyfan, hyd yn oed yr ystod oedd nesa at y clawdd, a honno'n llaith ac yn drwm i'r picwerchwyr blinedig. Hon fydde ei gampwaith terfynol am y dydd. Felly, yn naturiol ddigon, arafach o dipyn fydde taith y falwoden olaf hon, yn ymwybodol y gallai un cam gwag gan geffyl neu un troad cam ar olwyn arwain at ail lwytho, a'r drychineb fwya hyd yn oed, ohirio amser swper.

Yn y diwedd derbyniais y fraint o lywio pan fyddai yna getyn o lwyth ola, gyda gwŷr y picwerchi, y bois fu'n mwdylu a'r rhai fydde'n casglu'r crafion yn y cae, yn cael hwyl fawr wrth orffwys yn fuddugoliaethus ar yr ychydig wair oedd yn weddill ar y treiler. Gyda'r llafur chwyslyd drosodd a'r awch am swper yn cynyddu bob eiliad, dechreuai'r canu wrth iddyn nhw syllu i lawr ar weithwyr yr ydlan druain, yn dal wrthi'n slafo ar y llwyth cynt.

Yn nechrau'r ugeinfed ganrif aeth fy Wncwl Dafi o Gwmwernen Llanpumsaint i'r lofa yng Nghlydach Vale yn y Rhondda, i ganlyn ceffylau yn y pwll glo tan ddaear. Bob haf, adeg pythefnos gwyliau'r glowyr, dychwelai gatre, yn aml iawn adeg cynaeafau gwair. Un flwyddyn, daeth â ffrind gydag e, a'i gyflwyno i'r picwerchwyr ar y caeau. Dyn tal cyhyrog, siriol a sychedig oedd Stuart Campbell, a wnaeth ddatblygu i fod yn bitsiwr da mewn byr o dro.

Daeth cyfrinach arall i'r golwg hanner ffordd lawr ar y treiler un noson, wrth iddo ymuno'n sydyn yn y canu. Ar derfyn 'Calon Lân' lwyddiannus, 'Hisht,' medde Wncwl Dafi, 'fe ganith Stuart *Yr Holy City* i ni.' Cofiaf yn dda o hyd y dechreuad disgybledig, tawel a swynol, '*Last night as I lay sleeping, there came a dream so fair,*' a thinc olwynion y gambo'n gyfeiliant iddo. Yn raddol cynyddu a chyfoethogi wnaeth y llais disgybledig, nes iddo lenwi'r hewl fach a llifo dros y bryn. Erbyn cyrraedd y tro penelin ola, cyn disgyn tua'r clos, cyrhaeddodd ei uchafbwynt yn ffwl throtl, '*Jerusalem! Jerusalem! Sing all ye nations sing...*' Erbyn hyn ro'dd bois yr ydlan ar stop a phawb a'u golygon tua'r canwr, y gwragedd a'r cyllyll a ffyrc yn eu dwylo wedi llifo mas o'r tŷ, i flasu'r wledd. Wedi cyrraedd y clos yfodd Stuart boteled o seidr Coates ar ei ben. Yn llawn deilwng o'r wobr!

Er yr holl waith caled roedd yna lot o hwyl ond gallai'r cae gwair fod yn lle peryglus hefyd. Byddai'n rhaid cadw llygad ar y newydd ddyfodiaid dibrofiad. Boi'n gwitho mewn swyddfa yn y dre o'dd un o'r gweithwyr un flwyddyn, wedi dod i bitsho, ond yn rhy hael â'i gynghorion gwybodus o'r funud y dath e drwy fwlch y cae. Wrth fwynhau pum munud yn aros i'r treiler nesa gyrraedd ceson ni wers 'da fe'n ymwneud â rhagoriaethau'r *Typewriter*, a sut y byddai hyn oll yn siŵr o newid cefen gwlad am byth. 'Os neith hi'r gwaith yn lle'r bicwarch, fe wna i brynu un,' oedd ymateb ffraeth Griff Penrhiw wrth i'r treiler gwag gyrraedd a rhoi pen ar y ddarlith hirwyntog. Wedi codi'r nesa, daeth cyfle i foi'r swyddfa draethu 'mhellach ar nifer o bynciau roedd e'n arbenigwr arnyn nhw. Fel arfer, do's neb yn ysu am glywed sŵn y gambo yn nesáu a'r seibiant prin ar ben, ond y noson honno fe'i croesawyd!

Y llwyth ola, y mwdwl diwetha ac yna i fyny â'r fforched derfynol ar ben y llwyth yn sŵn y geiriau arferol o ryddhad, 'Hon buon ni'n whilo amdani trw'r nos'. I fyny ar ben y llwyth roedd John Bryncene wedi cadw un twll sgwâr trefnus i roi'r ddwy fforched ola. Un gorchwyl yn unig oedd bellach ar ôl, sef rhoi help llaw i'r llwythwr ddisgyn ryw ddeuddeg troedfedd tua'r ddaear. Yn ôl yr arfer, gosodwyd pen y ffyrch i mewn yn y gwir ar ochr y llwyth, er mwyn creu grisiau iddo droedio'i ffordd lawr. 'Gadewch e i fi,' mynte fe 'deall y cwbwl'. Plannodd ei bicwarch yn y gwair, a honno fydde cam ola John wrth ddod lawr. Ond yn groes i'r arfer rhoddodd e'r goes yn y gwair a dal y ddau ben pigog yn ei ddwylo.

'Nid fel 'na ti fod neud, y twpsyn,' oedd geirie plaen Dai Twm, a fynte wedi cael llond bola ar y parablwr erbyn hynny.

'Byddwch dawel, ddyn,' oedd yr ymateb gafodd yr hen Twmi druan.

Gyda holl bwysau ei gorff wrth ddisgyn, glaniodd troed John yn drwm ar goes y bicwarch olaf, ac fe dorrodd honno yn ei hanner. Rhwygwyd y blaen pigog o afael boi'r dre, cyn plannu ei hun fel picell ryfel ym mola John. Daliodd pawb eu hanadl mewn braw wrth ei wylio'n suddo i'r tir a'r darn fforch yn ei fola. Yr unig beth tebyg a welais i cyn hynny oedd golygfa mewn ffilmiau Cowbois ac Indiaid yn y Lyric yng Nghaerfyrddin.

'Well i chi fynd lawr i'r Inffirmari iddyn nhw ga'l gweld be sy ore i neud, John.' Dyna o'dd yr unig awgrym synhwyrol ac aeddfed a wnaeth y pechadur drwy'r nos.

'Na, bydda i'n iawn, boi bach,' medde John. Er rhyfeddod i bawb tynnodd y bicwarch mas o'i gorff a sychu ei blaen gwaedlyd yn llawes ei grys. Wedodd dyn y dre ddim gair wrth weld hyn, yn wir buodd e bron â llewygu yn y fan a'r lle. Na, aeth John ddim i weld meddyg, ac erbyn cyrraedd y clos roedd, yn ôl ei reddf fel gweithiwr caled a chydwybodol, yn cynnig rhoi help llaw i fois y sied i ga'l gwared ar y llwyth olaf. Ond, wedi hir berswâd, llwyddwyd i'w ddarbwyllo nad oedd fawr o waith i'w wneud yn y sied, ac y bydde hi'n well iddo fynd miwn i'r tŷ i gael ei swper gyda'r forded gynta. Doedd hynny ddim yn plesio o gwbwl, gan taw ar y forded ola bydde'r bois profiadol yn byta, a threfn gwaith trannoeth yn cael ei benderfynu. Miwn ag e heb unrhyw adwaith i'r ddamwain. Ond roedd yna un cliw bychan i ddangos nad oedd popeth yn hollol arferol, oherwydd gwrthododd yr ail blated o gig moch. Wedi dweud hynny, dylid ychwanegu na lwyddodd dyn y dre fyta hanner ei blated cynta, ac nid oherwydd ei fod yn clebran gormod oedd hynny, achos wedodd e yr un gair wrth y ford swper ac yn ddigon dywedwst yr a'th e gatre.

Yr oen swci

Am ryw reswm *Joey* fu enw pob oen swci yn Pantglas. Ar bob anifail arall gosodwyd enw unigryw fyddai'n ei neilltuo oddi wrth bawb arall, hyd yn oed os oedd yr enw hwnnw'n cael ei ailadrodd o un genhedlaeth i'r llall. Felly enwyd sawl buwch yn *Penwen* a cheffylau di-ri yn *Beauty*. Pam enwau Cymraeg i'r gwartheg ond Saesneg i'r ceffylau bob tro? Sa i'n gwbod, ond dyna fu'r drefen oesol yn ôl pob tebyg.

Ambell waith, fe gesech enw hollol addas o'dd yn ffitio'r cymeriad yn berffaith, fel *Prince* ein ci defed dda'th o Aberarth, oherwydd do'dd na'm gronyn o waith yn perthyn iddo fe. Dro ar ôl tro bydde Donald yn gweiddi cyfarwyddiadau arno adeg casglu'r da lawr o'r llethrau i'w godro. Gyda'r holl gymdogaeth yn dystion, bydde'r ddrama yn datblygu yn ddyddiol ar lwyfan eang y cwm. Clywid anogaeth a chyngor ac ambell air o ganmoliaeth hyd yn oed o enau'r meistr i ddechrau, cyn iddo'n raddol golli ei dymer wrth iddo gael ei anwybyddu'n llwyr gan yr anifail aristocrataidd. Gwyddai'r gynulleidfa, gan gynnwys Wili Parce, na fyddai'n rhaid aros yn hir cyn i'r ddrama fawr gyrraedd ei huchafbwynt, wrth i Donald golli ei dymer yn rhacs, a rhegi'r diogyn diwerth i'r cymylau. 'Ti werth mo'r ffy* i neb y co** dioglyd!' Byddai'r geiriau hyn yn eco o un ochor y cwm i'r llall, a chyrraedd clustiau Henri Howells yn Pentremawr, bron i filltir i ffwrdd. Dyma'r ciw i'r ci tywysogaidd droi ei gefen ar Donald ac ymlwybro'n araf am gysgod y clawdd, a'i holl osgo uchel ael yn awgrymu, 'Does yr un taeog bach yn siarad â fi Prince, Pendefig Dyfed, fel 'na.' Dal i bori'n hamddenol, yn mwynhau sbelen fach ychwanegol, wnâi'r gwartheg, yn llwyr ymwybodol fod pob sawdl yn hollol saff rhag dannedd yr hen Prince. Yn y diwedd, bydde'n rhaid i Donald ddringo'r llether i 'nôl y da ei hunan o dop Cae Cwnc neu o hirbell Cae Sied.

Ond yn ôl at yr ŵyn swci. Dim ots faint o seis o'dd e, na beth oedd ei gyflwr, na sawl diwrnod ôd o'dd e, cynted fydde fe'n cyrraedd y tŷ Joey fydde fe am weddill i oes yn Pantglas. Bob tymor wyna bydde 'na ddafad yn geni tri, un arall yn gwrthod ei hepil, neu ambell dro bydde dafad yn trigo ar enedigaeth yr oen, felly bydde 'na oen swci rywbryd neu'i gilydd yn cyrraedd ac angen cael ei fwydo a'i gynnal. Wedi hen arfer â chymryd y creaduriaid bach amddifad dros genedlaethau, ro'dd Mam yn gyfarwydd â'u hanghenion a'u cleme. Fe'm synnwyd fwy nag unwaith o weld truan bach oer, llonydd yn gorwedd yn gorff marw ar y pentan, ond wedyn mewn ychydig oriau yn prancian ac yn brefu yn swnllyd ar lawr y gegin. Dyna fyddai ei gipolwg ola o gegin y ffarm. Cyn gynted ag roedd e'n ddigon cryf, mas ag e i'r cartws ac yn ddigon pell o'r tŷ. Gwyddai Mam yn dda mor fuan y tyfent yn llawer rhy ewn i fod yn y gegin, cyn dechrau brefu am eu potel lath a gneud eu busnes dros bobman. Felly, gwnaeth Mam reol bendant. Bydde'n rhaid i bob oen dderbyn ei botel yn y cartws, yn ddigon pell o'r tŷ. Gweithiodd y drefen yn dda, a'r ŵyn swci yn dysgu mai'r clos o'dd eu cartref, yn y cartws caen nhw eu bwydo ac yno ro'dd eu gwâl i gysgu.

Er taw Joeys o'n nhw i gyd, er mwyn gwahaniaethu rhyngddynt, daeth yn arferiad i ychwanegu ail enw, felly Joey marw oedd yr un dreuliodd ddau ddiwrnod o flaen y grât cyn cropian 'nôl i dir y byw. Joey swci, swci a anfonwyd nôl at y praidd i bori'r adledd gwair yn y caeau top wedi iddo dyfu. Ond wedi symud y defaid i gyd i lawr beth amser ar ôl hynny i'r cae wrth y tŷ, pan welai Joey swci'r clos bydde fe'n cofio am ei blentyndod. Am ddiwrnodau bu'n brefu a brefu am ei botel lath, a hwnnw erbyn hynny yn glamp o hwrdd mowr.

Adeg y cynhaeaf gwair bydde'n rhaid casglu i gael help llaw, a daeth yn draddodiad i Jac hel porthmyn o'r marts i roi cymorth i ni 'da'r cywen fin nos. Un o'r gweithwyr gore hynny oedd Harri Clifton o Gaerfyrddin, yn gamster ar drafod bêls, ond gynted ag y taflwyd yr un ola i ben y sied, bydde ei holl fryd ar fynd i'r Tanners Arms yn y dre. Gwrthodai bob anogaeth i ymuno â'r criw yn y gegin am y swper cynhaeaf traddodiadol. Er bod Mam yn anhapus, cytunwyd bod Harri yn cael mynd i'r cartws at y crêt seidir Bulmers i aros am rywun i orffen ei fwyd a'i gario i'r dre.

Y noson honno, o weld symud yn y cartws, daeth Joey ato yn y gobaith annisgwyl o gael poteled ychwanegol o lath. Wrth ei weld, fe welodd Harri'r botel ar y silff gerllaw, ac yn ôl traddodiad cymdeithasol yfwyr i rannu drwy brynu rownd, a'i natur addfwyn yntau, dyma lanw'r botel a chynnig seidir i'r sychedig un. Er bod y blas yn wahanol plesiwyd Joey. Sawl poteled gafodd e, chawn ni ddim gwybod, ond pan ddethon ni mas o'r tŷ fe welon ni un o ryfeddode bywyd yng nghanol y clos. Dyna lle ro'dd yr oen swci ar ei benliniau ar lawr yn hanner rhochian a brefu, yn cwmpo ar i ochor wrth drial codi, a'i lyged yn agor a chau'n araf wrth iddo geisio gwneud synnwyr o'i gyflwr. 'Licet ti gal ymbach rhagor, fy ffrind?' medde Harri a fynte wedi ca'l llond bola hefyd erbyn hynny. Am bump o'r gloch fore trannoth d'o'dd pethe ddim yn edrych cweit mor ddoniol, pan ddihunwyd ni a'r cilog yn llawer rhy gynnar, gan frefu aflafar o'r clos. Yn ei unig hangofer mewn oes fer, ro'dd Joey yn sgrechen am ga'l rhywbeth i'w yfed, drwy niwlen ei ben tost.

Un flwyddyn daeth ôn itha mowr arall oedd angen gofal aton ni, ac yn gloi iawn fe berffeithiodd hwnnw gêm hwylus dros ben i ddarpar hwrdd. Pan welai rywun ar y clos symudai'n gyfrwys o dawel y tu ôl iddyn nhw, cyn hyrddio'i hunan a'i dopi y tu ôl i'w benliniau. Mae'n swnio'n ddoniol ond does 'da chi ddim syniad pa mor ddolurus oedd y boen annisgwyl. Fe fydden ni, oedd bellach yn gyfarwydd â'i strancie, yn wyliadwrus ac yn cadw llygad ar y diawl bach, ac os nad o'dd e i'w weld yn y cyffinie, taflem gip y tu ôl i ni, jyst rhag ofan.

Mab Wncwl Dafi, Clydach Vale oedd Horace, yn byw yn 66 Cementary Road, Maesteg, ac wedi agor busnes barbwr yno. Penderfynwyd y byddai'n syniad da i'w unig ferch, Margaret, o'dd tua'r un oedran â fi, ond yn uniaith Saesneg, dreulio gwyliau haf yn Pantglas er mwyn dod yn gyfarwydd â bywyd y wlad. Fe gadwodd Joey bant oddi wrthi am ddiwrnod neu ddou, efallai am nad oedd yn gyfarwydd â choesau merched neu ei fod yn clywed ei hiaith yn estron, ond cadoediad byr fu hwnnw. Ar yr ail brynhawn, safai Margaret yn hyderus ar waelod y clos, wedi cael ei dysgu gan Mam i fwydo'r ieir, ac yn hoffi pwysigrwydd ei swydd newydd wrth i'r Rhode Island Reds a'r Brown Leghorns glowcian o'i hamgylch wrth bigo'r Indian Corn roedd y ferch wedi ei rannu iddyn nhw. Fe welodd Joey ei gyfle, a hithe ddim yn ymwybodol o'i bresenoldeb, gallai fforddio mynd ychydig lathenni am yn ôl er mwyn cael hyrddiad iawn. Yn sicr hon fu ei glatsien ore, bwrodd hi mor nerthol nes i ddwy droed Margaret adael y ddaear, cyn iddi gwmpo yn fflat ar lawr, gan wasgaru ffowls i bobman yn glochdar aflafar. Er mai croten o'r dre o'dd hi, ware teg fe synhwyrodd yn weddol sydyn beth o'dd wedi digwydd. *'It was you, was it. Now shooee, go away. I'll never feed you again, you Cheeky Devil!'*

A dyna shwd gath e ei ail enw, Joey Cheeky Devil fuodd e byth wedyn. Ond, a'th e'n rhy bell. Galwodd ein Ficer addfwyn un prynhawn a thra ro'dd e'n trafod pryd i gynnal yr ymarfer pwnc gogyfer â'r Calan Hen yn Llandysul gyda Mam ar y clos, fe loriodd Joey y ffeirad a glaniodd yng nghanol y cachu ffowls. Dyna'i diwedd hi! Ar fore Mercher wedyn dath hi'n ddiwrnod mart arall ac i mewn i drelar Jac fy mrawd fu ei dynged. Rhaid bod Joey Cheeky Devil wedi sylweddoli bod dydd y farn wedi cyrraedd, wrth i glos ffarm Pantglas ddiflannu a'i deyrnasiad wedi dirwyn i ben.

Byd Addysg

Ysgol Llanpumsaint

Rown i bob amser o'r farn fod ein prifathro, Jac Johns yn athro hynod o oleuedig ac o flaen ei amser. Pan es i ymchwilio yn holl lyfrau'r ysgol gogyfer â'm cyfrol i ddathlu *Canmlwyddiant a Hanner Ysgol Llanpumsaint*, cadarnhawyd hyn oll. Af fi ddim i ailadrodd holl fanylder y gyfrol honno, ond dyma un neu ddwy enghraifft o'i ffyrdd creadigol o gyflwyno addysg. Bob prynhawn Gwener, y dasg oedd tynnu llun rhyw blanhigyn roedden ni, fel plant, wedi ei gasglu o ryw glawdd amser chwarae ar ôl cinio neu ar ein teithiau byd natur. Yn gartrefol wrth ysgrifennu, rown i'n anobeithiol wrth dynnu llun, o'i gymharu â'm merch, Rhianedd, gafodd radd Dosbarth Cyntaf yn y pwnc yng Nghaergrawnt. Bydde Johns yn ein rhyddhau i fynd mas amser chwarae ar brynhawn Gwener yn ôl y marcie a gawson ni am ein lluniau. Byddwn i bob tro o dan 5 mas o ddeg a phob tro ar waelod y rhestr. A dweud y gwir ro'dd dau ohonon ni'n anobeithiol ac un prynhawn dyma Johns yn rhoi 4 a 7/8 i fi. Gorfoledd, ro'n wedi maeddu'r diawl bach arall! Yna siom, wrth i Johns roi 4 a 15/16 i hwnnw, a do, cyrhaeddodd y drws o 'mlân i. Fi o'dd y diwetha mas i'r iard unwaith 'to, ond fues i byth wedyn ar ei hôl hi wrth feistroli'r Fractions! Cofio nhw'n mynd ati i godi cegin, twll mowr dwfwn ynghanol yr iard a ni fechgyn yn rhedeg ein cylche rownd iddo. Diogel? Wel chwmpodd neb miwn ac ymhen amser cethon ni ginio twym, yn lle'r brechdanau diflas a te wedi ei aildwymo ar y stôf yn ystafell y Babanod.

Wrth ein hannog ni blant i gyfieithu enwau ffermydd i'r Saesneg roedd hynny nid yn unig yn hybu dwyieithrwydd diddorol, ond hefyd yn sicrhau ein bod yn adnabod ein hardal ac yn ein ca'l i ystyried ystyron enwau'r ffermydd. Felly, daethon ni'n gyfarwydd â Ffynnonfelen (yellow well), Penllwynuchel (head of high bush), Frongoch (red breast) a Nantyrhebog (hawk's stream) a daeth yr enwau i olygu llawer iawn mwy i ni. Lle byddai plant mewn rhai ysgolion yn chwysu'n ddyddiol ar ddim ond syms a sillafu wrth wynebu her yr 11+, bydden ni'n cael hwyl wrth gydweithio mewn grwpie o bedwar yn gwneud gwaith project. Ni fydde'n cael gwneud yr holl benderfyniadau: Pwy fydde'n dewis cynllun? Pwy fydde'n llunio'r brawddegau? Pwy fydde'n ysgrifennu? Pwy fydde'n tynnu llunie? Ni o'dd ei ddosbarth olaf cyn iddo ymddeol.

Er mai bwydlen addysg Seisnig fu'n rheoli, ni theimlais unrhyw wrthwynebiad erioed at y Gymraeg yn Llanpumsaint ac mae hynny hefyd yn datgelu rhywfaint am Mr Johns. Pan ffurfiwyd Urdd Gobaith Cymru yn y 1920au roedd e'n flaenllaw yn gynnar iawn yn ei gefnogaeth ac yn un o'r rhai cynta i fynd â phlant i Wersyll Llangrannog.

Un bore yn 1949, es ar y bws lawr i adeilad mawr dierth yng Nghaerfyrddin, lle'r oedd lot o ddynion yn gwisgo clogyn mawr du. Ie, mynd yno i sefyll yr 11+ ro'n i. Gan fod fy Wncwl Dai (D Mansell Thomas) yn Gynghorydd Sir roedd e wedi cael golwg fach gyfrinachol ar y canlyniadau beth amser cyn y cyhoeddiad swyddogol. Dyna felly'r eglurhad am wincs rownd y gornel i Mam a'i haddewid y cawn i feic newydd os llwyddwn i. Da'th yr Hercules i Bantglas a llwyddodd pump ohonon ni o Ysgol Llanpumsaint fynd i mewn i'r Gram. Y pedwar arall oedd Meinir Lewis, merch y Ficer, Stanley Jones, Penbontbren, Gethin Burgess, Maenllwyd ac Arwyn Howells, Waunyrhelfa, sef nai i Jennie Eirian Howells gynt a Jennie Eirian Davies wedyn.

Yr Ysgol Ramadeg

Tipyn o newid byd. Rhedeg lawr yr hewl fach i ddal Bỳs Biheif a nes mlân Bỳs Dan Blosom, gyda'r seddi gore i gyd wedi mynd yn barod. Gwisgo cap ysgol cyn cychwyn cerdded lan y dreif tua'r adeiladau mawr, gyda'r llwybr yn rhannu wedyn yn ddau, y merched yn cerdded tua'r chwith i'w hysgol nhw a ninnau i'r dde. Yn llai ofnus o lawer wedi cael y dyco o fedydd ar y diwrnod cynta. Am y tro cynta daethom i gysylltiad â bois y dre, o'dd dipyn mwy ewn na ni. Ond wedi cyfnod o fygwth a thowlu enwau, 'Boscins,' medden nhw wrthon ni a ninne'n towlu 'gytersnaips' 'nôl atyn nhw, daethon ni'n eitha ffrindiau yn y diwedd gyda nifer o fois y dre. Roedden ni'n hen gyfarwydd â galw'r prifathro yn Llanpumsaint yn Mr Johns a Mr Jones (Dai Wein yn ei gefen) ond canfod yn awr fod gan bron pob un o'r athrawon, dynion i gyd, lysenwau. Stincs oedd yr athro Cemeg a Walrys oedd yr athro Bioleg, oherwydd bod ganddo fwstásh enfawr. Cawr o ddyn oedd Bwl yr athro Cymraeg ac un arall braidd yn ferchetaidd yn Siwsi. Roedd 'da ni athro da iawn yn dysgu Hanes ond oherwydd yr ychwanegiad ar lawes ei got, Patchi oedd e. A wedyn Spif, wel o'dd e'n edrych fel un! Byddai'r Prifathro Tudor Williams yn crwydro o amgylch i ganfod troseddwyr gan gario cansen fygythiol yn ei law. Wedi iddo ymddeol daeth Ben Howells, a phan briododd â'r Brifathrawes drws nesa bedyddiwyd hithau'n Benher. Ie, ar ôl y ffilm honno.

Wrth i'n bỳs aros tu fas i dŷ yn Heol Bronwydd bydde holl rialtwch y seddau cefn yn tawelu'n sydyn, achos bydde'r athro Ffrangeg yn camu miwn – Hwcer, neu W H Thomas yn swyddogol. Amser Rhyfel dodwyd ef yn gyfrifol am roi trefn ar warchodlu Bronwydd, a dyma un Home Guard gafodd fwledi go iawn, oherwydd yr ochr draw i'r Pil Bocs, tu fas tafarn Bronwydd, ro'dd na dymp arfau a ffrwydron enfawr ar gaeau Plas Glangwili. Un nosweth, wrth iddo aros am y bechgyn i gyrraedd daeth Mrs Ifans mas o'r drws a dweud 'Licech chi ga'l diferyn bach tra bo'ch chi'n aros, Mister Hwcer?' Ro'dd hi'n lwcus ei bod hi wedi hen adael yr ysgol! Ddegawdau wedyn, a minnau'n oedolyn, daeth ton o euogrwydd drosof pan glywes i fe'n siarad Cymraeg ar stryd Caerfyrddin, wrth gofio'r holl bethau beirniadol a hallt ddywedon ni amdano fe o fewn ei glyw. Nid fe oedd yr unig athro yno i gelu'r ffaith fod ganddyn nhw afael ar y Gymraeg. Amrywiol oedd safon y dysgu, gyda ffurfioldeb yr hen draddodiad gramadeg yn teyrnasu. Oherwydd fy niddordeb mewn Hanes mwynheais wersi Mr Thomas, ac roedd gwersi Saesneg Haydn Evans bob amser yn oleuedig. Câi ef ei adnabod wrth ei enw cywir.

Amser chwarae ac yn ystod yr awr ginio lawr â ni i waelod y dreif i wylio coesau'r merched drwy'r ffens wrth iddyn nhw chwarae pêl-rwyd neu denis, gydag ambell un yn siapus o boblogaidd. Y tu fas i'r dreif rhedai Mrs Jones ei siop, melysion yn swyddogol ond cadwai ffags Woodbine o dan y cownter. Pan wnaed fi'n Briffect yn y chweched dosbarth, dodwyd fi a'm cyfaill, Barry Long yn gyfrifol am gadw trefen o gylch y siop. Dau gadno i warchod y sied ffowls a chyfle arall i smoco fel trwper! Bydde pawb yn smoco bryd hynny. Anfonwyd fi â neges i ystafell y staff un egwyl. Pan agorwyd y drws doedd hi ddim yn bosibl gweld neb yn y mwg ac amhosibl oedd canfod pwy oedd pwy.

Roedd y ddisgyblaeth yn gallu bod yn llym ac i fechgyn y wlad, doedd dim yn fwy annheg na'r awr o *Detention* ar ôl ysgol. Wedi colli bỳs pedwar bydde gyda ni dros awr arall i'w gwastraffu cyn bỳs whech, gan gyrraedd gatre biti starfo. Bues yn ffodus i osgoi'r ddedfryd, ar wahân i ryw ddwywaith, gydag un ohonyn nhw'n profi'n i fod yn hanesyddol. Es lawr i'r dre wedi cael fy rhyddhau a chanfod tyrfa fawr stwrllyd yn llenwi sgwâr y Clos Mawr. Aeth yn fyddarol yno wrth i Ronnie Harris gael ei arwain allan, newydd ei ddedfrydu i farwolaeth am lofruddio'r pâr oedrannus o Langynin a ches y cyfle amheus i fod yno i'w weld.

Pêl-droed

Ar sawl achlysur drwy 'mywyd daeth ceisiadau cyson i fi ymuno â chymdeithas hen ddisgyblion y Gram, yr Old Maridunians fel y'u gelwir. Gwrthod wnes i bob tro ac roedd yna reswm, un a fu'n corddi am ddegawdau. Ar brynhawn Sadwrn bydde rhai ohonon ni'n chwarae pêl-droed i dîm Peniel A.F.C., a daeth hyn i sylw athro ymarfer corff yr ysgol. Gallech chi feddwl fod Ian Paisley yn cael cymundeb 'da'r Pab, yn ôl y ffỳs a wnaed gan yr ysgol, gan mai ond rygbi a gâi ei gydnabod yno. Pa hawl oedd gan ysgol drefnu ein Sadyrnau? Felly, safodd tri ohonon ni ein tir, a'r canlyniad fu ein gwahardd o'r holl wersi ymarfer corff am flwyddyn. Oherwydd hynny, bûm yn casáu rygbi am flynyddoedd a down i ddim yn drist pan gafodd yr athro bach milain hwnnw y sac am ddangos gormod o ddiddordeb yn un o fenywod y gegin, ac nid am ei gallu i goginio!

Mae'r tŷ bach twt hwnnw, sef ein hystafell newid, ar sgwâr Peniel yn dal yno o hyd. Cartre mam-gu Dai Dwbwl D (D D Davies) oedd yn rhedeg y sioe. Lle saif ysgol newydd Gynradd Peniel heddiw, dyna lle'r oedd ein cae chwarae, un digon safonol yn y dyddiau hynny. Daw rhai o'r timau y bydden ni'n eu chwarae i gof, fel Llandysul, Llanegwad a Meidrym, ar wahân i dimoedd y dre. Un Ionawr oer, cyrraedd ystafell fechan Clwb Ieuenctid Meidrym a newid

o amgylch y ford tenis bwrdd. 'Ymwelwyr yn gynta.'
Pobol garedig whare teg. A lifft i ni lan i'r cae ger tafarn
Maenllwyd mewn fan. Cysgodi rhag y gwynt a sythu o dan
glawdd noeth a dim pêl yn unman. Bron hanner awr wedyn
cyrhaeddodd ein gwrthwynebwyr, ac yn dilyn chwiban y
reff rhaid oedd dechre chware'n syth, heb gyfle i ystwytho
na dim. Yn stiff ac yn araf ro'n ni dair gôl lawr cyn pen
chwarter awr. Tactics C'mon Midffild ar eu gore!

Prifysgol Abertawe

O lwyddo yn Lefel A ces fy nerbyn i Brifysgol Abertawe ac yn
1956 rown i'n ffodus i fod yn un o'r cant cynta i gael lletya
yn Neuadd Breswyl gynta'r coleg, sef Neuadd Gilbertson yn
Blackpill. Roedd y neuadd rhyw filltir i'r gorllewin o'r coleg
ei hunan, ond taith fer oedd hi ar y rhamantus, hanesyddol
Reilffordd y Mwmbwls. Cyn hynny, nid o'wn i erioed wedi
cyfarfod â bron neb o wlad dramor, ond i Gilbertson daeth
nifer o fechgyn y tu hwnt i wledydd Prydain. Mae'n amlwg
i'r awdurdodau gynllunio bod yno drawsdoriad eang ac
amrywiol o fyfyrwyr yn ymuno i gyd-fyw yn 1956, gydag
ambell hen ben yn ein mysg o'r ail flwyddyn. Ar wahân i'r
niferoedd disgwyliadwy o dde a gogledd Lloegr derbyniwyd
wynebau lliwgar o wledydd yr Affrig, megis Kenya a Nigeria,
a deuthum yn ffrindiau mawr â chymeriad diddorol o
Zagreb, Iwgoslafia, bryd hynny. Ei enw oedd Predrang
Moesisc, cymeriad cryf a oedd yn benderfynol o lwyddo i
feistroli'r iaith Saesneg.

Warden cyntaf Gilbertson oedd Hugh Bevan, darlithydd
yn Adran Gymraeg y coleg, gŵr mwyn o hiwmor tawel ond
digon chwareus, serch hynny. Ni chafodd amser rhwydd
iawn ar y dechrau, yn bennaf oherwydd ymddygiad rhai
o'r myfyrwyr imperialaidd Seisnig, gyda'u rhagfarn amlwg
at bob iaith a diwylliant arall, heblaw am y Saesneg. Yn

wir, derbyniai'r Gymraeg lawer mwy o gydymdeimlad gan y myfyrwyr tramor, hwythau yn dangos ychydig o barch at ein hiaith mewn cyfnod pan nad oedd gan y Gymraeg unrhyw statws swyddogol y tu allan i eglwys neu gapel.

Dyma'r cyfnod pan ymosododd llywodraeth Eden ar Yr Aifft yn Suez. Hefyd, roedd dau o'n cydfyfyrwyr yn hanu o Ynys Ciprys, ar yr union adeg pan oedden nhw'n gwrthryfela ac yn brwydro am eu hannibyniaeth. Ar un noson o anfri paentiwyd sloganau mochynnaidd ar eu drysau a'u muriau ar ail lawr yr hostel. Trodd y sefyllfa'n frwnt o wleidyddol, pan welwyd gorymdeithio o blaid ac yna yn erbyn Suez, gyda myfyrwyr, darlithwyr, undebwyr ac eraill yn taflu bygythiadau a galw enwau ar ei gilydd ar strydoedd Abertawe. Ces brofiad annifyr dros ben, wrth i fi wylio'r orymdaith o blaid y Llywodraeth yn teithio i lawr y Kingsway a chlywed un o'm darlithwyr yn gweiddi sloganau brwnt i'm cyfeiriad. Ie, a hwnnw ychydig ddyddiau cyn hynny, fu'n pwysleisio pwysigrwydd pwyso a mesur dadleuon yn waraidd cyn dod i unrhyw gasgliad terfynol. Daeth y Cenhedloedd Unedig i osod trefn ar bethau, a phan ymddiswyddodd Eden, tawelodd y sefyllfa. Er hynny, arhosodd llawer craith, yn enwedig rhwng rhai o'r Saeson a'r tramorwyr wrth i'r ymgyrchoedd dros ryddid ledaenu dros diriogaeth yr hen Ymerodraeth Brydeinig.

Roedd Cymdeithas Gymraeg lewyrchus iawn er hynny yn y coleg ac ymunais yn llawen i fwynhau bwrlwm o weithgareddau, a chwrdd â chyfeillion newydd fel Cennard Davies, a'i acen gref o'r Rhondda, a Tal a oedd bron yn annealladwy o Abergynolwyn. Erbyn hyn, roedd Alun Jones, fy nghefnder o Lanpumsaint, wedi ymuno â'r coleg a'r Gymdeithas. Fe fyddai ei frawd, John a'm brawd inne, Donald yn mwynhau tipyn o hwyl wrth ddod â ni 'nôl i Abertawe a'r ambell Nos Sul wedi i ni fod gartre.

Yn Neuadd Gilbertson deuthum yn ffrindiau â grŵp o Saeson oedd yn rhannu fy hoffter o Jazz traddodiadol a thrwy hynny des yn gyfeillgar â'r darlithydd a'r awdur enwog Kingsley Amis wrth ei gyfarfod y tu allan i'r coleg lle roedd yn ddarlithydd yn yr Adran Saesneg. Bryd hynny, roedd Amis yn dipyn o rebel, yn gwrthryfela yn erbyn y sefydliad, nodwedd a wnaeth, yn anffodus, ddiflannu wrth iddo heneiddio. Rhoddodd ei nofel, *Take a Girl like You* a'r ffilm yn seiliedig arni, Abertawe ar y map. Trodd diddordeb y bechgyn ac Amis ei hunan, at Jazz cyfoes M J Q ac ati, oedd yn swnio i fi fel cath yn cerdded dros biano. Er hynny, cedwais y cysylltiadau a arweiniodd at gyfarfodydd mewn tafarnau fel yr Uplands a'r Rhyddings ac at bartïon hwyr tan oriau mân y bore yn nhŷ Kingsley Amis.

Rhyw ddwy fil o fyfyrwyr oedd yn y coleg bryd hynny, felly roedd llawer o gymdeithasu rhwng darlithwyr a myfyrwyr. Yn yr Adran Hanes, edrychid ar Neville Masterman fel boi anghyffredin iawn. Bydde'n cychwyn ei ddarlith foreol yn syth wedi iddo agor y drws a byddai pawb yn gwylltio wrth chwilio am ben neu bensil i gymryd nodiadau. O astudio Athroniaeth yn fy mlwyddyn gynta, bues yn ffodus i ddod o dan adain yr Athro J R Jones a Rush Rees a pharhaodd eu dylanwad yn gryf arnaf. Bu'n weddol amlwg mai Hanes fyddai'r pwnc dewisol am radd ac felly ymlaen â fi at Glanmor Williams ac i fwynhau dadlau ag e ynglŷn ag effaith y Ddeddf Uno 1536 ar yr iaith Gymraeg, a chwarae teg byddai'n barod i dderbyn rhai o'm gosodiadau pan fyddai tystiolaeth gen i.

Arhosais yn Abertawe i gyflawni blwyddyn o hyfforddiant i fod yn athro, er nad oedd angen blwyddyn gyfan i gyflawni hynny! Cofio dal trên yn y bore bach ar ddiwedd un tymor, yng nghwmni Alun Frongoch, ar ôl mwynhau noson dda yn Abertawe ac wrth gwrs fe gysgon ni'n dou yn sownd ar y trên cynnar y bore dydd Sul wedyn a mynd drwy orsaf Caerfyrddin. Pan ddihunon ni lan ro'n ni'n dou wedi cyrraedd Hendy-gwyn a hithau rhwng pump a chwech y bore. 'Chi'n lwcus na chyrhaeddoch chi Doc Penfro,' oedd unig sylw y gorsaf-feistr. Doedd dim amdani adeg hynny o'r bore ond cerdded ac yn y diwedd cyrraedd caffi ar ochor y ffordd. Oddi yno ffones i Donald, gan wbod y bydde fe wedi codi erbyn hynny. Ie, Donald oedd y Samaritan Trugarog a'n hachubodd ni y bore hwnnw a'r unig sylw a wnaeth e oedd dweud, 'Chi'n edrych fel dou newydd ddod mas o'r lock up.'

Byd Llencyndod

Llanpumsaint yr Arddegau

I lanw'r gaeafau bu'r Clwb Ieuenctid yn Neuadd Goffa Llanpumsaint yn ganolfan bwysig i ni fechgyn ifenc. Bob Nos Fawrth miwn â ni i'r Ystafell Fach yng nghefen y Neuadd, dan arweiniad hwyliog William John a bydde'r cardie a'r draffts yn dod mas, wrth i ni aros ein tro ar y bwrdd darts tu ôl i'r drws. Cawsom ddarlith a dadl a chyfle i drafod gwahanol bynciau ac ymarfer siarad yn gyhoeddus. Yna, wedi i bwysigion y Neuadd ildio i Emlyn Lewis y Ficer cawson ni allwedd i'r Neuadd fowr, a bois bach, dyna wefr oedd gweld y bwrdd tenis yn cyrraedd. Gweithiwr yn Co-op y Ffermwyr oedd William John, yn hapus o roi ei amser i'n rheoli ni'r ieuenctid. Yn rhedeg y sioe gydag e roedd John Phillips ac Elfyn Lewis, fy nghyd actorion yn ddiweddarach. Roedd gan William John ddawn hwylus o reoli a phob tro bydde angen gwneud rhywbeth yn y Neuadd, rhoi Beeswax er enghraifft, bydden ni i gyd yn ymateb iddo. Cyn hir caniatawyd i'r merched ymuno â ni yn yr ystafell fawr, a ches glamp o gusan ar ganol y llawr gan un ohonynt. Gallase William John fod wedi gwneud athro arbennig.

Aethom i ginio dathlu'r Clwb yn y Smiths Arms yn Foelgastell, a'r bechgyn yn dringo nôl miwn i'r bws, a blas y cwrw wedi rhyddhau'r tafodau'n ormodol gan arwain at regfeydd. Clywodd Jenkins y Ficer newydd nhw ar stepen y drws, felly dyma Vernon Llether yn ceisio rhoi trefen ar bethe – 'Iesu gwyn bois! Watsiwch y'ch ffycin iaith. Ma'r blydi Ficer 'ma!' Siglo'i ben wnaeth Gweinidog tal a main yr Efengyl. Wrth lwc chlywodd e ddim mohono fi'n dynwared ei bregeth ambell nos Sul wedi i ni'r bois fwynhau potelaid o bop a bag o greision yn y pentre.

Ar Goll

Efalle ei bod hi'n saff bellach olrhain hanes tender a'th ar goll. Ro'dd jobyn gwaith coed ishe ca'l i wneud yn y Neuadd ac yn lle rhoi'r gwaith i Ernest Rhydygar, saer y pentre, penderfynwyd gofyn am tenders, ac wrth gwrs dododd Ernest un miwn. Ond oherwydd iddo ychydig cyn hynny lifo darn o'r Bwrdd Snwcer, er mwyn jyst ca'l pishyn o bren handi, gellir tybio i'r pleidleisiau fynd yn ei erbyn. Cwyno wnath e pan gollodd y gwaith, a'r esgus a roddwyd iddo gan y pwyllgor oedd na dderbyniwyd cais ganddo.

Yn fuan wedyn, ymddangosodd neges yn adran *Lost and Found* y *Carmarthen Journal* fod y tender wedi mynd ar goll a ffrwydrodd pethau yn fwy byth. Ychwanegwyd at y benbleth gan ddatganiad y ferch a dderbyniodd yr eitem yn swyddfa'r Journal pan holwyd hi gan un o bwyllgor y Neuadd ynglŷn â phwy roddodd yr hysbyseb iddi. Dywedodd y ferch y bydde hi'n sicr o'i adnabod e, gan ei ddisgrifio fel hen ddyn yn gwisgo het ar ei ben, sbectol *national health* a barf. Ond tase hi wedi edrych mas drwy'r ffenest a'i ddilyn lawr Stryd y Brenin y bore hwnnw, bydde hi wedi gweld rhywun cymharol ifanc yn rhuthro i mewn i gar o'dd yn aros amdano, cyn diflannu.

Beth amser wedyn cafwyd sylw craff o enau'r Cynghorwr Lleol, Harri Bowen, pan holodd, 'Odi bois y colege wedi dod gatre 'to?' Oedd, roedd cyfle i ddatblygu'r ddawn o ddynwared ac i actio yn bodoli mewn pentrefi gwledig yr adeg honno.

47

Y Mart a'r Lloi Bach

Wedi bod yn y byd addysg tan hynny, teimlais yr angen i gymryd blwyddyn bant. Felly 'nôl gatre es i ac ail gydio mewn bywyd ar y ffarm a threulio tipyn o amser gyda'm brawd hynaf, Jac, yn y marts. Roedd Jac erbyn hynny wedi dod yn un o brif brynwyr a gwerthwyr lloi bach yng ngorllewin Cymru. Gan i'r ardal hon ddod yn un o'r cynta drwy Brydain i fod yn rhydd o'r clefyd TB, daeth galw mawr o bobman am ein stoc iach, lleol. Bydde Jac yn prynu lloi yn y marchnadoedd: Aberteifi ar ddydd Llun, lawr i San Clêr a Hendy-gwyn ar Ddydd Mawrth, dydd Mercher a Iau yng Nghaerfyrddin, gan orffen yr wythnos ar ddydd Gwener yng Nghastell Newydd Emlyn. Bydde'r lloi wedyn yn cael eu hanfon, naill ai ar y trên neu mewn lorïau, mor bell â gogledd Lloegr a'r Alban. Daeth y brodyr Bell o Dumfries yn gwsmeriaid pwysig a chyson dros y blynyddoedd.

Un jobyn pwysig ges i bryd hynny o'dd bwydo'r lloi gatre yn Pantglas, cyn eu llwytho i'r fan a'u gyrru nhw i ddal y trên yn Llandeilo. Fel arfer, wedi eu bwydo a'u llwytho, bydden ni'n eu gadael yn y fan am ryw awr i setlo ac i orwedd. Un diwrnod, cyrhaeddodd Jac 'nôl yn hwyr o'r mart, felly ras i'w bwydo a miwn â nhw a bant â fi'n syth. Wrth fynd rownd y tro cynta ar riw'r Graig, aeth y fan ar ddwy olwyn am ryw ddeg llath. Bu bron â thipo drosto, cyn glanio 'nôl ar y pedair olwyn. Doedd y lloi ddim wedi setlo lawr i orwedd, yn hytrach ro'n nhw i gyd ar eu traed yn y bac ac wrth fynd rownd y tro yn rhy gloi, ro'n nhw wedi mynd i gyd i'r un ochor a bron â throi'r fan drosto. Lwcus!

Bu'n gyfnod diddorol o gwrdd a chymysgu 'da bois y marts, cymeriadau unigryw fel Des Cridland, Harri Clifton a Danny Duxberry. Hoff hobi Harri o'dd cadw cwningod dof a chystadlu yn y sioeau lleol. Gorfod i Harri fynd i ryw sêl ar ddiwrnod Sioe Llandeilo, felly cynigodd Des a Danny fynd â'r cystadleuwyr i'r sioe. Cyntaf a trydydd gafodd y ddwy gwningen. Hawliodd syched y ddau stop yn nhafarn Yr Hanner Ffordd, ar y ffordd gatre, ond doedd neb o fois y marts yno i dalu am eu cwrw. Cafodd Danny syniad, sef rafflo'r ddwy gwningen ac aed ati i werthu tocynnau yn y ddwy ystafell orlawn Er tegwch, gofynnwyd i'r tafarnwr dynnu enw'r enillydd o'r hat a ddaliai'r tocynnau. Darllenodd hwnnw yr enw – Harri Cliffton Caerfyrddin. 'Fi'n 'i nabod e'. Ma fe newydd adel. Af i â nhw iddo fe,' gwaeddodd llais Des o'r cefen yn rhywle. Mae'n werth ca'l dwy hat weithie – dim ond enw Harri o'dd ar y tocynnau yn yr hat aeth i'r bar.

Y Stag an' Ffesant, Pont-ar-sais

Yn y chwedegau daeth hi'n haws byw yng nghefn gwlad gan fod bywyd yn fwy llewyrchus. Gyda mwy o arian ar hyd y lle, prynwyd tractors i ddisodli'r ceffylau ac wedyn gwelwyd car y teulu'n cyrraedd y clos. Wedi i'r mab hynaf ddysgu gyrru, a chael ei fenthyca ar Nos Sadwrn, byddai'n pigo ei ffrindiau lan a bant â nhw. Diolch i'r holl gwningod a ddaliwyd, roedd digon o arian poced i fwynhau tafarn, dawns, pysgod a sglodion cyn dod gatre a pheth newid mân yn dal yn y boced, efalle hyd yn oed yn newid o'r bunt wreiddiol. Ar hen strydoedd Caerfyrddin y Nelson Hotel ger yr hen farchnad oedd y lle gore am Bass a gêm o ddarts. Tra âi bois Alltwalis i'r Market House, y White Horse oedd hoff ffynnon bois Llanpumsaint ar nos Sadwrn. Y dre fu'r dynfa, nes i dro ar fyd ddigwydd i hen dafarn bach digon tawel a di-nod mas yn y wlad yn Pont-ar-sais. Ychydig o ffermwyr ac ambell deithiwr nawr ac yn y man welwyd yn y Stag and Ffesant cyn hynny, tafarn fu'n perthyn yn wreiddiol i Ystad Glangwili, Llanllawddog.

Yna, yn 1961 daeth Madge Jenkins yno, ffarmwraig o

Dresaith ar yr union adeg y digwyddodd y chwyldro ymysg y to ifanc. Dawnsio a jeifo i Bill Haley a Radio Luxemburg, addoli'r Beatles a herio'r genhedlaeth hŷn ynglŷn â hawliau dynol a sefyllfa'r iaith Gymraeg. Doedd 'na ddim croeso i'r gwallte hir neu fyr na'r trwseri tyn ymhobman, ond agorodd y wraig fusnes graff hon y drws led y pen i bawb. Gyda dwy ferch bert y tu ôl i'r bar gwelwyd y ceir yn anelu am y Stag ar nos Sadwrn, er ei fod bishyn tu fas i'r dre. Tyrrodd merched yno hefyd, gan gynnwys Beti Pante, chwiorydd Pentremawr a nyrsys Glangwili a rhai fel Lorraine Cwmwernen mewn cyfnod diweddarach. Cyn hir bydde'n broblem cael lle i barco, os na fyddech yno yn go gynnar, gyda cheir yn cyrraedd o bobman yn Sir Gâr a Cheredigion. Cryfhau wnaeth ein cysylltiadau ag ardal Pencader wrth gwrdd â Lona ac Alun Dolcoed, Dewi a Gillian Blossom, Anne Bronallt, merched Cwmhwplyn, bois Rhywlwyd ac eraill.

Bois y darts fydde'n rheoli'r bar gyda Dai Twm, Lewis 8, Philbo a Lyn Traed Gwlyb – ei droed wastod tu flân i'r llinell wen wrth daflu – yn anymwybodol o bob dim arall wrth chwarae am beints. Tipyn mwy o amrywiaeth yn y lownj, bechgyn wedi gwisgo'n barod am y ddawns nes mlân, trafodaethau politicaidd am Gymdeithas yr Iaith ac yna cyrhaeddodd bois yr FWA. Dwysáu wnaeth pethau wrth i drychinebau Tryweryn ac Aberfan danlinellu gwendid Cymru dan reolaeth Llundain, a chyn hir datblygodd Y Stag i fod yn un o ganolfannau Caio a'i fyddin. Bydden nhw'n galw'n amal yn ystod eu teithiau rhwng de a gogledd a Gelert, ci Dennis Coslett yn profi'n ffefryn wrth wneud ei driciau yn y bar. Daeth criw o wlad Israel i gyfweld Caio un noson a gan fod Arwyn Pentremawr yn hoff o holi perfedd pobl, gofynnodd pam eu bod yno. Ateb y criw ffilmio oedd ei bod yn bwysig cadw mewn cysylltiad ag arweinwyr y dyfodol. Diddorol oedd gwybod yr argraff o Gymru oedd gan wledydd eraill, bryd hynny, gan danlinellu ar yr un pryd pa mor effeithiol fu datganiadau Caio ar y cyfryngau.

Bychan oedd y lownj a honno'n orlawn yn amal, gan greu awyrgylch arbennig wrth i'r to atseinio i emynau Percy ar y piano, neu 'Gwŷr Harlech' o accordian Caio, a chawson ni gyfle i ryfeddu at ddawn y Meic Stevens ifanc. Pan wnaed estyniad a chreu ystafell fawr drws nesa, agorwyd hi gan Hywel Gwynfryn, er y collwyd peth o awyrgylch unigryw yr hen lownj orlawn. Aeth sôn am y Stag drwy Gymru gyfan, doedd dim paso i fod a ches gyfle i ddod i nabod beirdd fel Dic Jones a Tydfor Cwmtydu – cyfansoddodd gerdd i'w chyflwyno i Jane a fi ar ein priodas. Yn eu tro galwai perfformwyr fel Heather Jones a Dewi Pws ac ymgyrchwyr iaith o bob oedran. Neb yn paso heb alw! Yna wedi stop tap, câi criw dethol wahoddiad i'r ystafell fyw, a chyfle i lyncu brechdanau wrth wrando ar yr adroddwr digri, Lloyd Danfforddgar yn olrhain hanes 'Colli'r Cwrcyn' a chlasuron eraill o waith S B Jones Peniel. Os byddai Dai Twm ar goll ar nosweithiau fel hyn, byddai Madge yn siŵr o ddod o hyd iddo o dan yr optics atyniadol y tu ôl i'r bar!

Gyda'r holl gynnwrf a gwrthryfela ar droed, câi llythyron Neil ap Siencyn yn y *Western Mail* eu trafod yn y Stag, bomiau Mudiad Amddiffyn Cymru (MAC) a hefyd bygythiadau John Jenkins i'r arwisgo. Yn anochel felly, pwy gyrhaeddodd y Stag ond yr Heddlu Cudd. Llwyddodd y cynta i gael cyfnod o weithio y tu ôl i'r bar, ond un tu hwnt o ddibrofiad oedd hwnnw. Gofynnodd i fois y darts yn y bar, ar ôl eu trydydd peint, pryd a ble bydde'r bom nesa'n mynd bant. Er eu stranciau politicaidd, roedd llawer o gefnogaeth gudd i'r FWA, a theimlad bod y genhedlaeth hŷn wedi cysgu'n daeogaidd drwy gyfnod Tryweryn. Chwarae teg i Madge Jenkins, roedd hi yno yn Llys Abertawe i gefnogi ei chwsmeriaid pan aed â'r bechgyn o flaen eu gwath. Cymeriad lliwgar llawn bywyd fu Caio, yn wir rwy'n ei gofio'n dod i Pantglas i brynu ceffylau oddi wrth Jac fy mrawd. Ond fel y soniodd Lyn Ebenezer, chwalwyd ei iechyd yn dilyn y ddedfryd a gafodd gan y llys. A phan fu farw John Jenkins yn ddiweddar, prin y cafodd ei holl aberth yntau dros ei wlad y gydnabyddiaeth a haeddai. Gallaf ymhyfrydu a dweud i fi gael y profiad o siglo ei law unwaith.

Bydde Madge yn gallu gwneud yr annisgwyl. Un noson gofynnodd i'r ddau John, sef Frongoch a Llwyncroes, ein tacsis arferol, barcio tu fas drws y gegin. Wedi stop tap daeth yn hysbys pam. Llwythwyd crêt ar ôl crêt o gwrw i'r ddau fwt. Parti, mynte hi! Ble? holodd y bois. Bodalwyn – tŷ Madge yn Aberystwyth. Do'dd Llwyncroes heb ddreifio 'mhellach na Cei Newydd erioed cyn hynny, felly pan welodd e fast teledu Blaenplwyf meddyliodd fod ceir yn breco wrth fynd lan rhiw! Aeth yn barti hwyr i'r bore bach a'r holl rialtwch yn ybseto dwy athrawes barchus oedd yn lletya yn Bodalwyn, wrth i'r sŵn amharu ar eu cwsg lan lofft. Bwrw nôl drwy'r eira a'r rhew er mwyn cyrraedd gatre i odro, jyst cyn i neb godi. Anlwcus fues i! Cwates i yn y cwtsh dan stâr wrth i Donald godi i odro, ond clywodd fi'n bwrw yn erbyn rhyw stên. Ei sylw cysglyd oedd, 'Mynd neu dod wyt ti?'

Daeth yr holl beth i ben pan symudodd 'y fam i blant y chwyldro' yn barhaol i fyw yn Aberystwyth yn 1972, gan aros yno hyd derfyn ei dyddiau yn 2016. Llithrodd y Stag 'nôl i fod yn dafarn gwledig cyffredin ac erbyn hyn tŷ preifet yw e i bobol o bant. Gobeithio, serch hynny, bod yr hen furiau'n cofio'r cynnwrf a fu.

Byd Addysgu

Daeth yn amser i ailgydio yn y byd addysg a phori dwy'r *Times Educational Supplement* i ganfod swyddi. Anodd iawn fu dod o hyd i swyddi dysgu Hanes yng Nghymru yr adeg honno, gan mai prin iawn oedden nhw.

Er mai nifer fach o gyfweliadau ges i yn ystod fy ngyrfa, buont yn rhai anghyffredin a dweud y gwir. Wrth chwilio am fy swydd dysgu gynta bues i'n ddigon ffodus i lanio dau gyfweliad yn Lloegr o fewn dou ddiwrnod i'w gilydd, felly un tocyn trên fydde angen. Cyrhaeddes y cynta yn Bedford i ganfod dwy ysgol ochr yn ochr, a bod y swydd Saesneg a Hanes i'w rhannu rhwng y ddwy. Yn y coridor cyn y cyfweliad, datgelod athro wrtha i nad oedd y Prifathro a'r Brifathrawes drws nesa byth yn siarad â'i gilydd a bod 'na dipyn o gasineb yn bodoli rhyngddyn nhw. Gan fod yr ail gyfweliad draw yn Essex yn swnio'n fwy addawol ac yn swydd dysgu Hanes yn unig, penderfynais roi brêc ar bethe a cheisio gwneud yn siŵr yn y cyfweliad na fyddwn i'n cael cynnig y swydd gynta, er mwyn arbed y costau teithio. Y rheol oedd, os o'ch chi'n gwrthod derbyn swydd fyddech chi ddim wedyn yn gallu hawlio ceiniog yn ôl. Aeth y sioe yn ôl y disgwyl, wrth i'r Brifathrawes fynd yn frwd o'm plaid, ond yna dechreuodd y Prifathro daflu cwestiynau eithaf hiliol tuag ata i. Pwy o'n i'n feddwl o'n i, yn honni y gallwn ddysgu Saesneg i blant Lloegr, gan boeri ei frawddeg derfynol – *'We all know civilisation ends at Cardiff!'* Fel fflach ymatebais,

'*It depends which way you're travelling!*' Yn y distawrwydd sydyn trodd ei wyneb yn fwy sarrug byth, a theimlwn innau'n bles fod y costau teithio'n saff. Ond Na! Fi oedd yr unig ymgeisydd a chynigiwyd y swydd i fi; o wrthod collais y costau teithio wedi'r cwbwl.

Daeth haul ar fryn ddau ddiwrnod wedyn, wrth i fi gael fy apwyntio'n gyfrifol am ddysgu Hanes yn Ysgol y Bechgyn Culverhouse, yn South Ockendon, Essex. Miwn â fi felly i ysgwyd llaw â'r Prifathro cyfeillgar gan ofyn iddo ynghanol y drafodaeth hamddenol o dan ba Awdurdod Addysg y byddwn yn gweithio. '*Fayc!*' mynte fe, ac yna '*Fayyc!*'am yr eilwaith. O'n ni'n ffili deall pam bod y dyn bach addfwyn 'ma mewn siwt barchus yn dechre rhegi mor sydyn. Dyna 'mhrofiad cynta o acen de-ddwyrain Essex. Enw'r Awdurdod Addysg oedd *Thurrock*!

Ysgol Eilradd Fodern oedd hi mewn ardal o ystadau eang, wedi eu hadeiladu hanner ffordd rhwng Upminster a Grays ger afon Tafwys, i deuluoedd a gafodd eu symud allan o ardaloedd tlawd a difreintiedig dwyrain Llundain. Er eu moethusrwydd cyfforddus mewn fflatie modern, dyma gymdeithas anniddig ac anhapus. O edrych yn ôl, gellir gweld eu bod ar goll, yn gweld ishe yr holl agosatrwydd a diwylliant eu ffordd o fyw, yn yr hen gynefinoedd tlawd ond clos ar hyd strydoedd gorlawn yr hen *East End* yn Llundain. Nid jobyn hawdd oedd ceisio trosglwyddo bwydlen addysg y cyfnod i griw nad oedd yn gweld unrhyw bwrpas ynddi. Ond, roedd 'na nifer o fanteision o weithio yn Culverhouse. Roedd rhyw hanner cant o athrawon yn yr ysgol a dros draean ohonyn nhw'n Gymry, ac un wedi ei fagu ddim ym mhell o gatre, sef Ian Owens o Lechryd. Hefyd daeth cymdoges i fi, sef Magi o ffarm Bwlchtrap Nebo i Ysgol y Merched drws nesa.

Wedi dod i ddeall ei acen, bu'r Prifathro, Freddie Meen,

mewn gwrthgyferbyniad i arwyddocâd ei gyfenw, yn gefnogol iawn i fi a chaniatáu tipyn o ryddid dysgu o fewn y drefen yn y cyfnod hwnnw. Cefais ei gefnogaeth lwyr i lunio cwrs arholiad i Fwrdd RSA ar y pryd, gan fy annog i fod yn greadigol. Lluniais faes llafur i blant Lloegr a oedd yn cynnwys adrannau teg am Yr Alban, Iwerddon a Chymru, gan egluro hanes diwylliant a'r iaith o safbwynt y gwledydd hynny. Teimlwn fod hyn yn bwysig, yn hytrach na bod y gwledydd wedi bod yn rhyw dri chocyn hitio i fyddinoedd Lloegr dros y canrifoedd. Er siom i'r ddou ohonon ni, gwrthodwyd y cwrs gan y Bwrdd Arholi, ond teimlaf hyd heddiw y dyle'r math yna o Hanes gael ei ddysgu yn Lloegr, Teyrnas Unedig neu beidio.

Ar wahân i'r Cymry, daw nifer o athrawon unigryw, a oedd yno ar y pryd, yn fyw i'r cof, a'r crwydryn o Awstralia, Jeff Larsen yn gymeriad amlwg yn eu plith. Treuliai bob diwrnod yn ystod y gwyliau yn teithio cyfandir Ewrop, gan brysuro 'nôl o Tilberry jyst cyn y gloch gynta ar fore cynta'r tymor newydd. Ychydig iawn o holl drigolion y cyfandir sydd wedi gweld cymaint o Ewrop â Jeff. Amser cinio ar ddydd Gwener yn yr Ystafell Athrawon, yn ystod yr adeg hynny o'r flwyddyn, deuai rhywun o amgylch i gasglu bets ar y Grand National. Gorfod egluro i Jeff beth oedd y ras. Trannoeth lan yr M1 ag e i wylio'r ceffyl blân yn mynd hibo'r postyn. Ma popeth mor gyfleus yn Ewrop, medde fe. 'Os ti'n byw yn Awstralia ma pobman mor bell oddi wrth ei gilydd.'

Y Smog

Cofir am aeaf 1962 fel y flwyddyn y gwnaeth y smog gwaethaf daro ac aros dros ardal eang o Lundain a'r Tafwys. Yn anffodus, ro'n i 'na ar y pryd ac yn wath byth yn lletya yn Grays, ar bwys yr afon. Anodd egluro a chael pobol i gredu mor wael a thrwchus oedd y smog. I groesi'r hewl doedd dim pwynt edrych, achos welech chi ddim byd, felly gwrando byddwn i am sŵn car a chamu'n gros mor gloi ag y gallwn i. Oherwydd yr holl dywyllwch bydde'r ysgol yn agor am ddeg y bore ac yn cau am ddau wedi cinio. Bydde'r bysiau bob dydd yn llawn, achos eu bod nhw'n dipyn saffach na dreifio car. Rhai milltiroedd lan yr hewl roedd gwaith sement Purfleet, ac o agor drws y tŷ yn y bore dyna'r unig beth y gallwn ei arogli a'i flasu 'fyd.

Ar brynhawn Dydd Gwener dyma Alan Davis, un o'r athrawon, yn cynnig lifft i fi 'nôl i'r drws yn ei Morris Minor, dim ond i fi aros am ychydig bach er mwyn iddo orffen ryw jobyn. Aeth dros awr a hanner heibio a phawb arall wedi hen fynd. Pan ethon ni mas i'r tywyllwch a'r smog, cethon ni drafferth ffeindio'r car. Profodd iet yr ysgol yn fwy o benbleth, a gorfod i fi arwain e mas dan chwifio macyn o'i flaen. Problem arall nawr, ble o'dd y blydi hewl? Da'th bws dau lawr mawr o rywle gyda lampe niwl a gyrrwr mewn sedd uchel, felly cynghorais Alan i'w ddilyn. Bu'n rhaid i ni aros bob tro bydde'r bws yn casglu neu ollwng teithwyr, ond fe aeth Alan yn ddiamynedd ac aeth hibo'r bws i mewn i'r fagddu, ac allen ni ddim gweld dim wedyn. Agores fy ffenest gan weud wrtho ble'r o'dd y cwrbin fel y galle fe gropian 'i ffordd 'mlân. 'Mas ym bach... miwn â ti... Ma'r hewl yn troi i'r chwith... i'r chwith yn gloi!' Stopiodd mor sydyn nes i fi daro 'mhen yn erbyn fframin drws y car.

'Beth uffern ti'n neud?' holais.

'Edrycha!' mynte fe.

Ro'n ni mor agos i ddrws rhyw dŷ, fel y gallen ni weld y rhif arno fe – Rhif 4. Ro'dd y car bach wedi mynd i fyny dreif rhyw dŷ preifet. Ro'dd y bws buon ni'n ei ddilyn wedi diflannu erbyn hynny, felly buon ni'n aros fan 'ny nes i'r nesa ymddangos fel drychiolaeth o rywle. Ymhen oriau cyrhaeddon ni Grays o'r diwedd, wedi taith lafurus a hunllefus. Dyna'r smog wnaeth arwain at newid y gyfraith ac atal cynnau tanau agored yn Llundain. Mae pawb yn meddwl 'mod i'n mystyn tipyn ar y stori, ond na, mae'r profiad yn wir bob gair. Un ôl-nodyn diddorol. Bydde'r athro celf yn dreifio lawr o Brentwood bob dydd. O heulwen lachar ei gartre, bydde'n sydyn, yn ôl ei ddisgrifiad e, yn plymio i mewn i'r llyn mochynnaidd wrth gyrraedd Upminster, ac yna'n dychwelyd i'r haul nefolaidd yn y prynhawn wrth ddringo am gatre ychydig filltiroedd i ffwrdd. Ces dair blynedd adeiladol iawn yn Culverhouse o 1962, lle dysges i sut oedd rheoli plant a chyflwyno Hanes mewn modd deniadol, cyn priodi a dychwelyd i Gymru.

Ysgol Griffith Jones, San Clêr

Mewn cyfnod pan welwyd gweddill y wlad yn symud at addysg Gyfun, parhau â'r system o Ysgolion Gramadeg a'r 11+ oedd polisi Awdurdod Addysg Sir Gâr yn y chwedegau. Felly, agorwyd dwy ysgol Fodern mewn adeiladau newydd sbon i'r disgyblion hynny a fethodd yr arholiad 11+, yn ardaloedd San Clêr a Maes-yr-yrfa, Cefneithin. Fe'm hapwyntiwyd i Ysgol Griffith Jones, San Clêr gyda chyfrifoldeb am Hanes, Saesneg a'r Llyfrgell pan agorwyd y drysau am y tro cynta ym Medi 1965. Dyma ddalgylch ysgol amrywiol o ddiddorol. Ar wahân i ardal San Clêr ei hun, deuai carfan o ddisgyblion o Dalacharn, Pentywyn, Bancyfelin, Meidrym a Threlech, ac o amrywiaeth o gefndiroedd gwahanol. Y dyddie hynny, teimlai Talacharn dipyn yn ynysig, roeddech chi'n dod naill ai o Dalacharn neu ro'ch chi'n dod o bant a byddai'r 'bant' hynny'n cyfeirio at San Clêr, Caerfyrddin, Abertawe neu Lundain. Ro'ch chi i gyd yn yr un twba – o bant! Ar wahân i blant traddodiadol Pentywyn, deuai nifer o safle'r Ganolfan Filwrol Arbrofol yno, felly gallai ambell blentyn fod wedi derbyn ei addysg cyn hynny yn Aden, neu Giprys, neu yn wir unrhyw le arall lle'r oedd lleoliad y fyddin Brydeinig yn bodoli. Mewn gwrthgyferbyniad llwyr roedd plant hollol draddodiadol Gymraeg yn dod o Bancyfelin, Meidrym, Trelech a'r pentrefi gogleddol. Wrth ddrws y dosbarth un bore dyma'r bachgen hyn yn pwyntio'i fys bawd ata i, fel tasen ni yn y mart, 'Jyst y boi fi'n moyn 'i weld', mynte fe. Cael trafferth gyda'i waith cartre ro'dd e!

Hanner can mlynedd yn union wedyn cafwyd aduniad, pan ddychwelodd 7 o'r 14 o athrawon gwreiddiol i ail ymweld â'r adeilad a gawsai ei newid erbyn hynny yn Ysgol Gynradd. Bu farw chwech o'r athrawon eraill cyn yr achlysur, gan gynnwys y Prifathro anghonfensiynol ac arloesol, Islwyn Williams. Cyfnod traddodiadol oedd hwnnw a pholisi ceidwadol, saff oedd yn gyffredin, ond yn San Clêr fe gethon ni Islwyn. Dyma ddyn ar dân am newid pethau a mentro weithiau'n beryglus i arloesi ym mhob agwedd ar fywyd ysgol, gyda chriw o athrawon â'r dasg o addysgu yr anffodusion a fethodd yr 11+ annheg. Bu ef yn ysbrydoliaeth a gyfoethogodd holl addysg y plant yn ei ysgol.

O dan ei arweiniad, bu'n rhaid camu mas o'r hen feysydd llafur ac arbrofi a chynhyrfu bywyd yr ysgol. Ni fyddai Islwyn byth yn gweld problem dim ond atebion ac o fynd ato â syniad newydd yr ateb a gâi'r athro neu'r athrawes oedd, 'Go hed! Cerwch amdani!' Llwyddodd Graham Thomas i hyfforddi Islwyn Rees i ddod yn bencampwr Pole Vault, a daeth Eluned James i olynu Jean Maher ac ymestyn y maes gymnasteg yn yr Adran Ymarfer Corff. Daeth Susan Dobbs o'r 'Pelydrau' i'r Adran Gymraeg ac i ganfod cymar yn yr athro Daearyddiaeth, Don Phillips. A daeth Martin Walters yn fywiog i'r Adran Gelf. Pan adrefnwyd ysgolion yr ardal nes ymlaen, gan droi Ysgol Griffith Jones yn Ysgol

Gynradd a Chanolfan Trefnyddion Addysg, aeth nifer o'r athrawon hyn ymlaen i Hendy-gwyn, a honno bellach yn Ysgol Gyfun.

Dosbarthiadau Nos

Rhaid oedd agor drysau'r ysgol a thywys y plant i fod yn rhan o'r gymuned a chyn hir gwahoddodd y gymuned honno 'nôl yn dorfol drwy ddrysau'r ysgol i elwa'n awchus ar raglen eang o ddosbarthiadau nos. Mewn oes pan nad oedd y teledu, na holl gyfleusterau'r teclynnau ffôn wedi cyrraedd i deyrnasu, roedd oedolion yn awchu am wybodaeth ac am weithgaredd fin nos ac roedd Islwyn Williams yn ddyn digon brwdfrydig i ymateb i'r her honno.

O fewn ychydig flynyddoedd ffrwydrodd y dosbarthiadau nos ac roedd Ysgol Griffith Jones yn cynnig 25 o wahanol ddosbarthiadau ar dair noson yr wythnos. Gwnïo, Coginio, Crochenwaith a Drama ar Nos Lun. Dewis ehangach Nos Fawrth, gyda Chelf, Gwaith Coed, Trwsio Ceir, Jiwdo, Cadw'n Heini, Ffotograffiaeth, Hanes Lleol, a dysgu Cymraeg a Ffrangeg. Byddai Nos Iau'n ail gynnig rhai o'r cyrsiau poblogaidd gorlawn ac ychwanegwyd Weldio, Astudiaethau Gwledig ac Almaeneg at y fwydlen eang. Ar ben hyn oll byddai'r Clwb Ieuenctid ar nosweithiau Mercher ac Iau yn cynnwys ymarfer corff, gwaith basged, badminton a gwersi gitâr. Felly, roedd Goronwy, y gofalwr, ar ddyletswydd bron bob dydd a nos. Pan fyddai'r dosbarthiadau ar ben a phawb wedi tyrru gatre, bydde'r dryse i gyd yn dal ar agor a phob gole mlân ymhobman, tan i Goronwy ddychwelyd o dafarn y Corvus jyst cyn un ar ddeg i gloi. Mewn oes o ymddiried welodd neb unrhyw beth o'i le ar y drefen, ac aeth dim byd ar goll.

Ond hyd yn oed yn yr oes honno, gwelwyd bod ffiniau i awdurdod athro. Dai Rees, a oedd wedi dod i fyw i

Dalacharn, a reolai'r ystafell Gwaith Coed gyda disgyblaeth lem, oherwydd yr holl offer peryglus oedd yno. Clatsien ar gefen llaw gyda darn o bren oedd y gosb i unrhyw grwt diofal, a gan fod un bachgen, Gareth yn eitha lletchwith bydde fe'n ei cha'l hi'n amal. Gadawodd yr ysgol. Mewn rhyw flwyddyn wedyn cyrhaeddodd Dai yn hwyr un bore mewn tymer ofnadwy. 'Y blydi crwt Gareth 'na!' oedd ei gŵyn. Yn ara deg daeth yr eglurhad. Hanner ffordd rhwng San Clêr a Thalacharn roedd bois y Cyngor Sir yn atgyweirio rhan o'r hewl, a phwy oedd yng ngofal yr arwyddion Stop-Go, ond ein cyn-ddisgybl. Pan welodd Gareth gar Dai'n dod, cofiodd am y driniaeth a gawsai yn yr ysgol. Trodd yr arwydd yn Stop a cherdded bant! Digwyddodd yr un peth ar y ffordd gatre y prynhawn hwnnw hefyd. Cymerwyd wythnos i orffen y jobyn ar y darn hwnnw o hewl ac am weddill yr wythnos, bu'n rhaid i Dai druan deithio ar hyd nifer o hewlydd bach y wlad er mwyn osgoi dialedd ei gyn-ddisgybl.

Ar wahân i redeg yr Adrannau Hanes a Saesneg, bûm yn llenwi'r Llyfrgell â phob math o lyfrau gyda chymorth brwdfrydig Rhian Jones o Lyfrgell Sir Gâr. Bu ymateb y plant, methiannau'r 11+, yn syfrdanol. Byddai ein Llyfrgell yn orlawn bob egwyl ac amser cinio, a nifer y benthyciadau yn ein Llyfrgell oedd y gorau yn y Sir o bell ffordd. Ar ben hyn oll, fe'm perswadiwyd, gan yr 'arloeswr ar garlam', i gychwyn dosbarth nos ar Hanes Lleol. Erbyn 1970 aeth yn ddau gwrs ar ddwy wahanol noson, gydag ymweliadau â chestyll, eglwysi, cromlechi a gwahanol dai ar nosweithiau yn ystod tymor yr haf. Mae ardaloedd San Clêr, Talacharn, Pentywyn, Eglwys Cymun, Meidrym, Llangynin, Hendygwyn yn frith o hanes. Ar ben hyn, câi cynadleddau Hanes eu cynnal o dan arweiniad Tecwyn Lloyd o Adran Efrydiau Allanol Aberystwyth.

Yn yr ysgol ddyddiol, ceid projectau di-ri gyda'r

'Seashore' o dan arweiniad D V Davies a byddai disgyblion yn heidio tua'r arfordir. Gwelwyd hwy'n hwylio cychod Mirror Dingies ar hyd y Taf a'r Tywi ac allan tua'r môr o Lanyfferi. Doedd dim sôn am reolau Iechyd a Diogelwch bryd hynny, nag am lenwi ffurflenni asesu risg ac ati. Ar ben hyn oll byddai llawer o sioeau a chynyrchiadau ysgol yn cael eu llwyfannu. Ond roedd hyn i gyd yn gostus a chydag Islwyn yn ffili gweud y gair 'Na' mewn ateb i unrhyw gais oddi wrth yr athrawon, fe orwariodd lwfans yr ysgol. Aeth rhai cannoedd drosodd un flwyddyn, arian mawr bryd hynny, a daeth y Cyfarwyddwr Addysg ei hun mas o'i swyddfa ac i lawr i San Clêr. Cyfarfod digon anniddig fu hi yn swyddfa fechan Islwyn, gyda'r Cyfarwyddwr yn y diwedd yn bygwth ailfeddiannu llyfrau o'r ysgol i gwrdd â'r gost. Os do fe te! Collodd Islwyn ei amynedd yn llwyr. 'Gadwch y llyfre i fod lle ma nhw! Os y'ch chi moyn mynd â rhwbeth, cerwch â'r blydi carped ma o dan 'y nhrad i. Ofynnes i ddim amdano fe o gwbwl. Chi roiodd e miwn 'ma!'

Cilio wnaeth y Cyfarwyddwr yn weddol sydyn wedyn, i sgubo'r ddyled o dan ryw garped tipyn mwy yn Neuadd y Sir. Rhaid cyfadde serch hynny nad oedd Islwyn Williams yn boblogaidd gan bobl llawer mwy confensiynol nag e ac fe allai fod yn beryglus o anhrefnus, weithie. Achosai un Saesnes o lywodraethwr ben tost cyson iddo, a hithau'n elyniaethus i'r holl ddiwylliant Cymreig 'wthiwyd i lawr gwddwg ei hannwyl fab' oedd wedi methu'r 11+. Wrth gyrraedd ei ddrws un bore ataliais fy nghnoc arferol o glywed rhyw gwmpo mas uchel. Es 'nôl ato ychydig wedyn i'w gweld hi'n camu mas a diflannu lawr y coridor. 'Dewch miwn,' mynte fe a'i wyneb yn danllyd goch, 'Chi'n gwbod be sy' ishe ar honna? Bwch gafr ddwywaith y dydd!'

Ysgol Maes-yr-yrfa

Y Prifathro Islwyn Williams wnaeth fy stopio, ar frys fel arfer, yng nghoridor uchaf adeilad Ysgol Griffith Jones, San Clêr. 'Ma swydd Maes-yr-yrfa'n dod lan. Cerwch amdani!' A chyda chwifiad braich brysur diflannodd i ysgogi ryw aelod arall o'r staff ynglŷn â rhyw syniad newydd, cyn i fi ddeall ei neges, heb sôn am godi cwestiwn. Trannoeth, yn ei swyddfa, a minnau erbyn hyn ar ddeall mai swydd Prifathro oedd dan ystyriaeth ym Maes-yr-yrfa Cefneithin, dyma godi amheuon. Yn y cyfnod hwnnw gwelid bod swyddi uwch yn aml yn adlewyrchu traddodiad traed y meirw, gyda dyrchafiad yn disgyn fel gwobr am flynyddoedd lawer o wasanaeth, gwobr cyn ymddeol. A minnau ond yn 33 blwydd oed, braidd yn gynnar oedd hi. 'Go hed achan! Bydd e'n brofiad da i chi ga'l cyfweliad, ac yn help i'ch dyfodol.' Buodd y profiad o wasanaethu fel Is-Warden i'r Dosbarthiadau Nos yn San Clêr yn fodd i ehangu'r gorwelion y tu hwnt i gyfrifoldeb pwnc neu ddosbarth, ac yn fodd i werthfawrogi shwd o'dd eraill yn gweld y byd. A dyna fel y bu ar ddydd o wanwyn yn 1972. Cais miwn!

Pan ddaeth y newyddion y byddwn yn un o dri i wynebu'r Cyngor Sir llawn yn Neuadd fawr Caerfyrddin, sobrodd yr iwfforia o fod yn geffyl rasys mas am y tro cynta i fod yn galop, yn weddol gloi. Dyma sylweddoli 'mod i o bosib o fewn cyrraedd ysgwyddo cyfrifoldeb nid yn unig dros gannoedd o blant, ond athrawon, rhieni, llywodraethwyr a'r Awdurdod Addysg wrth gwrs. Teimlad ysgytwol ond un adeiladol iawn fel y datblygodd pethau. O flaen y fath dyrfa, sylweddolais na fyddai rhyw holi manwl y tu hwnt i'r tri chwestiwn amlwg arferol, felly bydde'n gyfle i gyflwyno fy athroniaeth bersonol ynglŷn ag addysg. Hyd yn hyn yn fy ngyrfa, rown i wedi dysgu'n reddfol heb feddwl llawer y tu hwnt i hynny. Es ati i roi trefen ar bethe.

Wedi amlinellu cyfrifoldebau amrywiol y swydd yn fewnol ac allanol, gan gynnwys yr adeilad a chyllid, y cyfan at wasanaeth plant ac athrawon, teimlwn yn hyderus o flaen y dorf boliticaidd. Heb os, bu fy mhrofiad wrth actio a llwyfannu yn gymorth mawr y diwrnod hwnnw. Yn hyderus iawn erbyn hyn, es ati i egluro shwd y byddwn yn defnyddio Hanes Lleol i ennyn diddordeb plant. Wrth ddysgu am holl gymhlethdodau crefyddol adeg cyfnod Cromwell es i hwyl. Cerdded miwn i'r dosbarth gan gyhoeddi fod Ficer Meidrym wedi ca'l y sac. Dylwn egluro fod y Ficer yno, y Parch W J Griffiths, hefyd yn un o arweinwyr blaenllaw y Grŵp Annibynnol ar y Cyngor. Wedi i'r plant sylweddoli mai at Stephen Hughes yn yr ail ganrif ar bymtheg y cyfeiriwn, roedd pawb yn awyddus i wybod pam. Daeth pwl o chwerthin o'r siambr, gyda'r Ficer yn wên fawr o glust i glust. Beth petawn i wedi ei ybseto? Fe'm hapwyntiwyd i'r swydd beth bynnag.

Wedyn, daeth cyfle i ymweld â'r ysgol am y tro cynta. Er cyrraedd yn hwyr yn dilyn ca'l pynctier ger Porthyrhyd, ces groeso cynnes iawn. O gerdded miwn daeth ton o ymdeimlad cartrefol o'r adeilad ei hunan, gyda'r cyntedd mawr agored a'i do gwydr yn goleuo fel rhyw sgwâr pentre cyfeillgar. Dyma lle mae'r coridor top a'r gwaelod yn cyfarfod â'r ffordd lan o'r adrannau crefft a chwaraeon, yn ogystal â mynedfa'r neuadd. Felly, dyma lle byddai'r gwahanol ddisgyblion ac athrawon yn cyfarfod, yn dilyn pob cloch newid gwersi. Ie sgwâr y pentre oedd y cyntedd 'na. Teimlwn naws deuluol gynnes yn teyrnasu drwyddi draw.

Fel yna y bu pethau am y pum mlynedd ar hugain nesa. Rhyw hanner ffordd drwy fy nghyfnod yno, ces fy mherswadio i gynnig am swydd arall, dyrchafiad i fod. Ar ganol y cyfweliad, a minnau mewn penbleth, ac i fod ateb rhyw gwestiwn arall, clywais fy hun yn dweud 'Rwy am fynd 'nôl i Maes-yr-yrfa.' Fel yna y bu, a wnes i erioed wedyn ystyried swydd arall, gan sylweddoli 'mod i'n berson teyrngar. Bûm yn deyrngar i'm hardal enedigol, yn deyrngar i gyfeillion, yn arbennig i rai bore oes, ac yn deyrngar i bob sefydliad y bûm yn ymwneud ag e. Felly yno y bues i, tan i fi ymddeol yn 1996.

Er holl gynhesrwydd yr ymweliad cynta, gwyddwn 'mod i am newid dau beth yn syth. O flaen drws y fynedfa roedd arwydd mawr negyddol yn gwahardd *Stileto Heels*. Lawr y dath e, oherwydd dylai'r neges y bydd person yn ei weld gynta wrth ymweld â lle fod bob amser yn groesawgar. Yn ail, pan ganai'r gloch i alw'r plant i mewn i'r ysgol, bydden nhw'n llunio rhesi militaraidd cyn ymdeithio i'r adeilad. Rhaid oedd dileu yr arferiad. Dylai pob un gerdded miwn fel y mynnai. Pethau bach, ond pethau pwysig yn fy athroniaeth i. Ond, roedd yna broblem dipyn mwy yn ymwneud â'r athrawon, oherwydd am resymau na wyddai neb pam, roedd o leiaf wyth ohonyn nhw ar delerau dros dro yn unig. Sefyllfa ansicr nad oedd yn deg â'r athrawon hynny, nac â dyfodol yr ysgol chwaith. Bu'n broses hir a chymhleth. Yn gyntaf, rhaid oedd edrych ar y cwricwlwm ac anghenion y disgyblion yn y dyfodol a cheisio cydweddu hynny â'r arbenigrwydd oedd ar gael.

Wedi datrys cymhlethdod yr athrawon dros dro a sicrhau swyddi iddynt, daeth cyfle i arloesi a chynnig pynciau newydd. Gyda'm cefndir ym myd yr actio, rown i'n awyddus i gynnig Drama fel pwnc ysgol. Ymateb negyddol gan ambell Lywodraethwr yn ôl y disgwyl, 'Rhowch ragor o syms a Saesneg iddyn nhw!' Bu Morley Lewis, Gweinidog Tabernacl Cefneithin, nai Elfed yr emynydd a thad Elfed Bach, y cawr ar goesau byr, yn gefnogol i'r syniad, a bu Norah Isaac, yn ôl ei harfer, yn brysur ar y ffôn. Cyn pen dim gofynnodd y Llywodraethwr negyddol i fi pa bryd y byddwn i'n hysbysebu'r swydd Drama, oherwydd ei bod hi'n bwysig symud 'mlân 'da'r oes. Felly, dyna gychwyn ar ffatri actio Maes-yr-yrfa a gweld Rhiannon Rees, wedyn Delyth Mai ac yna Carys Edwards yn datblygu talentau di-ri i lenwi stiwdios *Pobol y Cwm*. Ie, cyn-ddisgyblion Maes-yr-yrfa yw Eifion a Sara a hefyd D J, heb sôn am actorion eraill fel Carys Eleri ac Aled Pugh a ymddangosodd mewn meysydd amrywiol dros y degawdau wedyn.

Fel mewn sawl ysgol arall, datblygodd y sioeau Nadolig i fod yn uchafbwynt diwedd y tymor cyntaf, gyda'r disgyblion a'r athrawon yn cyfrannu mewn amryw ffyrdd dan arweiniad Delyth Mai Nicholas ar y dechrau. Bu dawn John James gyda'r gwahanol offerynnau yn ysbrydoliaeth i Gerdd, a rhaid talu teyrnged i wasanaeth hyfforddi teithiol Dyfed, a oedd yn griw mor weithgar a brwdfrydig. Parhau wnaeth y traddodiad i'r Ysgol Ddwyieithog hefyd. Efallai mai *Sŵn y Gân*, cyfieithiad *The Sound of Music*, fu'r uchafbwynt, ac fe'i comisiynwyd i fynd ar daith drwy Gwm Gwendraeth gan y Cyfarwyddwr Addysg, John Ellis. Defnyddiwyd Neuadd fawr Pontyberem ar sawl achlysur wedi hynny.

Bu apwyntiadau allweddol eraill a gwelwyd pobl fel James Rees a Delyth Armstrong yn cyrraedd ac yn parhau ar y staff tan iddyn nhw ymddeol. Fel yn Ysgol Griffith Jones, derbyniai dioddefwyr yr 11+ addysg amrywiol ac arloesol yn Ysgol Maes-yr-yrfa, gyda'r fwydlen yn ehangach nag a ganiatawyd yn yr ysgolion Gramadeg. Adeiladwyd Hovercraft i hedfan ar gae'r ysgol ac fe rwyfodd bechgyn mewn canŵs o amgylch Ynys Bŷr hyd yn oed, o dan arweiniad Steve Pugh Jones. Ffynnu wnaeth dosbarthiadau garddio Gareth Protheroe. Ac fe aeth Eisteddfod stwrllyd Dydd Gŵyl Dewi rhwng llysoedd Arthne, Non a Darog yn uchafbwynt cystadleuol tu hwnt.

Taith o ryw ugain munud oedd hi o 'nghartref yn

Bronwydd i'r ysgol, a chyfle i roi'r meddwl ar waith ynglŷn â threfniadau'r dydd. O bryd i'w gilydd bydde'r annisgwyl yn hawlio'r lle blaenaf. Ond anghofia i fyth yr annisgwyl un bore, hanner ffordd draw. Cyn dyddiau'r ffordd osgoi, ar waelod rhiw Nant-y-caws ro'n i'n dechre dringo yr ochr arall pan welais wreichion a chlywed sŵn mawr ro'n i'n meddwl oedd yn dod o'r ddau dŷ ar y chwith, islaw capel Phila. Yna, gwelais lori dancer olew yn ymlwybro lawr canol yr hewl yn araf bach tuag ata i a'r ddwy olwyn flaen yn troi yn ôl a mlân o'r chwith i'r dde heb unrhyw reolaeth arnyn nhw. Tynnes i miwn i iet y cae ar y chwith, ond allwn i wneud dim byd wrth i'r anghenfil anelu amdana i – arswyd llwyr – doedd 'na ddim gyrrwr yn y lori. Rhyw ddeg llath bant oddi wrtha i, dyma'r olwyn yn gwyro i'r dde ac fe foelodd y lori ar y clawdd gyferbyn. O ddod mas o'r car meddyliais i fi weld hen got ar ganol yr hewl nes lan. Wedi cerdded ati, doedd dim rhaid edrych yn fanwl, dyna i gyd oedd ar ôl o'r gyrrwr druan a gawsai ei wasgu i farwolaeth yn erbyn wal y tŷ. Daeth yr Heddlu a'r gwasanaethau brys yn fuan iawn wedyn, ond anwybyddais yr awgrym y dylwn fynd i'r ysbyty.

Es ymlaen yn syth i'r ysgol a chymryd y gwasanaeth boreol fel arfer. Ryw hanner awr wedyn, wrth drin y post dyddiol, torrais allan yn chwys diferol drosta i gyd a theimlwn mewn gwendid mawr. Awgrymodd y staff na ddylwn aros yn yr ysgol ac am unwaith derbyniais eu cyngor. Gan mai fi oedd yr unig dyst i'r ddamwain bu'n rhaid mynd i'r cwest, lle datgelwyd fod y gyrrwr wedi diodde trawiad ar y galon wrth yrru i lawr y rhiw.

Yn yr ysgol rown i'n awyddus bob amser i fod ar gael ac i gadw drws fy ystafell yn agored i blant, aelodau'r staff, rhieni, neu unrhyw un arall. Byddwn yn crwydro o amgylch yr ysgol, yn enwedig adeg egwyl a thros ginio. Teimlwn fod cadw mewn cysylltiad â phawb yn holl bwysig i gynnal yr awyrgylch yno.

Yn y dyddiau cynnar byddai Carwyn James yn croesi'r hewl o'i gartref i daro i mewn am gwpaned o goffi, ac un rheol ganddo; trafod llenyddiaeth neu gloncs lleol, ond dim rygbi. Ro'dd Carwyn James yn smygwr mowr. Cofio gofyn iddo beth fu ei broblem fwya wrth arwain taith fuddugoliaethus y Llewod i Seland Newydd, a chael ateb annisgwyl; 'Wrth fynd o le i le ffindo siop yn y bore yn gwerthu Players Navy Cut!' Rhannais ystafell gydag e ar un daith criced hefyd. Bydde fe'n tano'r ffag nesa o'r stwmpyn blaenorol; diffodd hanner stwmpyn y peth diwetha cyn mynd i gysgu ac wrth ddihuno yn y bore cropian amdani i'r blwch wrth ochor y gwely. Bu ei farwolaeth sydyn yn golled enfawr, nid yn unig i'r byd rygbi, ond i'r gymuned leol yng Nghwm Gwendraeth a Chymru gyfan.

Gofalwyr

Arweiniodd ambell gnoc ar y drws at greu syndod. Daeth gweinidog lleol i mewn un bore, ei wyneb yn fflamgoch a chaeodd y drws yn glep gan floeddio, 'Ffycin Diaconied!' Roedd gofalwr yr ysgol ar y pryd yn un ohonyn nhw. A sôn am ofalwr, bu Nigel Owens yn llenwi'r swydd ar un adeg ac yn effeithiol iawn hefyd. Bu'n ddisgybl ac wedyn yn dechnegydd cyn yn y diwedd symud ymlaen i ddyfarnu, dod yn fyd enwog, ond daliai i fod yn un o fois y Cwm ac yn deyrngar i'w fro enedigol.

'Nol yn y saithdegau, caniatawyd i ddisgyblion, na fyddai'n sefyll arholiadau ac yn ysu am gael gwaith, adael yr ysgol erbyn gwyliau'r Pasg.

Ddwy flynedd yn olynol, torrwyd y gwydr tân i greu hafog stwrllyd chwarter awr cyn y gloch derfynol. Penderfynais roi stop ar hynny drwy weithredu cynllun cudd. Yn fy swyddfa, rhoddais gyfarwyddid i'r Gofalwr newydd, Robert Sams i droi'r system larymau bant am dri o'r gloch i atal hynny. Am dri o'r gloch, serch hynny atseiniodd holl glychau'r ysgol fel yn y blynyddoedd cynt. Rhuthrais allan i'r cyntedd, a gweld môr o blant ac athrawon yn rhedeg i bob cyfeiriad. Yno hefyd safai'r Gofalwr a golwg fodlon iawn ei fyd ar ei wyneb.

'Beth ddiawl ry'ch chi 'di neud, ddyn?' holais.

'Wedoch chi wrtho i am roi'r larwm bant a 'na beth 'nes i!'

'Off o'n i'n feddwl!'

'Wel bant yw off, ond tefe? Be sy'n bod arnoch chi?'

Lawr yn yr Ystafell Dyblygu chwerthin wnath Nigel Owens wrth weld fod y gamddealltwriaeth yn ddoniol – Fi am i'r Gofalwr droi'r system bant ac ynte wedi rhoi'r larwm bant – i ganu. Ar ei ddiwrnod ysgol olaf y diwrnod hwnnw, roedd 'na un bachgen bach siomedig. Ac ynte ar fin ffugio ei fod yn dioddef o stumog dost, er mwyn ca'l gadael y dosbarth i dorri'r gwydr, beth glywodd e, o'dd yr holl glyche'n byddaru pawb, gan fod y Gofalwr wedi cael y bla'n arno fe.

Fel dau ffermwr roedd Robert Sams a finne'n deall ein gilydd i'r dim ac rown i'n gadel iddo ga'l oriau hyblyg. Buwch i'r mart neu'n fisi ar y seilej, câi agor yr ysgol a bant â fe am gatre. Ond wedyn, pan fydde galw arno fe i fod yn yr ysgol, galle fe fod gyda ni drwy'r dydd.

Un bore Sadwrn, a finne wrthi ar ganol agor rhych yn yr ardd, dyma Jane yn galw a dweud bod y Gofalwr ar y ffôn. Neges od iawn o'dd 'da fe,

'Cerddes i hibo'r Tŷ Gwydr ond do'dd e ddim 'na.'

'Wrth gwrs 'i fod e 'na 'chan!'

'Nadi, mae e wedi mynd. Dewch draw, os nad y'ch chi'n 'y nghredu i.'

Byddai Robert yn cerdded o amgylch yr ysgol ar ei ffordd

i Bontyberem bob bore Sadwrn. Fe, o'dd yn iawn wrth gwrs. Roedd Tŷ Gwydr Gareth Prortheroe a'i ddosbarth garddio wedi diflannu'n llwyr. Dadl ddiffrwyth wedyn 'da'r Cyngor Sir, gan mai yswiriant difrod yn unig oedd ganddyn nhw, achos doedd neb byth yn colli tŷ gwydr! Felly buodd yn rhaid i'r ysgol dalu am un newydd i Gareth.

Fisoedd wedyn daeth plismon lleol i ddweud eu bod nhw wedi ffindio'r tŷ gwydr. Wrth ganlyn rhyw fewnfudwr ar gyffuriau, archwiliwyd ei dŷ yng Nghefneithin, ac wrth iddo wneud cyfaddefiad llawn fe gawson nhw'r gwirionedd.

Daeth y plismon lleol i mewn i'm swyddfa a gwên fawr ar ei wyneb, *'Problem Solved,'* mynte fe. Eglurodd fod y gŵr wedi bod yn cadw'r holl blanhigion canabis yn nhŷ gwydr yr ysgol, a hynny yng ngwaelod ei ardd. Llwyddiant i'r heddlu, ond doedd y tŷ gwydr a hwnnw bellach yn ddarnau yn werth dim i ni bellach.

Ar ddechrau'r saithdegau roedd y wialen yn dal yn gosb gyfreithlon, ond beth amser cyn ei dileu'n swyddogol rown wedi rhoi'r gore i'w defnyddio. Cofio'r defnydd olaf a wnes ohoni'n dda. Mewnfudwr o grwt cas o Faesybont wedi ei ddal am yr eildro yn towlu cerrig at ddwy ferch fach, felly penderfynu rhoi gwers iddo. Bu'r gansen yn llechu tu ôl i'r gwresogydd am flwyddyn neu ddwy yn ddi-waith cyn hynny, ond chwalodd yn deilchion wrth roi'r gosb, yn wir roedd yn ddarnau mân dros y llawr i gyd.

Mas â'r crwt a miwn â Susan, yr ysgrifenyddes, i gyhoeddi fod dwy fam bryderus yr olwg o Gorslas, am fy ngweld ar unwaith. Rhaid bod rhywbeth mowr o'i le. Aeth y ddau ohonon ni ati i gasglu holl friwsion y bambŵ o lawr yr ystafell. Miwn dda'th y ddwy o'r diwedd i ddatgelu'r argyfwng mawr.

'Ni'n gwbod 'i fod e'n gofyn lot, ond all Kevin a John adel chwarter awr cyn y gloch ar ddydd Gwener. Ni 'di bwco mynd i weld goleuadau Blacpwl 'da bỳs Williams ac ma fe'n gadel am chwarter wedi tri.'

Rhyddhad! O'n i'n eitha parod i roi'r diwrnod cyfan bant i'r ddau.

Prifathrawon

Drwy'r wythdegau byddai ysgolion ardal Dinefwr, sef Llanymddyfri (Rowley Griffiths), Tre-gib (Glyn Davies), Rhydaman (Caryl Edwards), Gwendraeth (Bob Garrero) a finne ym Maes-yr-yrfa yn cydweithio'n rymus mewn consortiwm ar nifer o fentrau yn ymwneud ag addysg. Wrth ysgrifennu'r geiriau hyn bu farw Rowley, yr olaf ohonynt, a braint fu sefyll gyda thyrfa ar y strydoedd ar ddydd ei angladd, tyrfa a werthfawrogodd ei gyfraniad i Lanymddyfri. Collodd criced Morgannwg hefyd un o gefnogwyr mwyaf selog y gêm bedwar diwrnod.

Fel uned o bum ysgol enillwyd safle Compact i gyflwyno cyrsiau a chyfarpar newydd i'r disgyblion. Sefydlwyd Pwyllgor Cyswllt Diwydiant ac Ysgol, a oedd yn cynnwys arweinydd y swyddogion, Phil Drakeford, brawd y Prif Weinidog, Gwynfor Price o gwmni 3M's, Martin Jones o gwmni yswiriant, yn ogystal â brwdfrydedd John Davies, European Profiles. Bu'r byd diwydiannol yn allweddol i gynnig wythnos o brofiad gwaith arloesol i'r plant.

Amheus fu nifer ar y dechre gyda sylwadau fel hyn gan rai o'r byd gwaith: 'Byddan nhw'n stico'u bysedd miwn yn y peirianne... 'Da pwy gewn ni yswiriant?' Ro'dd rhai athrawon hefyd yn ddigon amheus: 'Pa les yw e i ni golli wythnos gyfan o wersi? Bydd e bownd o effeithio ar ganlyniade'r plant yn arholiade'r haf.' Ond cyn hir, gyda brwdfrydedd amlwg y plant yn profi'n allweddol, enillodd yr arbrawf ei safle, i ddatblygu'n rhan hanfodol o fyd addysg. Cofio un ferch aeth yn frwdfrydig at y fet ar ei phrofiad gwaith, i ddarganfod na allai hi oddef aroglau'r lle. Cafodd y cyfle i ddarganfod hynny mewn pryd fel y gallai newid gyrfa mewn pryd ac felly cwrs ei bywyd.

Wrth i fi sôn am ddial yn y bennod ar San Clêr daw atgof arall i gof yn ystod fy nghyfnod yn Ysgol Maes-yr-yrfa. Daeth Warden Traffig newydd i dre Caerfyrddin, un yn llawn brwdfrydedd, a chrwydrodd y prif strydoedd yn hela am ei brae. Y tu allan i hen wyrcws Caerfyrddin sylwodd ar gar ei gyn-brifathro o Gastell Newydd, a'i fod wedi parcio ar linellau melyn. Yn llawn gorfoledd, rhoddodd docyn ar ei ffenest, ond wedi ail feddwl penderfynodd mai gwell fyddai bwco'r chwech arall hefyd, rhag ofn i'w hen brifathro gwyno.

Ymhen rhyw hanner awr llifodd prifathrawon y Sir allan o Swyddfa Dr. Hedydd Davies mewn hwyliau drwg, gan na fyddai ceiniog goch ar gael iddynt ei wario ar gelfi am flwyddyn arall, yn dilyn y newyddion am yr holl gwtogi. Gwaethygodd eu hwyliau'n enbyd o weld y papurau parcio yn chwifio yn yr awel. Aeth y lle'n wenfflam: Caryl Edwards, Rhydaman am gael cyfreithiwr, George Bancroft, Hendygwyn yn taranu ac eraill yn ofni gweld y stori ar dudalen flaen y *Journal*. Oherwydd i fi gyrraedd y cyfarfod yn hwyr, ro'n i'n lwcus wedi cael lle yn y maes parcio priodol. Felly, o ran diawlineb es at Miss Wooloff, Prifathrawes awdurdodol Ysgol Cambria, a chynnig mynd i'r llys a rhoi geirda iddi. Roedd yr ymateb ar ei hwyneb yn bictiwr! Aeth Hedydd ar y ffôn a dyna fu diwedd y mater.

Er ein bod, o ran syniadau addysgol, yn bell iawn oddi wrth ein gilydd, rhaid cofnodi i Miss Wooloff a fi gydweithio'n hwylus wrth drefnu siaradwyr i ddod i gynadleddau disgyblion chweched dosbarth y Sir dan nawdd CEWC (Council for Education in World Citizenship). Yng Ngholeg y Drindod y câi y rhain eu cynnal, a dw i'n dal i gofio y gynhadledd honno pan lwyddason ni sicrhau presenoldeb trefnydd yr ymgyrch i ryddhau Nelson Mandela, i gynnal dadl â chynrychiolydd Llywodraeth Apartheid De Affrica. Gwanllyd iawn fu dadleuon hwnnw wrth iddo geisio amddiffyn apartheid, er mor gryf oedd ei acen. Flynyddoedd yn ddiweddarach, ar daith ar fy ngwyliau yn cerdded drwy diroedd tyfu grawnwin y wlad honno, clywais yr un acen arw yr Affricans, ond bellach un yn llawn balchder, wrth i'n harweinydd ddangos i ni'r fynedfa y cerddodd Mandela drwyddi i ryddid.

Cyfathrebu

Drwy'r wythdegau aeth cynadleddau addysg yn rhemp gyda galwadau cyson i'w mynychu ac weithiau byddwn yn cynadledda am ddeuddydd. Barnwyd bod y sesiwn gynta, wedi cinio mawr ganol dydd, yn un farwol, a dw i'n synnu dim. Wedi tri chwrs, heb anghofio'r gwin, câi'r ffenestri eu tywyllu, diffoddwyd y goleuadau a byddai'r taflunydd yn taflu gwybodaeth. Ond, wrth i'r cyflwynydd droi ei gefn at ei gynulleidfa bydde'r pâr cynta o lyged yn dechrau cau...

Y syndod mwyaf oedd sut y gallai unigolion y byd addysg anwybyddu rheolau sylfaenol cyfathrebu. Rhaid i athro, actor neu siaradwr gadw cysylltiad â'i gynulleidfa bob amser, mae'n sylfaenol bwysig eu bod yn gweld ei wyneb a'i lygaid. Roedd Hywel Teifi Edwards yn bencampwr ar wneud hyn. Cofio ei ddarlith ar Eisteddfodau'r Bedwaredd Ganrif ar Bymtheg i Antiquarians Caerfyrddin – talcen caled wrth ei gyflwyno i grŵp di-Gymraeg. Camodd 'nôl ac ymlaen, ei ddwylo'n chwifio ac yntau heb nodyn o bapur llwyddodd i hoelio'r gynulleidfa am awr gyfan. Yna, wrth iddo sylwi bod pen un hen ddyn bach yn yr ail reng yn dechrau cwympo, cododd Hywel ei lais a chafwyd y perl yma, 'That adjudication on the Crown competition was totally biased, and I can see the gentleman here in front of me is in total agreement.' Fentrodd y gŵr bach na neb arall chwaith gymryd napyn am weddill y ddarlith.

Drygioni

Yn awyrgylch gartrefol, agored yr ysgol bydde 'na dipyn o sbri a thynnu coes, ac yn amal iawn bydde Nigel Owens a Robert Sams ein gofalwr o ffarmwr yn ei chanol hi. Daeth gorchymyn gan yr awdurdod bod yn rhaid trafod rhyw fater cenedlaethol gyda'r holl staff, a threfnwyd cyfarfod wedi'r gloch ganu un prynhawn yn Ystafell yr Athrawon. Troi i adael ar ddiwedd y cyfarfod, ond ffili'n deg ag agor y drws; roedd hwnnw ar glo. Ro'dd rhyw ddeugain ohonon ni wedi ein caethiwo yno a phawb ar hast i fynd gatre.

'Odi pawb 'ma?' holodd un athro.

'Fi'n ffili gweld y gofalwr na'r technegydd,' medde rhywun arall.

Lwcus bod y Dirprwy, Ieuan Morgan yn ddigon main i fynd mas drwy'r ffenest. Roedd hi'n weddol amlwg ym mhoced pwy roedd yr allweddi ac ynte erbyn hyn yn ei lordio hi ar hyd yr ysgol. Yn dilyn hyn, ar Ebrill y cyntaf anfonwyd Nigel lan i siop fawr Leekes i gasglu teclyn gorchuddio ffenest, gorchudd nad oedd yn bodoli, wrth gwrs. Gyda staff Leekes miwn yn rhan o'r cynllun, anfonwyd ef o un adran i'r llall am amser cyn iddyn nhw gyda'i gilydd floeddio 'Ffŵl Ebrill'. Fynte, â gwên fawr ar ei wyneb, yn cydnabod iddo ga'l ei ddala.

Addysg Ddwyieithog

Dechreuais i ddysgu Hanes drwy gyfrwng y Gymraeg yn Ysgol Griffith Jones tua'r un adeg ag y bu Margaret Davies yn arloesi yn Ysgol Ramadeg y Gwendraeth. Wedi'r amheuon cynnar, daeth cymdeithas i werthfawrogi hyn

73

fel cam rhesymol a naturiol. Yn raddol, cynyddu wnaeth y fwydlen a chyn hir ychwanegwyd Daearyddiaeth ac Addysg Grefyddol. Cynyddu wnaeth y galw am addysg ddwyieithog gyflawn, gyda Rhydfelen yn esiampl i bawb a datblygiadau yng Nghaerfyrddin yn ychwanegu at hynny. Yn fuan wedyn, penderfynwyd adrefnu addysg Cwm Gwendraeth, ond gan fod tair ysgol bellach wedi eu sefydlu eu hunain yn yr ardal, tasg anodd fyddai honno, beth bynnag a gâi ei gynnig. Yn y diwedd, Ysgol Eilradd Pontyberem gollodd mas, er i'r Cynghorwr Howard Jones ymladd yn galed drosti. Ac i fod yn deg roedd yna dipyn o gydymdeimlad â sefydliad a fu'n boblogaidd ac yn effeithiol iawn yn ei ardal. Gallai seremonïau gwobrwyo'r cyfnod gael eu hanghofio'n weddol gloi, ond bydde 'na siarad am wythnose wedyn am y Te ym Mhontyberem – y byrddau'n orlawn ac arnyn nhw bob math o ddanteithion. Yn wir, bydde ambell gynghorwr yn gwneud mochyn o'i hunan!

Penderfynwyd mai dwy ysgol gyfun fyddai bellach, un cyfrwng Saesneg yn y Gwendraeth ac Ysgol Ddwyieithog ym Maes-yr-yrfa. Gwelwyd nifer o athrawon fu'n cefnogi addysg Gymraeg yn symud lan yr hewl o'r Gwendraeth i Faes-yr-yrfa, megis Margaret Davies, Elsbeth Jones, Ieuan Morgan, Wyn Thomas, Geraint Roberts, Anne Jones a Gaynor Hughes, i enwi ond rhai. Unodd y rhain gyda'r hoelion wyth oedd yn yr ysgol yn barod; athrawon fel Gwynallt Pryce, James Rees a Delyth Armstrong. Cefais y cyfrifoldeb o lywio'r fenter newydd, oedd yn ôl rhai yn arbrawf peryglus o fentrus. Ond tyfu a ffynnu a wnaeth yr ysgol gydag athrawon brwdfrydig a galluog eraill yn cyrraedd, megis Mair Ifans i'r adran Gymraeg a Julie Francis. Tyfodd yr ysgol o fod yn 196 disgybl yn wreiddiol, i groesi'r 700 erbyn i fi ymddeol, gan roi hyder i Gymreictod y cwm.

Bu'n rhaid troedio'n ofalus wrth ledaenu'r pynciau a gâi eu dysgu drwy'r Gymraeg. Ar un ochr tyfodd y brwdfrydedd a'r hyder am fwy, ond bu'n rhaid pwyso hyn gyda'r hen draddodiad fod rhai rhieni yn gweld rhagoriaethau yn eu dysgu drwy'r Saesneg. Araf deg piau hi; cyn bo hir, yr unig Saesneg a gaed mewn gwersi Mathemateg oedd y geiriau ar glawr y llyfr, am fod y plant a'r athro wedi penderfynu taw Cymraeg fyddai iaith y dosbarth. Cadwodd yr ysgol, nid yn unig ei henw da, ond yr awyrgylch agored, gartrefol, a chredaf o hyd i ffurf yr adeiladau ac yn bennaf 'sgwâr y pentre' o gyntedd, canolfan naturiol lle gallai pawb gwrdd, fod yn un ffactor pwysig yn hynny i gyd.

Rhaid peidio anghofio cynhesrwydd ac agosatrwydd naturiol Cwm Gwendraeth ac adlewyrchwyd hyn gan un digwyddiad arbennig. Wrth i bob ysgol yn ei thro wynebu'r Archwiliad Llawn Swyddogol byddai'r holl beth yn creu tensiwn a phryder a pharatoi gwyllt ymhlith yr athrawon am fisoedd cyn wythnos fawr y mewnlifiad o Arolygwyr. Daeth ein tro ni. Yng nghanol yr archwiliad, merch fach ddeuddeg oed yn cwrdd ag Arolygwraig yn y cyntedd un prynhawn ac yn gofyn iddi, 'A shwt ddiwrnod i chi wedi ga'l te?' Chwarae teg, aeth y sylw miwn i'r Adroddiad. Ac o sôn am do gwydr y cyntedd, ro'dd hwnnw'n hen gyfarwydd â llais Gwynallt Pryce yn cymopo plant, ond cododd y lefel dipyn yn uwch wrth i Elsbeth Jones daranu ar y ceffylau gwyllt yn y ciw cinio, 'Allwch chi fentro... Fi'n gweud 'tho chi nawr!' O'dd ar bawb ofon Boco!

Yn wahanol i'r byd cyfrifiadurol heddiw, yn y ganrif ddiwethaf, y ffôn oedd y prif gyswllt â'r byd y tu allan. Ymhob ysgol yr ysgrifenyddes felly fyddai'r allwedd a theimlaf o hyd nad ydyn ni wedi llawn werthfawrogi pa mor allweddol ydy'r swydd honno. Byddai rhai gofynion yn ddigon syml fel, 'Alla i siarad â Mrs Jones?' ond weithiau gallai'r mater fod yn fwy cymhleth. Yr Ysgrifenyddes brofiadol fyddai'n llywio'r alwad, yn ei chyfeirio at y person neu at yr Adran berthnasol a chadw pawb mewn hwyliau da. Bues i'n hynod o ffodus i weithio gyda Susan Roberts am dros ugain mlynedd a hefyd Wendy Tinnuche a Lesley Rees am gyfnodau hir. Dros y cyfnod, daethom i wneud defnydd o sgiliau arbenigol y ddwy olaf. Pan fydde'r ysgol efalle ar fai, byddai llais cynnes, goddefgar Wendy yn tawelu'r dyfroedd, ond os am sorto rhywun mas, gallai Lesley roi tipyn o fin ar ei llais, wrth benderfynu tynged yr alwad. Wrth ysgrifennu hyn, hynod o drist eleni oedd clywed am frawd Lesley, Mike O'Leary, un o'm hen ddisgyblion. Roedd wastod damed bach o dynnu co's rhyngon ni, fel y bu ar y nos Sadwrn ola honno yng Nghlwb Rygbi Nantgaredig, ddeuddydd yn unig cyn y cafodd ei lofruddio.

Cofio ca'l trafferth gydag un dyn bach crintachlyd lleol oedd yn casáu plant. Wrth daranu ar y ffôn dyma fe'n bygwth mynd â'i gŵyn yn syth at John Phillips, y Cyfarwyddwr Addysg. Iawn mynte fi, a thra boch chi wrthi ar y ffôn gydag e, gwedwch eich bod wedi rhegi'n frwnt ac wedi towlu un ar ddeg 'ffyc' at y Prifathro. Aeth y llinell yn farw a chlywes i ddim gair ganddo fe wedyn.

Er hynny daeth ambell gwmwl du. Buom yn ffodus i ddenu dau o'r athrawon addysg corfforol gorau oll yn Megan Williams a John Beynon, er taw ein caeau chwarae ni oedd y rhai gwaethaf yng Nghymru. Bob tro bydde hi'n bwrw glaw, safai'r dŵr ar wyneb yr hen wastraff glofaol, ac anwybyddwyd cais ar ôl cais i'r Awdurdod yn gofyn iddynt ddreinio'r safle. Wedi brwydr hir trefnwyd *Site Visit* i'r Cynghorwyr gan y Swyddog Addysg Ranbarthol. Mas y dethon nhw'n griw mawr i archwilio'r safle, ynghanol tywydd crasboeth un mis Mehefin pan oedd wyneb y cae fel concrit. Un cyfrwys oedd Dr John Protheroe!

Llwyddodd John Beynon i ddatblygu nifer o chwaraewyr rygbi talentog, gyda Dwayne Peel yn un yn eu mysg, ac ef a berswadiodd Nigel Owens fod ganddo ddawn dyfarnu. Collwyd y ddau, Megan a John i'r gelyn cancr. A dyna hefyd fu tynged Sian Ifans a wnaeth gymaint i gynnal ein cysylltiadau ag ysgol Balatonalmadi yn Hwngari. Ychydig dros flwyddyn wedi i'r wlad adennill eu rhyddid ro'n i ar daith ysgol yno. Ar y bws i lawr prif stryd Budapest dyma fi'n codi i bwyntio'r safleoedd lle bu gwrthryfel 1956. Yn sydyn, trodd wynebau'r plant i'r cyfeiriad arall yn hollol. McDonalds! So nhw'n gwastraffu amser cyn symud miwn, ydyn nhw! Wy'n dal mewn cysylltiad o hyd â'r hen Brifathro, Sandor. Bu cyfnewid llwyddiannus hefyd gydag ysgolion yn yr Almaen a De Ffrainc.

Wrth i'r ysgol dyfu, aeth prinder ystafelloedd yn broblem. Er i'r Cyfarwyddwr Addysg, John Phillips, ei olynydd, John Ellis ac wedyn Dr Hedydd Davies fod yn gefnogol, mewn cyfnod o gwtogi a diffyg arian, ni ellid ehangu. Felly, bob tro y bydde'r plant yn gorlifo, llawer o'r tu allan i'r dalgylch, ac un teulu bob dydd yn dod o Lanwrtyd, bydde caban arall dros dro'n cyrraedd cyn ei gwneud yn sied barhaol. Wedi i'r trydydd caban ar ddeg gyrraedd, es ar y ffôn i ofyn i'r Awdurdod newid enw'r ysgol yn Maes-y-mobiles, a chael pesychad sych fel ateb! Ond ymhen amser ac ymhell ar ôl fy nyddiau i, yn dilyn adrefnu pellach bu cryn adeiladu ar y safle. Yn y frwydr hir am adeiladau rhaid cydnabod cyfraniad teyrngar llywodraethwyr yr ysgol dan arweiniad cadarn a diflino y Cadeirydd, Keith Lewis am gyfnodau hir ac ef yn gyn-reolwr Pwll Glo lleol. Eraill a ddaw i'r cof yw D T Davies Dryslwyn, Wyn Ifans a Huw Voyle o Landdarog, Howard Jones Pontyberem, Terry Davies Gorslas a Cefin Campbell o Menter Cwm Gwendraeth. Cymeriad hoffus iawn hefyd oedd yr hen E O James o Lanon, byth yn dweud llawer mewn cyfarfod, ond byddai'n cydio yn fy llawes wedi'r cyfarfod yn y coridor, pan fyddai problem ganddo i'w thrafod er mwyn sôn amdani'n dawel heb ddim ffys. Gwelodd D T Davies ei ganfed pen-blwydd a chofiaf yn dda am y bore hwnnw pan gyfarfu â Sandor o Hwngari yn fy swyddfa, a finne'n gwrando arnyn nhw'n cyfnewid enwau pentrefi yn y wlad honno, fel tasen nhw'n siarad am bentrefi yng Nghwm Gwendraeth. Yn ei gyfrol, *Dianc i Ryddid* mae D T yn disgrifio sut y gwnaeth trigolion y wlad ei gynorthwyo i osgoi cael ei ail gipio gan y Natsïed adeg y Rhyfel.

Mewn cyfnod arloesol a chynhyrfus aeth nifer o ysgolion ati i gynnig meysydd llafur ac arholiadau newydd; felly i Megan Williams, datblygiad hollol naturiol fu penderfynu cynnig Dawns fel pwnc Dull Tri i'r Cydbwyllgor Addysg yng Nghaerdydd. Gan fod Megan yn cael ei chydnabod fel arbenigwraig ledled Cymru ac yn Feirniad Dawns mewn Eisteddfodau Cenedlaethol, mater bach fu disgwyl am y cadarnhad o Gaerdydd. Aeth amser heibio, felly dyma fi'n mynd ar y ffôn i holi. Ces fy mhasio o'r naill berson i'r llall rhwng seibiadau hir, a heb hyd yn oed fiwsig i'm diddori. Yn y diwedd dyma fi drwodd i'r Pennaeth ei hun, Mel Jones, dyn rown i'n gyfarwydd ag e ac yn dipyn o ffrindiau. Ond Mel gwahanol oedd hwn heddi, yn fyr ei eiriau a braidd yn swrth ac yn bell. Mewn ateb i'm cais am gadarnhad i'r pwnc, atebodd yn swta mai cyfrifoldeb y Cydbwyllgor oedd amddiffyn safonau. Wfftiodd fy honiad fod hwn yn bwnc safonol gan ddweud nad oedd unrhyw urddas yn perthyn iddo. Collais fy nhymer a holi pa hawl oedd ganddo fe sarhau pobl fel Rudolph Nureyev, Fred Astaire a'u tebyg fel y gwnâi. Aeth y ffôn yn ddistaw am beth amser, cyn iddo ofyn, pa bwnc ro'n i'n siarad amdano. 'Dawns, achan,' mynte fi.

'O blydi hel,' mynte fe. 'Darts wedon nhw wrtho i!'

Do, yn naturiol fe dderbynion nhw y cwrs, wrth gwrs, a phob tro y bydde Mel a fi'n cwrdd ar ôl hynny, bydde un ohonon ni bownd o wneud ystum taflu dart at y bwrdd.

Cedwais y gyfrinach, fy addewid i fi fy hunan, y byddwn yn ymddeol yn chwe deg oed, ac fe gedwais at yr addewid. Felly, gwneud cyhoeddiad i bawb ar yr un pryd fyddai decaf, a dyna fel y bu. Ac wedi trosglwyddo'r awenau i'm holynydd, Iwan Rees, drannoeth y diwrnod ysgol olaf, es 'nôl i glirio fy ystafell. Ar ôl pum mlynedd ar hugain yn y swydd, cerddais mas oddi yno gyda dim ond llond dau fag du o ddeunydd.

Wrth fynd yn ôl i gyngherddau neu Ginio Nadolig blynyddol roedd yn braf cael ail gysylltu gyda phobl a sgwrsio am y dyddiau a'r digwyddiadau a fu. Yn raddol, newidiodd y cyfarchion wrth i fi gyrraedd yr Iard o fod yn, 'Helô! Shwd i chi, Syr?' i un rai blynyddoedd wedyn yn, 'Prynhawn da. Alla i'ch helpu chi?' Sylweddolais fod yna genhedlaeth o blant wedi diflannu a'i bod hi'n hen bryd i finnau eu dilyn.

Bûm yn ffodus o'r profiadau amrywiol a ges mewn ysgolion a chael y cyfle i greu ac i arloesi: rhyddid i redeg yr Adran Hanes yn Culverhouse; cychwyn ysgol newydd yn Griffith Jones gan osod sylfaen i'r Adrannau Hanes a Saesneg a datblygu llyfrgell brysur; ym Maes-yr-yrfa wedyn diwygio'r Ysgol Fodern cyn gwthio cwch i'r dŵr yn yr Ysgol Ddwyieithog a'i gweld yn aeddfedu. Er cydnabod y chwyldro mewn cyfathrebu yn y ganrif hon, rwy'n dal yn ffyddiog mai ysgolion uwchradd o ryw 500 i 700 o ddisgyblion yw'r unedau delfrydol. Digon mawr i gynnig ehangder o ddewis heb golli'r ymdeimlad cartrefol, o gymdeithas a nabod ei gilydd.

Byd y Ddrama

Does dim amheuaeth fod yr elfen yn y teulu ac felly yn y gwaed. Yn ddiweddar iawn, wrth ymchwilio i hanes lleol yr ardal, des o hyd i dystiolaeth bod fy nhad, sef Tom Thomas, Y Pant, Nebo, Llanpumsaint, yn ddynwaredwr o fri. Mae'n debyg y byddai'n creu adloniant mewn gwahanol gartrefi, yn ôl traddodiad yr oes, hyd oriau mân y bore. Dyna lle bydde fe ar ôl swper hwyr o flaen y tân, yn dynwared cymeriadau lleol a digwyddiadau trwstan y gymdeithas wledig yn hanner cyntaf y ganrif ddiwethaf. Bu farw'n ifanc, ac mae'r brith gof sy 'da fi ohono, yn anffodus, yn un o ddyn tost mewn dioddefaint. Felly fe golles y fraint a'r mwynhad o'i glywed e wrthi'n perfformio.

Er hynny, daw llu o atgofion i'r meddwl wrth gofio am fy mrawd, Donald; dynwaredwr a oedd yn hoff o wthio'r cwch ymhellach bob tro, a chreu sefyllfaoedd ffug fyddai'n gweddu'n berffaith i oes y sgetshys teledu, genhedlaeth yn ddiweddarach. Am a wn i, ni fu un o'r ddau ar lwyfan. Cofiaf yn glir iawn y tro cynta i fi droedio ar lwyfan, a hynny yn neuadd Llanpumsaint yn cyflwyno dwy ddrama fer gan Eic Davies, *Randibŵ* a *Cwac Cwac* fel rhan o gast Aelwyd yr Urdd.

Does gen i ddim cof o fod yn nerfus, prin bod amser i hynny dan law ein cynhyrchydd nerthol, sef y Ficer, Emlyn Lewis. Rodd hi'n fraint cael bod yno rwy'n cofio hynny, oherwydd dyma'r llwyfan lle bu cwmni enwog Dan Matthews yn cyflwyno ei ddramâu adeg y rhyfel – trannoeth, bydden ni'r plant yn troedio'n bregethwrol o amgylch iard yr ysgol yn dynwared 'Malachi Jones BA BD'. Ar yr un llwyfan gwelwyd W R Evans a Bois y Frenni yn canu'r caneuon gogleisiol 'Y Blacowt', a 'Dwy bunt yr Erw, Bois', penillion digri a chyfoes a godod dipyn ar galonnau pobl ar nosweithiau tywyll y gaeafau du adeg y rhyfel. Ac roedd 'Anti Henrietta o Chicago' yn ychwanegu haen Americanaidd go gyfoes i'r holl hwyl a ninnau wedyn yn dynwared y caneuon.

Ond anghofiais am un arferiad pwysig. Rown i wedi bod ar y llwyfan hwnnw cyn hynny, yn ystod y cyngherddau croesawu'r milwyr gatre; gatre o ble do'n i ddim yn siŵr, ond roedd yn esgus i gael cyngerdd a thipyn o sbri. Croesawyd yr alltud lleol yn ôl yn ei lifrau, i eistedd ar y llwyfan i wrando ar yr eitemau, Cofiwch, bron yr un rhai fyddai'n perfformio bob tro. Roedden ni blant yn rhan o eitem Jones Panteg, y tiwniwr piano sychedig, a wariai ran helaeth o'i amser yn nhafarn y Railwe, fel bydde'r ceiniogau'n caniatáu. Y bonws mawr i ni, bois y ffermydd, oedd y gwahoddiad i de gan Mrs Morris Panteg ar ôl ysgol, ar ddydd y cyngerdd; cael bara jam a jeli, cyn i Jones ein galw i'r parlwr i ymarfer. Sais oedd ein harweinydd, felly *'You are my sunshine'*, a *'It 'aint gonno rain no more'*, oedd ar y fwydlen i'w hymarfer ar ôl te. Byddai'r practis yn mynd yn iawn, am wn i, ac yna bant â ni blant mas i'r ardd i chwarae. Y drafferth oedd yr oriau rhwng y practis a'r llwyfan. Mewn ymgais i lenwi ei hun ag ychydig o'r *'dutch courage'*, gallai Jones fynd dros ben llestri a daethon ni i sylweddoli'r newid aruthrol yn ei gymeriad a ddigwyddai rhwng y practis yn y parlwr a'r perfformiad ar y llwyfan. Nid ni o'dd mas o diwn bellach! Gan ddibynnu ar faint o folied ro'dd e 'di ga'l, gallai'r perfformiad ddirywio i lefel ffars, gyda'r gynulleidfa, barchus fel arfer, yn ca'l sbort fawr wrth ein gweld a'n clywed yn perfformio. Y diffyg dealltwriaeth rhwng bysedd Jones a nodau du a gwyn y piano oedd yn gyfrifol, er na fydde fe'n cytuno â'r cyhuddiad.

Un tro fe luniwyd sgets – un plentyn i ganu mas o diwn yn fwriadol, Jones o'r diwedd yn canfod y troseddwr ac yn rhoi cosb ffug drwy ei daro â gwialen ar ei law; yna byddai diweddglo llwyddiannus wrth i ni ganu'r darn yn gywir. Popeth yn iawn yn y practis, tipyn o hwyl, ac fe fyddai'r gynulleidfa wedi bod wrth eu bodd pe bydden nhw wedi clywed y perfformiad hwnnw. Erbyn wyth o'r gloch newidiodd cymeriad yr arweinydd; ymlwybrodd i'r llwyfan a golwg gas arno, a dirywiodd safon ei actio yn y sgets nes ei fod yn fygythiol iawn. Yn y fersiwn buom ni'n ei hymarfer, wrth iddo holi *'Who's singing out of tune?'* roedd un o'r merched lleiaf i fod godi ei llaw yn bryderus, ond bydde fe yn ei hanwybyddu cyn canfod y gwir bechadur, sef y bachgen mwyaf wrth gwrs. Nid fel 'na y bu pethau ar y llwyfan. *'Hand out!'* taranodd wrthi, cyn taro llaw y ferch fach ddiniwed yn galed. Sgrechodd y groten ddieuog nerth ei phen, gan ddal ei llaw yn boenus wrth ddianc mewn dagrau o'r llwyfan at ei rhieni. Er mwyn arbed y sefyllfa, trawodd Jones nodau'r hen ffefryn, *'It 'aint gonna rain no more'*. Anghywir fu'r broffwydoliaeth wrth i'n harweinydd anghyfrifol gael ei erlid o'r llwyfan gan rieni'r ferch fach.

Ni fu llewyrch ar bethau wedyn, ac fe ddaeth hi'n 'full stop' arno mewn cyngerdd arall, pan fu'n rhaid i Mrs Morris ei erlid o'r dafarn, i'r neuadd a phob cam lan i'r llwyfan, gan chwifio gwialen fedw yn glos wrth ei gwt, er mawr ddifyrrwch i bawb. Ond er mor drychinebus y perfformiadau, erys yr hen ganeuon yn y cof o hyd.

Emlyn Lewis

Yn Llanpumsaint yr adeg honno, yn fuan ar ôl i'r rhyfel orffen, ffurfiwyd cangen hynod lwyddiannus o'r Urdd. Daeth côr merched yr Aelwyd, dan arweiniad Decima Morgan Lewis, sef gwraig y ficer, yn enwog, drwy gynnal cyngherddau di-ri ledled y wlad, gan goroni'r cyfan â pherfformio yn Gray's Inn Road yn Llundain, a chystadlu yn yr Eisteddfod Ryngwladol yn Llangollen yn yr un gystadleuaeth â chôr enwog bellach Obenkirchen o'r Almaen. Roedd rhyw hanner dwsin ohonon ni fechgyn wedi mynd i Langollen i gefnogi'r merched ac felly yn eistedd yn y babell fawr pan gamodd y plant bach o'r wlad roedden ni i gyd wedi ein hen ddysgu i'w chasáu, ar y llwyfan. Daeth 'Y Crwydryn Llon' (Happy Wanderer) yn fyd enwog, ond anghofia i byth y wefr o wylio'r côr yn ei chanu am y tro cynta yno, ag Edith Mûller yn arwain a'i brawd Karl ar y bas dwbl. Diflannodd llawer iawn o gasineb tuag at yr Almaenwyr mewn llai na phum munud. Mae'n debyg i Dylan Thomas fod rhywle yn y gynulleidfa gan ddweud am eu perfformiad, 'They sang like pigtailed angels!'

Merched yn unig oedd yng nghôr yr Aelwyd. Cheson ni'r bechgyn ddim cynnig canu a'n job ni oedd actio mewn sgetshys a dramâu. Ro'n ni'n ddigon hapus ar hynny, gan ein bod yn cael mynd ar dripiau i'w cefnogi yn Llangollen a hefyd i Eisteddfod Genedlaethol yr Urdd. Cododd problem yn dilyn ein hymweliad ag eisteddfod Machynlleth, gan nad oedden ni wedi gofyn caniatâd i golli diwrnod o'r ysgol heb sôn am ddau. Clywsom gan ffrindie fod y prifathro'n ynfyd grac ac y bydde fe am ein gwaed ni ar y Dydd Llun canlynol. Ffonies i'r ficer, Emlyn Lewis i sôn wrtho am y broblem ac fe alwodd e ni'r bois at ein gilydd i ddod i'w dŷ ar y Nos Wener. Dywedodd wrthon ni am ddweud ein bod yn cystadlu mewn parti cydadrodd a rhag ofn y byddai'r prifathro, Tudor Williams yn gofyn i ni adrodd, buodd wrthi'n ein hyfforddi i gydadrodd cerdd. Er i'r prifathro ddweud y drefen wrthon ni, nes ein bod ni'n mystyn, yn ffodus ni ofynnodd i ni gydadrodd!

Caem bregethe bywiog gan Emlyn Lewis yn aml yn yr eglwys. Un prynhawn Sul gwresog o haf, anodd oedd cadw ar ddi-hun yn y cwrdd prynhawn wedi cinio mawr a bowlened o bwdin reis. Yn wir, cwympodd fy mrawd, Jac i gysgu. Stopodd Emlyn ei bregeth a rhoi gorchymyn i'r Warden. 'Rhowch bwt i Jac. 'Sdim ots 'da fi i fod e'n cysgu drwy'r bregeth, ond wy'n tynnu'r lein ar y chwyrnu!'

Bu'r profiad o ymddangos ar lwyfannau amrywiol iawn mewn gwahanol neuaddau ar draws gorllewin Cymru yn ddiddorol ac yn addysgiadol gan fod y cynulleidfaoedd yn amrywio'n fwy na'r llwyfannau hyd yn oed, wrth i ni berfformio'r dramâu *Randibŵ* a *Cwac Cwac*. Dysgon ni fod comedi'n anifail bach bregus iawn; y llinell oedd yn tynnu'r to lawr gan chwerthin mewn un pentre, yn gallu cwympo'n fflat mewn distawrwydd mewn canolfan arall. Buan hefyd i ni sylweddoli fod chwaeth cynulleidfa weithiau yn diystyru safon yr actio a bod ymdrech i oractio pan fydde pethe'n cwympo'n fflat yn saff o ladd y ddrama'n llwyr; 'sdim ateb i'w ga'l bryd hynny, dim ond gweddïo am fynd gatre ac anghofio am y perfformans.

Weles i neb ohonon ni'n nerfus bryd hynny, gan ein bod yn ddigon ifanc i beidio gofidio dim am yr hyn allai fynd o'i le, ac o ystyried cymaint o berfformiadau a fu, mae'n syndod cyn lleied o bethe aeth o chwith. Rhaid rhoi llawer o'r clod am hynny i'r cynhyrchydd diflewyn ar dafod. Fe wyddai Emlyn Lewis yn union beth ro'dd e'n moyn ac felly bant â'r cart fydde hi, heb ddim gronyn o siarad wast. Bydden ni'n ca'l ein gweithio'n galed mewn rihyrsal ac âi Emlyn drwy focs cyfan o fatshys Swan, gan aildanio ei bibell dro ar ôl tro, wrth roi trefen ar yr actorion dibrofiad.

Dysgodd ni hefyd i ymateb i unrhyw sefyllfa anghyffredin. Cofiaf chwarae rhan potsiwr mewn un ddrama fer. Cyn ymddangos ar y llwyfan penderfynwyd y byddai'n syniad da i fi wthio pen y gwningen drwy'r drws, cyn i fi ei dilyn i mewn ac felly ca'l y gynulleidfa i chwerthin cyn i'r potsiwr ymddangos. Mae'n debyg mai gorhyder wnaeth i fi wthio'r drws i mewn yn lle ei dynnu fe am mas, ac aeth y gwningen, oedd wedi ei stwffio beth bynnag, yn sownd yn y drws. Panig llwyr wedyn wnaeth i fi geisio adfer y sefyllfa, drwy dynnu'r drws am mas a'r gwningen yn dal yn sownd ynddo fe. Bu bron i'r set gwmpo gyda'r holl wthio a thynnu gwyllt, a blew'r gwningen ffug yn gwasgaru dros yr holl le. Erbyn hyn, roedd yr actorion ar y llwyfan wedi hen redeg mas o linellau, a'r dorf bellach yn cael hwyl wrth weld ein problem, a rhai'n credu ei bod hi'n rhan o'r act. Wrth i fi ymladd yn ffyrnig â'r drws, ces gic nerthol yn fy nhin, oglau baco yn fy nghlust a fe'r ficer yn sibrwd yn ffyrnig, 'Cer rownd yr ochor draw, y twpsyn. Defnyddia dy ben, fachan!' O gyrraedd y llwyfan o'r diwedd bu'n rhaid creu llinellau yn sydyn iawn: 'Fi 'di dod â cwningen fach i chi. Dda'th neb draw i'r drws i'w derbyn hi, so penderfynes ei gadel hi draw yn y drws fan co am nawr, achos mae hi'n gwynto tamed bach.' Chwarddodd y dorf unwaith 'to, y tro hwn mewn gwerthfawrogiad efalle i ni ddod mas o drwbwl.

Daeth y cyfnod cyffrous hwnnw i ben a ninnau dipyn yn fwy profiadol ar ôl rhyw dri deg o gyngherddau mewn neuaddau gwahanol a chynulleidfaoedd amrywiol iawn ar hyd a lled siroedd Caerfyrddin a Cheredigion. Profiadau unigryw!

Dan gyfundrefn estron yr ysgol ramadeg, ni ddatblygwyd sgiliau actio na doniau canu yr un ohonon ni, ffaith sy'n gondemniad llwyr ar fethiant sefydliad ffroenuchel, hunanbwysig ysgolion gramadeg. Addysg estron Seisnig gawson ni. Felly, bu bwlch yn ein datblygiad. Drwy gydol y blynyddoedd o addysg ramadeg ni ddaeth yr un cyfle i ddatblygu sgiliau actio hyd yn oed drwy gyfrwng y Saesneg, ac eto ymfalchïai'r gymdeithas leol yn yr addysg odidog y credent ein bod yn ei derbyn. Dyna'r prif reswm i fi wrthod pob cynnig dros y blynyddoedd i ymuno â chymdeithas y cyn-ddisgyblion, yr *'Old Maredunians'*.

Yn y Brifysgol

Wedi ymsefydlu yn y Brifysgol yn Abertawe dyma ail gydio yn yr actio wrth ymaelodi yn y Gymdeithas Gymraeg yn y coleg. Yno, o gyfarfod â chydfyfyrwyr o gefndir cyffelyb, aethon ni ati i ddewis, ymarfer a pherfformio dramâu Cymraeg; cawson ni dipyn o hwyl oherwydd, y tro hwn, myfyriwr oedd yn cynhyrchu; yn ddibrofiad ond yn ddigon hyderus i roi tro arni.

I fi, yn y coleg, dyma gyfle gwych i ddatblygu fy nawn dynwared i'r eithaf, gan gynnwys lleisiau ac ystumiau darlithwyr coleg, a hyd yn oed araith Nadolig y Frenhines. Yn fuan iawn datblygodd rhai ohonyn nhw i fod yn ffefrynnau a byddai galw amdanynt dro ar ôl tro mewn tafarnau wrth i'r cwrw lifo fin nos. Tynnai ffug glod Elisabeth yr Ail i Trinidad a Thobago, wrth iddyn nhw ennill annibyniaeth ac ymuno â'r Gymanwlad y to i lawr bob tro – nid âi'r cyferbyniad rhwng sefyllfa'r ynysoedd hynny â sefyllfa Cymru ar goll gan fy nghynulleidfa, wrth flasu'r hwyl.

Llecyn o Gymreictod oedd y 'Gym Gym', ac yno byddai pedwar ban byd yn cwrdd. Daeth acenion Y Rhondda, Abergynolwyn, Caernarfon, Beulah, Dolgellau a Dowlais Top i'r glust, ynghyd â thafodiaith unigryw Ton Pentre o enau'r anfarwol Cennard Davies. Yn fuan iawn aed ati i ddysgu dramâu a llunio deunydd Noson Lawen gan gynnwys nifer o sgetshys, a dyma fi mewn maes arbrofol cyffrous newydd, ac yn gyfle i ddatblygu talent. O'r diwedd dyma lwyfan cyhoeddus i'r holl berfformiadau a'r mwynhad a gaed cyn hynny, mewn tafarnau a thai preifat yn hwyr ar sawl noson dros y blynyddoedd. Oeddwn, rown i'n barod ac yn falch o dderbyn yr her hirddisgwyliedig. Cynhaliwyd nifer o nosweithiau llawen hwyliog ac ysgafn mewn neuaddau pentref yn ardal y coleg, ac ynddynt rhoddwyd i fi'r rhyddid i arbrofi a gwthio'r ffiniau i gyfeiriadau newydd.

Tan hynny, yn yr iaith Gymraeg y bûm yn actio'n gyfan gwbwl, oherwydd yn yr Ysgol Ramadeg, darllen Shakespeare y tu ôl i ddesg oedd swm a sylwedd byd y ddrama. Yn fy mlwyddyn Ymarfer Dysgu yn Abertawe, daeth cyfle i actio yn y ddrama, *The Pillars of Society* gan Henrick Ibsen, y dramodydd enwog o Norwy.

Cwmni Drama Averley

Wedi i fi sefydlu fy hun yn fy swydd dysgu gynta yn Culverhouse, De Ockendon yn Swydd Essex yn 1962 daeth cyfle i ymuno â Chwmni Theatr lleol, 'Averley Children's Theatre' fyddai'n mynd o amgylch ysgolion cynradd y cylch i berfformio. Athrawon oedd y cast a bydden ni'n mynd ati i ymarfer a llwyfannu ar ôl diwrnod o addysgu. Tipyn o hwyl, digon o symud a gwisgo lan, ambell ffeit gleddyfe ar lwyfan, fel arfer yn y rownd, hynny yw gyda'r gynulleidfa o blant yn amgylchu'r actorion. Gwraig o'r enw Mary Collyer fydde'n cynhyrchu; ond wedyn, gogyfer â'r ddrama nesa, dyma athrawes ddrama ifanc yn ymgymryd â'r swydd. Doedd hon ddim yn cymryd lot o nonsens, roedd hi o ddifrif.

Dechreuais gefnogi Arsenal yn 1950, ac rwy'n dal i wneud ac yn edmygydd mawr o Arsene Wenger. Felly, yn y cyfnod hwnnw, a minnau mor agos at Lundain, awn i'w gweld yn Highbury yn amal. Llwyddais i gael tocyn i'r gêm gwpan yn erbyn Lerpwl un Nos Fercher, ac felly collais yr unig rihyrsal drama ers i fi ymuno â'r cwmni, a'r unig dro erioed i fi fethu bod mewn ymarfer, heb reswm digonol. Os do fe te! Ces uffarn o row cyn cychwyn y rihyrsal nesa ac fel actor cyfrifol do'dd dim pwynt trial amddiffyn fy hunan. Felly, cynigais fynd â'r ferch danllyd o gynhyrchydd am ddiod wedyn i'w thawelu. Diweddglo'r stori yw i fi a Jane briodi yn 1965. Alun Frongoch oedd y gwas priodas ac adroddodd gerdd gan ein cyfaill o fardd, Tydfor, i'n llongyfarch.

Dychwelon ni i Gymru erbyn yr haf. Buodd y ddau ohonon ni'n ddigon ffodus i sicrhau swyddi dysgu yn Sir Gâr. Aeth Jane yn athrawes drama i'r hen Ysgol Eilradd Fodern, Ystrad Tywi, yn Nhre Ioan ger tref Caerfyrddin a finne i San Clêr.

Talacharn a Dan y Wenallt

Adeg y Chwedegau cynnar doedd neb wedi clywed am *Dan y Wenallt* ond roedd *Under Milk Wood* yn destun siarad cyffredin, yn amrywio o'r cefnogwyr brwd i'r gwrthwynebwyr cul, crefyddol. Oherwydd y câi perfformiadau eu cynnal yn Talacharn bob tair blynedd, eu hail adrodd eu hunain a wnâi'r safbwyntiau a'r dadleuon. Gwynne D Evans, y dramodydd o Gefneithin, oedd y cynhyrchydd cynta, a throsglwyddodd yr awenau wedyn i weinidog Priordy, Caerfyrddin, a gâi ei adnabod fel y Parchedig T James Jones ar y pryd, ond un y des i i'w adnabod, fel sawl un arall wedyn, fel Jim Parc Nest – y cynhyrchydd gorau i fi gael y fraint o weithio gydag ef. Daeth yr alwad i Jane a minnau ymuno â'r cast a dyna gychwyn ar ddigwyddiad fyddai'n ail ymddangos bob tair blynedd. Oherwydd bod tair blynedd yn gyfnod eithaf hir a'r ffaith y byddai ffurf y cynhyrchiad yn newid bob tro, ni wnâi aelodau'r cast fyth flino ar *Under Milk Wood* ac erbyn i gyfieithiad Jim, *Dan y Wenallt*, ymddangos daeth brwdfrydedd newydd i'r holl fenter.

Gwnaethom nifer o ffrindiau newydd gan gynnwys rhai aeth ymlaen i'r byd proffesiynol ac S4C, fel Buddug Williams. Roedd un aelod o'r cast yn gymeriad unigryw, Peter John o Grymych. Deuai'r ciw ganddo bob tro'n ddigon uchel, ond doedd dim sicrwydd beth fydde'r ciw hwnnw. Cymeriad a lenwai'r llwyfan ym mhob ymddangosiad. Ymhlith y cast hefyd roedd Rhiannon Rees a Delyth Mai, dwy o athrawesau drama Ysgol Maes-yr-yrfa wedyn.

Rheolwr y llwyfan am flynyddoedd oedd Bryn Davies, Cross Hands neu Bryn Bach fel y cyfeirid ato gan bawb. Dyn roedd y ddrama'n llifo'n gryf drwy ei wythiennau. Daethon ni'n gyfarwydd â'i gyfarwyddiadau munud ola; fydde pethe byth yn daclus cyn y rihyrsal ola, a rhyw awr cyn y perfformiad cynta, bydde nifer o bethe eto heb gael eu cwblhau yn hollol. Hyn oll yn ddigon i gynhyrfu unrhyw gynhyrchydd. Ond nid Jim, ro'dd e'n hen gyfarwydd â ffordd Bryn, ac yn hollol hyderus y deuai pethe i fwcwl cyn i'r llenni godi oherwydd y ffydd oedd ganddo ynddo. Un arferiad nerfus ro'n i'n euog ohono oedd cerdded ar y llwyfan rai munudau cyn dechrau'r perfformiad, er mwyn sicrhau fod y props i gyd yn eu lle. Hollol ddiangen, ond dyna 'yn ffordd i o dawelu'r nerfau cyn dechrau. Noson gynta *Milk Wood* a dyma fi'n sleifio ar y llwyfan a gweld Bryn yn sefyll yno â brwsh paent gwlyb yn ei law. 'Pan fyddi di'n gneud dy entry, gofala beidio cyffwrdd yn y drws, ma fe'n dal yn wlyb,' medde fe'n hollol hamddenol.

Oedd, roedd yr ymadrodd Seisnig, *'It'll be alright on the night!'* yn ffito'n gywir iddo. Ond, mae lwc yn rhedeg mas ambell waith, a dyna fu ei dynged ar noson agoriadol arall o *Milk Wood*. Y flwyddyn honno, sef 1975, penderfynwyd gosod yr holl actorion mewn rhyw fath o focsys, gyda dim ond yr ysgwyddau a'r pennau yn weladwy i'r gynulleidfa. Yr unig brops fyddai newid penwisg wrth newid cymeriad gyda golau'r sbot lamp yn goleuo pan siaradai'r cymeriad. Felly, cap postman i Jacyraca, yna, estynnwn het liwgar i gymeriad Syr Wili Watsh, ac wrth orffen yr olygfa bydde'r gole arna i'n diffodd a gallwn ymlacio yn fy sedd tan fy ngolygfa nesa. Roedd hyn mor syml gan nad oedd angen amseru dod 'mlân na gadael y llwyfan. Fe weithiodd pethau'n hwylus iawn drwy'r rihyrsals ond heb ddefnyddio'r goleuadau sbot, gan fod Bryn wrthi'n datrys yr elfen honno.

Daeth y noson agoriadol a sylwais fod wyneb Jim, ein cynhyrchydd, ychydig yn llai hyderus nag arfer, bod yna sawl trafodaeth, lled ddirgel wedi bod rhyngddo fe a Bryn, a bod hwnnw hefyd wedi dechrau whilmentan a stablan ymysg y gwifrau yng nghefen y neuadd. Dechreuon ni'r ddrama heb lenni, wrth gwrs gyda'r golau'n llachar ar actor y Llais Cynta, ond hanner ffordd drwy ei araith agoriadol, ffindiodd hwnnw ei hunan mewn tywyllwch llwyr. Chafodd yr actor nesa, sef yr Ail Lais, ddim gole o gwbwl. Buan iawn dyma ni'n sylweddoli ein bod ni'n gorfod dweud ein llinellau mewn tywyllwch, ond yn waeth na hynny ar ôl ymlacio, pan nad oedden ni fod cymryd rhan, yn sydyn deuai fflach o olau llachar ar ein hwynebau. Erbyn yr ail hanner, llwyddodd ein trydanydd arloesol i oleuo ambell gymeriad pan oedd yn perfformio, ond goleuwyd sawl un arall pan na ddylai a golwg llawn embaras ar ei wyneb, gan nad oedd ganddo linellau i'w dweud.

Y switshis ga'th y bai! Yn dilyn y perfformans, yn y Browns Hotel roedd ymwelwyr o'r Iseldiroedd ar bererindod llenyddol, oherwydd eu hedmygedd o Dylan, yn llawn canmoliaeth, er ychydig yn ddryslyd oherwydd yr hyn a welsant yn y perfformiad. Pan holodd un ysgolhaig barfog Bryn ynglŷn ag arwyddocâd y patrwm goleuadau, wnaeth ateb hwnnw fawr ddim i'w oleuo; *'We are a forward looking group who like to experiment, you see!'* Ond datryswyd y broblem erbyn yr ail berfformiad. Cyfarwyddwyd Bryn i gynnal y golau'n gyson ar bob actor; yna, pan na fyddai gan yr actor ran yn y chwarae, plygai ei ben, fel na fyddai dim ond ei het yn weladwy. Canlyniad hynny oedd symleiddio'r plot goleuo, yn ogystal â sicrhau llwyfan yn llawn o hetiau lliwgar. Cafodd Bryn ganmoliaeth uchel!

Daeth yn batrwm hwylus o gyflwyno *Under Milk Wood* a *Dan y Wenallt* am yn ail â'i gilydd a heb fawr ddim trafferth, gan fod pawb yn hen gyfarwydd â'u llinellau yn y ddwy iaith. Yna, cafwyd datblygiad pellach, pan gafodd Jim y syniad o gael perfformiad dwyieithog; y ddadl oedd fod nifer o bentrefi'r ardal bellach, yn gymysgedd o'r ddwy iaith, a byddai pobol yn troi o'r naill iaith i'r llall ac ambell waith yn newid iaith hyd yn oed wrth siarad â'r un person. Gan fod hyn oll yn wir, ni ellid dadlau â'r rhesymeg. Ond, wrth gymryd y llwyfan fel Jacyraca'r Postman ces ofon ofnadwy. Deuai ciw mewn un iaith, a byddai gofyn i fi ateb y cymeriad yn yr iaith arall. Fues i erioed yn teimlo mor Jacyraca'n ddryslyd ar lwyfan ac ro'n i'n chwys diferu erbyn diwedd y perfformiad. Diolch byth taw dim ond unwaith y cyflwynon ni'r ddrama fel yna!

Bu diwrnod y perfformiad olaf yn un hynod i fi am reswm arall. Bob haf, byddwn yn trefnu pethau er mwyn osgoi gwrthdaro rhwng galwadau'r ddrama a chwarae criced. Fel arfer llwyddwn i wneud hynny gan osgoi unrhyw drafferthion. Ond noson olaf yr ŵyl ar y 30ain o Orffennaf 1975 cododd problem. Roedd gêm bwysig gatre gan Dalacharn yn erbyn Penfro yng nghynghrair Sir Benfro a chan 'mod yn un o'u bowlwyr allweddol fe'm perswadiwyd i chwarae yn y gobaith y bydden nhw'n batio gyntaf yn y prynhawn. Nid fel hynny y bu, a dyna lle rown i'n bowlio nerth fy nhraed ar ôl te, mewn ymgais i orffen pethe. Yn y diwedd rhaid oedd ffugio cael niwed, er mwyn gadael y cae a rhuthro o ystafell newid y criced i ystafell newid y ddrama cyn cael fy ngholuro. Rhwng y chwys, y paent a'r powdwr roedd golwg arna i, fy ngwyneb i'n fflamgoch; ond daeth pethau i fwcwl yn y diwedd. Cafwyd perfformiad da a do, fe enillon ni'r gêm griced 'fyd.

Perfformio *Dewin y Daran*

Flwyddyn cyn hynny, yn 1974 cynhaliwyd Eisteddfod Genedlaethol Caerfyrddin, wedi ei lleoli ar gae Dolgwili ger Glangwili. Ymysg y bwrlwm o baratoadau penderfynwyd llwyfannu pasiant enfawr hanesyddol sef *Dewin y Daran* ac roedd tua 100 o gast. Gyda chlwstwr o olygfeydd mewn cestyll a thafarnau, llu o filwyr a rhialtwch tyrfa, aeth y dasg o benderfynu shwt i gyflwyno'r fath sioe yn y pafiliwn mawr yn dipyn o ben tost. Gyda chast mor fawr a symud cyflym o olygfa i olygfa, roedd cario meics, fel y gwnaeth cast *Nia Ben Aur*, mas o'r cwestiwn. Penderfynwyd yn y diwedd mai'r unig ffordd o berfformio'r sioe yn glywadwy i'r dyrfa fawr yn y pafiliwn, oedd recordio'r holl eiriau cyn y perfformiad, chwarae'r tâp ac ymarfer yr actorion i symud a meimio'u geiriau i gydredeg â'r tâp.

Mae'n swnio'n gymhleth iawn ond wedi ymarfer, ymarfer ac ymarfer daeth yr holl gast i gydymffurfio a chydweithio'n wyrthiol, er nad oedd y mwyafrif wedi bod ar lwyfan mewn drama erioed o'r blaen. Mewn un olygfa dafarn stwrllyd a meddwol i ragflaenu cyfansoddiadau yr enwog Ficer Pritchard o Lanymddyfri, perswadiodd Jim, Cliff Jones, chwaraewr llwyau dawnus o Lanpumsaint, i fywiocáu'r olygfa. Wedi'r recordio ac ar y nosweithiau ymarfer i'r tâp, dal i chwarae a wnâi Cliff, oherwydd chwarae teg iddo, byddai trial meimio chwarae llwyau'n anodd dros ben. Bu'r perfformiad y tu hwnt i'n gobeithion, popeth yn hwylus a'r dorf ar y diwedd yn rhoi bonllef o gymeradwyaeth. Wrth i'r cast ymadael, a'r maes wedi gwacáu, safai Jim yno'n fwriadol er mwyn diolch i bob un yn unigol. Des i mas yr un pryd â Cliff,

'Diolch yn fowr, Arwyn, a diolch o galon i ti Cliff, am berfformiad arbennig iawn,' meddai Jim.

'Do,' mynte Cliff, 'Wharies i'n gyts mas heno!'

Bu Cliff yn teithio o amgylch y wlad gyda'i fan yn llawn bwydydd tŷ amheus eu hoedran, a doedd y clêr a'r picwns yn y fan ddim yn ennyn hyder y cwsmeriaid a dweud y gwir. Prynodd Jim unwaith faryn o Fruit and Nut ganddo ac esgus cwyno mai dim ond un gneuen oedd ynddo. 'Buest ti'n lwcus i ga'l *un* 'chan,' atebodd Cliff.

Roedd chwe mil o gynulleidfa yn y pafiliwn gorlawn ac ynghanol y perfformiad cawson ni storom enbyd o law tarane. Bu'n Eisteddfod hynod o lwyddiannus, er y tywydd, a hyd yn oed ar y Sadwrn olaf, pan ddirywiodd y Maes i fod yn fôr o fwd, daeth 24 mil i'r maes i glywed Côr Meibion Pontarddulais yn trechu Côr Meibion y Rhos yn y brif gystadleuaeth corau meibion. Gan 'mod i ar ddyletswydd fel Clerc y Llwyfan drwy'r wythnos, rown i'n falch o gael mynd bant am wylie yr wythnos wedyn.

Dramâu Cwmni'r Dewin

Ody, mae hi'n hollol amlwg shwt cethon ni'r enw ar y Cwmni, a ffurfiwyd wedi Eisteddfod Caerfyrddin, a'r aelodau bron pob un wedi ymddangos yn *Dewin y Daran* a chyda Jim yn dal i fod yn cynhyrchu ac ysgrifennu'r dramâu i ni'n ogystal. Bu'n gyfnod hynod o brysur ac yn un llewyrchus a chynhyrchiol.

Soniais yn barod am gynyrchiadau *Under Milk Wood* a *Dan y Wenallt* yn 1975, ond bu'n flwyddyn ddiddorol oherwydd un digwyddiad arall hefyd. Yn nechrau Mis Ionawr 1975 penderfynwyd gwneud ffilm o hanes *Diwygiad*

93

Mawr 1905, sef diwygiad Evan Roberts i BBC2. Roedd nifer o'r golygfeydd yn rhai torfol ac roedd angen llawer iawn o ecstras i greu cynulleidfaoedd, felly gwelwyd carfan uchel iawn o gast *Dewin y Daran* ynddi. Darlledwyd *The Revivalist* ar BBC2 ym mis Mawrth a defnyddiwyd llun ohono i fel un o'r diwygwyr tanbaid ar flaen y credits. Yn y golygfeydd torfol hynny rhaid oedd creu cynnwrf er mwyn cyfleu holl brofiad heintus Diwygiad 1905. Erbyn gorffen, gallwn werthfawrogi pa mor hawdd oedd cael eich sgubo gan yr holl donnau o frwdfrydedd ac emosiwn i ymuno â'r Diwygiad.

Yn niwedd Ionawr 1976 dyma ddechrau ymarfer *Wil Angladde*, ffars o hiwmor du yn ymwneud â chyrff a chladdu wedi ei lleoli mewn mynwent. Y cynhyrchydd a'r dramodydd oedd T James Jones ac roedd cast o bump – Ruby Jones o Hendy-gwyn, Elfyn Lewis o Lanpumsaint, Cyril Williams o'r Crown Stores, Caerfyrddin, Malcolm Evans, brawd Ernest o Gross Hands a finne. Gan 'mod i'n chwarae cymeriad Wil ro'dd tipyn o waith dysgu 'da fi ac ro'n i ar y llwyfan drwy gydol y ddrama. O edrych yn ôl at y cyfnod hwnnw, mae'n syndod i fi heddi shwt o'n i'n dod i ben â phopeth. Ar wahân i fod yn Brifathro Ysgol Maes-yr-Yrfa, byddwn yn chwarae golff bron bob penwythnos yn y gaeaf, yn chwarae mewn cynghrair Badminton ganol wythnos, criced drwy'r haf, a gatre, roedd 'da ni ddwy ferch fach, Rhianedd a Gwenfyl, yn bump a chwe oed. Byddwn i hefyd yn mynd 'nôl a mlân gatre i helpu ar ffarm Pantglas yn gyson. Yn ychwanegol at hynny cawn hi'n anodd mynd heibio, heb alw, yn y tafarndai lleol, oedd bryd hynny'n ganolfannau cymdeithasol bywiog, buddiol a phwysig.

Rywfodd, serch hynny, gwnâi bopeth gwympo miwn i'w lle'n drefnus. Cofiaf fod Jim yn fedrus iawn wrth drefnu ymarferion, gan osgoi'r golff a'r criced, osgoi'r nosweithiau pan fyddai Elfyn 'On Call' yn ei swydd electroneg a byddai'n cydymffurfio â galwadau siop nwyddau Cyril. Newidiai'r noson ymarfer yn ystod yr wythnos yn amal er mwyn cael pawb at ei gilydd. Llwyfannwyd *Wil Angladde* gynta yn Theatr Haliwell yng Ngholeg y Drindod Caerfyrddin, ac er ein bod yn nerfus am fod y ddrama yn gwthio'r ffiniau bryd hynny, cafwyd derbyniad da; yn wir, dderbynion ni ddim ymateb negyddol o gwbwl. Efallai fod y ffaith i ni ei pherfformio ar Ddydd Ffŵl Ebrill wedi helpu pethe! Daeth sylwadau canmoliaethus gan Gwynedd Jones, a oedd wedi ei blesio'n fawr gan y perfformiad. Yn hwyrach yn y mis cafodd trefnwyr yr Ŵyl Ddrama ym Mhontrhydfendigaid dipyn o sioc wrth weld arch yn cael ei ddadlwytho o hers a gawsom ei fenthyg gan Ken Morris. Doedd neb wedi marw, jyst un o'r props oedd e! Ac yntau'n chwarae gatre, cafodd Elfyn dipyn o hwyl arni yn neuadd Llanpumsaint, a mwy o hwyl wedyn yn y Railwe yng nghwmni cadeirydd y noson, Alun Frongoch.

Aed â'r ddrama wedyn i Eisteddfod Genedlaethol Aberteifi, eisteddfod y llwch, a chawsom ein hysgwyd oherwydd digwyddiad anghyffredin iawn. Ddeng munud cyn i'r llenni godi syrthiodd gwraig yn y rhes flaen yn swp ar ei hyd ar y llawr. Cariwyd hi i'r cyntedd er mwyn iddi gael awyr iach. O gofio beth oedd cynnwys y ddrama, medde un o'r cast, 'Os ody honna wedi marw, sdim un ffordd y gallwn ni berfformio'r ddrama hon fan hyn heno.' Wrth lwc, wedi llewygu ro'dd hi oherwydd y gwres a dychwelodd ymhen tipyn i'w sedd gan ymateb i'r ddrama drwy chwerthin yn iach.

Digwyddodd rhywbeth hynod arall yn ystod y perfformiad hwnnw. Yn yr olygfa yn y fynwent, roedd yr arch a Cyril ynddi yn y bedd. Daeth y plismon lleol i'r llwyfan, ac yn nodweddiadol o blismon drama cawsom y geiriau, 'Ho! Ho!

Beth sydd yn mynd ymlaen fan hyn te?' Plygodd i lawr ac edrych i mewn i'r arch. Dyw helmed fenthyg byth yn ffito ac ro'dd hi'n rhy fowr i Malcolm. Fe gwympodd miwn ar ben Cyril, gan greu ton o chwerthin annisgwyl mewn golygfa ffug ddwys. Aeth yn don o rialtwch wrth i'r helmed atgyfodi ar ôl i'r plismon ofyn i'r corff, 'Pas yr helmed 'nôl i fi, wnei di!' Ie comedi ddu oedd hi!

Ararat oedd y nesa, drama roedd Jim yn ei hysgrifennu ar y pryd, gan lwyddo i orffen pob act, jyst cyn y rihyrsal nesa. Fi gafodd ran Noa, pregethwr wedi llithro ar gyfeiliorn ac yn chwilio am gysur yn y botel. Er y bu'n rhaid i fi ymlafnio i ddysgu ambell i fonolog hir a chymhleth, mwynheais chwarae'r cymeriad, wrth fynd â hi i Grymych, Llangain a Neuadd San Pedr Caerfyrddin.

Daeth y Crown Stores, siop fwyd Cyril Williams, a oedd drws nesa lawr o adeilad y Llyfrgell bresennol gyferbyn ag eglwys San Pedr yng Nghaerfyrddin, yn ganolfan ymarfer ddifyr am sbel, gyda Cyril yn cicio bilie'r tacs llwyd o'r neilltu, wrth i ni droedio lan lofft i'r ystafell fyw. Yno hefyd y cychwynnwyd ymarfer *Gair i Gall* a *Bedi'r Ots*, dwy o'n dramâu byrion mwyaf llwyddiannus, a dwy hollol wahanol i'w gilydd. Golygfa dafarn gaed yn *Bedi'r Ots*, gyda dau o'r hen rapscaliwns, Elfyn a Cyril, yn 'yfed arian y dôl', dan reolaeth ddiarffordd y dafarnwraig, Mrs Holloway, a chwaraewyd gan fy ngwraig, Jane. Tarfwyd ar eu mwynhad gan ymddangosiad y plismon lleol. Dyn byr o daldra, bach iawn a dweud y gwir, o dan pum troedfedd oedd John Phillips o Lanpumsaint, felly o'i wisgo mewn siwt a helmed plismon lawer rhy fawr iddo, denwyd y gynulleidfa i chwerthin, dim ond wrth weld ei olwg. Ychwanegwyd at yr hwyl wrth i'r ddau ddihiryn yn raddol feddwi'r heddwas drwy brynu gwydred ar ôl gwydred o chwisgi iddo. Diweddglo'r holl rialtwch yw ymddangosiad Indian yn gwisgo tyrban

Ben a Marged Nantglas, Llanpumsaint –
Hen Dad-cu a Mam-gu.

Llun cyntaf ohonof gyda fy rhieni Tom
a May ym Mhant-y-Fedwen, Nebo 1937.
Bet, chwaer Mam, sydd i'r chwith.

Fy nhad, cyn ei waeledd, gyda
'mrawd Jac ar y chwith a Donald
ar y dde yn y 1930au.

Wrth y gwair ym Mhant-
y-Fedwen – Mam-gu Yr
Hendy yn y canol.

Prince y ci bonedd, Mam yn y cefen, Sarah, sef merch Bet, a finne.

Ro'n i'n weddol ddiniwed, bryd hynny!

Mam ar hewl fach Pantglas yn dod gatre ar ôl siopa.

Tîm pêl-droed bechgyn Llanpumsaint yn y 1950au. Rhes gefn: Harri Cwmcreigiau; Dai Green (rheolwr); Eifion Ifans; Gwynfor Davies; Arwyn Thomas; Stanley Jones; Edwin Green; Gethin Burgess. Rhes flaen: Dilwyn Davies; Alun Jones; David Henry Davies; Brian Jacob; Dewi George.

Dyddiau Ysgol ger mynedfa Ysgol Ramadeg Caerfyrddin – Barry Long yw'r un tal yn y canol.

Dyddiau coleg y tu fas i Neuadd Breswyl Gilbertson, Blackpill, Abertawe, 1957.

Dydd ein priodas ar 21 o Ebrill 1965.

Arddangosfa Hanes Lleol yng Ngholeg Gwerin Griffith Jones, San Clêr 1970.

Tîm Badminton Ysgol Griffith Jones – Y Prifathro arloesol, Islwyn Williams ar y chwith a fi ar y dde.

Tîm Criced Talacharn tua 1970. Yn y tu blaen, i'r dde o'r capten Barry Jackson mae John Jenkins, fi a Jeff Watts.

Y tu fas i Meysydd gyda'r Prifathro Sandor Czuczor a'i wraig, adeg cyfnewid rhwng Ysgol Maes-yr-yrfa ac Ysgol o Balatonalmadi, Hwngari 1993.

Amser cinio yn fy swyddfa yn Ysgol Maes-yr-yrfa.

Dau'n llawn drygioni – Robert Sams y gofalwr a'r technegydd, Nigel Owens.

Ffarwelio â
Keith Lewis,
Cadeirydd
Llywodraethwyr
Ysgol Maes-yr-
yrfa.

Gyda staff Ysgol Maes-yr-
yrfa wrth ymddeol yn 1997.

Mr. Arwyn Thomas

Hwn, heb wers o'r gorffennol - a roddodd
I'n gwreiddiau ddyfodol:
Ei dasg oedd codi ysgol
A'i rhoi i rai ar ei ôl.

(Prifathro Maesyryrfa 1972 - 1997)

Tudur Hallam.

Englyn gan
Tudur Hallam.

Wrth Aros Godot – gyda John Phillips ac Elfyn Lewis – yn yr Eisteddfod Genedlaethol yng Nghaernarfon 1978.

Diweddgan gyda John Phillips.

Cast *Tri Chryfion Byd*, Twm o'r Nant. Ar y chwith yn y cefn, Geraint Roberts a finne (Y Diafol).

Diweddgan – Jane yn coluro Elfyn Lewis – Ruby Jones wrth ymyl y cynhyrchydd, Jim Parc Nest.

Beio'r botel yn y ddrama *Arrarat*.

Cliff Jones Llanpumsaint – fy athro chwarae llwyau!

Theatr Felin-fach
Yn cyflwyno

Y Twrch Trwyth

gan T James Jones

Delyth Wyn, Llion Williams, Einir Siôn, Jaci Evans ac Arwyn Thomas
Cyfarwyddwr Huw Emlyn

Y tro diwethaf ar y llwyfan.

Llun cyntaf Clwb Criced Bronwydd 1978. Rhes gefn: Chris Peregrine; Ray Lewis; Ronwydd Williams; Trevor Benwell (tad y clwb); Gerald Vaughan; Melfyn Jones. Rhes flaen: Nigel Roberts; Wynne Jones; Arwyn Thomas; Colin Lewis; Ogi; Dai Nam.

Y cyfleusterau yn Cnwcyderi i'r tîm criced 1979.

Gosod y llain criced cynta gyda Wynne Panteg.

Alan Jones Morgannwg yn agor yr ail bafiliwn gyda Dorian Taylor a Dave Elliot.

Gyda'r ŵyr, Cian yn trin y llain.

Y cyfleusterau heddiw o'r Cnwc.

Defnyddio'r peiriant bowlio wrth hyfforddi.

Wrthi'n dyfarnu.

Tair merch yn
llwyddo yn yr
arholiad dyfarnu
yng Ngholeg
y Drindod
Caerfyrddin.
Steve Watkin
Morgannwg
– canol yn y cefn.

Ar gwrs golff
Caerfyrddin gyda'r
ddau gricedwr,
Byron Jones a
Dave Elliot.

Arwyddo llyfr canmlwyddiant Clwb
Golff Caerfyrddin.

Troedio llwybr
Arfordir Sir Benfro.

Cerdded llwybr
Clawdd Offa.

Dosbarth Ysgol yn Vietnam.

Pibydd ar gopa Machu Picchu yn Peru.

Eira mawr ar glos Pantglas.

Un o luniau Rhianedd.

Donald – y brawd a gollwyd.

Pen-blwydd olaf fy mam yn 99 oed – Jane a fi a 'mrawd, Jac.

Dathlu ein Priodas Aur yn 2015. O'r chwith, Gihan (gŵr Rhianedd), Bud (partner Gwenfyl), Cian, ni'n dau, Rhianedd gyda Kal a Gwenfyl gyda Tegid.

Yr wyrion - Kal gyda Tegid wyneb i waered.

yn chwilio am help gan fod 'y moped wedi rhedeg mas o betrol!' Ie, fi oedd hwnnw!

Adeg yr egwyl bydden ni'n troi y set oddi amgylch ac ynddo bwlpud, er mwyn cyfleu golygfa mewn hen gapel. Drama ddwys a difrifol yw *Gair i Gall*, yn ymwneud ag argyfwng addoli a chau capeli, ffenomena sydd wedi dod yn llawer amlycach a difrifol erbyn heddiw. Mewn ffordd roedd *Gair i Gall* wedi rhagweld y dyfodol a'r hyn sy'n digwydd i'r capeli yn awr. Un aelod, a honno'n hen wraig ffyddlon, sydd ar ôl bellach yn y capel. Chwaraewyd hi'n dyner gan Ruby Jones, aelod oedd yn dal yn ffyddlon i'r gweinidog cymysglyd ond teyrngar, John Phillips. Roedd y capel i'w gau a daw'r derbynnydd oeraidd a chas i mewn, cymeriad rown i'n ei chwarae. Mae'r dadlau'n adlewyrchu'r tyndra sydd rhwng glynu wrth yr hen safonau ac wynebu gwedd fydol a masnachol y byd newydd. Yn niweddglo'r ddrama, ceir tipyn o ymladdfa ac ymrafael yn y pwlpud rhyngo i a John. Gan fod y ddwy ddrama mor wahanol roedd hi'n bosibl plesio pawb – y rhai traddodiadol nad oedd yn hoff o olygfeydd mewn tafarn, gan y bydden nhw'n mynd gatre'n fodlon, wedi mwynhau *Gair i Gall*.

Wedi agor yn Neuadd Bronwydd yn Chwefror 1978, cawson wanwyn prysur wrth ymweld â Llandeilo a Llandyfaelog a phenderfynu cystadlu yng Ngŵyl Ddrama'r Foel, oedd mewn bri ar y pryd. Yno, cipiodd *Gair i Gall* y wobr gyntaf a daeth *Bedi'r Ots* yn drydydd. Ychydig ddyddie cyn teithio i'r gogledd, i aros dros nos yn y Cann Office, cynhaliwyd ein hymarfer olaf yn y Crown Stores gan fod Cyril wedi gwerthu'r lle ac wedi ymddeol. Buon ni wedyn yn eu perfformio yn Theatr Felinfach ac yna yn Neuadd Llanpumsaint, lle bu Emily Davies yn bwrw ei llinyn mesur, fel rhan o gystadleuaeth y Ddrama Fer yn Eisteddfod Genedlaethol Caerdydd.

Cyrhaeddodd y ddwy eu huchafbwynt pan ddaethon ni'n gyntaf yn y gystadleuaeth honno yn y Sherman yng Nghaerdydd, gyda Llwyndyrys yn ail a chwmni Caerdydd yn drydydd. Ond mae mwy i'r stori. Drwy'r amryw deithiau mewn gwahanol neuaddau a llwyfannau daethon ni'n hen gyfarwydd â newid y set dafarn rownd am olygfa'r capel a'r pwlpud. Beth oedd yn wahanol yn y Sherman oedd i ni ddod ar draws criw llwyfan cyflogedig ac felly chawson ni ddim mynd yn agos at y set wrth iddyn nhw ei gosod ar y llwyfan. Y nhw oedd yn trafod popeth. Pan ofynnwyd a fydden nhw'n symud pethe ar ôl y ddrama gynta, daeth yr ateb swta, *'You'll be lucky! We'll be down the boozer by eight!'* Felly aethon ni ati yn ôl ein harfer, ond oherwydd fod dwylo dierth wedi bod wrthi, ni osodwyd pethe'n iawn ac yn bendant doedd y pwysau ddim yn gorffwys fel y dylen nhw fod ar y set. Aeth y perfformiad yn dda a theimlwn fod gwerthfawrogiad y gynulleidfa'n gynnes. Daeth y *finale* a'r ymrafael terfynol yn y pwlpud, ac fel dau reslwr roedd John a finne'n hen gyfarwydd sut i gydio yn ein gilydd yn ystod y ffeit. Efalle, oherwydd ein bod yn synhwyro fod pethe'n mynd yn dda, fe roen ni ychydig yn fwy o ymdrech i mewn yn y gwthio, ac yn sydyn aeth popeth yn ddu pan syrthiodd y set ar ein pennau wrth i'r llenni gau yn y *finale*. Bu'n rhaid i ni ymladd ein ffordd mas am y 'Curtain Call' i gymeradwyaeth fyddarol hir y gynulleidfa, yn syllu'n hurt ar ddarn o'r bar yn y ddrama *Bedi'r Ots* yn hongian dros y pwlpud. Yr oedd arwyddocâd y symbolaeth yn adrodd cyfrolau, a chyda chymaint o ganmoliaeth i'r cynhyrchiad, yr actio a'r set wefreiddiol roedden ni'n fud. Holodd un o selogion y ddrama, 'Shwd lwyddoch chi amseru'r ymladd â chwymp y set?' Taw piau hi ambell waith!

Dramâu Norah

Yn ystod holl brysurdeb 1977/8 llwyddais i ddarganfod yr amser a'r egni i fod mewn drama arall a chwmni arall, oherwydd allech chi ddim byth ddweud 'Na' wrth Norah Isaac. Drama dditectif oedd *Y Fflam Leilac*, y bûm yn actio rhan ynddi nôl yn nyddiau'r Coleg. Aeth cynhyrchiad Norah hefyd ar daith yn 1978, i Bontargothi a Llanddarog, Ysgol y Strade, Porth Tywyn a Felinfach. Roedd honno'r noson wedi i fi fod yn Llandyfaelog gyda *Gair i Gall* a *Bedi'r Ots*. Pan orffennwyd gyda'r wythfed perfformiad yn Trimsaran daeth cyfnod prysur ond difyr a diddorol iawn i ben. Dau gynhyrchydd hollol wahanol. Lle byddai Jim yn drwyadl a manwl iawn, yn enwedig ynglŷn â symudiadau, roedd Norah dipyn yn fwy llac ynglŷn â ble ro'ch chi ar y llwyfan, ond wiw i chi roi gair neu dreiglad mas o'i le.

Flynyddoedd yn ddiweddarach, adeg cyfnod prysur iawn yn yr ysgol, daeth galwad ffôn frwdfrydig gan Norah a'i bryd ar gynhyrchu *Tri Chryfion Byd*, anterliwt Twm o'r Nant. Ei bwriad oedd ei llwyfannu yn union fel y gwnaed yn yr hen ffeiriau yn y ddeunawfed ganrif ar ben hen gart. 'Mae'n swnio'n ddiddorol, Norah ond wir i chi, alla i ddim cymryd rhan y Diafol. Ry'n ni'n fisi ofnadw yn yr ysgol, ynghanol nifer o apwyntiade ac mae adrefnu'n digwydd o fewn yr ysgol.'

'Chi'n gwybod beth mha nhw'n ddweud, Arwyn, *If you want something done, ask a busy man*! A dim ond rhywun o'ch profiad chi all wneud tegwch â rhan y Diafol.'

Ro'dd hi'n gwbod shwt o'dd seboni! Addewais ailfeddwl ond o fewn tridiau ces alwad daer arall oddi wrth y wraig benderfynol iawn ac ildiais. Aeth yr ymarferion yn ddigon hwylus, ar wahân i orfod dysgu monolog hir y cymeriad Angau, a hynny mewn Cymraeg oedd yn perthyn i'r ddeunawfed ganrif. Gŵr di-Gymraeg o Flaenafon yw ein cymydog drws nesa ac aeth i gredu, siŵr o fod, 'mod i'n wirioneddol yn dechre ei cholli hi ar y penwythnose, wrth i fi droedio 'nôl a 'mlân yn yr ardd gefen yn parablu a gweiddi ryw nonsens annealladwy iddo fe. Mae araith Angau yn un hir a cheisiwn gychwyn yn araf ac yn isel gan godi fy llais yn raddol nes cyrraedd at uchafbwynt o floeddio cas. 'Na dechneg bu Hitler yn gamster arni!

O'r diwedd, llwyddais i gael trefen arni, ar wahân i un llinell ryw dri chwarter ffordd drwyddo, lle byddwn yn baglu ac yn colli fy rhediad a'r rhythm bob tro. Hen garreg drafferthus ar ffordd lefn. Trefnwyd dau berfformiad yn Neuadd Porthyrhyd ger Llanddarog gyda'r lle'n orlawn ar y ddwy noson. Sylweddolais y bydde'n rhaid i fi fod yn ofalus gyda'm symudiadau heriol a bygythiol oherwydd roedd yr hen gart yn ddigon sigledig, yn symud o dan bwysau'r actorion. Do'dd dim ishe lot o ymdrech i gwmpo bant, felly o fod ychydig yn fwy cynnil wrth symud, penderfynes roi tamed bach yn fwy i mewn i'r geirie. A chan ei bod yn holl bwysig cynnal rhediad y rhythm tan yr uchafbwynt, penderfynes adael y llinell drafferthus mas. Aeth pob dim yn iawn, gyda'r perfformiad yn plesio pawb. Daeth Norah o amgylch i longyfarch, 'Portread clodwiw, Arwyn Thomas. Ond er na sylwodd y gynulleidfa, peidiwch meddwl nad o'wn i 'di sylwi i chi, yn hollol fwriadol, adael allan un llinell o waith Twm.'

Rown i wedi sôn wrthi am y llinell drafferthus yn ystod ymarferiadau, ond denu ateb digon swta ganddi a wnes, na ddylid ymyrryd â gwaith awdur. Ond whare teg iddi, cyn y perfformiad ola daeth ata i a dweud, 'Chi oedd yn iawn Arwyn a'r hen Twm oedd yn anghywir!'

Wrth Aros Godot – Caernarfon 1979

Hon oedd yr her fawr. Penderfynodd Jim y gallai'r cwmni ymrafael â chymhlethdodau Samuel Becket drwy fynd ati i lwyfannu cyfieithiad Cymraeg Saunders Lewis o *Waiting for Godot*. Cychwynnwyd ymarfer yn nechrau Mis Bach ac roedd y troeon cynta gatre yn Meysydd. Ynghanol hyn oll, atgyfodwyd *Gair i Gall* am un tro arall i'w pherfformio yng Nghapel Heol Undeb, Caerfyrddin, a dyna fu diwedd y ddrama honno i'n cwmni ni. John Phillips a finne ddewiswyd i ymgymryd â'r ddau brif gymeriad yn Godot. Estragon o'n i gyda John yn cymryd rhan Vladimir; Cyril Williams oedd Pozzo ac Elfyn Lewis druan yn gorfod diodde rhan Lucky. Cymerwyd rhan y groten fach gan fy merch, Rhianedd, mewn blwyddyn a fu'n anodd iddi, gan ei bod hi'n dioddef o glefyd prin a dirgel, Henock Shonlein Papura.

Yn ei fywyd bob dydd prifathro Ysgol y Dderwen Caerfyrddin oedd John, sefyllfa handi dros ben, oherwydd cyn gynted â bod y plant wedi diflannu a'r glanhawyr wedi cymhennu'r Neuadd, i mewn â ni i ymarfer tua hanner awr wedi pedwar. Yn gwmni amatur dielw, allen ni ddim fforddio hurio ystafelloedd, felly, mewn tai, neu drwy ddrws cefen sefydliadau oedd yr unig leoedd lle gallen ni ymarfer. Bu hi'n gyfnod digon anodd i ni ein dau fel prifathrawon, yn syth wedi diwrnod o waith, i fynd ati i ymrafael â chymhlethdodau drama Becket. Un o gryfderau Jim fel cynhyrchydd fu'r ymarfer ac ymarfer cyson, ac erbyn dechrau Ebrill roedden ni wrthi bob cyfle posibl, ac ar y 9fed a'r 10fed o'r mis buon ni wrthi drwy'r dydd. Fe dalodd hyn ar ei chanfed wrth i ni ennill y gystadleuaeth yn Y Foel – dod yn gyntaf drwy gyflwyno Act Gyntaf *Wrth Aros Godot* ac roedd 13 cwmni yn cystadlu. Bu tipyn o ddathlu yn y Cann Office lle'r arhoson ni dros nos. Fore trannoeth rown i ar yr hewl yn gynnar, yn teithio lawr i Arberth i chwarae gyda Chlwb Criced Bronwydd yng nghystadleuaeth Cwpan y Pentrefi.

Aed ati wedyn i ddod â'r ail act i fwcwl, a bu perfformiadau er mwyn ei hymarfer. Dim ond rhyw hanner cant o dyrfa ddaeth i'r Drindod, ond roedd hi'n gynulleidfa ddeallus. Yna, aethon ni i Felinfach, fy hoff lwyfan. Cyn teithio am y Genedlaethol, a'r ddrama'n awr yn gyflawn ac wrth fodd ein cynhyrchydd, aethon ni i Neuadd Cross Hands, am ein perfformiad terfynol. Roedd addewid cadarn Bryn Bach yn seinio yn ein clustiau, y caem ein herio o flaen cynulleidfa orlawn a deallus. Wrth orffen coluro sylweddolon ni na chlywn y bwrlwm arferol o seddi'n llenwi yn y pellter, ac o weld, roedd y seddi i gyd yn wag. Honnai Bryn mai bws Llanelli o'dd yn hwyr, ond ar ôl oedi am chwarter awr arall aed ati i lwyfannu *Wrth Aros Godot* o flaen Bryn a'r gofalwr, ac fe ddiflannodd hwnnw ar ôl rhyw ugain tudalen, yn ôl Hetti, ein promptwraig. Ond bu'r profiad yn werthfawr, oherwydd cawson ni dro arni mewn lle dierth, er ei bod yn llawer rhwyddach chwarae o flaen neuadd lawn, nag mewn neuadd â sŵn eco gwag ynddi.

Teithio drwy dywydd stormus ar yr 8fed o Awst i aros yn Neuadd Eryri'r Coleg Normal ym Mangor. Y noson wedyn aethon ni i Ysgol Syr Huw Owen i lwyfannu Godot ym mhrif gystadleuaeth y ddrama hir yn Eisteddfod Genedlaethol Caernarfon. Cawson ni hwyl dda arni ac ennill Cwpan Bae Colwyn a £250 o wobr, yn ogystal â derbyn beirniadaeth ganmoladwy iawn gan y beirniad, Edwin Williams. Roedd gwell i ddod. Ces y newyddion drannoeth 'mod i wedi ennill Cwpan Olwen Mears, fel yr actor gorau yn yr holl gystadlaethau yn ystod yr wythnos ac roedd 58 o actorion wedi perfformio. Mawr fu'r llongyfarch ar y Maes ar y dydd Sadwrn hwnnw, cyn i fi brysuro gatre i bigo wal y tŷ, cyn i'r adeiladwr lleol, Ronwydd Fronfras gyrraedd.

Mae'n ddrama gymhleth dros ben fel y gwŷr y rhai sy'n gyfarwydd â gwaith Samuel Becket. Dyw Godot byth yn cyrraedd, er yr holl aros, a chred rhai fod Becket yn dipyn o dynnwr coes. Gofynnwyd i fi'n amal egluro ystyr a phwrpas y ddrama. Gallaf grynhoi hynny mewn un olygfa – bwrdd yng nghornel un o dafarndai Bangor wedi'r perfformiad, John a finne'n eistedd mewn tawelwch wrth i holl densiynau'r actio ymbellhau. John, wedi cymryd llwnc, yn holi, 'Beth o'dd hi obiti te?'

Distawrwydd, yna wedi llwnc, atebais, 'Sa i'n gwbod!'

Hir ddistawrwydd a llwnc arall o'i beint gan John, 'Na finne 'fyd!'

Heb yn wybod i ni, ro'dd y ddau ohonon ni wedi mynd i siarad yn null ac arddull Becket, hyd yn oed wedi gadael y cymeriadau ar y llwyfan.

Yn syth wedi Calan 1980 aed ati i ail ymarfer *Wrth Aros Godot* unwaith eto, er mwyn ei pherfformio yn Theatr Clwyd ar y 12fed o Ionawr. Yn dilyn y perfformiad bues i, Elfyn Lewis a John Phillips y tri ohonon ni o Lanpumsaint yn cloncan yn ddifyr gyda Jennie Eirian Davies, oedd yn y gynulleidfa, gan ddwyn i gof hanesion am fro ein mebyd, gan iddi hithau gael ei geni ynghanol y pentre, yn Llandre.

Wythnos yn ddiweddarach cafwyd ein perfformiad olaf yng Ngholeg Addysg Cyncoed, Caerdydd. Er mor galed fu'r profiad o ddysgu'r llinellau ac ymarfer, roedd yn flin gen i ffarwelio â'r cymeriad, Estragon. Cymerwyd rhan y ferch yn y ddau berfformiad olaf gan Gwenfyl, fy merch ifanca oherwydd bod Rhianedd ar ei ffordd i Ysbyty Ladywood ger Birmingham am driniaeth i'r clefyd Shenock.

Yn gynnar yn Ionawr 1981 penderfynon ni berfformio *Diweddgan (Endgame)* drama unwaith 'to gan y dramodydd Samuel Becket. Hon oedd drama gomisiwn yr Eisteddfod Genedlaethol ym Machynlleth. Ond cyn hynny gwrthodai

Bedi'r Ots ddiflannu a dyma ei hail godi i gystadlu yng Ngŵyl Ddrama Pontrhydfendigaid. Felly aethon ni ati'n syth i ymarfer y ddwy ddrama ochr yn ochr â'i gilydd. John Ogwen oedd beirniad y Bont, ac wedi'n perfformiad cynta ar yr 28ain o Fawrth daeth y newyddion i ni gyrraedd y rownd derfynol.

Ni oedd yr olaf i berfformio ar y 25ain o Ebrill allan o rhyw hanner dwsin o gwmnïau, oedd yn anfanteisiol i ni. Wedi eistedd a gwylio ac aros rhwng newid setiau bob tro roedd pobl wedi mynd yn flinedig ac anesmwyth. Doedden nhw ddim yn ymateb fel bydde cynulleidfaoedd fel arfer a phan ddeuai chwerthin byddai'n aml yn ddibatrwm. Am unwaith doedden ni ddim yn bles o gwbwl â'n perfformiad. Er hynny llwyddwyd i ddod yn ail.

Rhaid adrodd un stori fach wrth ddychwelyd o'r perfformiad cynta yn y Bont. O ail wneud 'Bedi' methwyd dod o hyd i gerbyd addas i gario'r set. Fel arfer, roedd gan Cyril Williams ateb parod, 'Pidwch becso dim, fi'n nabod ffarmwr bach yn Felin Gwm a fe ga i fenthyg ei Landrover a'i dreiler e clatsh. Dim ond gofyn sy isie.' Ac fel 'ny y bu hi. Wedi golchi'r tail oddi ar y treiler ac er gweld bod tipyn o rwd arno, penderfynu y gwnâi'r job yn iawn. Wedi llwytho, bant â ni gyda Cyril yn dreifio a gweddill y cast yn teithio mewn ceir. Fel arfer ar ôl y perfformiad, bydden ni'n mynd lawr i'r dafarn agosa am un bach er mwyn ymlacio. Wrth i ni archebu un bach arall penderfynodd Cyril ddechre ar ei ffordd 'nôl o'n blaene ni, a chan fod John Arfon i fod cwrdd â'i wraig yng Nghaerfyrddin, penderfynodd Ruby fynd yn ôl yn syth gyda Cyril.

Beth amser wedyn a'n gwydrau bellach yn wag, dyma'r gweddill ohonon ni'n mynd am ein ceir. Ar y ffordd dywyll a thawel yr adeg hynny o'r nos, allan o Bontrhydfendigaid am Dregaron mae yna dro digon cas yn yr hewl. Wrth gyrraedd y tro, beth welson ni ond y Landrover wedi tynnu miwn ar y borfa ger rhyw iet ac yng ngolau'r car gwelon ni gip o Ruby hanner ffordd drwy dynnu ei theits bant, a chip o Cyril yn cuddio y tu ôl i'r clawdd. Pwy feddylie a ninne ddim wedi amau fod dim yn mynd mlân rhyngddyn nhw! Ai dyna pam ei bod hi wedi gwrthod diod arall er mwyn cadw cwmni i Cyril? Shwd o'n nhw wedi llwyddo i gadw pethe mor dawel, ac am ba hyd ro'dd hyn wedi bod yn digwydd?

Wel ro'n ni i gyd yn hollol anghywir, achos ffanbelt y Landrover o'dd wedi torri a Ruby yn cynnig ateb i'r broblem. Rhaid eu bod nhw'n bâr da o deits achos, fe baron nhw bob cam 'nôl i Gaerfyrddin gyda'r ceir yn dilyn mewn confoi, jyst rhag ofon. Da iawn M&S!

Mor gyflym mae amgylchiadau mewn bywyd yn gallu troi o dynnu coes a chael sbort i wynebu tristwch. Prin wythnos wedi ei berfformiad olaf yn *Bedi'r Ots* dioddefodd Cyril druan drawiad ar y galon. Bu farw yn Ysbyty Glangwili a bu ei angladd yng Nghapel Bethania, Caerfyrddin ar y 5ed o Hydref, yn un o'r angladdau mwya a welwyd yno erioed, a thros ugain o weinidogion yn bresennol. Cymeriad lliwgar a hoffus, bob amser yn rhuthro i rywle'n llawn brwdfrydedd gan daflu ei wallt hir gwyn yn ddiamynedd yn ôl. Un noson, a ninnau wedi ffili cael lle i ymarfer dyma Cyril yn dweud 'Dewch lan lofft i'r Crown Stores!' Ac wrth fynd lan stâr dyma fe'n cicio rhyw ddwsin o amlenni llwyd o'r ffordd. 'Bilie tacs OHMS y'n nhw,' medde fe ac wedi rhoi cic arall iddyn nhw ychwanegodd, 'Pidwch becso obiti rheina, dw i ddim!'

Os o'dd pobl yn meddwl fod Godot braidd yn od, dilynwyd y ddrama honno gan *Diweddgan* oedd yn llawer mwy hynod ac afresymol – dyma Theatr yr Absŵrd ar ei heithaf. Pedwar ohonon ni oedd yn y cast. Hamm oeddwn i, yn gymeriad dall mewn cadair olwyn, gyda'i was Clov, sef John Phillips, yr unig un oedd yn symud ar y llwyfan, ac yn wir yn ffili bod yn llonydd. Mae tad a mam Hamm, sef Nagg (Elfyn Lewis) a Nel (Ruby Jones), ill dau heb goesau ac yn byw mewn biniau ar y llwyfan. Mae Clov yn chwarae pob math o driciau ar ei feistr dall, disymud wrth windio'r cloc a neidio o'i gwmpas. Er mwyn fy helpu i greu'r ddelwedd o ddyn dall rown i'n gwisgo sbectol haul.

Un o driciau bythol Clov oedd siarad â Hamm un ochr iddo ac yna cripian yn dawel i'r ochr arall, cyn clywed ei ateb, a fydde'n cael ei anelu i'r ochr anghywir. Roedd symudiadau John o amgylch y llwyfan yn ddoniol iawn. Yna, mewn un ymarfer dyma Jim yn dweud wrtha i,

'Rhaid i ti gadw dy lyged ar gau, Arwyn.'

'Pam, Jim? Achos 'sneb yn galler gweld bo nhw ar agor drw'r sbectols tywyll 'ma.'

'Iawn. Ond os cedwi di nhw ar gau, fyddi di ddim yn gwbod i ble mae John wedi symud.'

Cynhyrchydd gwych! Gan 'mod i nawr yn wir ddall fe greodd hyn gyfleoedd di-ri i Clov ychwanegu mwy o dricie, er difyrrwch i'r gynulleidfa. Dechre brawddeg un ochr i Hamm a'i gorffen hi yr ochr arall, a chael fi i ateb ar yr ochr chwith pan oedd John wedi symud draw i'r dde, ac yn y blaen. Gwnaeth hyn dipyn i ysgafnhau drama dywyll i'r gwylwyr. O bryd i'w gilydd bydde'r ddau yn y biniau'n codi clawr i ymuno yn y ddrama, ond ro'dd hi'n anodd i Ruby ac Elfyn orfod bod yn llonydd yn eu cwrcwd am gyhyd ar lwyfan. Yn y diwedd mae'r Hamm hunanol ar ei ben ei hun yn y byd. Er yr holl amgylchiadau anghyffredin, fe wnaethon ni i gyd fwynhau perfformio *Diweddgan*, efallai am ei bod mor wahanol.

Bu yna ymarfer cyson drwy fis Gorffennaf cyn anelu am y Genedlaethol. Arhoson ni yng ngwesty Ashleys, Aberystwyth ac yna teithio i Lantwymyn i lwyfannu

Diweddgan ar y 6ed a'r 7fed o Awst. Aeth y ddrama yn dda ac roedd hynny'n ryddhad i ni oherwydd ei bod hi'n ddrama gomisiwn. A bu'n wythnos well fyth i fi'n bersonol wrth i fi ddychwelyd drannoeth i gipio pum wiced i Bronwydd yn erbyn Felinfoel. Ail atgyfodwyd *Diweddgan* i'w llwyfannu ym Mhontarddulais ar y 4 dd o Dachwedd ac yna'n derfynol yn Theatr Felinfach, ie fy hoff lwyfan, ddwy noson wedyn. Oherwydd annwyd trwm bu'n rhaid i fi ddoso'n drwm cyn mynd ar y llwyfan yn y ddwy. Credwch neu beidio, drwy yfed moddion!

John Phillips yn ateb yr alwad

Yng nghinio Gym Gym y flwyddyn honno, 1982 yng ngwesty Tanardy, The Guardsman yr adeg hynny, penderfynodd Cwmni'r Dewin ddal ati, er bod Jim yn gadael. Roedd ei ddawn fel cynhyrchydd a dramodydd wedi creu argraff fawr arnon ni, ond roedd Caerdydd a'r cyfryngau'n galw. Buom yn ffodus o gael y cyfle a'r profiad o weithio gyda chynhyrchydd mor arbennig am gymaint o amser.

Er yn llawn bwriadau, ni chydiodd neb arall yn yr awenau wedi ymadawiad Jim ac er yr holl ewyllys da diffrwyth fu'r blynyddoedd nesaf. Aeth John Phillips ymlaen at waith teledu wedi iddo ymddeol o fod yn brifathro Ysgol y Dderwen yng Ngorffennaf 1984. O edrych yn ôl, mae'n biti mawr na wnaeth neb arall gydio yn yr awenau oherwydd erbyn hynny roedd y cwmni'n brofiadol ac yn dalentog a'r gallu ganddyn nhw i gydio mewn unrhyw fath o ddrama. Yn bersonol, doeddwn i ddim yn awyddus i gamu i fyd y cynhyrchydd ac erbyn hynny, heb fod yn snobyddlyd, yn llawer rhy brofiadol i gamu'n ôl i ryw bantomeim pentrefol. A chyda gwaith ysgol yn prysuro o ddydd i ddydd, chwarae a hyfforddi criced, ac wedi llwyddo i ddod yn Ddyfarnwr Criced Gradd 1 a chychwyn hyfforddi eraill i'r un cyfeiriad, aeth pethe'n fisi iawn. Er hynny tase rhywun wedi cnoco'r drws a dweud dere i chwarae'r cymeriad yma mewn drama, fe fyddwn wedi cydio yn y cyfle. Dyna ni, dyna shwd drodd pethe mas!

Yna, yn y diwedd dyma John Phillips yn ymateb i alwad Dramâu'r Cwlwm i ail ffurfio, gan ddechrau ymarfer comedi Ifan Gruffydd, *Harri'r Wythfed*. I dŷ John, yn Gwylfa Llanpumsaint yr ethon ni am yr ymarferion cynta. I ymuno ag Elfyn Lewis a finne o hen Gwmni'r Dewin, daeth eraill o'r pentre, Colin Lewis, Margaret Ffynnonlas a Helen Davies Gwili Vale. Wedi'r noson honno, Festri Capel Bethel, Llanpumsaint fu'r lleoliad i'n hymarferion. Cofiaf un digwyddiad hynod yn dda.

Byrdwn y ddrama oedd bod ffermwr bach gwledig wedi cael ei dwyllo o rai miloedd o bunnoedd gan ddyn a merch yn honni eu bod am dalu'n hael am y fraint o ffilmio ar dir y ffarm. Fi oedd y cynhyrchydd ffilmiau sham, yno i dwyllo'r diniwed ac mewn un olygfa rown i danio sigâr enfawr a chwythu mwg dros y lle i greu argraff. Nawr, gan 'mod i wedi rhoi'r gore i smygu ers 1984, ar ôl oes o bwffian ers yn blentyn, down i ddim yn edrych ymlaen at danio'r sigâr 'ma. Llwyddais i greu esgusodion a gwneud hynny ymhob rihyrsal, ond yn y Dress Rihyrsal dywedwyd wrtha i ei bod hi'n angenrheidiol, er mwyn amseru'r geiriau a'r symudiadau. Taniais ac wedi ychydig bwffs bant â fi o'r llwyfan. Bore trannoeth roedd 'y ngwefusau wedi chwyddo ac roedd 'yn siarad i'n dew, ond diolch byth, erbyn y prynhawn roedd y panig drosodd a'r chwydd wedi diflannu. Gyda dwy noson o berfformiadau o'n blaen penderfynwyd ei bod hi'n ormod o risg tanio wedyn, a bu'n rhaid ffugio'r holl beth. Erbyn heddi, daeth teclynnau bach sy'n goleuo i greu'r argraff o smocio ar y farchnad. Un peth da ddaeth o'r digwyddiad, bellach gwn yn bendant nad oes yna berygl yn y byd i fi byth ail ddechrau smocio.

Bu diwrnod y perfformiad cynta yn un trist. Yn y bore rown i yng Nghwmpengraig, Drefach Felindre yng nghwmni nifer o ddyfarnwyr a chricedwyr rhyngwladol. Rown i'n un o gludwyr arch y dyfarnwr o Rydaman, David Evans a fu farw'n sydyn iawn ynghanol ei yrfa. Wedi dychwelyd o'r Amlosgfa daeth cyfle i ymlacio cyn y perfformiad cynta. Roen ni'n hollol bles â'r ddau berfformiad yn Neuadd San Pedr Caerfyrddin, yn arbennig yr ail, a ninne wedi ennill hyder fel cast. Ail gynnwyd yr hen fflam!

Flwyddyn yn ddiweddarach, sef Ebrill 1991, rown i'n ôl yn Neuadd San Pedr. Yr un cwmni, yr un cynhyrchydd, yr un actorion, yr un awdur, ond drama newydd ganddo, sef *Randibŵ*. Y tro hwn chwaraeais hen ficer braidd yn sigledig o ran ei droedio a'i synnwyr. Mwynheais greu'r cymeriad, gyda rhai o'r gynulleidfa o'r farn iddyn nhw gael eu hatgoffa o W M Jenkins, hen Ficer Llanpumsaint. Tebyg iawn fod peth gwir yn yr honiad, gan 'mod i'n fy llencyndod wedi dynwared tipyn ar yr hen ficer annwyl.

Yr actio'n dod i ben

Wedi ymddeol o'r gwaith a byd y ddrama hefyd, yn sydyn daeth galwad arall. Jim eto! Bu'r ymarfer i'r ddrama, *Y Twrch Trwyth* a'r perfformiad cynta yn theatr gynnes, gyfeillgar Felinfach a chyfle i rannu llwyfan â Llion Williams, Delyth Wyn, Einir Sion a'r seren lleol, Jaci Ifans, gyda Huw Emlyn yn cynhyrchu. O edrych ymlaen cymaint at y profiad, od iawn oedd i chwarae cymeriad, a fyddai'n gwrthdaro cymaint â chymeriad Llion, ond eto doedden ni ddim yn taro gair â'n gilydd ar y llwyfan. Cafwyd hwyl arni er hynny ac aethon ni wedyn i Grymych, teyrnas Peter John cyn gorffen yn Theatr Llanelli. Erbyn hyn trist nodi i fi weld bod cynulleidfa'r ddrama lwyfan yn lleihau.

Yna gwnes un ymddangosiad ola ar lwyfan yn *Malwod Mawr* gan Menna Elfyn, gan chwarae rhan hen ffarmwr ffraeth yn gwisgo wellingtons – atgoffwyd rhai yn y gynulleidfa yn Bronwydd fod tebygrwydd mawr rhwng y cymeriad â Dai Twm, cymeriad lliwgar iawn yn lleol a chymydog i fi pan o'n i'n byw yn Pantglas.

A dyna hi. Bellach dw i ddim yn gweld ishe golff na chriced, ond rhaid cyfadde fod yna ychydig o hiraeth o hyd am fyd y ddrama, gwefr arbennig y *Curtain Call* o flaen cynulleidfa fyw a rheiny wedi eu bodloni. Y cyffur perffaith!

Byd y Chwaraeon

Criced – Cae Pantycelyn a thu hwnt

Tri ohonon ni yn ein cwrcwd y tu ôl i hen sied flinedig ger
y bwlch miwn i gae pori Pantycelyn, ochor draw i'r hewl i'r
Cae Chwarae presennol yn Llanpumsaint. Fan'na roedd ein
Lords ni, ein cae criced. Tu fiwn i'r sied roedd Nic, Vidi gŵr
Mali Post, a rhywun arall. Rhain fydde'n dewis tîm criced
Llanpumsaint i wynebu Cwmduad bant. Mater o ysgrifennu
enwau fydde'r chwech i saith cynta, ond dibynnu ar bethe
erill fydde'r aelode i ddilyn. Falle bydde lle i un neu ddau
grwt i lanw lan. Dyna pam o'n i'n clustfeinio y tu ôl i'r sied
hollbwysig ac yn gallu gweld rhyw damed ohonyn nhw drwy
dwll bach rhydlyd yn y sinc.

Enw Nic yn gynta, fe'n agor y batio, a Trefor Thomas y
bowliwr cyflym yn go gloi wedyn. Rhywle sha rhif naw aeth
hi'n drafodaeth fowr a lleisie'n codi. Vidi yn moyn gadel Dai
Green mas, achos yn ôl y llyfr sgorio, ro'dd e' wedi bod mas
bob tro heb sgorio'r un rhediad. Gan ei fod e'n dala'r bat
fel rhaw ro'dd e mas fel arfer ar y belen gynta. Twymodd
pethe'n uwch ac uwch nes i Nic weiddi ar dop i lais, 'Chi'n
ffili gadel Dai mas, achos ma 'i gar e'n dala whech!' Wy ddim
yn cofio'r sgôr ond colli nethon ni. Ro'dd 'da nhw fowliwr
cywir a pheryglus, Tattersall Nantyclawdd, Cwmduad, a do,
fe gath e Dai mas ar y belen gynta. Ond yn bwysicach na
dim, dethon ni i gyd 'nôl yn saff yng nghefen ei gar e.

Ie, dyna flas o'r criced gwledig bryd hynny, wrth chware

ar gae pori gwartheg Pantycelyn ger afon Gwili. Doedd 'na ddim cefndir criced yng nghefn gwlad nes diwedd y pedwardegau, ond daeth yn boblogaidd yn gyflym iawn yn y pumdegau. Pawb yn awyddus i droi at chwaraeon wedi cyfnod diflas y rhyfel. Bydde Llanpumsaint, Cynwyl, Cwmduad ac yn rhyfedd iawn yn achlysurol, Cwmffrwd yn chware'n gystadleuol iawn yn erbyn ei gilydd. Roedd yna dîm yn Bronwydd hefyd yn defnyddio cae ffarm Troedyrhiw, ond timau o'r dre fydden nhw'n cystadlu yn eu herbyn, fel arfer. Daeth cystadleuaeth Cwpan William Edwards yn hynod o boblogaidd yn y dre, honno'n denu tyrfaoedd i wylio ar y cae ger y bont, lle heddiw saif Curries a'r Range a chyn hynny, Dyfed Seeds. Roedd timau gan bawb bryd hynny: yr Heddlu, Neuadd y Sir, y Swyddfa Bost, Athrawon yr Ysgol Ramadeg, ond y pencampwyr fel arfer fydde Abergwili. Wedi ffynnu gyda'i garej geir, agorodd William Edwards siop i werthu dillad ac offer chwaraeon gan gynnwys offer criced wrth gwrs. 'Sneb bron yn sylweddoli i'r dyn busnes craff yma, a fu mor ddylanwadol yng Nghaerfyrddin, gael ei eni a'i godi yn Llanpumsaint, yn Llety'r Gïach, adfail ger Rose Cottage, cartref Cliff y llwyau wedyn.

Cyntefig a pheryglus oedd chwarae ar gae pori ac wrth ddewis lle i roi'r wicedi bydde angen cadw llygad manwl am y tail da. Yn amlach na pheidio y bêl ac nid y bowliwr fydde'n penderfynu pa lwybr bydde hi'n ei dilyn. Bu techneg Nic wrth agor y batio yn effeithiol, bob amser yn symud ei goes a'r bat mlân ac os bydde hi'n taro'r pad a'r dyfarnwr pen draw o'r un enwad â chi, ro'dd gobeth goroesi. Collodd y Parchedig Emlyn Lewis ddau ddant wrth wynebu Trefor Thomas. Dau ddant da medde'r Ficer – rhai pwdwr yn ôl Trefor!

Taith gyffrous fu hi pan ddaeth gwahoddiad i fynd

bob cam lawr i Lanyfferi i chwarae ar y traeth. Gan ein bod wedi dod mor bell a chyrraedd yn saff penderfynodd Mister Wilkins, y dyn yswiriant, y bydde'n decach i ni fatio'n gynta fel bod rhai o'r bechgyn yn cael hoe fach wedi bod cyhyd yn y ceir. Roedd y wicedi ar fat hir ar wyneb y tywod a'r ffin, sef dau bostyn rhyw ddeg llath ar hugain y tu ôl i bob pen y wicedi, yna'r creigiau yn ffin un ochor a'r môr yr ochor arall. Rhyw dri i bedwar deg sgorion ni – ddim yn rhy ffôl falle. Ond erbyn i Lanyfferi fatio gwelwyd bod y llanw yn nesáu'n gyflym a'i bod hi erbyn hynny'n llawer haws taro'r bêl dros y ffin miwn i'r môr. Wlyches i 'nhrad fwy nag unwaith wrth nôl y bêl a doedd pêl wlyb fawr o help i'n bowlwyr ni. Chymerodd hi fawr o amser cyn iddyn nhw ennill. Llais yn llawn siomedigaeth a diflastod o gwt y car ar y ffordd gatre, 'Pidwch byth trysto Dyn Inswrans'!

Erys un atgof o'r pedwardegau yn fyw yn y cof. Ces fynd ar wyliau i Gaerloyw at fy modryb, Bet – bocs yng nghornel y gegin yn llawn o fflachiadau eira, a gweld fy set deledu gynta a dysgu am *Muffin the Mule*. Llawer iawn pwysicach, rhyddid i fynd ar y bws i Cheltenham i weld sêr India'r Gorllewin yn chwarae yno a chasglu llofnodion rhai fel Weekes, Walcott, Ramedhin a Valentine, bechgyn diymhongar a chyfeillgar. Arweiniodd hyn at oes o ddilyn Morgannwg a des yn gefnogwr cadarn y gêm dri ac wedyn pedwar diwrnod, yn San Helen, Gerddi Soffia, Bae Colwyn a thu hwnt. Yn y cyfnod euraidd hwnnw, pan enillodd Morgannwg y bencampwriaeth lawr yn Taunton yn 1997, prin y byddai unrhyw faes parcio criced yn Lloegr, heb bresenoldeb bysiau Blossom, Pencader, rywbryd yn ystod yr haf. Mae John Williams Abertawe yn dal wrthi'n trefnu teithiau i'r cefnogwyr er i'r firws darfu ar y trefniadau y llynedd. Daeth cyfnod euraidd y criced lleol i ben yn y chwedegau a bu'n rhaid i griced aros tan yr wythdegau cyn blasu cyfnod tebyg arall.

Yr hyn sy'n ddiddorol, er mor gyntefig oedd y safon yn lleol, bydde tyrfa'n casglu ar gae Pantycelyn i wylio, gan gynnwys gwragedd a merched ifenc. Llawer iawn mwy nag sy'n gwylio tîm talentog Bronwydd heddiw yn Adran Gyntaf Cynghrair De Cymru. Rhyfedd o fyd!

Pêl-droed – Chwech Bob Ochor

Wrth lwc roedd llawer yn digwydd yn ein harddegau. Gwywo wnaeth y criced, a phêl-droed ddaeth i hawlio'n sylw. O'r wythdegau ymlaen gwelwyd Gwili Rangers yn cystadlu yng Nghynghrair Ceredigion, ar gae chwarae iawn, gyda goliau iawn, rhwydi a hyd yn oed baent gwyn dros y cae.

Nôl yn y pumdegau bydden ni'n lwcus i fenthyca cae pori rhyw ffermwr pan fyddai'n siwtio hwnnw a dwy got fowr bob pen yn gôl. Carto'r bêl wedyn ar feics lan i Lleine yn Nebo, cae Penbontbren neu'r Dole yn y pentre, neu tychan lan am Ffynnonhenri. A chyn cystadleuaeth Chwech Bob Ochor Alltwalis bu'n holl bwysig ymarfer ac ymarfer. Roedd hi'n oes aur y gystadleuaeth bryd hynny gyda chystadlaethau yn Rhos, Llangeler ac un fawr ym Mhencader, lle bydde tyrfaoedd yn dod i wylio.

Roedd gwersylloedd yr Urdd hefyd yn boblogaidd. Ro'n ni i gyd wedi cael hwyl yn Llangrannog ac yn edrych 'mlân at wersylla yng Nglan Llyn ac wy'n beio Alltwalis am i fi golli'r cyfle o fynd yno. Dwy noson cyn mynd ro'n i'n chwarae yn Chwech Bob Ochor Alltwalis, a finne ar fin saethu am y gôl ces wthiad yn y cwrt cosbi, ac fel bechgyn y Premier League heddi, taflais fy hunan ar lawr i wneud yn siŵr o gael y gic gosb. Cyn ei chymryd hi, lawr â fi 'to mewn poen ofnadwy, pont yr ysgwydd wedi torri. Felly ta, ta Glanllyn!

Clwb Criced Talacharn

Ar y ffordd mas drwy ddrws eang newydd Ysgol Griffith Jones daeth dyn bach o ran taldra, ond llais dipyn yn uwch a medde fe, 'Ti yw Arwyn Thomas, ife? Ti'n gallu whare criced, so dere lawr i Talacharn i whare gyda ni. Tîm da 'da ni a ni ishe bowler.' Ble gath e'r wybodaeth, dyn a ŵyr, ond arweiniodd y gwahoddiad sydyn o enau Jeff Watts, Larni a hwnnw'n siarad Cymraeg, at flynyddoedd o bleser.

Mae Parc Woodford ar safle bendigedig uwchlaw'r pentre a'r castell, gyda golygfeydd hyfryd o Afon Taf yn llifo i Fae Caerfyrddin. Pobl o dras gwahanol, nid Cymry cynhenid yw tarddiad Y Larnis, yn wreiddiol wedi eu tywys yno gan y Normaniaid i wasanaethu'r castell yn y Canol Oesoedd, 'run fath â phoblogaeth De Sir Benfro. Er i bethau newid yn sylweddol erbyn heddiw, 'nôl yn y chwedegau roedd yna dipyn o ymdeimlad eu bod nhw'n wahanol i'r pentrefi Cymraeg cyfagos. O'dd gyda chi Dalacharn a phobman arall yn Off. Galle rhywun fynd i San Clêr, Caerfyrddin, Abertawe neu Lundain, dim ots ble – ro'dd e wedi mynd Off. Felly roedd Jeff Watts yn unigryw am ei fod e'n siarad Cymraeg. Abercorran oedd yr enw Cymraeg gwreiddiol ar y lle, ac fe red afon Corran heibio'r castell mawreddog.

Braidd yn nerfus o'n i wrth wynebu'r gêm gynta, heb chwarae bron o gwbwl ers dyddiau Llanpumsaint yn y pumdegau pan ddiflannodd yr holl griced yn lleol. Heb chwarae o gwbwl adeg cyfnod y Brifysgol, na chymryd at y gêm yn Essex chwaith. Efallai fod edrych ymlaen at ddychwelyd gatre i'r ffarm yn hawlio blaenoriaeth adeg y gwyliau bryd hynny. Er syndod i fi, fe es miwn i rythm bowlio'n syth; falle ei fod e fel reido beic, unwaith mae e 'na, mae'n aros 'na! Yn syth ro'n i'n aelod o'r tîm, ond mater hollol wahanol oedd ca'l eich derbyn fel un ohonyn nhw, fel Larni. Yn ystod y tymor cynta, er fy llwyddiant ar y cae, teimlwn mai rhyw *Hired Gun* o'wn i. Yna ar unwaith, am resymau cudd i fi, ces fy nerbyn fel aelod o'u cymdeithas – yn Larni o'r diwedd! Ac rwy'n dal i fod felly. Bob tro af i lawr 'na'r dyddie hyn, daw galwad dros y stryd i 'nghyfarch i, neu bydd braich yn chwifio mas o ryw gerbyd i'm cydnabod.

Mae yna Borthfaer a Bwrdeiswyr yn rheoli tiroedd Talacharn, y dull tri chae, canoloesol sydd yno o hyd i osod y tir, sefyllfa unigryw yng Nghymru. Symudodd Dai Rees yno'n gynnar yn ei fywyd a bu'n Glerc i'r Cyngor am ddeng mlynedd ar hugain. Ond pan awgrymodd Dai fod manteision i awgrym gwyllt y Cyngor Sir am greu ffordd osgoi o gwmpas Talacharn, daeth ymateb y Porthfaer yn sydyn o eglur, '*Shut up boy! Thee's only just cwm 'ere!*'

Arwydd pendant iawn i fi gael fy nerbyn fu'r gwahoddiad i Frecwast Mawr y Porthfaer yn dilyn gwasanaeth am chwech y bore yn yr Eglwys. Bolied o wledd yn gynnar y bore. Y prif westai'r bore hwnnw oedd Prif Gwnstabl Dyfed. Gan fod popeth drosodd erbyn canol y bore, ro'n i'n ffili deall pam fod tyrfa fawr yn dal i loetran ar hyd y stryd, neb yn symud i fynd gatre, na symud i unman arall chwaith. Yna, daeth car mawr swyddogol i gasglu'r Prif ac wedi lot o ysgwyd llaw bant aeth e yn y modur swyddogol. Cyn ei fod wedi clirio top y rhiw, agorodd drws y Browns a phob tafarn arall ac mewn llai na dwy funud ro'dd y stryd yn hollol wag. Arwydd amlwg iawn nad oedd y rheol cau tafarnau ar y Sul yn berthnasol i Dalacharn yn y chwedegau ar ddiwrnod Brecwast y Porthfaer, o leia.

O 1966 hyd 1983 chwaraeais yn gyson bob haf i Dalacharn, y rhan fwya o'r gemau hynny yng Nghynghrair Sir Benfro ar gaeau deniadol fel Carew, Cresselly, Stackpole, Lamphey heb anghofio Hendy-gwyn, jyst lawr yr hewl. Y lle anodda i ddod o hyd iddo oedd Llanrhian, reit mas yn y wlad ar dir ffarm unig, gyda thair gwahanol ffordd ddryslyd i'r cae. Mae cof poenus 'da fi am fy ymweliad â'r cae hwnnw. Roedden nhw newydd ddechrau chwarae ar un rhan o gae mawr, gyda weiren drydan i gadw'r gwartheg draw y tu hwnt i'r ffin. Trawyd y bêl dros y ffin a'n jobyn i oedd ei hôl hi. Daeth gwaedd o'r sied fod y trydan wedi ei droi bant. Iawn, diolch. Felly ar fy ffordd 'nôl cydiais yn dynn yn y weiren yn fy nwy law wrth gamu drosti hi. Ces sioc ofnadwy mewn man tyner iawn, iawn! Pwl o chwerthin uchel o'r sied. 'Dyna'r trydydd un i ni ei ddala 'leni! Ha! Ha!' Er hynny, des i'n ffrindie da gyda Chymry Llanrhian gan edrych ymlaen at y peint wedi'r gêm yn y Slwp ym Mhorthgain, a chael cyfle i sgwrsio ag Alun, eu batiwr agoriadol talentog ac arlunydd, sy'n dal wrthi yno. Erbyn hynny hefyd, clywyd mwy a mwy o Gymraeg yn nhîm Talacharn wrth i Clive Jones o Gaerfyrddin, Aled Gwyn o Henllan Amgoed a meibion Perris Davies San Clêr ymuno. Aeth y mab ieuengaf, Aled ymlaen i chwarae i Carew a Chymru.

Am flynyddoedd bues i'n agor y bowlio gyda John Jenkins, un cyflym a medrus, ond cecrus ar adege. Gêm ola'r tymor yn niwedd Awst a John a checryn arall o waelod Sir Benfro yn cwmpo mas drwy'r prynhawn. Lawr i dafarn y Corporation ger y sgwâr aethon ni, ond y noson honno, oherwydd bod llanw uchel Awst ar ddod miwn, doedd neb i barcio ym maes parcio'r pentref. Anwybyddodd y cecryn o Sir Benfro y rhybudd, felly un car yn unig welwyd ynddo. Drwy ffenest y bar wedyn gwelon ni'r môr yn agosáu ac awgrymodd rhywun ei bod hi'n well rhybuddio perchennog y car. 'Na,' mynte John, 'Weda i wrtho fe yn 'yn amser 'yn hunan!' Arhosodd nes bod y don yn lapio yn erbyn piben yr Exhaust cyn cyhoeddi, 'Hei, Pal, dwi'n credu fod problem 'da ti,' cyn arwain pawb mas i wylio'r dyn bach yn gorfod codi i drwser dros ei bengliniau, er mwyn cyrraedd y cerbyd a hynny yn droednoeth.

Fel y soniais gynt, mae Orchard Park yn safle godidog, uwchben y pentre, yn edrych lawr ar y castell a'r môr y tu hwnt. Mae'n arferiad eitha cyffredin i gricedwyr daflu golwg ar ragolygon y tywydd fore'r gêm, ond ar wahân i ambell bysgotwr falle, fi fyddai'r unig un i edrych pa amser fydde penllanw'r môr. Am y tro cynta galla i ddatgelu beth fu'r gyfrinach fawr. Bydd bowlwyr cyflym yn symud y bêl tuag at neu i ffwrdd oddi wrth y batiwr, gan ddefnyddio cyfeiriad y gwynt yn gymorth i wneud hynny. Fel arfer, bydd y gwynt yn chwythu o gyfeiriad Pentywyn, sef y de-orllewin ac felly fe wyddai pob batiwr profiadol beth i'w ddisgwyl a sut i ymateb. Yna, sylweddolais un dydd fod awel y môr yn cymryd drosodd o'r cyfeiriad arall am ryw hanner awr cyn y penllanw, felly gallwn symud y bêl i'r cyfeiriad arall. Ces sawl wiced annisgwyl pan ddigwyddai hynny er syndod i bawb. Ond y tric oedd perswadio'r capten i fi ga'l bowlio ar yr amser tyngedfennol hynny. Bu'n gyfnod hapus iawn yn chwarae i'r tîm ac rwy'n dal mewn cysylltiad o hyd â'r pentref unigryw hwn.

Clwb Criced Bronwydd

Bore Sadwrn oedd hi yn 1977 a finne, yn ôl fy arfer, yn mynd lawr i'r siop a'r Swyddfa Bost, oedd 'da ni bryd hynny yn Bronwydd.

'Llongyfarchiadau,' medd Wernos y siopwr wrtha i.

'Am beth?' holais.

'Ti yw Cadeirydd Clwb Criced Bronwydd.'

Penbleth lwyr oherwydd doedd y fath sefydliad ddim wedi bodoli ers y pumdegau. O dipyn i beth daeth rhagor o wybodaeth. Sais o Gaerfaddon oedd wedi prynu tŷ yn Bronwydd ac o weld nad oedd tîm criced yma, roedd wedi ethol swyddogion a ffurfio Clwb cyn hyd yn oed galw cyfarfod. Fe wnaeth e hynny wedyn a denu pobl leol fel

Wynne Panteg, Colin Lewis, Russell Davies (a chwaraeodd i'r tîm gwreiddiol ddegawdau 'nghynt), a Ronwydd Fronfras. Fe ddysgon ni'n go gloi mai dyn ar hast oedd Trevor Benwell ac er nad oedd cae chwarae yn y pentre aeth ati i drefnu cyfres o gemau gogyfer â 1978. 'Fe chwaraewn ni bant bob gêm!' A bant ethon ni i Stackpole, Tregwyr, Pontyberem, Llanilar, Talacharn wrth gwrs ac i gaeau eraill. Benthycwyd Cae Cnwcyderi y flwyddyn ganlynol, a digon cyntefig oedd y cyfleusterau: newid dan y sied wair, te yn y boudy nes ymlaen, a bwced rownd y bac pan fydde natur yn galw. Ond cam wrth gam datblygodd y cae hwnnw yn gartre parhaol i ni yn y diwedd.

Ni welai Trevor anawsterau dim ond atebion, felly yn 1980 dyma Bronwydd yn noddi gêm i Forgannwg yn San Helen, ar yr union adeg pan o'n i'n gorfod benthyca peirannau i dorri porfa yn ein cae chwarae! Y syndod mwya wrth gyrraedd Abertawe y diwrnod hwnnw fu sylweddoli bod Viv Richards a Joel Garner, y ddau gawr o India'r Gorllewin, yn ffrindiau personol i Trevor. Gydag ymdeimlad cryf o berthyn i gymdeithas bryd hynny, gwelwyd bron yr holl bentref yn frwdfrydig wrthi ar y maes chwarae ac wedyn yn codi'r ystafelloedd newid a'r lolfa i ymlacio erbyn 1985. Cam pwysig ymlaen o'r boudy a'r sied wair! Dychwelodd Alan Jones, arwr Morgannwg, ffrind cyson a hyfforddwr i nifer o'n bechgyn gorau ni, yn ôl eilwaith yn 2008 i agor ystafelloedd tipyn mwy moethus i'r Clwb, diolch i ffrwyth llafur lleol unwaith eto.

Wedi tair blynedd yn Gadeirydd bûm yn Gapten, ond yn bwysicach sefydlais dimau ieuenctid a'u datblygu i gystadlu yng Nghynghrair Ieuenctid De Cymru, a chyn hir roedd timau i bob oedran o 11 i 16 oed. Er bydde nifer o chwaraewyr yn symud i ffwrdd, neu'n rhoi'r gore iddi, aeddfedodd digon o chwaraewyr yn gyson i gynnal a chryfhau'r tîm cyntaf a'r ail. Erbyn hyn mae'r tîm cyntaf yn Adran Gyntaf Cynghrair De Cymru a'r ail dîm yn y Drydydd o'r saith Adran sy'n bodoli.

Llwyddais i chwarae nes 'mod i'n chwe deg pump a chedwais ati i ofalu am y llieiniau chwarae nes i fi gyrraedd fy saith deg. Dros y blynyddoedd, er yr holl waith cyson a chaled ar adegau, mwynheais yr amrywiaeth yn y gwaith. Byddai pob tymor yn wahanol ac weithiau, oherwydd ein tywydd amrywiol, byddai pob wythnos hyd yn oed yn wahanol hefyd. Mae tirmon criced yn frid arbennig o bobol a bu'n fraint derbyn cynghorion gan bobol fel George Clement, San Helen ac wedyn gan Len Smith, Gerddi Soffia. Cofiaf un o gynghorion cynnar George wrth iddo dynnu ar ei bib, 'Os nad yw'r tywydd a'r amgylchiade yn iawn i weithio ar y sgwâr, cofia taw'r lle gore i ti yw'r dafarn.' Sylwer bod y Cricketers y drws nesa i San Helen, braidd yn rhy bell i fi, ond derbyniais weddill ei gyngor doeth. Erbyn hyn trosglwyddais yr awenau, ond yn 83 oed, fi sy'n dal i hau hadau a gwrteithio y sgwâr, yn yr hen ddull gan ddefnyddio fy llaw.

Ymunodd Bronwydd â Chynghrair Gorllewin Cymru yn 1983 i chwarae yn erbyn Aberystwyth (Llanilar gynt), Talybont, Aberaeron, Aberporth, Coleg Aber (Senior Commoners) ac yn nes ymlaen Llandysul. Cyn hir ffurfiwyd cynghrair i'r ail dimau, a daeth teithiau i Dregaron, Penrhyncoch a'r Gwerinwyr yn Synod Inn lle'r oedd Emyr Llew a'i feibion. Daeth galwad ffôn un nos Wener yn nechrau Medi, oddi wrth Aled Gwyn. Roedd Cymry Caerdydd un bowliwr yn brin gogyfer â'u taith i'r gorllewin i chwarae yn erbyn y Gwerinwyr drannoeth. Gan 'mod i wedi addo mynd i rywle arall gwnes esgusodion, ond yna, ei ddadl derfynol o'i enau pryderus oedd hyn, 'Ma'n rhaid i ti whare 'chan. Gronda! Ma tîm cryf ar y diawl 'da nhw – doi fardd

Cenedlaethol!' Pa wahaniaeth wnâi hynny i'r sgôr wyddwn i ddim, a chware wnes i, ta beth. Anodd gwrthod Aled.

O edrych yn ôl bu'r wythdegau ac i mewn i'r ddegawd nesa yn oes aur arall i'r gêm griced yn lleol, oherwydd ar wahân i'r cynghreiriau uwch, ffurfiwyd nifer o glybiau lleol i chwarae gemau cymdeithasol. Byddai Occasionals Bronwydd dan Wynne Panteg yn teithio i Lansteffan, Llanegwad a Llanwrda. Ffurfiwyd timau gan athrawon Bro Myrddin a Maes-yr-yrfa a byddai'r tafarnau lleol fel Y Stag, Y Railwe a'r Roc wrthi hefyd. Yng nghanol y bwrlwm sefydlwyd cystadleuaeth Ugain Pelawd ar nos Fercher i Hendy-gwyn, Talacharn, San Clêr, Llansteffan, Caerfyrddin a Bronwydd. Roedd rhywbeth wedi'i drefnu bob dydd o'r wythnos – Ieuenctid Nos Lun, Mawrth a Iau, Gwili-Taf Nos Fercher a'r gemau cyfeillgar Nos Wener, cyn troi dau dîm mas am y Sadwrn a'r Sul. Ac fel tase hyn ddim yn ddigon trefnwyd cystadleuaeth dan do yng nghanolfan Hamdden Caerfyrddin dros Suliau'r gaeaf. Yn ychwanegol at y timau uchod ymunodd Drefach a'r Gwerinwyr yn yr hwyl gaeafol. Hyn i gyd mewn oes cyn i'r teledu lwyddo i reoli meddyliau a throi pobl yn wylwyr llawn amser, bron.

Dyfarnu a Hyfforddi

Cymhleth ac eang fu rheolau criced erioed. 42 o reolau ond gyda chymalau di-ben-draw yn ychwanegol, a gaiff eu newid neu eu cymhwyso'n gyson. Es ati i'w hastudio ac eistedd arholiadau'r ACU (Association of Cricket Umpires) dan arweiniad trylwyr a chadarn y diweddar Stan Richards o Sir Benfro, gan lwyddo mewn arholiad ysgrifenedig ac yna un llafar. Roedd yr arholiad llafar yn llawer mwy anodd, achos yn y llafar, y gair cynta a ddaw mas o'r geg a dderbynnir fel ateb, felly doedd dim amser i feddwl na chyfle i newid meddwl. Bellach, gallwn ddyfarnu mewn unrhyw gynghrair neu gwpan, ond parhau wnaeth yr ysfa i chwarae, felly cyfyng fu'r cyfleoedd i ddyfarnu. Oherwydd hynny, fe'm perswadiwyd i ddod yn hyfforddwr dyfarnwyr yn y gaeaf, ac yn dilyn rhagor o arholiadau llwyddais i ddod yn Hyfforddwr Dosbarth Cyntaf i Dde Cymru. Daeth fy nghyfaill yn Adran Caerfyrddin o'r ACU, Arwyn Williams yn arholwr llafar hefyd, a bu Colin Davies, Malcolm Jones, Billy Ifans, John Homer a Huw Jones yn aelodau ffyddlon o'r Gymdeithas.

Am flynyddoedd teithiais drwy oerfel y gaeafau i gynnal dros ugain o ddosbarthiadau yn Llandysul, Drefach, Llanybydder, lawr i Sir Benfro, a gwahanol leoliadau yng Nghaerfyrddin, gan gynnwys Banc Barclays, Y Clwb RAFA a Choleg y Drindod. Aeth rhai aelodau ymlaen i sefyll arholiadau ond bodlonodd eraill ar ddysgu mwy am y rheolau er mwyn gwella eu penderfyniadau ar y cae, ac yn y diwedd, hynny oedd bwysica. Cofio un ysgolhaig o foi hedfanodd drwy'r arholiadau ond a drodd mas yn drychinebus fel dyfarnwr ar y cae, wrth iddo ildio i ddylanwad bowlwyr cyfrwys a galwadau croch ac uchel y maeswyr. Yn ddiddadl, ein prif lwyddiant fu Jeff Evans, Drefach; aeth drwy holl broses yr arholiadau i esgyn yn Ddyfarnwr Dosbarth Cyntaf i Siroedd Lloegr a theithio'r byd i ddyfarnu dramor. Newydd ymddeol mae Jeff o fyd dyfarnu'r dosbarth cyntaf, rhyngwladol.

Gan fy mod wedi treulio cymaint o amser gyda'r Ieuenctid yn naturiol ces fy nhynnu i mewn i'r byd hyfforddi, ac eto'n ffodus i ddod dan ddylanwad dyn arbennig iawn, sef Tom Cartwright, oedd â'r ddawn o wneud y cymhleth yn syml. Erbyn hyn mae lluoedd wedi derbyn trwydded hyfforddi ond prin yw'r goreuon. Ces y fraint o weithio ychydig gyda Tony Cottey, un o'r goreuon, gyda'r gallu i gywiro batiwr rhyngwladol, ond hefyd yr amynedd i wella'r crwtyn mwya clymercyn. Collwyd hyfforddwr talentog i Gymru a Morgannwg pan symudodd i Sussex. Mae'r stori adroddodd Nigel Owens amdana i'n eitha gwir. Cerdded coridor Maes-yr-yrfa un amser cinio gwlyb i gadw trefen, a gweld dau grwt yn chwarae criced. Clatsh! Ffenest yn torri a'r batiwr bach yn derbyn cerydd annisgwyl, 'Gronda ma! Os ti'n whare'r ergyd na 'to, gna'n siŵr fod dy benelin chwith di'n llawer uwch!'

Rhaid talu teyrnged i John Pricket hefyd, athro yn Ysgol Coedcae, Llanelli. Heb ei fwrlwm ef a'i ddyfalbarhad byddai criced ysgolion y Sir wedi bod yn wanllyd iawn. Er gwaetha'r tywydd drwg a holl ymyrraeth arholiadau ac wedyn y gwyliau haf, sicrhaodd John fodolaeth cystadleuaeth yr ysgolion. Ar ddydd ei ymddeoliad gadawodd fwlch mawr na ellir ei lanw. Bellach, y clybiau sy'n cynnal yr holl hyfforddi, a'r cystadlu yn adran yr ieuenctid, ac mae rhai ohonyn nhw'n gwneud gwaith arbennig o dda. Bu Bronwydd yn ffodus pan fu'n rhaid i fi roi'r ffidil yn y to, daeth Cliff Jenkins yn gynta, ac wedyn Stephen Phillips i gynnal ac ehangu ar y gwaith. Erbyn hyn, gan fod nifer o hyfforddwyr yn yr ardal, daeth digon o gyfleoedd i'r bechgyn ac i'r merched hefyd.

Erbyn hyn mae'r holl ymfudwyr yn bla yn ein pentrefi, ond rhaid cydnabod dylanwad dau Sais allweddol i Glwb Criced Bronwydd ynghyd â chyfraniadau teyrngar y bechgyn lleol. Soniwyd am Benwell eisoes, yna ymgartrefodd John Homer yma ers yr wythdegau a daeth ei waith diflino a'i arweiniad cyson a chadarn yn allweddol. O'r holl chwaraewyr rhaid nodi i Byron Jones gyfrannu'n gyson am ddeugain mlynedd gan sgorio cannoedd di-ri. Mor bell ag y gwyddon ni, Bronwydd yw'r unig gae criced gyda Blwch Sgorio uniaith Gymraeg ac mae'n syndod pa mor gyflym mae ymwelwyr yn cyfarwyddo ag e.

Teithiau Criced

O'r cychwyn cynta bu teithiau criced yn elfen hanfodol yng Nghlwb Bronwydd. Gan i Benwell ddod o Wlad yr Haf, trefnodd deithiau rhyngon ni a chlybiau fel Evercreech, Shepton Mallet, Chew Magner, Charlton Mackrel a Temple Cloud ar hyd y blynyddoedd. Pobol ffein iawn gewch chi yng Ngwlad yr Haf, yn garedig a chyfeillgar dros ben. Rhy gyfeillgar unwaith pan gynigodd Cadeirydd Evercreech, oedd hefyd yn swyddog tarw potel lleol, dywys pedwar o'r bechgyn, nad oedd yn chware'r prynhawn hwnnw, fynd â nhw am dro o amgylch y ffermydd lleol. Dychwelodd y car a'u dadlwytho jyst cyn amser te. Bu eu hymgais ar 'Hen Wlad Fy Nhadau' wrth bwyso yn erbyn coeden yn hollol aflwyddiannus! Y scrympi lleol cryf gafodd y bai. Wrth ddychwelyd gatre o daith arall, torrodd y bws o Lambed i lawr a'n gadael drwy'r nos ym maes parcio yr hen Bont Hafren. Dihunodd un o'r gwragedd lan tua pump o'r gloch y bore a chyhoeddi wrth bawb, 'Jiw Jiw! Sa i ariod wedi cysgu gyda chymint o ddynion o'r bla'n!'

Trist nodi, erbyn heddiw, mai prin iawn yw'r gemau criced cyfeillgar ac eithriad yw gweld ymwelwyr o bant. Ond un adeg bydde 'na o leia un gêm gyfeillgar bob Sul ac ymwelwyr yn cyrraedd yn gyson o Loegr a hyd yn oed o Awstralia. Deuai Cymry Caerdydd yma'n gyson dan arweiniad Dafydd Hywel, a deuai Dewi Pws â nifer o sêr y cyfryngau yn gwmni iddyn nhw. Ar achlysur diwrnod mawr codi arian i Gronfa Goffa Grav, daeth y rhan fwyaf o gast *Pobol y Cwm* ac ymunodd Nigel Owens â nhw i fod yn arwerthwr llwyddiannus ar y dydd. Ymgyrch codi arian arall wnaeth dynnu sylw fu chwarae gêm, heb egwyl, drwy holl oriau'r dydd hiraf sef 21ain o Fehefin at Elusen Plant Mewn Angen. O bedwar y bore tan bron hanner awr wedi deg y nos bu galw ar nifer ohonon ni fod wrthi. Profiad od iawn fu cipio wiced cyn brecwast! Rhyfeddach fyth i eraill fu gorfod chwarae am bron i ddwy awr cyn mynd i'r gwaith. Yn anffodus, criced cystadleuol yw unig ddiddordeb y byd cyfoes, felly a'th lot o'r sbri a'r sbort ar goll am byth.

Oherwydd cymhlethdod trefnu'r holl amrywiol gemau sylweddolais y byddai'n symleiddio pethau taswn i'n gwneud y jobyn hynny fy hunan. Aeth pethau'n hwylus ar wahân i un achlysur. Dydd Llun Gŵyl y Banc oedd hi a ninnau'n paratoi i groesawu clwb ar daith i orllewin Cymru o Swydd Gaerloyw. Gadewais hwy yn ciniawa yn y dafarn leol er mwyn cwblhau'r paratoadau ar y cae. Wrth fynd heibio'r ystafell newid clywais acen gref Birmingham, ond gan fod y trigolion hynny wedi treiddio i bob man, feddyliais i ddim rhagor am y peth. Pawb mas ar y cae wedyn, a dau fatiwr cynta'r ymwelwyr yn barod i wynebu'r bêl gynta, ond dyma fws yn cyrraedd y maes parcio i ddadlwytho tîm o gricedwyr, ie o Gaerloyw! Anamal bydd batiwr yn gorfod egluro pwy yw e, a dyma'r ateb: *'We're Lucas from Brum. Cwm 'ere Bank 'oliday last year!'* Heb anfon gair pellach at neb, dyma nhw jyst yn cyrraedd Bronwydd. Cafodd yr ymwelwyr chwarae'i gilydd cyn te, Aeth Caerloyw am gatre ac fe chwaraeon ni Lucas wedyn.

Byd Hanes

O edrych yn ôl, bu'r hoffter o ddarllen a'r diddordeb mewn hanes yn rhan reddfol ohono i o'r cychwyn. Es drwy holl lyfrau llyfrgell Ysgol Llanpumsaint yn weddol fuan, a 'nôl gatre do'dd dim yn well 'da fi na dringo i ben Cae Cnwc ar ddiwrnod o heulwen haf ac agor tudalennau llyfr. Yn yr ysgol ramadeg wedyn, des dan ddylanwad athro oedd mor frwdfrydig wrth gyflwyno'r pwnc. Tomos Histori neu Patchy, oedd hwnnw. Bu dewis Hanes fel pwnc gradd yn syml o naturiol yn y Brifysgol, wedi clywed darlithwyr fel Neville Masterman a Ieuan Jones yn traddodi. Wedyn, datblygodd yr Athro Glanmor Williams i fod yn ddylanwad mawr arna i. Er ei holl ymchwil a'i lyfrau dysgedig ar Gymru, cynrychioli agweddau'r sefydliad Prydeinig roedd e ar nifer o achosion. Dysgais lawer wrth ddadlau ag e mewn tiwtorials, ac i fod yn deg, os oedd gen i dystiolaeth gadarn i'm dadleuon, roedd e bob amser yn barod i gydnabod hynny. O wau hanes lleol i'r patrymau ehangach, cenedlaethol a byd eang, dysgais lawer wrth ddarllen gwaith Bob Owen, Croesor; ac yn ystod fy nghyfnod yn San Clêr wedyn, bu'n fraint gwrando ar Tecwyn Lloyd, un a oedd yn byw lan yr hewl. Ond, y dylanwad mwya oedd fy arwr o hanesydd, John Davies.

Yn Essex, anodd fu ceisio dod o hyd i gysylltiadau lleol addas wrth gyflwyno Hanes i ddisgyblion, a oedd fel finne, newydd gyrraedd yr ardal. Roedden nhw wedi ffarwelio â hen strydoedd difyr yr *East End* o Lundain, ac ymadael

126

â'u holl gysylltiadau a'u diwylliant lleol. Talcen caled oedd hi a'r unig beth y gallwn ei wneud oedd cynnwys cymaint o hiwmor â phosib wrth gyflwyno meysydd llafur Hanes oedd yn gwbwl anaddas iddyn nhw. Er cael cefnogaeth frwdfrydig y Prifathro, gwrthodwyd y maes llafur Hanes a gynigiais i'r Bwrdd Holi RSA; maes llafur a fyddai wedi cyfleu'r Deyrnas Unedig yn fwy teg o safbwynt y tair gwlad a orchfygwyd gan Loegr.

Tir ffrwythlon San Clêr

Ond daeth eto haul ar fryn, goleuni llachar fel y digwyddodd hi. O gyrraedd San Clêr, cefais ryddid a chefnogaeth frwd i gyflwyno hanes Cymru a gwneud hynny drwy roi lle amlwg iawn i Hanes Lleol. Roedd dalgylch Ysgol Griffith Jones yn gyfoethog o amrywiol ar gyfer hynny. Yn San Clêr Isaf roedd castell uwch ben hen borthladd Afon Taf, a safle'r Priordy a'r Eglwys Normanaidd; datblygodd San Clêr Uchaf yn dilyn dyfodiad y rheilffordd yn y 1850au; gwelwyd canol y pentre yn ffynnu wrth i heol A40 brysuro drwodd yn yr ugeinfed ganrif. Digonedd o ddeunydd i'w drosglwyddo i'r disgyblion. Dair milltir i ffwrdd, ger aber Afon Taf, roedd bwrdeistref hanesyddol Talacharn, neu i ddefnyddio'r enw Cymreig gwreiddiol, Abercorran. Mae castell mawr yno ond yn bwysicach fyth mae'r hen drefn o Borthfaer a Bwrdeiswyr yn dal i fod yn weithredol, a dull y tri chae o osod y tir yn rheoli. Unwaith y flwyddyn cynhelir gwasanaeth yn yr eglwys am 6 o'r gloch y bore i'w ddilyn gan Frecwast y Porthfaer – clamp o wledd. Yna, unwaith bob tair blynedd, bydd taith hollol agored i'r bwrdeiswyr a phawb arall i gerdded o amgylch yr holl dir – 'Beating the Bounds'. Taith o bron i ugain milltir, ond bydd cyfle i segura wrth alw'n aml mewn amryw gartrefi am gwrw a bwyd. Bob blwyddyn bydd rhai yn ffili cyrraedd gatre cyn nos!

Pentywyn wedyn, a'i gysylltiadau â'r môr. Saith milltir o dywod, lle byddai ceir fel Babs yn rasio gynt, ac yno hefyd mae ardal gudd y Weinyddiaeth Amddiffyn sydd wrthi'n saethu rocedi dirgel. Llanddowror, cartref Griffith Jones a Hendy-gwyn â'i gysylltiadau â Hywel Dda a'r Abaty Sistersiaid. Tua'r gogledd mae digon o hanes yn ymwneud â phentrefi Meidrym, Llangynin, Trelech a Llanboidy. Bron iawn y gallwn ddweud fod dalgylch yr ysgol hon wedi ei greu at y pwrpas o gyflwyno Hanes Lleol.

Ar wahân i garfan o blant milwyr y Weinyddiaeth, a fyddai newydd gyrraedd o wledydd tramor yn amal, roedd pawb arall yn rhan o'u cynefin traddodiadol a chefndir eu cymdeithas yn eu gwneud yn ddisgyblion Hanes Lleol naturiol. Gyda'r ysgolion nos yn ffynnu, ymatebais i'r alwad. Pan gefais rwydd hynt i gyflwyno Hanes drwy'r Gymraeg teimlwn fod popeth wedi disgyn i'w le. Bellach, nid rhestr o ddyddiadau brenhinoedd Lloegr, na brwydrau tramor yr Ymerodraeth Brydeinig oedd ar fwydlen gwersi Hanes y disgyblion, ond adlewyrchiad yn y dosbarth o rai pethau a glywsant o enau eu tad-cu a'u mam-gu. Arweiniodd hyn at brojectau unigol o wir ddiddordeb iddynt, gydag un ffarmwr o grwt wrth ei fodd yn cymharu enwau cyfoes eu gaeau â'r rhai oedd ar Fap y Degwm yn 1840. Daeth Hanes yn fyw fel pwnc iddo.

Wrth i'r Ysgolion Nos ehangu daeth galw i gynnal dosbarthiadau ar Hanes lleol. Yn fuan iawn chwyddodd y dosbarth heibio i ugain o aelodau ac wedyn i ddeg ar hugain, bob Nos Fawrth. Daeth trafodaethau hanes yn brif bwnc yr wythnos yn aml yn siop y cigydd lleol, sef Eynons, wrth i Eddie'r perchennog ddatblygu'n ddisgybl disglair a brwd. Bu Ficer Eglwys Cymyn yn ffyddlon dros y blynyddoedd hefyd, a chyn hir daeth galwad i fi redeg ail ddosbarth ar y Nos Iau. Pan ddeuai'r haf byddwn yn trefnu nifer o

ymweliadau â llefydd o ddiddordeb. Ar wahân i'r cestyll,
eglwysi a chapeli, aem ymhellach draw i gromlech Gwâl y
Filiast yn Llanboidy er enghraifft.

Wrth ymweld ag adfeilion hen eglwys ar ffarm Llandeilo
Abercowin, nid nepell o Afon Taf, daeth stori fach ddifyr
i'r amlwg. Rhyw ganrif yn ôl bydde'r ffarm yn gwneud
caws ac yn ei werthu ym marchnad Caerfyrddin. Aeth y si
ar led ymysg y glowyr oedd yno'n prynu yn y farchnad mai
Caws yr Atgyfodiad oedd y caws gore o bell ffordd. Ar y
ffarm, wrth ddefnyddio darn o hen garreg fedd o adfeilion
yr eglwys i wasgu'r caws, ymddangosai'r geiriau ER COF
AM ar y darnau caws i'w gwerthu. Allech chi ga'l gwell
cyhoeddusrwydd yn yr oes grefyddol honno?

Wedyn, dan anogaeth Adran Efrydiau Allanol Coleg
Aberystwyth, bûm wrthi yn ardal Castell Newydd Emlyn.
Bu'n gyfnod prysur tu hwnt hyd at 1972, pan gymerodd
cyfrifoldebau Prifathro drosodd wrth ymadael ag ardal San
Clêr.

Ni lwyddais i wneud ymchwil adeg fy nghyfnod ym Maes-
yr-yrfa. Gyda chyfrifoldebau'r swydd, yr actio, y criced
a'r golff, yn ogystal â holl ofynion y cartref a chodi teulu,
bu'n rhaid aberthu'r ymchwilio i Hanes. Byddwn yn dal i
draddodi ambell ddarlith yn lleol i wahanol gymdeithasau,
heb orfod chwilota rhyw lawer, drwy ailgylchu yr ymchwil
a wnaed eisoes.

Cyfrol Hanes Bronwydd

Wedi ymddeol ac ymgyfarwyddo â'r rhyddid newydd gan
sylweddoli nad oedd clychau yn fy rheoli bellach, dyma
ddychwelyd ati i ymchwilio. A minnau yn byw bellach yn
Bronwydd ers 1969, penderfynais mai casglu hanes yr ardal
honno fyddai'r project cynta.

Cyn i'r trên cynta gyrraedd yn 1860 prin hanner dwsin

o dai oedd yn y pentref, ond roedd llawer mwy o hanes. Filltir i'r de mae Plasty Cwmgwili, cartref i'r teulu Philipps ers y bymthegfed ganrif – sylwer ar y sillafiad unigryw i'w cyfenw. Ychydig ymhellach i'r gogledd bu Gwaith Haearn Pentre Morgan yn brysur iawn yn y ddeunawfed ganrif yn defnyddio golosg y gelltydd cyfagos. Araf fu tyfiant y pentre, ond gyda'r orsaf yn ganolbwynt iddynt, adeiladwyd 31 tŷ rhwng 1871 a 1939. Yna, codwyd ystadau Gelli Aur a Bronyglyn a dyblwyd maint y lle yn y 1970au. Creodd hyn weithgarwch cymdeithasol byrlymus o amgylch ardal y Neuadd a'r cae criced.

Erbyn hyn gwelwn fod colli'r siop a'r Swyddfa Bost yn y pentref wedi bod yn ergyd farwol i'r ymdeimlad o berthyn i gymdeithas. Pan redai Wernos a Gail y siop, dyma lle byddai'r cwsmeriaid yn ymgasglu ac yn cael clonc ac o ganlyniad byddai cyfeillgarwch yn ffynnu. Byddai Wyn Pentan yn foreol yn cyfnewid ei glonc yno, ac erbyn un ar ddeg bydde bron pawb ym Mronwydd yn gwbod y stori ddiweddaraf o Lanpumsaint. A finnau wedi byw yma ers hanner can mlynedd bu'n arferiad 'da fi godi llaw ar bawb wrth yrru heibio. Wy'n dal i neud, ond mae'r dieithriaid sy'n byw yma bellach yn rhyw edrych yn ddigon amheus arna i ac anaml y byddan nhw'n ymateb. Beth bynnag, bu casglu ac olrhain yr hanes yn bleser a theimlwn yn bles iawn wrth ddod o hyd i luniau nodweddiadol o'r cyfnod cyffrous a fu. Lansiwyd *Llyfr Hanes Bronwydd* yn y Neuadd newydd yn 2002.

Diddorol a heriol fu canfod tarddiad yr enw – Bronwydd Arms – oedd wedi datblygu'n destun trafod ac anghydweld rhwng rhai gwybodusion lleol. Ai'r orsaf drenau neu'r dafarn roddodd yr enw i'r pentre? Wedi gneud ymchwil manwl llwyddais i brofi fod y dafarn yn eiddo i ystad y Bronwydd ger Henllan a gellir gweld yr adfeilion yno o hyd ar dir ffarm i'r gogledd o'r bont. Ar dir yn perthyn i'r ystad honno yma adeiladwyd tafarn ar groesffordd y ddwy heol, ymhell cyn i'r trên cynta chwibanu ei ffordd lan y cwm. Caiff hyn ei gadarnhau gan fapiau'r Degwm a Chyfrifiad 1841. Dymchwelwyd yr hen dafarn yn 1980, ond aed ati i osod plac ar yr hen leoliad. Lle digon tawel fu yma cyn dyfodiad y rheilffordd a bu'n rhaid aros tan ail ran yr ugeinfed ganrif cyn gweld datblygiad sylweddol. Er hynny, drwy ychwanegu hanes pentref Cwmdwyfran gerllaw, llwyddwyd i gasglu digon o ddeunydd i greu cyfrol swmpus.

Cyfrol Hanes Llanpumsaint

Yn y cyfamser, rown i eisoes wedi bod wrthi'n ymchwilio hanes ardal Llanpumsaint gan mai hon fydde'r gyfrol nesa. Am fod fy hen gartre yn Pantglas rhwng y ddau bentref, roedden ni fel teulu wedi byw â'n traed yn y ddau le. Roedd y cefndir teuluol i gyd o Lanpumsaint ac yno awn i'r Eglwys ac i'r Ysgol Gynradd. Ymhen amser daeth Mam yn aelod yn Eglwys Sant Celynin, Bronwydd ac oherwydd fod y pentref hwnnw'n nes ac ar y ffordd i'r dre, daethon ni'n fwy a mwy o ffrindiau â'r bobl yn yr ardal honno. Yn bersonol, er hynny, cadw cysylltiad â chyfeillion Ysgol Llanpumsaint wnes i.

Yn Llanpumsaint mae'r hen Garreg Hir ger gallt Blaenduad wedi bod yno ers pedair mil o flynyddoedd, Carreg Ogham yn yr Eglwys ers tua'r seithfed ganrif, a Phyllau'r Saint yn Cwmcerwyn o ddyddiau'r Derwyddion. Felly, rhaid oedd troedio bob cam lawr y canrifoedd o'r cyfnod cynnar i'r byd cyfoes. Er mai pentre bychan oedd yr hen bentref, eto mae iddo fôr o hanes o fewn ergyd carreg. Cartrefi Martha Llwyd a Jennie Eirian drws nesa i'w gilydd ynghanol y pentre, lle mae plac i'r ddwy bellach, ysgol a oedd yn 150 oed yn 2014, Capel Methodist, dwy siop a gweithdy'r gof unwaith, a ffatri wlân wrth yr ysgol. Datblygodd y pentref uchaf wedi 1860 wrth i'r orsaf drenau brysuro, ac ymhen amser agorwyd Tafarn y Railway, Swyddfa Bost, ffatri wlân arall ac wedyn Farmers Co-op. Daeth lluniau, cymeriadau a storïau di-ri i lenwi'r tudalennau. Lansiwyd *Hanes Llanpumsaint* yn y Neuadd Goffa orlawn yn 2004.

Llyfr Canmlwyddiant y Golff

Daeth cnoc ar y drws yn 2005 – Terry James un o fy hen gyfeillion yng Nghlwb Golff Caerfyrddin. Ymunais 'nôl yn 1966 ar gychwyn y cyfnod euraidd pan drodd y gêm o fod yn rhywbeth crachaidd, dosbarth canol, i fod yn gyfle bywiog i bawb fwynhau'r gêm. O'r saithdegau ymlaen daeth golff mor boblogaidd nes bod rhestrau aros cyn ymuno mewn sawl clwb, a bu hynny'n wir am Gaerfyrddin hefyd. Ar ôl gorffen chwarae ar y penwythnosau, bydde hwyl fawr yn y Clwb. Cyn pen awr neu ddwy clywyd y muriau'n atseinio i'r canu emynau, gyda bechgyn Llandysul, Bois Gomerian, Dai Lewis, Jams y Fet a Byron, ar flaen y gad. Erbyn y cyfnod hwnnw, allen i ddim ffitio popeth miwn, felly penderfynais chwarae golff yn y gaeaf a chriced yn yr haf a dyna fu'r patrwm wedyn. Medde un Capten wrtho i, 'Pan fydd y gwenoliaid yn gadel, ni'n gwbod dy fod ti ar y ffordd 'nôl 'ma!' Wrth wynebu ymddeol, disgwyliwn y byddwn yn chwarae golff yn llawer amlach, ond y gwrthwyneb ddigwyddodd. Es yn ôl at Hanes, es i gerdded arfordir Sir Benfro, Clawdd Offa, a dilyn afonydd Gwy a'r Wysg o'u tarddiad tua'r môr, a threuliais lawer mwy o amser ar y ffarm gatre yn Pantglas. Yn wir, rhois i'r gore i chware golff yn fuan wedi troad y mileniwm.

Ta beth, neges Terry oedd holi a fyddwn yn fodlon ysgrifennu hanes y Clwb, fyddai'n gant oed yn 2007. Pwysleisiodd y bydde gen i rwydd hynt i fynd ati fel y mynnwn. Felly, gofynnais am help Geraint Griffiths – Twg i'w gyfeillion a Three Iron i ddarllenwyr hanesion wythnosol y golff yn y Jyrnal.

O fynd ati, diddorol oedd darganfod i'r arloeswyr cynnar fynychu tri gwahanol safle cyn ymgartrefu yn Rhydymarchog. Ces rwydd hynt i ddarllen holl ddogfennau'r clwb, ond wnaeth neb ddatgelu bod y rhan fwyaf o'r rheini wedi cael eu llosgi mewn tân bach cyfleus ar waelod y maes parcio wrth glirio'r lle cyn codi'r adeilad newydd yn y nawdegau. Felly, bu'n rhaid i fi dreulio diwrnode lawer yn pori drwy ddegawdau o'r *Carmarthen Journal* er mwyn llanw'r bylchau.

Er hynny, cafodd Geraint a fi lot o hwyl wrth ymweld â chyn-gapteiniaid a'u cyfweld. Rhai'n ddiddorol dros ben ac yn hael gyda'u chwisgi, ond un neu ddau arall heb nemor ddim i'w gyfrannu. Un noson, wedi parcio ym Mhorthyrhyd aeth yn ddadl fawr rhyngo i a Twg yn y car, ble'r oedd Jac Edwards yn byw. Twg yn mynnu ein bod yn y pentre anghywir a finne'n anghytuno'n ffyrnig. Felly doedd dim amdani ond ei ffonio. Atebodd Jac, 'Fi'n y'ch gweld chi'n siarad yn y car tu fas i'r tŷ. Pam na ddewch chi miwn te?'

Daeth y llyfr i ben yn llwyddiannus ac mewn pryd cyn y dathliadau mawr yn 2007. Wrth edrych drwyddo nawr, gwelwn i'r saithdegau a'r wythdegau fod yn oes aur o fwynhad bywiog mas ar y cwrs ac wedyn yn y bar, gyda bechgyn Llandysul, Llansaint a San Clêr yn morio drwy'r emynau di-ri. Bellach, byseddu teclyn ffôn mewn tawelwch yn y bar yw hi.

Canmlwyddiant a Hanner Ysgol Llanpumsaint

Wedi canmlwyddiant y Clwb Golff, daeth hi'n

ganmlwyddiant a hanner Ysgol Gynradd Llanpumsaint. Aeth tri ohonon ni ati i drefnu aduniad i'r cyn-ddisgyblion hynaf, a bu cydweithrediad a chyfraniadau Margaret Griffiths a Llew Tomos yn allweddol – Te mawr yn y Neuadd a chyfle i ail ymweld â'r adeilad hanesyddol. Efallai nad yw William Williams, a aned ar ffarm Tredarren ger y pentre, yn boblogaidd drwy Gymru, oherwydd ei gysylltiad â 'Brad y Llyfrau Gleision', ond roedd yn arwr mawr yn lleol. Ef a dalodd am adeiladu'r ysgol a dyfodd o nerth i nerth dros gyfnod o gant a hanner o flynyddoedd. Rown i wedi ysgrifennu ychydig am yr ysgol yn llyfr *Hanes Llanpumsaint*, ond penderfynwyd y dylwn chwilota'n fanylach drwy'r cofnodion ac ychwanegu hefyd gyfraniadau hen ddisgyblion o wahanol gyfnodau, yn adrodd eu hatgofion. Rhoddodd Alun Frongoch drefen ar y gyfrol cyn ei chyhoeddi.

Cafwyd diwrnod lansio cofiadwy a phawb drwy'r Neuadd am gael eu dwylo ar y gyfrol cyn troi i weld eu llunie ynddi. Rhoddwyd label i bawb ei wisgo ac arno'r enw yr adweinwyd hwy yn yr Ysgol – felly Elfed Cwmwernen ac nid Elfed Davies oedd e am y diwrnod. Gwelwyd y labeli Ray Uwchwili, Nellie Penllwyniorwg a John Esgair ymhlith y dyrfa. Wrth fynd drwy'r gorchwyl o arwyddo llyfrau, er i hanner canrif fynd heibio, hawdd felly oedd adnabod pawb, diolch i'r label. Wrth gael y cwestiwn, 'Ti'n nabod fi te?' 'Odw, odw,' cyn edrych lan ac yna ansicrwydd yn lledu dros fy wyneb. Ro'dd y diawl bach wedi troi'r label wyneb i waered. Ond, llwyddes i blesio pawb arall drwy eu henwi'n gywir.

Yn ystod y dydd cawsom i gyd gyfle i ail ymweld â'r hen ysgol, i gyfnewid straeon a hanesion, a gweld fod y tŷ bellach yn rhan o'r adeiladau dysgu.

Cofio a Mwy

Ers 2010 bûm yn cyfrannu pwt bach i gyhoeddiad newydd lleol, ffrwyth mewnfudwyr i'r ardal. Ei enw oedd *Village Voice* ond wedi i fi ddechre cyfrannu, llwyddais i ail enwi'r ochr Gymraeg yn *Llais y Llan*. Gan fod y cyhoeddiad bob yn ail fis yn ddwyieithog gofynnwyd i fi fod yn un o'r cyfranwyr, ac erbyn hyn bydd erthygl gen i ymhob rhifyn. Bydd fy narnau yn amrywio o fod yn deyrngedau i'r ymadawedig megis Elfyn Lewis, Madge Stag, Elfed Cwar a Dai Twm, weithiau ambell hen hanesyn fydd ynddo, neu dynnu coes. Gwnaeth y cylchgrawn ymledu yn ei apêl i ardal Bronwydd hefyd.

Ymysg fy erthyglau fe ddatgelais fod yna nifer o fechgyn lleol wedi colli eu bywydau yn y Rhyfel Byd Cyntaf a bod yr holl hanes wedi naill ai fynd yn angof, neu wedi ei anwybyddu'n fwriadol. Er bod rhyfela a lladd yn wrthun i fi, teimlwn ei bod yn gyfrifoldeb arna i fel hanesydd i ddatgelu'r gwir. Er tegwch i'r bechgyn a aberthodd gymaint, roedden nhw'n haeddu cael eu cofio 'run fath â chofebion lleol i'r milwyr a gollwyd yn yr Ail Ryfel Byd. Ychwanegwyd cofebion iddyn nhw felly yn Llanpumsaint a Bronwydd yn dilyn yr erthygl.

Wedi pori drwy hen rifynnau *Llais y Llan*, dewisais amrywiaeth o gyfraniadau amrywiol, o fwyara i gasglu calennig a theyrngedau. Profodd cyfres fach ar ystyron a chefndir enwau tai a ffermydd yn boblogaidd iawn. Gobeithio bydd hynny o gymorth i'w cadw. Felly tipyn o gawl pwdin cymysg fu *Cofio a Mwy*.

Teithiau Tramor

Aeth Jane a fi ar ein taith dramor gynta yn 1966, ac roedd iddi ddiweddglo digon cyffrous. Fel yn hanes pawb arall, dod yn haws a digwydd yn amlach a wnaeth y teithiau tramor yn ystod yr ugeinfed ganrif a'r ganrif hon, o leiaf tan y cyfnod presennol. Ein taith olaf oedd taith ar afon Duro yn Portiwgal yn 2019. Do's dim pwrpas rhestru llwyth o fanylion dibwys am y gwahanol deithiau gan eich bod chi'r darllenwyr wedi dod yn hen gyfarwydd â theithio'r byd. Er hynny, mae rhai digwyddiadau a phrofiadau mewn gwledydd arbennig yn haeddu sylw.

Gwersylla mewn pabell wnaethon ni wrth deithio drwy Ffrainc a'r Eidal yn 1966 gan fwynhau jengyd yn llwyr rhag sŵn a sylw'r cyfryngau. Stopio ychydig filltiroedd o Calais ar ein noson ola. Yn y Caffe cwrdd â Sais ac egluro o ble ro'n ni'n dod a hwnnw'n datgan, *'Been in the news that place, Carmarthen. One of your Welsh chappies got into Parliament!'* Wedyn y Ffrancod lleol a'r gyrwyr lorïe yn methu deall pam bod yr ymwelydd hwn o Pays de Galles yn mynnu prynu diod i bawb yn yr ystafell. Aeth ein pleidlais bost dros Gwynfor Ifans yn saff cyn i ni adael Cymru, ac erbyn hyn mae'n rhan o hanes.

Flwyddyn wedyn gwelodd ein pabell ei thaith olaf i Iwerddon. Cael gwlychfa ofnadwy ger Killorglin, helpu hen wraig i dynnu buwch mas o ffos ddofn yn Connemara, ac ychydig lan yr hewl canfod eglwys newydd sbon gyda'r harddaf a welais erioed. Yn y llyfr ymwelwyr sylw'r dyn o Ogledd Iwerddon oedd, *'Typical of Popery!'*

Lleol fu hi am y degawd nesa wrth i'r plant dyfu a dod i adnabod Tresaith, Llangrannog, Y Cei, Pentywyn a Telpyn ger Amroth, cyn mentro 'nôl dramor. Daeth mordeithiau ar afonydd Ewrop yn ffefrynnau wedyn a buon ni ar y Rhein, y Daniwb, Rhon, Sein a nifer o rai llai. Heb os, gosododd prydferthwch hamddenol y Douro yn Portiwgal yr afon honno ar y brig o bell ffordd. Er bod cwmnïau fel Noble Caledonia a Viking yn cynnig cyfleusterau moethus a gwasanaeth effeithiol iawn ar eu teithiau ar afonydd, roedd llawer gormod o Americanwyr arnyn nhw, hyd at 80% weithiau. Syrffedu ar egluro pa ran o England do'n i ddim yn byw ynddi. Ond un ffordd o gau eu cegau oedd adrodd cymaint ro'n ni wedi mwynhau ein hymweliad â Cuba ar derfyn y nawdegau.

Hedfanon ni i Havana ac wedi cyrraedd y ddinas, hedfan wedyn i Santiago de Cuba yn y de, cyn treulio pythefnos yn teithio 'nôl lan drwy'r wlad mewn bws mini bychan. Cawsom stopio a gweld lle bynnag a beth bynnag ro'n ni'n moyn. Ysgol gynradd fechan o 12 disgybl yn eu gwisgoedd glân hyfryd, a gofyn i'r Prifathro a oedd peryg iddi gau. Edrychodd yn syn arna i cyn ateb, 'O na dim o gwbwl. Yn yr ysgol lan rhewl dim ond 8 plentyn sy yno ac mae'n gweithio'n iawn.' Mae hiwmor iach a gwreiddiol yn perthyn i bobl Cuba, yn llwm, ond mae bron pawb ar yr un safon byw. Mor wahanol i'n hymweliad â Jameica flynyddoedd wedyn, lle'r oedd tlodi ofnadwy mor amlwg weladwy, ochr yn ochr â moethusrwydd y breintiedig.

Daw Vietnam a'i phobl yn uchel ar fy rhestr hefyd. Teimlwn yn hollol saff a diogel yno drwy'r tair wythnos a dreulion ni'n teithio'r wlad o Ddinas Ho Chi Ming (Saigon cynt) bob cam i Hanoi a'i llynnoedd. Ein harweinydd yno oedd Americanes ychydig dros ugain oed, ond un hynod o effeithiol a threfnus ac wedi meistroli'r iaith frodorol. 'Fory ni'n ymweld â My Lai!' mynte hi, a dim mwy. Y drefn fyddai trosglwyddo'r awenau i arweinydd lleol. Ac felly y bu y tro hwnnw.

Gŵyr pawb i uned o filwyr America mewn hofrennydd gyrraedd y pentref tawel hwnnw pan nad oedd ond gwragedd a phlant yno. Cafodd y trigolion eu saethu bob un a'u taflu i mewn i gwter fawr. Aeth y milwyr â dyn camera gyda hwy fel tyst i'w buddugoliaeth fawr. Gwelsom olion y bwledi a lluniau'r holl drigolion cyn erchylltra'r lladd. Y llun gwaethaf i fi oedd hwnnw o'r milwyr yn eistedd yn hamddenol yn yfed coffi a mwynhau mwgyn yn dilyn y gyflafan. Wedi ymweld â rhai lleoedd arbennig bydde'r bws mini yn llawn mân siarad fel arfer, ond wedi'r ymweliad hwnnw â My Lai ni ddywedodd neb air am dros awr. Yn hwyrach y noson honno, a hithau yn dal mewn sioc, cyfaddefodd yr Americanes na wnaeth neb ddatgelu'r hanes hwnnw iddi yn y gwersi hanes yn America.

Buom, fel cymaint o'n cenhedlaeth, yn mwynhau teithio mor ddidrafferth drwy Ewrop i gael blas ar wahanol wledydd a mwynhau eu hieithoedd, eu diwylliannau a'u dinasoedd heirdd. Trist nodi i'n haelodaeth o'r Undeb Ewropeaidd gwâr gael ei ddisodli bellach gan genedlaetholdeb cul, yr hen ymerodraeth bwdwr. Bu Peru, Cuzco, Machu Picchu a'u mynyddoedd a hanes yr Incas yn brofiad arbennig hefyd. Er byddai'n well 'da fi pe na bawn wedi gorfod bwyta'r mochyn cwta hwnnw!

Gwyliau bach digon cyffredin oedd cael cyfle i gerdded y Lovados a bwyta fy ffordd o amgylch Funchal. Dyna yw tynged yr ymwelwyr a lifa i Madeira. Dyna a ddisgwyliwn i hefyd wrth lanio yno ar wyliau un mis Medi, a dyna gawson ni am rai diwrnodau. Yna, penderfynon ni aros am un noson mewn gwesty ar gopa mynydd ucha'r ynys, gyda'r bwriad o gerdded ychydig drannoeth i fwynhau'r golygfeydd mewn tywydd heulog mwynaidd. Pan ddihunais yn y gwesty a phob dim mor lachar o olau, credais am ennyd i ni gysgu'n hwyr, nes sylweddoli fod bopeth yn wyn tu fas a gwyntoedd ofnadwy'n chwythu. Roedden ni ynghanol storom enbyd o eira a hwnnw'n lluwcho dros bob man. Doedd dim trydan, na staff yn y gwesty, ar wahân i swyddog diogelwch dros nos. Llwyddodd hwnnw i gynnu tân bach i dwymo ychydig arnon ni, y deg ymwelydd o dan warchae.

Am ei bod yn ofnadwy o oer llusgais fy hun allan. Roedd yn rhy beryglus i geisio sefyll ar fy nhraed a bu'n frwydr dod o hyd i ddrws y car wrth i fi 'nôl ein cotiau i'n cadw ni'n dwym. Erbyn diwedd y prynhawn llwyddodd y Frigâd Dân i anfon un cerbyd lan aton ni. Roedd lle i'r gwragedd y tu fiwn ond buon ni'r dynion bron â rhewi ar y daith lawr yn yr awyr agored. Ar ôl rhyw hanner milltir ar y ffordd i lawr, diflannodd yr eira, ond roedd yn arllwys y glaw. Erbyn cyrraedd Funshal do'dd hi ddim hyd yn oed yn bwrw! Trodd y gwesteion cyfforddus yn y gwesty moethus yr aed â ni iddo i edrych mewn rhyfeddod ar y ffoaduriaid a gawsai eu gadael i mewn. O ddychwelyd i'r copa cyn diwedd yr wythnos mewn car benthyg, prin y gallwn weld y cerbydau yn dal o dan drwch o eira. El Nino gath y bai!

Gogledd Iwerddon

Yn dilyn degawdau dedwydd o deithiau i'r Iwerddon Rydd aethon ni i Belfast beth amser yn ôl, ac elwa ar gynnig cynhyrfus i ymweld ag ardaloedd y gwrthryfel. Aeth dyn y tacsi â ni a dangos strydoedd yr helynt a'r gwrthdaro, a rhoi cyfle i ni gamu mas nawr ac yn man. Yr hyn a'm tarodd oedd pa mor agos i'w gilydd oedd y ddwy ochr, Falls Road a'r Shankill Road o fewn ergyd carreg, a Murlun Bobby

Sands mor agos at un y Fam Frenhines, ac at Jac yr Undeb. Mewn un man, weiren yn unig oedd yn gwahanu'r ddwy ochr, ac roedd y negeseuon bygythiol yn dal yn weladwy. Er mai canol dydd oedd hi, gallwn deimlo'r tensiwn dan yr wyneb hyd yn oed bryd hynny flynyddoedd wedi Cytundeb Gwener y Groglith.

Ond profiad hollol wahanol fu ein hymweliad â Derry. Ymwelson ni â thafarn bach yn ardal y Derry Rydd er mwyn blasu'r awyrgylch a'r Guinness! Wrth geisio talu dywedodd y dyn tu ôl i'r bar nad oedd newid ganddo ac y cawn i dalu pan fyddwn yn prynu'r rownd nesa. Beth na wyddwn i ac y gwyddai e'n iawn oedd bod y cerddorion ar fin cyrraedd i gychwyn y Craic. Setlwyd y bil rai oriau wedyn tua hanner nos!

Teulu'r Meysydd

Wedi dychwelyd i Gymru, ein cartref cynta oedd tŷ yn Heol Drindod, Tre Ioan, Caerfyrddin yn 1965. Er yn gyfleus i deithio i San Clêr, drws nesa i Ysgol Ystrad Tywi, yr ysgol lle gweithiai Jane, ac er ei fod yn agos i'r dre, gwyddwn mai 'nôl yn y wlad y bydden ni. Felly, pan ddaeth Meysydd y Bronwydd ar werth yn 1969 dyma fynd amdani. Llwyddon ni gael morgais am ddwy fil a hanner, sy'n swnio'n ddim heddiw, ond yn ôl un dyn bach hollwybodus lleol, 'Mae e wedi crogi 'i hunan am oes!' Mae'r morgais wedi hen ddiflannu ac ry'n ni yma o hyd, yn 2021. Bu newid sylfaenol o'n hamgylch dros yr hanner canrif i ni fod yma yn y pentre'; byw mewn tai ac nid mewn cymdeithas mae pobl bellach.

Ganed Rhianedd ar Ebrill y 1af cyn gadael Tre Ioan yn 1969, ac yna, Gwenfyl yma ar Noswyl Nadolig yn 1971. Gan na phriododd un o'm brodyr, y nhw fu'r unig wyrion i fwynhau awyrgylch a rhyddid fferm Pantglas, gan roi llawer o bleser i'w Mam-gu. Cawsant lawer o fwynhad gyda'r ddau geffyl, yno ar y caeau ac wrth fynd i wahanol sioeau a chystadlaethau. Sefydlodd Jane Ysgol Feithrin yn Bronwydd gyda Margaret Mathews. Bu hefyd yn cynhyrchu nifer o sioeau a dramâu yn Ysgol Ystrad Tywi ac wedyn yn Ysgol Cambria. Roedd yn aelod o Gwmni'r Dewin wrth gwrs!

Aeth ein dwy ferch i ysgol gynnes Cynwyl ac yna ymlaen i Fro Myrddin. Llwyddodd Rhianedd i ennill gradd dosbarth cyntaf mewn Celf yng Nghaergrawnt ac aeth Gwenfyl i Fangor i raddio mewn Daearyddiaeth. Wedi treulio cyfnod yng Nghaeredin dychwelodd Gwenfyl i ardal Penylan o Gaerdydd, gan barhau yn ei gwaith fel gweithiwr cymdeithasol, ac ymwneud â mabwysiadu plant. Newydd gychwyn yn Ysgol Bro Edern mae'r mab Tegid. Yn dilyn cyfnod yn Cilrhedyn a San Clêr ymunodd Rhianedd â'i chwaer yn y ddinas. Pan gyrhaeddodd Gihan o Skri Lanka yma ac yntau yn gricedwr talentog, dyna egluro diddordeb sydyn ac annisgwyl Rhianedd yn y gêm, ar wahân i'w hymroddiad â Homeopathy a Chelf. Mae Kalina'r mab hefyd yn artist addawol. Ei mab hynaf yw Cian sydd bellach yn un ar hugain ac yn mwyhau bywyd y ddinas ond yn dechrau teimlo'r dynfa 'nol tua'r gorllewin. Y gobaith yw y byddant yn cadw a chynnal Pantglas yn y teulu.

Colli fy ffrind gorau – fy mrawd Donald

Nos Wener arall, ac edrych ymlaen at ymlacio ar ôl wythnos brysur, flinedig ym mis Tachwedd 1992. Canodd y ffôn ychydig wedi pump. Wyddwn i ddim pwy o'dd yn siarad a dim ond un frawddeg awdurdodol a llym glywes i, 'Dere lan i Pantglas ar *un waith!*' Yna aeth y ffôn yn farw. Gwyddwn fod rhywbeth mawr o'i le. Pan gyrhaeddais y clos, yno roedd Jac, 'y mrawd hyna, yn cerdded mewn cylchoedd ac yn mwmblan penbleth o eirie – Donald. Tractor. Hewl y Banc. Rhedais am yr hewl honno a thri chwarter ffordd lan gwelais y Ffergi wedi moelyd a chorff marw 'mrawd yn gorwedd ar wyneb yr hewl.

Erbyn hyn, ro'dd rhiw Graig yn wenfflam o oleuadau a seiren y Frigâd Dân, yr Heddlu ac yna'r Ambiwlans yn cyrraedd. Cofio dweud wrth fy hunan, 'Rhy hwyr bois bach, rhy hwyr.' Nid bod yn feirniadol oeddwn i, dim ond crynhoi'r sefyllfa. Cyn hir cyrhaeddodd y camerâu teledu ac mae'n drueni iddyn nhw ga'l eu hatal rhag dod i'r clos. Rhoddwyd yr argraff, o'r lluniau a dynnwyd o bellter, fod hewl Banc Pantglas yn hewl anghyffredin o beryglus. Mewn gwirionedd mae'n hewl gadarn, hollol ddiogel a saff, un y byddai Donald yn mynd ar ei hyd deirgwaith neu fwy y dydd. Daeth cenedlaethau o lwythi gwair i lawr arni.

Hyd y dydd heddi, wyddon ni ddim beth achosodd i'r tractor ddringo'r clawdd chwith, yr ochr ddiogel, a throi wyneb i waered, wrth i Donald gario dwy fêl o wair i'r gwartheg yn y cae nesa. Bu damcaniaethu lawer: rhywbeth ddath drosto; awyren neu'r ci wedi tynnu ei sylw; un o'r gwartheg wedi neidio lawr i'r hewl. Archwiliwyd y Ffergi a do'dd dim o'i le arni cyn y ddamwain. Un pâr o lyged welodd beth ddigwyddodd, ond ni allai Carlo'r ci ddweud wrthon ni beth welodd e. Buodd hwnnw hefyd, druan ag e, ar goll yn cerdded mewn cylchoedd am ddiwrnode. Pan fydda i'n mynd lan i'r caeau ar y Banc, bydda i'n gneud pob ymdrech o hyd i osgoi mynd heibio'r sbotyn yna. O'dd, ro'dd e'n fwy na jyst brawd, fe o'dd 'yn ffrind gore i.

Bu'n sioc i'r holl gymdogaeth, a phawb mewn galar o golli ei bersonoliaeth fywiog a hapus. Ef oedd gatre'n rhedeg y ffarm tra oedd Jac bant yn y mart bob dydd. Yn bwysicach byth, Donald o'dd yn gofalu am Mam a hithe erbyn hynny yn 93 oed. Bob dydd wedyn tan yr angladd, gwelwyd y clos yn llawn ceir, yn cyrradd i gydymdeimlo, a Mam druan yn llefen y glaw. Ar ôl y ddamwain bues i'n cysgu yn Pantglas, ac er bod galw arna i i fynd gatre i gasglu rhai pethe, lwyddes i ddim gadael y clos am dridie, oherwydd bod pobol yn cyrraedd mor gyson. Sawl gwaith cyrhaeddes ben yr hewl fach a gorfod mynd 'nôl – car arall yn dod. Gan taw fi oedd erbyn hyn yn trefnu'r angladd, teimlwn fod yn rhaid i fi gwrdd â phawb fydde'n dod i gydymdeimlo.

Roedd Eglwys Llanpumsaint bron yn rhy fach i'r holl berthnase, Capel Caersalem gerllaw yn orlawn a channoedd tu fas yn gwrando ar yr uwchseinydd. Yn ystod yr emyn olaf torrais lawr i lefen o'r diwedd, rhywbeth nad o'n i wedi ei wneud cyn hynny. Claddwyd ef yn y fynwent ymysg ein perthnasau, ac yno bydda inne hefyd, o dan y tir a fu unwaith yn sanctaidd i'r Derwyddon.

Gair Amdana i Fy Hunan

Ychydig ddyddie cyn yr angladd, dechreuodd y trydydd bys ar fy llaw dde grafu, a dyna ddechre'r ecsema cythreulig a ledaenodd dros fy nghorff, i'm poeni byth ers hynny. Cyd-ddigwyddiad trist fu i gyfaill mawr arall, Tydfor, y bardd o Gwmtydu, gael ei ladd mewn damwain tractor debyg iawn, ddegawd ynghynt.

O ran fy iechyd, yn fy arddegau cynnar bues i'n ffodus iddyn nhw ddarganfod Streptomycin, oherwydd nad o'dd fy nghorff yn derbyn Penicillin – hwnnw'n wenwyn llwyr i fi. Fyddwn i ddim wedi goroesi'r TB, oni bai am y Streptomycin bryd hynny. Dyna'r pris a dalais am yfed llaeth yn syth o deth y fuwch yn y boudy, ond drwy wyrthiau'r cyffur newydd, llwyddais i wella'n llwyr, a byw bywyd iach i weithio a chwarae.

Yn union wedi ymddeol a theimlo'n anhwylus, darganfuwyd 'mod i'n dioddef o glefyd y siwgr, ond drwy lwc a gofal, llwyddais hyd yn hyn i'w reoli drwy fwyta'n ofalus. Roedd llawer gwaeth i ddod yn 2010, yn anffodus ces y newyddion 'mod i'n dioddef o ganser ar y colon. Ond wedi llawdriniaeth wyrthiol yn Ysbyty Treforys, therapi cemo a radiotherapi, cario bag am flwyddyn, gwellodd popeth yn llwyr. Un o'r rhai lwcus?

A minnau'n 83 bellach, er na ddaw henaint wrth ei hunan rwy'n dal wrthi. O ddewis byddwn wedi dewis byw fy mywyd mewn gwlad rydd gyda llun rhywun fel Glyndŵr ar yr arian, ond o edrych yn ôl ar hanes y byd dros y cyfnod mae 'na lawer o le i deimlo'n ddiolchgar hefyd.

Cymeriadau

Leino newydd a Thafarn Bronwydd

Er bod y Bronwydd Arms yn swno'n fawreddog ac wedi etifeddu'r enw o ystad fawr y Bronwydd yng Ngheredigion, un ystafell fechan, rhyw bedair llath o led ac wyth yn ei hyd, o'dd y lle i gyd. Rhyw dwll yn y wal a elwid yn hatsh, oedd ffynnon y cwrw, gyda Mrs Ifans y tu ôl iddo, fel petai ar deledu anferth. Ond roedd y tafarn bach mewn safle delfrydol, ar groesffordd y brif hewl tua Cynwyl ac Aberteifi, yr hewl ganol i orsaf y rheilffordd ac ymlaen i Lanpumsaint ac yna'r heol fach lawr dros y rheilffordd ac Afon Gwili tua'r ffatri wlân.

Felly, galwai cwsmeriaid yno o bobman, a chan fod Mrs Ifans yn gwerthu petrol hefyd, aeth yn arferiad gan lawer i stopo yno'n gyson: bois y ffatri, bois y cwar, gwybodusion Glangwili, a llawer un fel Jones Red Ink y swyddog treth, a weithiai mewn swyddfa yn y dre. Wrth gwrs, mas yn y wlad, roedd 'na ffermwyr ymhobman ac fe wnâi Mrs Evans fusnes bach eitha teidi. Gyda chymaint yn galw ar ôl gwaith yn eu hesgidiau trwm, ro'dd 'na dipyn o draul ar y leino ar lawr y bar. O'r drws i'r hatsh ro'dd e waethaf, a wedyn dan ford y ffenest lle bydden nhw'n chwarae Tippit ac yn symud eu traed drwy'r amser. Bydde Edgar Glangwili a John Ffynnonwiber yn stablad a llusgo'u sgidie 'nôl a mlân wrth gwato'r bwtwm – lot o 'wêr an têr' mewn blwyddyn. Do'dd dim cweit cymaint o droelio o dan y ford chwarae cardiau – y gêm od honno ro'n nhw'n galw Ffat arni.

Daeth yr amser i ga'l leino newydd, a gan fod Robert Yorath yn barod i roi e lawr am gwpwl o beints, roedd hi'n werth mynd amdani. Y bore wedi ei osod ro'dd y cwbwl yn sheino, gallech chi bron weld 'ych llun ynddo fe. 'Bydde'n rhaid rhybuddio'r ffermwyr i sychu eu traed yn y borfa cyn dod miwn heno,' meddyliodd Mrs Ifans, 'a chadw llygad ar Glyn Pistyllgwyn gan fod tail da ar 'i ôl e'n amal.' Wrth y drws ffrynt, medde hi wrth Ffynnonwiber, 'Watshwch John, ry'ch chi 'di camu yn rhwbeth. Cerwch draw at y borfa fan'co!' Aeth y neges o un cwsmer i'r llall, oherwydd do'dd neb am ybseto'r landladi. Ro'dd hi'n cau ar y dot am ddeg fel ro'dd hi, a do'dd neb am roi esgus iddi droi'r cloc mlân!

Hwyliodd y noson i'w phatrwm hamddenol arferol. Tipyn o sŵn wrth i Edgar chwareus gyhuddo Elvet Cwar o gwato dau fwtwm, ac yna Clem Barrett yn honni fod Elvet wedi towlu un bwtwm i'r llawr. Daeth Wat y Siop drws nesa miwn am ei beint o Mild arferol.

'*Put it on my account, Mrs Evans!*' medde Clem.

'Allen i feddwl 'i fod e mewn rhyw hotel fowr yn rhwle,' mynte hithe.

Un o Jacs Abertawe oedd Clem, yn rhedeg siop sbêr-parts ceir yn y dre. Chelech chi ddim byd bant 'da fe yn y siop, ond roedd e'n itha hael mewn tafarn, whare teg.

Tawelach o lawer o'dd y ford gardie, gyda Stan Penbont ac Arwyn glanhau simneie yn astudio'r cardiau'n ofalus. Yr unig sŵn anarferol o'r cyfeiriad hwnnw oedd ambell ebychiad o enau cegog John Dolwar, wrth iddo siarad â'i gi. Gorweddai Huckleberry Hound wrth ei draed. Alle fe ddim mynd i unman ta beth, achos bod John wedi clymu ei dennyn yn sownd yn ei gadair.

Daeth y noson i ben ac am dair munud wedi deg yn union, dyma'r landladi miwn drwy'r drws a dechre clirio'r gwydre, gydag ambell un yn dwbwl dagu wrth geisio gorffen ei gwrw cyn iddi gydio yn ei wydryn. Yn sydyn craffodd yr hen wraig o dan y ford gardie. 'Mowredd annwyl, be sy wedi digwydd fan hyn?' A phan edrychodd Huck lan ati, ro'dd stribyn o'r leino newydd yn hongian mas o'i geg. Sgathrodd y dynion o'r ffordd tra symudodd Mrs Ifans y ford i ddatgelu yr anfadwaith. Tra bod ei berchennog wedi bod yn claddu ei beints, roedd y ci wedi bod yn fisi yn tynnu a chwalu darn mawr o'r leino mas o gornel y stafell, lle gwnaeth Rob gyflawni campwaith mor deidi y bore hwnnw.

'O'dd y ci'n dawelach nag arfer heno,' oedd sylw Stan Penbont. 'Dim rhyfedd.'

Am unwaith doedd gan ei berchennog fawr iawn i weud, 'Sorri Mrs Ifans! Huck, ti 'di bod yn noti boi.'

'Noti boi wir! Pidwch dod â'r ci 'na miwn byth 'to. Chi'n deall, John?'

Aeth pawb yn fud. Drwy'r holl flynyddoedd o feddwi ac ambell gwmpo mas gwyllt, chafodd yr un dyn erioed ei wahardd o'r tafarn bach. Hyd yn oed pan dorrodd Elvet goes y brwsh llawr newydd, wrth chware ambwyti; dim ond rhybudd gath e 'da hi. A'r un ddedfryd roddwyd pan daflwyd peint dros un o fois y Tippit am gafflo. Ond heno derbyniodd Huckleberry Hound y gosb eitha, am iddo fwynhau gneud rhywbeth newydd, cyffrous.

Agorwyd fel arfer y noson wedyn yn union am hanner awr wedi pump, er y gwyddai Mrs Evans na fydde hi'n debyg o weld neb cyn chwech; ond dyna oedd rheole'r drwydded, a rhaid cadw ati i'r llythyren. Aeth 'nôl i'r gegin yn ôl ei harfer, yn sydyn clywodd sŵn troed ar y fflagen tu fas. Aeth i'r hatsh; trafeiliwr siŵr o fod. Agorodd y drws led y pen ond, ddaeth neb miwn. Od! Yna clywodd rhyw sŵn anghyfarwydd fel petai'n dod o'r leino ar lawr a phen John Dolwar yn ymddangos ar waelod y drws wrth iddo gropian i mewn ar ei bedwar.

'Pidwch ca'l ofan, Mrs Ifans, dim ond fi sy 'ma!'

Daeth gwên o faddeuant dros ei hwyneb, ond i John yn unig roedd y maddeuant. Roedd Huckelberry Hound wedi gweld ei gêm olaf o gardie ac wedi blasu ei leino olaf ar y blaned hon.

Left Hand Drive

Ro'dd John bant o'r hewl am yr eildro erbyn hyn, a'r Bobis yn cadw llygad barcud amdano. Galle John Dolwar gerdded i'r tafarn lleol yn Bronwydd, ond roedd dydd Sul yn broblem. Oherwydd ei syched, bydde'n anwybyddu apêl ddirwestol Capel Cwmdwyfran a rheolau cau tafarnau ar y Saboth yng Nghymru. Rhaid fydde ffeindio lifft i'r Clwb RAFA yn y dre. Gan nad oedd bysie ar ga'l ar y Sul, a phob lifft bron yn anelu am gapel neu eglwys, ro'dd hi'n dalcen caled ca'l lifft. Ond rhywsut, rhywfodd bydde'r hen John yn llwyddo i gyrradd ei fangre bersonol bob Sabath.

Yr ail broblem wythnosol o'dd ffindio lifft gatre, gan fod y Clwb yn cau am un o'r gloch. Tase fe'n aros ar agor drwy'r dydd, fydde dim anhawster. Do'dd dim pwrpas troedio strydoedd gwag Caerfyrddin a chinio Sul ei fam yn aros amdano, felly cadwai lygad barcud ar y mynd a dod i'r bar wedi hanner awr wedi deuddeg. Pwy a ŵyr pwy ddele miwn. Ambell un o Cynwyl falle, a dyna lifft i'r hewl dop; prynu peint i foi o Bencader a'i berswadio i fynd gatre drwy Bronwydd; geiriau caredig i ddyn bach o Abergwili i'w redeg e lan beth o'r ffordd; os bydde'r cwbwl yn ffili, tacsi amdani.

Y Sul hwnnw do'dd dim lot miwn yn Clwb y RAFA am ryw reswm. Yna hwrê! Da'th Glyn, cyn dafarnwr y Roc and Ffownten, ac yn byw yn Gelli Aur ac felly'n pasio'i gartre. Nabyddodd y llall 'fyd, mab yng nghyfraith Glyn, gartre ar wylie o'r fyddin yn yr Almaen. Gwd. Ro'n nhw bownd o ga'l doi beint, ac fe bryne fe'r ail cyn gofyn am y lifft. Dim problem gan fod Glyn yn falch o gwrdd â'i hen gwsmer. Daeth yr alwad derfynol; gwacawyd y peints a mas â nhw.

'Tw *sitter* sy 'da fe, so af fi i'r gwt, gan taw ti sy'n mynd mas ginta,' medde Glyn.

Eisteddodd John mewn steil yn sêt flaen y car tramor, posh. Bant â nhw lan Heol y Brenin, bryd hynny, ac o amgylch ochr ogleddol Eglwys San Pedr. Arhosodd y car, wrth gyrraedd yr hewl fawr, godderbyn ag Oswald Davies. Aeth dau gar heibio o'r dde ac yna o'r chwith ymddangosodd sgwad car llachar yr Heddlu yn prowlan yn fygythiol, araf. Yn sydyn trodd capie swyddogol y ddau blismon a syllu ar John. Dyma sgŵp! Roedden nhw wedi dal y diawl bach yn gyrru'n anghyfreithlon, a hynny ar y Sul hefyd, ac yn feddw siŵr o fod. Gallent weld 'Promotion' yn ymddangos ar y gorwel. Daeth golwg bryderus dros wyneb y gyrrwr, ond syllodd John 'nôl atyn nhw gyda rhyw hyder heriol newydd. Cododd ei ddwylo a heb olwyn o'i flân gwaeddodd arnyn nhw, '*Nothin to do with me!*'.

'*Bloody foreign car! Left hand drive!*' oedd ymateb y bobi wrth sbarduno bant a gobeth am 'bromotion' wedi diflannu.

Em Trapwr

Yn y pum a'r chwedege bydde rhai'n ca'l dydd Sadwrn bant, ac eraill yn rhydd ar ôl hanner dydd; felly, bydde'r tafarne'n llawn. Fel llawer i un arall, gwariai Emrys beth amser yn y dre, cyn dod 'nôl i'r Bronwydd Arms yn y Mini bach. Hwnnw wedyn yn ca'l ei barco ger sied Cyril i'r gogledd o'r pwmps petrol. Gan y bydde fe yn y dafarn am weddill y dydd, ro'dd e'n edrych yn saffach yno, fel rhan o'r sefydliad fel petai. Bydde Em yn gadel am gatre am hanner awr wedi naw'n brydlon, gan fod y bobis yn newid shifft am ddeg. Gan taw dreifo lori'r Co-op o'dd ei waith e, do'dd e ddim ishe tynnu sylw heb ishe at ei daith fach gatre ar Nos Sadwrn. O'dd bobi Cynwyl, whare teg iddo, yn gwbod sut i gau llygad, ond allech chi'm trysto'r hen batrols 'na yn enwedig ar y penwythnos, ac ar ôl deg y nos y bydde'r bois busneslyd 'ny mas yn prowlan. Er taw dreifo lori'r Co-op ro'dd e 'radeg hynny fe'i hadnabyddid fel Em Trapwr am mai trapo cwningod o'dd un o'i jobs cynnar.

Dydd Sadwrn bach arferol o'dd hi ac Em wedi mwynhau. Ond erbyn naw o'r gloch ro'dd yr hen beswch yn cynyddu, oherwydd yr holl Woodbines ro'dd e wedi'u smoco drwy'r dydd. A phan fydde fe'n dechre ca'l pwl ar hanner brawddeg, âi'r pwl mlân a mlân.

'O'n i'n mynd lan â llwyth o gêc i ... whwwf ... Benw ... hfff... whwwf ... Benllwyn ... wwwhhfff ...'

Yna, bydde Wat y Siop, o'dd yn gwbod hanes pawb a phopeth, yn trial 'i helpu, 'Lan i Benllwyniorwg.'

'Whwwwff... fff ... Nage achan ... whhwwff... Penllwynuchel!'

Rodd hi'n anobeithiol gorffen y stori a phesychodd yr hen frawd ei ffordd mas i'r awyr iach am ychydig o ryddhad. Erbyn iddo ddod 'nôl a gwacáu ei beint ola o Mild arbennig Mrs Evans, ro'dd y cloc ger bocs y Blind ar y silff ben tân yn ymlwybro am hanner awr wedi naw.

'Hwyl, Em. Wela i ti wthnos nesa.'

'Gwd te, Em!'

Gwyddent o brofiad na ddeuai unrhyw gyfarchiad 'nôl heblaw am hanner dwsin o Whwwffs. Dyna pryd byddai Wat yn tynnu ei bib mas cyn cyflwyno ei frawddeg arferol, 'Ma'n hen bryd iddo fe baco'r ffags 'na lan a smoco rhywbeth teidi!'

Mewn rhyw ddeg munud agorodd y drws i ddatgelu pen ein harwr wedi dod 'nôl. Anarferol iawn.

'Ma'r Mini'n pallu ... whwwff ... mynd!'

'Os wyt ti mas o betrol pam na lenwi di'r Mini?' gofynnodd Cyril.

'Ma fe'n starto'n iawn ... whhff... pallu... whhhhffw mynd ma fe!'

I arbed y darllenwr orfod ymlwybro drwy bwffs di-ri yn ystod y munude nesa, dyma grynodeb o'r trafod dwys a fu. Barn bendant un arbenigwr oedd mai'r *Crown wheel an'pinion* oedd ar fai. Fynte wedi clywed a hoffi'r gair yn rhywle, siŵr o fod. Plygs mynte un o borters Ysbyty Glangwili. Datganodd un arall, gyda chryn brofiad o fod wedi gweithio gyda mecanic, fod rhaid newid y carborator. 'Ti'n siŵr bod oil 'da ti ynddo fe?' holodd un arall.

Ybsetodd hyn Em. 'Sa i'n dwp ...hfffww... fi'n dreifo lori bob blydi dydd. Ta beth ... hffffw ... hwwff ma'r car yn rhedeg yn iawn. Pallu symud ma'r diawl!'

Yn anochel ro'dd rhaid mynd mas i weld a chan fod cymaint o wybodaeth amhrisiadwy ar gael, aeth poblogaeth y tafarn bach un ystafell i gyd mas i fusnesu. Yn y dyddiau hynny, ar adeg hynny o'r nos, prin iawn oedd y drafnidiaeth; a gweud y gwir a'th dim un car hibo drwy gydol y ddrama. A'th Em miwn i'r car bach, tanio a refio lan fel ryw Jaci Stewart, ond sefyll yn ei unfan wnaeth y Mini.

'So fe'n gêr 'da ti!' medde John Ffynnonwiber, mas o gornel ei geg drwy'r ffag rowlo'i hunan.

Ffrwydrodd Em. 'Wrth gwrs bod e yn gêr. Ddim ddo ces i 'ngeni ... hfffwww... Ma rhwbeth mowr yn rong!'

Agorwyd y bonet ac yn yr hanner tywyllwch, dan fflachiad ambell i leiter ffags, archwiliwyd holl rannau corff y car bach. Wedi'r holl archwilio, daethon nhw i gasgliad unfrydol: do'dd 'da neb syniad beth o'dd yn bod.

Yna cofiodd y boi o'dd wedi bod 'da'r mecanic beth o'dd

hwnnw'n neud pan o'dd e'n stympt, 'Starta fe lan to, Em, i ni ga'l un bip fach arall.'

Geiriau doeth tu hwnt. Taniodd y peiriant a refodd y dreifwr fflat owt. Yna sylwodd John Pistyllgwyn, o'dd wedi crwydro rownd sha bac y car, fod yr olwynion ôl yn troi fflat owt, ond nad oedd yr olwynion blaen, na'r car yn symud modfedd.

'Ffyc ffyc! Fi'n gwbod be sy'n bod. Ma'r ddwy whil ôl yn sownd yn y lein ddillad a ma nhw off yr hewl!'

Y gwir o'r diwedd. Pan rifyrsodd Em 'nôl ynghynt yn y dydd, a'th 'nôl dros lein ddillad Mrs Ifans. Ro'dd hi wedi casglu'r dillad cyn iddo gyrraedd. Wrth barco, roedd y Mini wedi crwydro dros y welten, ac erbyn hyn roedd hanner y car yn hongian yn yr awyr, a dim ond y lein ddillad o'dd yn ei arbed rhag cwympo'r deugain llath i'r hewl waelod am Lanpumsaint. Y syndod mwya oedd fod y lein wedi dal holl bwyse'r car.

Fel digwyddodd hi, ma dynion tri chwarter meddw, dibrofiad, yn gallu cyflawni gwyrthie weithie. A'th y bois rownd cefen y car a lawr am y dibyn, a rhoi dwy ysgwydd dan ei ben ôl i'w godi uwchben y lein ddillad, dau arall yn gwasgu'u pwyse ar y bonet a bant â fe. Ro'dd hi bryd mynd, achos ro'dd hi bron yn ddeg o'r gloch!

Ond, chwarae teg, ffindiodd e amser i droi'r ffenest lawr a gweiddi ar Cyril, 'Rho bobo un miwn iddyn nhw a gwed thenciw!' Gymaint o'dd yr argyfwng, fel nad o'dd sôn am y peswch!

Yfa gwrw Cymru'r diawl

Gan nad oedd 'y nghartre yn Meysydd ond chwarter milltir lan yr hewl o'r Bronwydd Arms galwn am beint yn fynych ar y ffordd gatre o ryw gyfarfod, neu ymarfer drama yn y saithdegau. Gan y bydde'r drysau'n cau'n brydlon am ddeg, do'dd na'm perygl i sesiwn ddatblygu. Y noson honno, galwes yn ôl fy arfer, wedi ca'l dwy awr o ymarfer gyda Chwmni'r Dewin. Wrth nesáu at y drws roedd sŵn o'r bar yn awgrymu fod y lle'n llawn, ond do'n i ddim yn barod am yr olygfa nesa.

Wedi agor y drws allwn i weld dim, oherwydd y cwmwl mwg trwchus yn hedfan mas, a sylweddoles yn go gloi nad mwg pib Wat, na Woodbines Dai Twm oedd y rheswm, ond mwg sigârs. O gamu i mewn a chyfarwyddo ychydig â'r tawch, gwelwn fod pawb yno'n smoco, neu yn treial smoco sigârs mawr tew a rhai'n ca'l trwbwl mawr meistroli'r mwgyn drud. Gwnaed y dasg yn anoddach, oherwydd sylweddoles eu bod nhw'n feddw gaib. Ond nid pawb. Safai un dyn ar ei draed yn chwerthin ei ben bant – Elvet y Cwar a dwy botel fowr o chwisgi, un ymhob llaw. Bob tro y dwedai rhywun rhywbeth, a ro'dd tipyn 'da nhw i gyd i weud erbyn hynny, arllwysai Elfed joch o chwisgi i mewn i'w beint, fel fforffit.

'Dere miwn i'r parti, Pantglas, i ti ga'l llwnc bach o hwn,' mynte fe.

Rodd Dai Twm fel sach o dato yn y cornel gyda'i sigâr wedi cwmpo miwn i'r blwch llwch ar y ford. Wrth nesáu at yr hatsh gwelwn Wat ar y sgiw, yn goleddu fel coeden mewn storom.

'Dylet ti fod 'ma' ynghynt ... hic... Mae'n neis ca'l ymbach o newid ambell waiff,' mynte Wat. Gwthiodd y sigâr hanner ffordd miwn i'w geg, a sylwes fod ei bib yn ei boced dop, yn dal ynghyn.

'Watshwch na losgith hi'ch poced chi.'

'Paid becso mo'r dam ... os odi'r babi'n cachu lond y pram,' oedd yr unig ymateb tolciog wrth iddo estyn ei beint hanner gwag a derbyn cymundeb arall o law Elvet.

Golwg fach ddigon cymysglyd oedd ar wyneb Mrs Ifans wrth i fi ofyn am beint.

'O'n i'n meddwl taw prynu dwy botel o White Horse i fynd mas o'dd e'. Fydda i'n falch o weld stop tap yn dod heno.'

Dyna pryd y sylweddolais fod dieithryn, yn slwmp ar y stôl ger y sgiw, ac ro'dd golwg lipa ar hwnnw hefyd.

'I aawnly caim in to payye for moi petrol and oim pissed. Oim from Brummie and oi'v got to get to Newcastle Oimlyn. Oi dawnt even know this blawk whose party it is!'

'Yfa gwrw Cymru'r diawl,' medde Elvet, gan lanw'i wydr unwaith 'to. 'Bydd e yn y clawdd cyn bod e'n cyrraedd Hermon, myn uffarn i!'

Daeth y diwedd yn sydyn wrth iddi hi alw TIME, dipyn yn gynt na gofynion y gyfraith, a'u troi nhw mas fel gwartheg o'r boudy. Cariwyd rhai i'r wal yr ochr draw, yn y gobaith y caen nhw adfywiad yn yr awyr iach. Chwerthin yn dawel wrth ei hunan a wnâi Elvet a dringo miwn i'w lori. Ei ddiléit oedd meddwi pobol erill. Bu'n noson dda, hyd yn oed yn well na'r noson pan feddwon nhw bobi Cynwyl y llynedd; mynd ag e gatre wedyn a'i roi i bwyso ar ddrws ei dŷ, cyn rhoi cnoc gadarn a'i baglu hi.

Ni ŵyr neb beth ddaeth o'r Brymi bach. Doedd dim sôn am ddamwen na dim, ond alwodd e byth wedyn yn nhafarn y Bronwydd.

Wil Gwili

Hen lanc yn byw sha Llangeler o'dd Wil Gwili. Bob tro ethe fe i'r dre yng Nghaerfyrddin, ro'dd rhaid galw yn y Roc ar y ffordd gatre. Tafarn rhwng Bronwydd a Cynwyl o'dd y Roc. Bryd hynny bydde gyda ni blismyn gwlad, a'r calla ohonyn nhw'n defnyddio'u synnwyr cyffredin yn amlach na'r pensil. Un noson, tynnodd car Wil Gwili mas o gornel parcio'r Roc gan anelu am gatre, a heb yn wybod iddo ymddangosodd car bobi Cynwyl a'i ddilyn. Erbyn cyrraedd fflaten garej ceir Henri, a'th yr heddwas hibo a'i dynnu miwn.

Trodd Wil ei ffenest lawr, 'Shw mae. Shw mae. Mae hi'n nosweth ffein. Gwir! Gwir!' Bydde'r cymeriad unigryw hwn yn gorffen pob brawddeg gyda'r geiriau, 'Gwir! Gwir!'

'Nosweth dda, William. Nawr fel bo'ch chi'n diall, y rheswm stopes i chi o'dd achos fod y gole ôl ddim mlân 'da chi'

'Wel 'nôl ma nhw fod! Ie. Gwir! Gwir!'

Daw'r ysfa gynhenid hyd yn oed i hen lanc, a chan taw aflwyddiannus fu ei ymdrechion i ddenu wejan fach, daeth cyfle o'r newydd o ddudalennau cyffrous y *News Of the World*. Hysbyseb oedd yno am ddol nwydus, ramantus ac egnïol. Dol na fydde byth yn ca'l pen tost ac yn barod amdani cyn neu ar ôl godro! Dol na fydde'n costi ceiniog ar ôl cyrradd drwy'r post a chan ei bod yn dod am bris teg iawn adeg y sêl, ro'dd y cyfle'n rhy dda i'w golli. Ac ar ben popeth, beth alle fod yn well na 21 diwrnod o 'Free Trial' cyn talu dime?

Y broblem oedd fod yna bobol fusneslyd sha Cwmduad a'r postmon yn un o'r gwaetha. Gan nad o'dd Wil Gwili byth yn derbyn unrhyw barsel drwy'r post, fe fydde'r diawl bach yn siŵr o bipo miwn ynddo fe i fusnesu. 'Na hi wedyn; o fewn diwrnod, bydde tri neu bedwar plwy wedi clywed y stori, gan gynnwys pobol y capel.

Wrth fwynhau peint un Nos Fercher wrth y bar yn y Roc, tynnodd fan goch Ei Mawrhydi lan tu fas, a dyma'r boi â'r cap yn rhoi dou barsel papur brown ar y cownter.

'Sbesial deliferi,' dwedodd wrth y tafarnwr. Yn amal, y dyddie hynny, bydde'r postman yn gadel parseli yn y tafarn lleol i'w casglu gan bobol yr ardal.

Mae ychydig alcohol yn cyflymu'r meddwl, medden nhw a do's dim angen ystyried gormod i weld i ba gyfeiriad ymlwybrodd meddwl yr hen lanc. Cytunodd y tafarnwr ar

unwaith i dderbyn parsel gydag enw William Gwili arno,
ac ymhen wythnos dyma fe'n cyrraedd. Y noson honno un
peint yfodd ein harwr a hwnnw ar ei ben cyn carlamu gatre
a rhwygo'r papur brown i ollwng y gyfrinach fawr mas i ole
dydd.

'Ie. Gwir! Gwir!' Efallai iddo'i chwythu hi lan yn ormodol.
Efallai iddo neidio ar ei phen hi'n rhy sydyn o drwm. Efallai
fod nam arni cyn dod mas o'r pacyn. Ond yn bendant, doedd
y darn fflat o rwber ar lawr y parlwr ddim byd tebyg i'r llun
nwydus â'r bronnau uchel croesawgar ar y pishyn papur. Y
fath siom!

Wedi hôl yr hylif riparo pynctiers beic o'r sied, gwelodd
fod y rhwyg yn y rwber yn un enfawr, a rhoddodd y stwff
pynctiers 'nôl ar y silff. Roedd anfon yr offeryn diffygiol yn ôl
mas o'r cwestiwn, gyda rhywbeth mor gyfrinachol a delicet
â hyn. Bydde'r tafarn yn siŵr o ofyn gormod o gwestiyne a
dod o hyd i'r gwirionedd ac wedyn bydde'r cwsmeried i gyd
yn neud sbort am ei ben. 'Rhaid meddwl obiti'r peth! Gwir!
Gwir!' medde Wil Gwili wrth ei hunan.

Gan nad o'dd hast i neud dim am dair wythnos, gadel
pethe i fod fydde ore. Efalle fod llawer i ddol yn ddiffygiol
a falle wedyn na fydden nhw'n cwrso am ei arian. Aeth
mis heibio ac wythnos arall ac ymddangosai fel petai
damcaniaeth ein harwr yn weddol agos ati. Ond, yna'r nos
Fercher ganlynol, wedi galw yn y Roc ar y ffordd gatre o'r
mart, tynnodd y tafarnwr e i gornel y bar.

'Ti'n gwbod y parsel 'na gest ti o'r General Rubber
Company. Ma nhw wedi hala bil a remeinder. Ishe i ti
dalu.'

'Hen stwff gwael o'dd e' ta beth. Sgrifenna 'nôl a gweud
wrthyn nhw, *owner dead* – Gwir! Gwir!' a mas â fe gatre'n
syth. Alwodd e ddim yn y Roc am sbel wedyn, gan newid ei
ffynnon a blasu cwrw'r Bronwydd a'r Blw Bel yn Cynwyl.

Aeth mis heibio ac aeth y mater yn angof, ond galwodd yn y Roc unwaith 'to a'r esgus parod ganddo iddo ga'l pwl o dostrwydd.

Hanner ffordd drwy ei ail beint, dilynodd y tafarnwr e mas i'r toiled,

'Gronda nawr, William bach, os odw i'n neud ffafre â phobol, fi'n disgwl eu bo nhw'n setlo'u bilie. Wy wedi ca'l y ffeinal rimeinder nawr.'

Gan gau ei gopys ar frys, anelodd ein harwr am y drws gan daflu ei sylw terfynol.

'Sori. Sori. Sgrifenna 'nôl a gwed – *owner still dead*. Gwir! Gwir!' A bant â fe!

Hywel Llygod

Un eitha da wrth ei waith o'dd Hywel Llygod, yn gwbod yn iawn shwd a ble i osod y gwenwn neu'r trap. Ro'dd tipyn o alw amdano yn yr ardal 'nôl tua chanol y ganrif ddiwethaf, ond fe ddatblygodd ddawn fwy arbenigol fyth. Yn greffus wrth ofalu am ei fola, daeth yn gamster ar ddewis ac amseru ei ymweliadau â gwahanol ffermydd hael cefn gwlad, gan gyrraedd bob tro ar yr amser iawn. Bydde rhai'n mwynhau brecwast mowr hwyr wedi holl waith godro'r bore, eraill yn porthi te deg hael. Bydde'r bwyd ar y ford o tua hanner awr wedi un ar ddeg gan y rhai a gâi ginio cynnar, eraill yn amrywio eu hamser tan ryw ddau o'r gloch a the wedyn gan eraill rywbryd o dri 'mlân. Bydde ein swyddog yn trefnu ei ymweliadau yn ôl trefn bwyd y ffermydd a chwant ei stumog. Yn naturiol, fydde cinio mawr hwyr ddim yn mynd gyda gormod o jam a sgons yn gynnar yn y prynhawn. Gan fod llygod yn bla yn y wlad yr adeg hynny bydde, 'Dewch miwn at y ford, Hywel. Ni ar fyta!' yn fiwsig i'w glustiau ac fe'i clywai yn ddyddiol.

O dipyn i beth ehangu a lledaenu wnath ei fola nes gneud y

weithred o blygu lawr yng nghorneli sguborie i drin trap neu wenwn yn weithred anghyffyrddus iddo. Felly, pan dda'th jobyn y War Ag, o'dd hwnnw jyst y job iddo fe, oherwydd câi ddal i drefnu ymweliadau â ffermydd fel arolygwr. Ei waith fydde sicrhau bod y ffermwyr wedi aredig yr erwau penodol i dyfu bwyd, yn ôl gorchymyn y llywodraeth adeg y rhyfel. Fydde dim penlinio poenus mewn corneli tywyll bellach, dim ond wac fach i fwlch clawdd i fwrw llygad. Ond os newidiodd natur ei waith, doedd y fordydd bwyd a ddewisai heb newid dim.

Tra parodd y rhyfel, gwelwyd pob arad yn troi yr erwau gorfodol, ond pan estynnwyd y cynllun ar ôl cyhoeddi heddwch, bu nifer o amaethwyr gorllewin gwlyb Cymru yn llai teyrngar. Beth oedd pwrpas trio aeddfedu ŷd mewn shwd hinsawdd anobeithiol o wlyb? I lawr yn nyffryn Tywi hawdd o'dd i Hywel roi pip dros ben iet i gadarnhau bod y tir wedi ei droi'n goch, cyn arwyddo dwy bunt yr erw i'r amaethwr. Ond fel yr âi'r caeau'n fwy llethrog âi'r cerdded yn faich wrth iddo lusgo'r bola mawr lan y rhiwie. Dysgodd fod edrych ar y tir cyn eistedd wrth y ford yn fantais. Wel, fel arfer, ar wahân i'r diwrnod hwnnw pan wedodd y boi 'ma wrtho fod yr arad wedi torri a'i fod e'n disgwl swche newydd; wedyn pan a'th e 'nôl i'r tŷ, dim ond dished wan o de gafodd e, a dim ond un llwyed o siwgwr a dim byd arall. Chafodd hwnnw ddim maddeuant, na'r ddwy bunt yr erw am aredig!

Fe dargedai Pantglas ar brynhawn dydd Gwener, dyna pryd y bydde Mrs Thomas yn coginio ei downyts blasus i'w bwyta dros y penwythnos. Ond, yn digwydd bod, ar un dydd Gwener arbennig, dyna'r union ddiwrnod ro'dd hi wedi mynd bant 'da'r Côr i ganu am y dydd yn rhywle. Ond, a'th Donald lawr i gwrdd â fan Jory ar ei rownds. Clywodd rester arferol hirfaith Jim Jory yn un ribidirês diddiwedd wrth iddo agor drws cefen y fan – "Ma chi, digon o ddewis heddi 'to... Bara, byns, torth fowr, torth fach, caws, cacennau...' ac yn y blaen lawr nes cyrraedd – 'toffi rolls a toffi recs a stecs o bwdin bara...' Bydde'r cwsmer yn torri ar ei draws pan fydde fe am brynu un o'r nwydde a enwyd cyn i Jim ddechre unwaith eto ar ei rester unigryw. Diddordeb penna Donald o'dd y dwsin o fyns mawr Jory a'r rheiny'n arogli'i dwym neis, jyst mas o'r ffwrn.

Pan gyrhaeddodd Hywel y prynhawn hwnnw ei eiriau cynta oedd, 'Well i ni fynd i weld y ca nawr, cyn ca'l te,' medde fe, ond dangos ei siom wnaeth e wrth iddo glywed am y Côr wedi mynd bant; ceisiodd anghofio am ddelwedd a blas hyfryd y downyts.

'Na,' medde Donald y gwesteiwr cyfrwys, 'ma popeth mas ar y ford a'r tecil wedi berwi.' Cododd ei galon wrth glywed arogl heintus byns Jory a gweld y soser llawn menyn catre. A'th dwy lawr yn go handi wrth i'r forwyn wrywaidd dabo slagen fowr o fenyn ar yr un nesa. O'dd hyd yn oed Hywel yn llanw, ond dim ond hanner yr un gynta ro'dd Donald wedi ei byta, gan ei fod e mor fisi yn bwydo'r gwestai. Mewn ymateb i honiad Hywel ei fod e'n llawn, ateb parod Donald oedd, 'Sdim pwynt gadel un ar ôl 'chan, o's e nawr?' Ildiodd unwaith eto. Cynted iddo'i gwthio lawr, a dwbwl dagu wrth wneud, ro'dd ein ffermwr ar ei draed.

'Cystal i ni fynd lan i ben y banc, achos sdim help 'da fi odro heno a bydd yn rhaid cwrdd â'r bỳs pan ddaw'r Côr gatre!'

O amgylch y tŷ ac adeiladau mas ffarm Pantglas mae 'na lethrau eitha serth a rhaid troedio am ryw ddau can troedfedd cyn cyrraedd y caeau top, sy'n hollol fflat; yn wir gallen nhw fod yn feysydd pêl-droed hyd yn oed. Dyna lle y dylai Donald fod wedi aredig chwe erw, yn ôl gofynion yr awdurdodau. Byddai Hywel yn gallu cadarnhau i'r aredig gael ei gyflawni pe bai'r gwaith wedi ei wneud. Aethon nhw drwy'r iet i mewn i Gae War Tŷ gyda'i gilydd cyn i Donald ddechre camu'n gynt, fel rhyw gystadleuydd rhedeg marathon cyfrwys, gan agor ychydig bellter rhyngddo a Hywel. A hwnnw'n tychan a'r byns yn dechre gwasgu arno, ceisiodd Hywel arafu pethe,

'Jiw ma golygfa bert o fan hyn. Ife Rhydargaeau ni'n galler gweld draw fan 'na?'

Aeth y pellter rhwng y ddau bron yn ugen llath. 'Ble ma'r ca 'ma, fi fod 'i weld?' holodd.

'Reit lan ar y top! Ma sbelen 'da ni i fynd 'to.'

Cyn cyrraedd y clawdd rhwng Cae Sied a Cae War Tŷ mae'r tir yn codi tipyn yn fwy serth, felly sbardunodd Donald mlân yn gynt yn fwriadol. Bu'n rhaid i Hywel druan stopo, gan fod y byd yn dechre troi rownd, byns Jory yn gwasgu arno ac yn corddi yn ei fola. Roedd y chwys a'r cochni ar ei wyneb yn brawf ei fod e mas o wynt yn gyfan gwbl.

'Y ca pella yw e ar bwys yr hen hewl Rufeinig,' gwaeddodd Donald yn y pellter. Suddodd calon ein swyddog o gofio ei fod wedi sylwi ar ei leoliad ar y map yn y Swyddfa.

Wedi adennill ychydig mwy o anal, gwaeddodd, 'Gwedwch wrtho i, ody popeth yn iawn lan 'na?

'Odyn, odyn. Popeth yn champion,' medde Donald a dod 'nôl ato.

'Grondwch 'ma. Ma 'ym bach o hast arna inne 'fyd. Os arwydda i, pidwch gweud gair wrth neb 'mod i heb fod lan 'na,' meddai wrth dynnu'r ffurflen swyddogol mas o'i boced frest.

Wrth i gerbyd ein swyddog adael y clos ac wrth weld wyneb gwelw Hywel, chwifiodd Donald ei ffarwél yn hapus arno. Ond cynted ag y diflannodd ei gar lawr yr hewl fach, trodd at Prince, y ci, gan weiddi'n fuddugoliaethus, 'Diolch byth am fyns Jory!' Bydde'n rhaid iddo fynd draw i Langeler at y gof yn weddol gloi, i weld a o'dd e wedi riparo'r arad.

Atodiad: Achau'r Teulu

Rhyw ddeng mlynedd 'nôl es ati i olrhain achau fy nheulu, ac fel pawb arall sydd wedi mentro i'r maes, daeth yr anawsterau a'r hunan feirniadaeth i'r wyneb yn syth. 'Trueni na se'n i wedi gofyn i Mam' ac 'O, Damo! Wy'n siŵr bydde Mam-gu'n gwbod yn iawn.' Rhy hwyr bois bach.

Rhaid sylweddoli hefyd y gall hanes teulu fod yn hynod o anniddorol i bawb arall y tu allan i'r cylch bach cyfyngedig. Sawl tro, fel hanesydd lleol, ces fy ngwahodd i ddatrys cymhlethdodau nifer yn y maes hwn, weithiau gan ymwelwyr brwdfrydig wedi dychwelyd o leoedd mor bell ag Awstralia ac America, yn chwilio am ryw gysylltiad lleol. Dysgais y gall fod yn beryglus derbyn tystiolaeth gan eraill heb iddyn nhw gynnig prawf. Wrth olrhain y teulu 'nôl i ddechrau'r bedwaredd ganrif ar bymtheg, daeth archwilio cofrestrau a chasglu tystysgrifau'n waith pwysig er mwyn canfod y gwir. Unwaith, bues yn dilyn bywyd gwas ffarm anghywir, am fod 'na ddau o'r un oedran, yr un enw ac yn byw yn yr un plwyf. Llofnod y tad iawn ar ei dystysgrif priodas wnaeth fy arbed rhag dilyn y perthynas anghywir.

Ffaith a amlygwyd yn syth oedd i 'nheulu bron i gyd fyw o fewn cylch o ryw ugain milltir i Lanpumsaint. Daeth ochor fy nhad o Lanybydder lawr i Lanfynydd a Llanllawddog cyn cyrraedd Llanpumsaint. Cangen o deulu fy mam hefyd o Lanllawddog, a'r llall o Gilrhedyn drwy Dre-lech a Chynwyl cyn cyrraedd yma. Mor bell ag y gwn i, aeth neb tua Awstralia nac i'r Amerig, ar wahân i un Richards a orfodwyd i ffoi draw yno pan gafodd ei adnabod ar gefen ceffyl fel un o Ferched Beca.

Amaethwyr a gweision y tir oedd y rhan fwya ohonyn nhw, gydag ambell saer coed ac un neu ddau siopwr yn eithriadau. Hyd yn hyn, bu'r ymchwil yn ddiddorol, heb fod yn rhy anodd, ar wahân i un neu ddau achos, wnaeth hawlio cryn ddyfalu, amynedd a dyfalbarhad. Am awn i, wnaeth neb ohonyn nhw ei ffortiwn, wnaeth neb lithro i drybini mawr, na chwaith orfod pwyso ar y plwyf am gynhaliaeth. Maen nhw'n ymddangos fel teuluoedd gweithgar, yn barod eu cymwynas ac yn gefnogol i berthnasau pan wnâi ergydion creulon bywyd daro. Effeithiodd rhai o'r ergydion hynny arna i'n bersonol: ni welais yr un tad-cu oherwydd i'r ddau gael eu lladd ar y rheilffordd cyn fy ngeni; bu fy nhad farw pan oeddwn ond yn wyth mlwydd oed; yna, yn 1992, collais fy ffrind gorau, fy mrawd Donald mewn damwain tractor.

Bu pedwar cartref yn ganolfannau pwysig i'r teuluoedd ymhell i mewn i'r ugeinfed ganrif. Ar ochr fy nhad, Dole ar gyrion pentref Llanpumsaint a Gwili Vale reit yng nghanol y pentre oedd yn bwysig. Roedd ochor Mam yn hanu o Nantglas Isaf fry i'r gogledd a Chwmwernen llai na milltir o'r Dole. Falle bydd ymweld â phob un yn eu tro yn ffordd hwylus o ganlyn y stori.

Nhad, Tom Thomas

Cangen Dolau

Jonathon Thomas (1812) Llanybydder + Judith (1813)
Llanfihangel Rhos y Corn

Thomas Thomas (1837) Llanegwad + Anne Jones (1846)
Llanegwad

Samuel Thomas (1870) Llanfynydd + Sarah Williams (1875)
Llanpumsaint

Tom Thomas (1897) Llanewydd + May Thomas (1898)
Cynwyl

John (1922) – **Donald** (1923) – **Arwyn** (1937)
Pant-y-Fedwen

Llwyddais i fynd 'nôl i'r 19eg o Ebrill 1836 lle mae cofrestr
Eglwys Rhos-y-corn, yn cofnodi priodas Jonathon Thomas,
fy hen, hen dad-cu o Lanybydder a aned yn 1811 â Judith a
aned yn 1813, o'r plwyf hwnnw. Yno, mae llawysgrifen daclus
y priodfab yn cadarnhau iddo dderbyn addysg yn rhywle, ac
mae'r ffaith i'r pâr lwyddo i symud i ffarm chwe deg erw, sef
Tirbedw, Llanfynydd yn yr oes lom honno, yn dyst fod 'na
ychydig o gyfoeth yn gefen iddyn nhw. Erbyn 1861, maen
nhw gyda chymorth y mab, Thomas wedi ehangu Tirbedw
i saith deg erw

Wrth ymweld â Tirfynwent, Llanfynydd heddiw, dim ond
adfail o ychydig gerrig sydd yno erbyn hyn, ond unwaith
safai mewn rhes o fythynnod bach, ger yr afon ar yr ochr
ddwyreiniol, y tu ôl i'r eglwys. Dyma gartref Thomas, (mab
Jonathon a Judith) a'i briod, Anne .

Gan nad Thomos oedd yr hynaf, felly yn nes ymlaen,
gwelir ef yn was ar ffermydd yn Llanegwad. Ond druan ag
e, bu farw'n ifanc, yn ei bedwardegau i adael baich aruthrol

ar ysgwyddau Anne druan, gyda'r chwech o blant. Doedd Thomas, a enwyd ar ôl ei dad, ond yn rhai misoedd oed. Gallwn ddychmygu'r cyfrifoldeb a'r pwysau trwm yn yr oes honno a fyddai'n disgyn ar y plant hynaf, a dim ond un ar ddeg oed oedd Samuel. Gwelais ei fod yn was ffarm yn ei ardal enedigol ar noson cyn ei briodas yn Blaen-nant-y-mab ac wedyn bu'n gweithio yn y cwar cerrig yn Cwmdwyfran. Yn weithiwr cydwybodol a phenderfynol o wella'i fyd, cyflogwyd ef gan y Great Western Railway erbyn cyrraedd y Dole. O fencer i ganger, ac yna'n arweinydd dros eraill.

Fe oedd gyrrwr y troli a drawodd yn erbyn injan ar dro yn y lein ger Cwmdwyfran, ar 21ain o Fehefin, 1934. Gorchmynnodd ef fod y pedwar gweithiwr arall yn neidio bant mewn pryd, ond dal wrth y llyw wnaeth Tad-cu pan drawyd y troli gan y trên. Ffrwydrodd ac aeth ar dân, ac fe'i lladdwyd yn y fan a'r lle ar ddiwrnod hiraf y flwyddyn, ac yntau ar fin ymddeol y flwyddyn honno.

Er iddo gael ei eni yn Woodcock Lodge ger Pentre Morgan, Cynwyl yn 1897, un o blant y Dole oedd Nhad, Tom Thomas, yr ail blentyn, ond mab hynaf Samuel a Sarah Thomas. Rhyddhad mawr fu symud draw i'r Dole, rywbryd rhwng 1901 a 1905, oherwydd gwasgwyd tri theulu gwahanol i ystafelloedd cyfyng y Lodge cyn hynny. Annie oedd yr hynaf, Mam Frances, Pantygof heddiw. Fy nhad, Tom oedd wedyn ac aeth y brawd nesaf, Jac yn goedwigwr i Benllegaer ger Abertawe, tra daeth y nesa, David Mansel (Dai Benzol neu Dai Home Cottage) yn dra adnabyddus, fel arweinydd Cyngor Sir Gaerfyrddin ac Ustus Heddwch. Priododd Hannah â glöwr, sef Luther, ond arhosodd y cyw melyn olaf, sef Agnes yn y Dole. Daeth yn fam i dri bachgen, Gwynfor, Dilwyn a Robert. Diddorol sylwi fan hyn i Aled, mab Dilwyn, ddychwelyd i'r Dole i gynnal y traddodiad teuluol ac enwi ei fab yntau'n Jac, ar ôl ei hen dad-cu.

Yn ôl at fy nhad, aeth yn was ffarm i Pantiouar Nebo a chyfarfod fy mam jyst lawr yr hewl yn Yr Hendy. Wedi priodi yn 1922 cychwynnon nhw eu bywyd priodasol ym Mhant-y-Fedwen, pellter llwybr o Bantiouar ac yno ganed fy nau frawd, John a Donald. Bedair blynedd ar ddeg wedyn des i i'r byd. Mewn llun a gefais yn ddiweddar, ces fy unig gip o'm tad yn holliach, oherwydd aeth yn sâl yn fuan wedi symud i Pantglas. Er iddyn nhw feddwl mai dyna oedd ore ar y pryd, mae'n dal yn boen i fi hyd heddiw, fod cymdogion wedi mynd â fi am wythnos o wyliau i Abertawe yn ystod dyddiau olaf fy nhad. Yno, yn rhyw wyth oed, synnais weld tyllau enfawr ar y ffordd, cyn sylweddoli i ganol y ddinas gael ei fomio adeg y rhyfel. Wrth edrych yn ôl, bydde hi wedi bod yn well petawn i wedi cael aros gatre i rannu'r galar yn 1946.

Cangen Gwili Vale

David John + Mary John

David John Williams (1795) Llanllawddog
(a newidiodd ei gyfenw) + Rachel (?)

John Havard Williams (1791) Caerfyrddin + Rachel Alban
(1796) Llanpumsaint

John Williams (John) (1840) Llanllawddog +
Hannah Williams

Sarah Williams (1870) Llanpumsaint + Samuel Thomas
(1870)

John Williams a sefydlodd Siop Gwili Vale, ar ôl dod lawr o Fwlch Bychan, Nebo. Magwyd ef yn Cwmere, tŷ haf bellach, sydd ynghanol y goedwig, ryw hanner milltir i'r gogledd o Eglwys Llanllawddog. Yn yr eglwys honno y bedyddiwyd pob un o 11 o blant David a Rachel John, yn dilyn eu priodas yno yn 1828. Hi o Lanfihangel-ar-Arth, ond fe'n fachan lleol. O ddarganfod manylion ei fedydd yma ar y 4dd o Fehefin 1795 – David the son of David and Mary John – sylweddolais fy mod wedi cyrraedd y man pellaf posibl yn ôl, wrth edrych am enwau hen, hen, hen dad-cu a mam-gu.

Sylwais fod anghysondeb – wedi i'r 11 gael eu bedyddio'n Johns, newidiodd dau o'r bechgyn eu cyfenw i Williams erbyn priodi. Ar y cychwyn dechreuais amau 'mod i'n trafod dau wahanol deulu wrth ymchwilio, ond ar ôl rhagor o dwrio a chymharu enwau a dyddiadau yn fanwl, daeth prawf mai un teulu sydd yma. Ni wnaeth Rachel ailbriodi chwaith, yn dilyn marwolaeth ei gŵr. Y brawd arall a aeth yn Williams oedd Charles yr ieuengaf a dyna yw e ar ddydd ei briodas yn 1876. Erys y dirgelwch! Falle fod y cigydd ddim yn hoff o John John.

Bu John, a aned tua 1791, a Rachel, a aned yn 1796, yn ffermio'r lle nes i'w mab John ddychwelyd. Mae un Cyfrifiad yn nodi mai ei swydd oedd 'Butter Carrier' – anghyffredin iawn o ystyried bod cefn gwlad mor dlawd yr adeg hynny. O ystyried agosatrwydd Ffosyfran i blasty moethus Glangwili, Llanllawddog, gellir deall pwy oedd yn ei gyflogi. Daw cysylltiad uniongyrchol â Llanpumsaint i'r amlwg wrth i'r Gofrestr Priodasau nodi fod Rachel Alban a John Havard wedi eu huno mewn priodas yno ar y 29ain o Dachwedd 1819, ac wedi byw yno cyn symud i Ffosyfran. Un o San Pedr, Caerfyrddin yw John Alban, yr unig un o'm cyndeidiau, hyd y gwn, i gael ei eni mewn tref. Ond gwelwyd nifer â'r cyfenw Alban yn byw yn ardal Llanpumsaint yr adeg hynny, megis yn Bedw Bach a Pantygof, sy'n dal yn y teulu.

John a Hannah, oedd fy hen dad-cu a mam-gu. Gan i'r ddau hanu o blwyf Llanllawddog, digon naturiol iddyn nhw briodi yn yr Eglwys honno yn 1861. Un o Havards Ffosyfran,

safle heulog hyfryd o hyd yng Nghwm Llanllawddog, oedd
Hannah, wedi ei geni yno yn 1838. Diddorol sylwi iddyn
nhw gychwyn eu bywyd priodasol yn Llanegwad cyn symud
i Fwlch Bychan, Nebo. Felly, ai dyma'r cliw o sut y cyfarfu
Sara o Gwili Vale a Sam o Lanegwad y tro cynta? Mae'n
werth bet o bunt, siŵr o fod!

Ni fu rhaid i Sarah Williams ar y pryd – Mam-gu Dole,
deithio ymhell i'w phriodas ar fore'r 18fed o Dachwedd,
1892. Y cyfan wnaeth hi oedd croesi'r hewl o Siop Gwili Vale
i borth Eglwys Llanpumsaint, a phriodi Samuel Thomas.
Fe'i ganed ar ffarm 35 erw Bwlch Bychan yn Nebo yn 1870,
cymdogion agosaf Pant-y-Fedwen, lle y'm ganed i sbel ar ei
hôl hi. Hi oedd pumed plentyn John a Hannah Williams.

Dim boi i'w ddala 'nôl o'dd John a mentrodd agor siop
y cigydd ynghanol pentre Llanpumsaint wrth i safonau
bwyd godi a mwy o bobol yn gallu fforddio bwyta cig. Aeth
Gwili Vale o nerth i nerth a chyn hir gwerthwyd tipyn o
bopeth yno. Heb os, bu bod ar bwys yr eglwys a'r capel
Methodistaidd yn hwb i brysurdeb y siop, a rhaid cofio bod
yr ysgol a'r Ffatri Wlân jyst lan yr hewl. O fewn tair blynedd i
farwolaeth John Williams yn 1906 daeth un o'r meibion 'nôl
i redeg y busnes. Dychwelyd o Glydach Vale yn y Rhondda
wnaeth e, ac un o'r pentref glofaol hwnnw oedd ei wraig.
Mae 'na gysylltiad ehangach yn ein taro, oherwydd dyna lle
byddai Dafydd Lodwick Jones, o deulu Cwmwernen, teulu
Mam, yn mynd yn ddiweddarach i ofalu am geffylau'r pwll
glo ac ymgartrefu yno. Parhau'n brysur wnaeth Gwili Vale
drwy gydol hanner cynta'r ugeinfed ganrif, ac fel plentyn
ysgol yn y pedwar a'r pumdegau, yno bydden ni'n gwario'n
ceiniogau i rannu melysion â'n ffrindiau; ond tŷ preifat
ydyw erbyn hyn.

Ochor Mam

Cangen Nantglas

Joshua Thomas (1803) Cilrhedyn + Amey Howell (1800)
Cilrhedyn

Benjamin Davies (1807) + Margaret (1819) –
Rhieni Margaret

Benjamin Thomas (1838) Trelech + Margaret Davies
(1845) Cynwyl

John Thomas (1875) Cynwyl + Margaret Jones (1875)
Llanllawddog

May Thomas (1898)

Ar y 9fed o Orffennaf 1822, mae cofrestr eglwys Cilrhedyn yn
nodi priodas Joshua ac Amy Thomas. Erbyn 1841 maent yn
ffermio yn Nhrelech gydag wyth o blant o gwmpas y bwrdd.
Daw un ferch arall sy'n datgelu cliw pwysig. Mae Anne ar
Gyfrifiad 1851 yn wyth oed, wedi ei geni yn Nantglas, felly
rhaid eu bod wedi symud yno erbyn 1843. Bu farw Joshua
ar Orffennaf 28ain 1864 chwe diwrnod yn unig ar ôl priodas
ei fab Benjamin, ac fe ddaeth hwnnw felly yn feistr sydyn ar
Nantglas.

Merch hynaf Benjamin a Margaret Davies oedd Mam-
gu Nantglas Mam, un o un ar ddeg arall o blant ar ffarm
fawr dau gan erw Clymache ger Cynwyl Elfed. Diddorol
sylwi pa mor agos i Glymache oedd Cydawell, lle ganed
fy mam. Erbyn hyn mae gen i ddwy ffeil anferth, ffrwyth
dilyn tynged holl blant y teuluoedd niferus 'ma, ond wna
i ddim eu dilyn yn y llith hwn ar wahân i nodi enwau rhai
canghennau – Llwynglas Nebo, Parcgwyn Llangyndeyrn.
Eto, rhaid cofnodi fod yna ymdeimlad hudol cynnes â'r holl

ddisgynyddion wrth ddwyn i gof atgofion Nantglas. Rhaid mai dylanwad Ben a Marged fu'n gyfrifol am hyn, dau fu mor uchel eu parch drwy'r holl gymdogaeth. Treuliodd Mam lawer o'i hamser yno, a dyna lle'r oedd hi, fwy na thebyg, pan anghofiwyd amdani hi gan y Cyfrifydd yn 1911. Roedd sôn am haelioni Mam-gu Nantglas drwy'r holl gymdogaeth, yn wraig addfwyn a chymwynasgar gyda chonsýrn amlwg am yr holl gymdeithas. Sonnir iddi fwydo a chynnal llawer o dlodion yr ardal, a dywedwyd na fyddech chi byth yn gadael aelwyd Nantglas yn waglaw. Hi fu arwres fy mam.

Honnir i Dad-cu Nantglas fod yn ddyn cadarn, yn rhannu ei gonsýrn am gymdeithas gyda'i wraig, ond eto i gyd yn Dori rhonc! Dywedir iddo gyfeirio at Lloyd George fel 'Dai bach Caernarfon' ac iddo wrthod casglu ei bensiwn pan ddaeth hwnnw ar gael iddo ar ôl 1911. Bu'r ddau fyw'n hir i oroesi nifer o'u disgynyddion o dan simnai lwfer yr hen aelwyd gynnes, fry uwch ben Llanpumsaint. Claddwyd y ddau ym mynwent lethrog, hynafol Capel y Bedyddwyr, Ffynnonhenri, Benjamin ar y 30ain o Hydref 1922 yn 84 oed, a Marged ar y 25ain o Chwefror 1932 wedi cyrraedd 87.

Trydydd plentyn o un ar ddeg oedd John i Benjamin a Marged Thomas Nantglas Isaf, ffarm gan erw, gyda golygfeydd godidog o'r gogledd uwchben dyffryn y Gwili a Llanpumsaint. Rhieni Benjamin fu'n gyfrifol am gychwyn teyrnasiad y Tomosiaid yn Nantglas

Rhaid troi at y drychineb. Wrth ddychwelyd o farchnad tre Caerfyrddin ar ddydd Sadwrn ym Mehefin 1902 cerddodd John a Marged i lawr y lein o orsaf Llanpumsaint, y ffordd fer i'w cartref newydd, Derwen Groes. Gyda basged siopa drom ar ei fraich, eisteddodd John ar ochr y trac, tra prysurodd ei wraig am gatre at y ddwy groten fach. Blinder ac effaith ychydig o ddiod ynghynt yn y dydd, efalle a achosodd iddo gwypo i gysgu, a chlywodd e mo'r trên yn agosáu. Bu farw o anafiadau difrifol yn Ysbyty Caerfyrddin i roi terfyn ar holl obeithion y teulu bach. Newydd symud lan yn y byd oedden nhw o Gydawell i'r Dderwen, ffarm dipyn yn fwy. Bu'n angladd druenus gyda theulu niferus Nantglas yn llenwi'r eglwys.

Margaretta Mary Thomas (May Pantglas)

Oherwydd na welais yr un tad-cu a bod 'Nhad a'r ddwy fam-gu wedi marw pan oeddwn yn ifanc iawn, yr unig ddylanwad mawr arna i oedd Mam. Wedi ei geni yn Cydawell, Cynwyl ar y 3dd o Dachwedd 1898, bu fyw am 99 blwyddyn. Hi oedd yr hynaf o dair merch; tra aeth Lizzie i Gaerloyw arhosodd Esther y drws nesa i'w mam yn yr Hendy, gan gymryd drosodd y swydd o fod yn bostman gwlad i ardal Nebo. Addysg Seisnig gaed bryd hynny, felly er i berthynas Mam a fi fod yn hollol drwy'r Gymraeg, llythyr Saesneg fyddai'n cyrraedd bob tro pan es i ffwrdd. Ar yr ochr gadarnhaol, bu safon dysgu Sol Ffa a chanu yn uchel iawn yn yr ysgol, gan lwyddo i greu cenedlaethau o gantorion a ddaeth yn aelodau yng nghôr adnabyddus Llanpumsaint.

Rhoddodd byd y canu fwynhad i Mam ar hyd ei hoes, mewn eglwysi, capeli, eisteddfodau a chorau. Roedd ganddi lais alto cyfoethog a bu galw cyson amdani i ganu mewn corau a chymanfaoedd, tan iddi gyrraedd y naw deg oed. Barn rhai oedd tase hi wedi byw mewn oes neu amgylchiadau gwahanol y gallasai fod wedi gwneud enw iddi hi ei hun fel cantores, ond a fyddai wedi dymuno hynny sy'n gwestiwn arall. Bu'n uchel iawn ei pharch gan bawb oedd yn ei hadnabod a gwerthfawrogwyd ei chyfraniad cynnes i gymdeithas. Gellir cydnabod dylanwad ei mam-gu Nantglas arni yn y cyswllt hwn.

Cangen Cwmwernen

John Jones (1802) Cynwyl + Anna (1811)
Penboyr – rhieni Benjamin

John Griffiths (1822) Abergwili + Margaret (1822)
Abergwili – rhieni Mary ac Esther

Benjamin Jones (1850) + Mary Griffiths (1849)
+ Esther Griffiths (Ail Wraig)

Elizabeth Cwmwernen (1884) – merch Esther

Marged Jones (1870) Llanllawddog – merch Mary

+ **John Thomas** (1875) Nantglas

May (Pantglas), Lizzie (Caerloyw) ac Esther Bethoron

Oherwydd marwolaethau cynnar, cyffredin iawn fu ail
briodi ac ail blanta ddwy ganrif yn ôl ac felly buodd hi
yn Cwmwernen. Pan fu farw Mary'n ifanc, ailbriododd
Benjamin, ond yn llai cyffredin nag arfer, priododd chwaer
ei wraig gynta, sef Esther, oedd yn ddi-briod yn 34 oed.
Dyma fi nawr yn wynebu dirgelwch mwyaf dyrys yn yr holl
dwrio achau. Ble bu'r briodas? Roedd angen cadarnhad a
thystiolaeth arnaf. Diffrwyth fu archwilio drwy gofrestrau
eglwysi Llanpumsaint, Llanllawddog a Chynwyl Elfed ac un
neu ddwy arall. Yn y diwedd fe'm gorfodwyd i bori'n boenus
o araf drwy Gofrestr Cenedlaethol Cymru a Lloegr gyda
dau enw llawer rhy gyffredin, Benjamin Jones ac Esther
Griffiths. O'r diwedd darganfûm iddynt briodi yn Swyddfa'r
Cofrestrydd yng Nghaerfyrddin ar y 23ain o Dachwedd
1882. Achoswyd cymlethdod pellach wrth i enw ei dad
gael ei gofnodi'n wahanol ar y Dystysgrif fel William Jones
– John Jones yw e ar ddogfennau eraill bob tro. Bu farw
Benjamin o wenwyn gwaed, Scrofula, ar yr 20fed o Ionawr

1883; er hynny ganed un ferch iddynt, Elizabeth a arhosodd yn Cwmwernen.

Un o blant Cwmwernen oedd Mam-gu'r Hendy, Marged Jones, un o blant Mary yn y briodas gyntaf, er iddi gael ei geni yn 1870 yn Troedrhiwnewydd, plwyf Llanllawddog, tyddyn 12 erw rhwng Pont-ar-sais ac Alltwalis, cartref ei mam. Ymsefydlodd ei rhieni, Benjamin, yn wreiddiol o Cynwyl a Mary, merch Troedrhiwnewydd, yn Cwmwernen Llanpumsaint. Aeth Tom, y mab, i ffermio Penllwynuchel, Nebo cyn symud ymlaen i Lantywi lan, Llanegwad. Diddorol sylwi i Benjamin fod yn was yno pan briododd y tro cynta ac i'w fam, pan oedd yn weddw, symud i dyddyn bach yn Felinwen; enw hwnnw oedd Lantywi.

Mae 'na ddirgelwch heb ei ddatrys yno'n rhywle. Dilynodd Dafi mab Tom ef lawr i ffermio Lantywi lan o Penllwynuchel. Merch Tom oedd Myfi Gilfach Llanddarog, mam Marion ac Eluned. Mab Tom oedd Benja Alltyfyrddin, Felinwen, tad Gwenfyl a Morfudd y Mochyn Du. Aeth Dafi Lodwick yn llawer pellach, i byllau glo Clydach Vale. Arhosodd William yn llawer nes at gatre i roi help llaw i'w chwaer weddw yn yr Hendy, Nebo.

Bywyd caled ac anodd gafodd Mam-gu'r Hendy, Marged Jones. Bu farw ei mam yn 1882. Ganed merch iddi yn 1892 bedair blynedd cyn ei phriodas, collodd ddau fabi cyn geni Mam ac yna colli ei gŵr yn y ddamwain yn 1902. Ond aeth y ferch hynaf, Anne yn weinyddes, a bu yn fendith aruthrol iddi, wrth frwydro i godi ei theulu bach. Bu ei brawd, William yn gefen hefyd nes iddo yntau farw yn 1919. Ond llwyddodd hi i gael swydd fel postman gwledig, i ddosbarthu llythyron draw dros ardal Nebo hyd at orsaf Cynwyl. Dyma swydd fyddai'r ferch ifancaf, Esther Bethoron a oedd yn byw drws nesa iddi, yn ei dilyn. Unwaith y gwelwyd y tshyrns llath ar ben heolydd y ffermydd, ni fu'n rhaid cerdded mor bell; miwn âi'r llythyr i'r tshyrn wag.

Mae gen i rai atgofion amdani, y mwyaf byw wrth ei gweld yn godro yn y boudy yn Pantglas. Hi fagodd fy mrawd hynaf Jac am flynyddoedd – yn ôl yr hen draddodiad teuluol o anfon yr hynaf at ei fam-gu. Bu hithau yn Troedrhiwnewydd am gyfnod, ac aeth fy mam i Nantglas hefyd. Cofio ei gweld yn rhoi pryd o dafod llym i Jac am iddo brynu buwch ar y farchnad heb ganiatâd ac yntau'n llefen y glaw i'r bwced godro. Ofer fu'r bregeth, oherwydd cyn hir datblygodd 'Jac y Lloi Bach' i fod yn un o brif borthmyn marchnadoedd gorllewin Cymru.

Rhaid mai Nadolig 1944 oedd hi pan ddihunais mewn siom i ganfod fod Santa wedi fy anghofio. Codi i'r llawr i ganfod Mam yn rhuthro i mewn ac egluro ei bod newydd weld Santa yn gadael anrhegion yn y gegin fach. Rhaid ei fod yn hwyr iawn wrthi eleni! Llyncais y stori ond y gwir oedd bod Mam newydd gyrraedd gatre, wedi bod yn gwylad Mam-gu lan yn yr Hendy; bu hi farw ar y 13eg o Chwefror 1945.

Teulu Cwmwernen – yr ail briodas

Gyda llaw, roedd Wmffre, yn enedigol o Gynwyl ac yn dipyn o gymeriad; priododd ag Elizabeth, sef unig ferch Benjamin Jones yn ei ail briodas ag Esther. Symudodd Wmffre i fyw i Cwmwernen at Elizabeth. Cawsant saith o blant. Ben yr hynaf a arhosodd yn Cwmwernen ac mae'r traddodiad teuluol yn para wrth bod Carwyn, mab Elfed, yr olaf o dri o blant Ben ac Eluned, nawr yn byw yno. Cofir am Ben Cabetsh fel cymeriad ffraeth ym marchnad Caerfyrddin ac mae Lorraine ei ferch wedi etifeddu'r ffraethineb hwnnw. Aeth Esther i Frongoch i godi teulu o bump o blant sy'n cynnwys Nancy yr hynaf o'r plant ac Alun, sy'n golygu'r gyfrol hon. Aeth eraill o'r teulu i Brynteg Peniel a Pantycelyn yn Llanpumsaint. Os am wybodaeth fanwl o holl gysylltiadau'r teuluoedd ar raddfa eang, Morfudd, merch Nancy yw'r arbenigwraig, gyda channoedd o enwau dan ei chesail

O'r pedwar cartref hanesyddol, braf nodi parhad teuluol mewn dau ohonynt o hyd, a hynny mewn oes mor gyfnewidiol ac ansicr. Erys y teulu yn Dole a Cwmwernen.

Y Prawf DNA

Beth amser yn ôl gofynnwyd i fi fod yn rhan o ymchwil DNA gan Broject Cymru DNA yn gysylltiedig â rhaglen *Heno*. Braidd yn ofnus o'n i o gael y canlyniadau, rhag ofn bod yna rhyw gysylltiadau Normanaidd cas yn cuddio yn y cefndir! Ond canlyniadau pendant clir a ges i, ac yn bwysicach na dim calonogol o dderbyniol. Oherwydd natur yr ymchwil bu'n gymorth mawr fy mod yn gallu cadarnhau cefndir a lleoliad fy nghyndeidiau yn ôl i tua 1800. Sampl o boer yn unig fu angen i fi ei roi iddynt er mwy iddynt allu datgelu fy hanes dros filoedd pell o flynyddoedd yn ôl, gan ddangos fod cefndir fy nhad a'm mam yn hollol wahanol.

Roeddwn yn Grŵp Pioneers H ar ochr fy mam, gyda'r DNA gwreiddiol yn mynd yn ôl 60,000 o flynyddoedd i Affrica. Yna, wrth i'r Oes Iâ Olaf wanhau, tua 9,000 o flynyddoedd yn ôl, ymledodd y bobl allan o'u hogofâu yn Sbaen a Ffrainc ac anelu am Brydain wrth iddynt ganlyn y ceirw a'r anifeiliaid eraill. Byddent wedi cerdded draw bryd hynny dros diroedd, cyn i'r môr ein gwahanu a'n gwneud yn ynys. Mae DNA y bobl hyn yn dal yn amlwg, yn enwedig yn Iwerddon, Cymru a hefyd Gwlad y Basg. Felly ochr fy mam oedd y gwragedd cyntaf i gyrraedd Cymru ac aros yno.

Datgelir cefndir dynion gan y y cromosom, ac rwy'n perthyn i'r Grŵp RIb-S145. Mae Rib yn gyffredin iawn yn Ewrop, ac S145 yn amlwg iawn ymhlith y Celtiaid.

Aethant allan o Affrica, croesi'r Môr Coch, dilyn yr afon Daniwb cyn cyrraedd Cymru tua 2,500 C.C. Pobl y Bicer a Cheltiaid oedd y rhain, a wnaeth gyflwyno eu hiaith unigryw sy'n wahanol iawn i 90% o ieithoedd eraill y byd. O'r iaith honno y tarddodd Gwyddeleg, Gaeleg, Manaweg, Cymraeg, Cernyweg a Llydaweg. Felly, gallaf honni i ni fod yma ers tro byd. O wybod tipyn am fy achau erbyn hyn, mae'n rhesymol dadlau, mwy na thebyg, i'r ran fwyaf o'm perthnasau sefydlog rannu'r DNA hwn.